SUBSTANTIAL KNOWLEDGE

ARISTOTLE'S METAPHYSICS

SUBSTANTIAL KNOWLEDGE

ARISTOTLE'S METAPHYSICS

C.D.C. REEVE

HACKETT PUBLISHING COMPANY, INC.
INDIANAPOLIS/CAMBRIDGE

For further information, please address:
   Hackett Publishing Company, Inc.
   P.O. Box 44937
   Indianapolis, IN 46244-0937

   www.hackettpublishing.com

Cover and interior design by Abigail Coyle.

Cover photograph: "The Inheritance of Form." Reproduced by permission of the artist.

Library of Congress Cataloging-in-Publication Data

Reeve, C.D.C., 1948–
    Substantial knowledge : Aristotle's metaphysics / C.D.C. Reeve.
        p.   cm.
    Includes bibliographical references and indexes.
    ISBN 0-87220-515-0 (cloth : alk. paper)—ISBN 0-87220-514-2 (pbk. : alk. paper)
        1. Aristotle—Contributions in metaphysics. 2. Metaphysics. 3. Aristotle—
    Contributions in philosophy of substance. 4. Substance (Philosophy) I. Title.

    B491.M4 R44 2000
    100′.92—dc21   99-052539

The paper used in this publication meets the minimum standard requirements of American National Standard for Information Sciences—Permanence of Paper for Printed Materials, ANSI Z39.48-1984.

∞

For
George and John

not many behold God
he is only for those of 100
percent pneuma

—Zbigniew Herbert
"Report from Paradise"

TABLE of CONTENTS

CONTENTS

CONTENTS

INTRODUCTION

Everything that is something—as Socrates is a man, pale a color, in the garden a location, ten pounds a quantity, or two o'clock a time—is a being. And what makes something a being, according to Aristotle, is its relationship to substance. Hence the account of substance is the centerpiece of his metaphysics, and of his science of being qua being. But the account itself is notoriously difficult—so difficult, in fact, that it is commonly viewed nowadays as an inconsistent amalgam of different accounts, developed at different times.

In the supposedly early *Categories,* so the story goes, the canonical or primary substances are particular instances (Socrates) of universal species (the human species), which, with genera, are substances only in a secondary sense. In the supposedly later *Metaphysics,* by contrast, secondary substance is abandoned, Socrates is treated as a compound of matter and form, and form alone is identified as primary substance. Even within the *Metaphysics* itself, moreover, distinct strata are discernible, with the celebrated middle books (VII–IX)—*die Substanzbücher* as a recent anthology revealingly calls them—containing Aristotle's fully mature views. Since divine substance (God) is not discussed in these books, it is not a crucial part of those views, and so may be safely ignored or downplayed.

In those same middle books, however, Aristotle claims that primary substances must be both ontologically primary (the fundamental beings) and epistemologically primary (the primary objects of scientific knowledge). At the same time, he is explicit that universals (specifically, definable universal essences) alone enjoy epistemological primacy, since they are the first principles of the sciences. It seems to follow that primary substances must be universals. But this conclusion he just as firmly rejects. The result is a dilemma of sorts, which I call the *Primacy Dilemma.* In my view, Aristotle's attempt to solve it is the central project of his entire epistemology and metaphysics—one that leads him to abandon Platonism and become an Aristotelian.

If I am right, the Primacy Dilemma has a key role to play in one of the most portentous episodes in the history of philosophy. That alone would be enough to ensure its importance. But its implications for the interpretation of Aristotle are equally significant. For it is the problem to which the *Categories* and *Metaphysics* (as well as many others of Aristotle's works) constitute what will emerge as a coherent unified response. The Dilemma is as much a challenge to contemporary Aristotle scholarship, therefore, as it was a challenge to Aristotle himself—especially so, indeed, because his response to it so crucially involves his theology.

Needless to say, anyone who proposes so significant a departure from more-or-less received wisdom is guaranteed to have bitten off more than he can thoroughly chew, and certainly more than he can hope to demonstrate—especially to those already heavily invested in such wisdom. My much more modest goal, therefore, is to lay out my own views in as vivid and straightforward a way as possible, in the hope that a clear target will attract equally clear criticism. Here, I want to say, is an account of Aristotle's metaphysics that represents it as well worth any philosopher's while. If it deserves to be added to the repertoire of such accounts, I will be well satisfied. If it is a contender, so to speak, it is all that I could reasonably hope it to be.

I would be guilty of false modesty, however, if I did not also say this. Many of the individual texts I discuss—especially when taken in isolation—certainly admit of interpretations other than the ones I defend, and many of those I cite pretty much as proof texts have this status only when taken together with other texts similarly treated. Such holism must surely be any reader's default position. Hence, though each individual interpretation I propose may be controversial when taken by itself, it is immensely strengthened by the fact that it fits into a unified reading of a large number of texts, drawn from a wide variety of Aristotle's works, which can be seen as addressing a single problem in a philosophically perspicuous way. Piecemeal criticism, as a consequence, is unlikely to do much to threaten my views. Indeed, piecemeal interpretation, often taking the form of a near obsessive focus on a few texts, is precisely what I want to challenge. To see Aristotle right, we need—daunting as the prospect may be—to see him whole.

Holism needn't be incompatible, of course, with the view that an author's thought develops over time and so may contain fundamental changes in doctrine, and real or apparent inconsistencies. But holism is to some degree in tension with such developmentalism—especially when, as in the case of Aristotle, independent dating of texts is difficult or impossible, so that developmentalist hypotheses largely piggyback on interpretative ones. If one can uncover doctrinal unity in such an *oeuvre,* therefore, developmentalism's role is diminished. No doubt some of Aristotle's writings do represent earlier stages of his thought than others, but on the central metaphysical and epistemological questions with which I am concerned, I see little evidence of any fundamental changes of mind. For me, then, issues of chronology are of relatively little significance, and I have usually said nothing about them. Rather, I have written as if Aristotle's metaphysics were a single, atemporal entity contained in the totality of the texts that make up the Corpus Aristotelicum. With appropriate caveats and provisos, some of which I have entered explicitly, that is what my researches seem to me to have revealed it to be.

My catholicism extends even to citing texts that are possibly (*Metaphysics* XI) or probably (*De Mundo, De Coloribus, Problemata*) not by Aristotle, but that are included in the traditional collection of his surviving works. I have done so, however, to bolster an interpretation made on independently well-attested grounds, never as its sole basis. These texts merit our (guarded) attention as inspired by Aristotle, if nothing else.

One more comment about holism. It is a feature of holistic accounts that notions introduced, and claims made, without much explanation or defense become fully intelligible only when their place in the entire interpretation is finally revealed. This is certainly the case here. A wise and charitable reader will keep his or her criticisms in reserve, therefore, waiting until the end to see whether or not they are satisfactorily answered.

The reader I have had primarily in mind, I should say, is not the Aristotle expert, or the one whose interest in Aristotle is mostly scholarly—though I hope that experts and scholars will find some grist here for their fine-grinding mills. Rather, I have thought of someone with a sufficiently developed interest in the central issues of philosophy to want to engage with Aristotle in an exploration of them—a painter, as it were, not already of Aristotle's school, who would like to apprentice himself or herself to a master, so as to learn to see and to paint better.

To keep the exposition as accessible and uncluttered as possible I have discussed the secondary literature exclusively in the footnotes, and only to support an interpretation of my own, to wrestle with an objection I found particularly instructive, or to acknowledge a significant debt. I have rarely cited something just because it is eminently citable or often cited. But there are no doubt many debts I should have acknowledged that I have simply forgotten or overlooked, and many occasions on which I have been unwittingly anticipated in some of my proposals.

Some debts of a more general sort, however, merit acknowledgment here. Alan Code, Marc Cohen, and Mohan Matthen commented helpfully and encouragingly on a very impressionistic and underargued early draft. Alan subsequently read a much longer and more polished version. His detailed and perceptive comments (especially on what is now Chapter Nine), together with his own papers, published and forthcoming, resulted in numerous improvements both small and large. Paul Bullen and Teresa Robertson read the penultimate draft and made numerous suggestions for improvements both stylistic and substantive. Jacques Brunschwig, Aryeh Kosman, and David Sedley kindly let me see their unpublished papers on *Metaphysics* XII. Mary Louise Gill and Stephen Menn sent me offprints of their papers. I thank all of them very warmly for their help.

John Cooper deserves separate mention. He has been involved in every project I have undertaken for Hackett. His incisive criticisms have invariably led me to see and do better. Working with him has been an education. I can pay him no greater compliment.

Deborah Wilkes, my editor at Hackett, also deserves separate mention. Without her enthusiasm, generosity of spirit, and sparkle—without her faith in it and me—*Substantial Knowledge* would not exist in its present form.

Finally, I acknowledge a debt of a different sort to the Stillman Drake Fund, the Summer Scholarship Fund, and the Dean of the Faculty at Reed College, Peter Steinberger, for providing generous computer resources and research materials of various sorts.

ABBREVIATIONS

Citations of Aristotle's works are in normal form: abbreviated title, book, chapter, Bekker page, column, and line. Line numbers, which are to the Greek text, are only approximate in translations. The abbreviations used are these:

APo.	*Analytica Posteriora*
APr.	*Analytica Priora*
Cael.	*De Caelo*
Cat.	*Categoriae*
Col.	*De Coloribus*
DA	*De Anima*
Div. Somn.	*De Divinatione per Somnia*
EE	*Ethica Eudemia*
EN	*Ethica Nicomachea*
GA	*De Generatione Animalium*
GC	*De Generatione et Corruptione*
HA	*Historia Animalium*
Int.	*De Interpretatione*
Long.	*De Longaevitate*
MA	*De Motu Animalium*
MM	*Magna Moralia*
Mem.	*De Memoria*
Met.	*Metaphysica*
Mete.	*Meteorologica*
Mu.	*De Mundo*
PA	*De Partibus Animalium*
Ph.	*Physica*
Pol.	*Politica*
Pr.	*Problemata*

Prt.	*Protrepticus*
Resp.	*De Respiratione*
Rh.	*Rhetorica*
SE	*De Sophistici Elenchi*
Sens.	*De Sensu*
Somn.	*De Somno*
Top.	*Topica*

Translations are my own, though many derive—occasionally with minimal changes—from those already published. I have found Fine and Irwin, *Aristotle: Selections,* Furth, *Aristotle Metaphysics: Books Zeta, Eta, Theta, Iota* (VII–X), and the various volumes of the Clarendon Aristotle Series particularly helpful. All necessary Greek is transliterated and explained. When a text receives extended or narrowly focused comment, it appears as a block quote with a beginning citation set entirely in italics. References back to such a text are also set in italics. Materials in square brackets are my additions.

ONE

PLATONISM

1.1 Separation

To what he regards as a perennial question of metaphysics Aristotle returns a lapidary answer: "Indeed what was long ago pursued, is now, and always will be a source of problems—the question what is being *(to on)?* is just the question what is substance *(ousia¹)?*" (*Met.* VII 1 1028ᵇ2–4). Substance, then, is the key to being. The key to substance is another matter, but a necessary condition (at least) of substancehood is not in doubt: "If one does not suppose the substances to be *separated,* and in the way that among the beings the particulars are said to be, one will destroy substance as we wish to speak [of it]" (XIII 10 1086ᵇ16–19). Separation *(chôriston),* then, must be our first topic.²

We may best approach it by looking first at things that are not separate: "None of the other things besides substance is separate, for all of them are said of substance as of a subject *(hupokeimenon)*" (*Ph.* I 2 185ª31–32).³ Thus being predicated of a substance—being an attribute—seems to be a sufficient condition of not being separate. Moreover, the latter seems itself to be a sufficient condition of being ontologically dependent: "All other

---

¹ The term *ousia* is an abstract noun derived from the verb *einai* ('to be'). Aristotle speaks (1) of a thing, such as Socrates, as an *ousia,* and also (2) of the *ousia* of Socrates. When used as in (1), *ousia* is standardly translated as 'substance'—a convention I have followed. When used as in (2), however, it is often translated as 'essence'. I have followed this convention, too, though I usually indicate when it is *ousia* that is translated in this way, and when it is *to ti esti* ('the what-it-is'), *to ti en einai* ('the what-it-is [for an F]-to-be [a G]'), or *to einai* ('the being [of F]').

² *Chôriston,* like other words with a *-ton* ending, may mean 'is actually separate from *x*' or 'is separable from *x*'. For reasons that will become clear, I think that *as applied to substance,* it has the former connotation.

³ Also *Met.* V 8 1017ᵇ13–14, VII 1 1028ª33–34, 3 1028ᵇ36–1029ª2.

things are either said of the primary substances as subjects or in them as subjects.[4] This is clear from an examination of cases, e.g., animal is predicated of man and therefore also of the particular man. For were it predicated of none of the particular men it would not be predicated of man at all. Again, color is in body and therefore also in a particular body. For were it not in some particular body it would not be in body at all. Thus all the other things are either said of the primary substances as subjects or in them as subjects. So if the primary substances did not exist, it would be impossible for any of the other things to be anything" (*Cat.* 5 2ª34–ᵇ6). Attributes, then, are all the beings besides substances. They are predicated of substances, and so are inseparable from, and ontologically dependent on, them. By parity of reasoning, the separation of substances should involve at least three things: being separate from attributes; not being predicated of them; and being ontologically independent of them. We shall look at these in turn.

Aristotle usually characterizes substances as separate *tout court,* not as separate *from something.*[5] Nonetheless, the very meaning of *chôriston,* which is formed from *chôrizein* ('to separate'), carries the implication that there is such a thing. Why, then, does Aristotle appear to cancel that implication? The natural explanation is surely this. Attributes are *all* the beings besides substances, so that substances, in being separate from them, are separate from everything else. Hence there is simply no need to specify what in particular they are separate from.

As an attribute is something predicated of a substance, so a substance is an ultimate subject of predication: "A substance—that which is called a substance most strictly, primarily, and most of all—is that which is neither said of a subject nor in a subject" (*Cat.* 5 2ª11–13). Because an "examination of cases" (2ª34) reveals such subjects to be particulars of some sort, for instance, a particular man (Socrates) or a particular horse (Bellerophon),

---

[4] The differences between said of and in are discussed in 4.6. For present purposes they may be ignored.

[5] Noticed by Devereux, "Separation and Immanence in Plato's Theory of Forms," 78–83. On his view, substances are separate *tout court* because "they exist on their own, i.e., they do not depend on some underlying subject for their existence." Suppose, however, that they do depend for their existence on attributes in some other way, e.g., because no substance can exist without attributes of some sort. Then why would the fact that they do not depend on attributes as *on an underlying subject* be so ontologically significant?

we can understand why this is true. For particulars do seem to be logical
subjects. No surprise, then, that substances are characterized as being
separate "in the way that particular beings are said to be," or that being
separate is regularly associated with being a this *(tode ti)*—a particular.[6]

If a particular substance were ontologically independent of its attributes,
it seems that it would have to be possible for it to exist without them. In
Aristotle's view, however, this is not possible: "If something comes-to-be,
clearly there will potentially (but not actually) be a substance from which
the coming-to-be will arise and into which that which passes-away has to
change. Will, then, any of the others [the non-substances or attributes]
belong to this actually? I mean, will that which is only potentially a this and
a being, but which is neither a this nor a being unqualifiedly, have any
quality or quantity or place? If it has none of these [actually], but all of
them potentially, that which in this sense is not [anything] will be separate,
and furthermore the principal and perpetual fear of the early philosophers
will be realized: the coming-to-be of something from nothing. On the
other hand, if being a this and a substance do not belong to it, while some
of the other things we have mentioned [viz., attributes] do, then attributes
will . . . be separate from substances [which is impossible]" (*GC* I 3
317ᵇ23–33). Apparently, then, Aristotle's substances are not ontologically
independent of attributes.[7]

Attributes, however, do not depend for their existence on a particular
substance; any substance that has them will do. Hence the parallel claim
about substances shouldn't be, as we supposed, that a particular substance
can exist whether or not it has any attributes, but that substances in general
can exist whether or not attributes do. It is the latter claim, therefore, that
we must evaluate.

On an *ante rem* (or Platonist) theory of attributes, attributes can exist
uninstantiated by particulars. On an *in re* theory, like Aristotle's, they
cannot: "if everyone were well, health would exist but not sickness, and if
everything were white, whiteness would exist but not blackness" (*Cat.* 11
14ᵃ7–10). Hence the ontological dependence of attributes—and the cog-

---

[6] E.g., *GA* IV 3 767ᵇ34–35; *Met.* V 8 1017ᵇ25, XI 2 1060ᵇ1–2. The significance of calling something *tode ti* is further discussed in 4.5.

[7] It is noteworthy, too, that Aristotle never advocates the weaker view—
attributed to him, e.g., in Burnyeat, *Notes on Book Zeta of Aristotle's Metaphysics*, 4—
that a substance is ontologically independent of its coincidental (or non-necessary)
attributes considered as particular property-instances or tropes.

nate ontological independence of substances—must be formulated differently by these theories. It seems, then, that if *in re* attributes were ontologically independent of substances, it could only be because *they were instantiated by something else,* since they cannot exist uninstantiated by particulars of some sort. This is exactly how we see Aristotle thinking in the following text: "Heat and straightness [and whiteness] can be present in every part of a thing, but it is impossible for all of it to be hot, white, or straight [and nothing else]. For then the attributes would be separate" (*Long.* 3 465^{b}12–14). Whiteness would be separate from substance, notice, not if it existed entirely uninstantiated, but if it were instantiated by a being that was wholly and exclusively white. Such a being is clearly not an Aristotelian substance, however, on the order of Socrates or Bellerophon, but something more like the Platonic form of whiteness, which is indeed white and nothing else.[8]

Substances can exist, then, whether or not their attributes exist through being instantiated by something else. Attributes, on the other hand, cannot exist unless they are instantiated by Aristotelian substances, since such substances are (in Aristotle's view) the only ultimate subjects of predication. The separation of substance from attributes is not only intelligible, therefore, but entirely of a piece with their inseparability from it.

Because substances are ontologically independent of attributes, they are prior in substance to them: "for those things are prior in substance [to other things] which they surpass in existing separately" (*Met.* XIII 2 1077^{b}2–3). Thus being a substance and being prior in substance seem to come to much the same thing. For being a substance entails being separate, which entails being ontologically independent, which entails being prior in substance.[9]

---

[8] A similar line of thought is also detectable in *Ph.* I 4 188^{a}6–13: "Attributes are not separate [from substance]. If colors [e.g., white] and states [e.g., healthy] are mixed together [as Anaxagoras supposes], then, if they should be distinguished, we shall have a white [thing] or a healthy [thing] that is nothing else and is not predicated [of substance]. Hence Anaxagoras' Mind is absurd: it is seeking the impossible, since it wishes to distinguish them and this is impossible, whether with respect to quantities or with respect to qualities—quantity, because there is no smallest magnitude, quality, because attributes are not separate [from substance]." Platonic forms are discussed in 1.2.

[9] Elsewhere, however, Aristotle seems to distinguish ontological independence from substantial priority: "A thing is said to be prior to other things where if it does

There are, however, three other sorts of priority, or primacy, enjoyed by substances that are of potentially greater interest:[10]

Met. VII 1 1028ª31–ᵇ2 Something is said to be primary in many ways. All the same, substance is primary in all of them: in account, in knowledge, and in time. For none of the other things that are predicated is separate, but only this one. And *it* is primary in account, since the account of substance is of necessity present in the account of each of them. Indeed, we think we know each thing most of all, e.g., man or fire, when we know what it is, rather [than when we know its] quality or quantity or place, since even each of these we know only when we know what the quality or the quantity is.

Priority in account and in knowledge are adequately explained here for present purposes—we shall have more to say about them later. Priority in time is more difficult. Initially, it seems to be just ordinary temporal priority: "Other things are prior with respect to time; some by being further from the present, i.e., in the case of past events (for the Trojan War is prior to the Persian, because it is further from the present), others by being nearer the present, i.e., in the case of future events (for the Nemean Games are prior to the Pythian, if we treat the present as beginning and first point, because they are nearer the present)" (*Met.* V 11 1018ᵇ14–19).[11] If priority in time were such simple temporal priority, however, substances would have to be able to exist before their attributes. But that, as we saw, is not possible. For though substances can exist whether or not their attributes are instantiated by other things, they cannot exist without attributes themselves.

---

not exist, the others will not exist, whereas it can exist without the others; there is also [priority] in time, and with respect to substance" (*Ph.* VII 7 260ᵇ17–19). The explanation for this equivocation probably lies with Plato, since he seems to have identified both natural and substantial priority with such independence: "A thing is prior with respect to its nature and substance when it is possible for it to be without other things but not them without it: this distinction was used by Plato" (*Met.* V 11 1019ª1–4). For clarity's sake, I shall refer to ontological independence alone as substantial priority.

[10] *Proteron* (prior) and *prôton* (primary) are the superlative and comparative of the same adjective. Thus something is primary in a given class if it is prior to everything else in that class.

[11] Also *Cat.* 12 14ª26–9.

What then is priority in time? Aristotle never explicitly tells us.[12] But his use of the notion is remarkably consistent: in one way, actuality (form) is prior in time to potentiality (matter); in another, potentiality is prior in time to actuality. The following text describes both cases and explains the difference between them: "In time it [actuality] is prior [to potentiality] in this sense: that which is actual, which is identical in form but not in number [to the potential being with the same form], is prior. I mean that to this particular man already existing in actuality, and to the corn, and to what is [actually] seeing, the matter and the seed and what is capable of seeing, which are potentially man and corn and seeing, but not yet actually, are prior in time; however prior in time to these are other things that are actually [man, corn, seeing], from which these come-to-be. For always out of that which is potentially that which is actually comes-to-be by agency of that which is actually, e.g., man out of man, musician by agency of musician, always when something is first moving; and the thing that moves [it] is already actually [what it is moving it to be]" (*Met.* IX 8 1049^{b}17–27). Priority in time seems, therefore, to be the sort of priority exhibited by F to G, when F is (part of) the explanation of the temporal phenomenon of G's coming-into-being. More particularly, the primacy in time characteristic of substances is the primacy of actuality to potentiality: "However [actuality] is also prior in substance, first, because the things that are posterior in coming-to-be are prior in form and in substance (e.g., male adult is [prior] to boy and man to seed; for the one already has the form that the other doesn't) and because everything that comes-to-be proceeds toward a first principle and an end (for that for the sake of which [something is] is a first principle, and the coming-to-be is for the sake of the end), and the actuality is the end, and it is for the sake of this that the potentiality is acquired. For animals do not see in order that they may have sight, rather they have sight so that they may see" (IX 8 1050^{a}4–11). It follows—and this is the most significant result for our purposes—that what is prior in time need not preexist what it is prior to.

To see this, consider the eternal spatial movement of the heavens. It is primary in time because it is the efficient cause of all the other types of movement. But it was not going on at a time when no other types of movement existed, since there have always been other types of movement

---

12. Though he does perhaps hint at the view I attribute to him at *Met.* IX 8 1050^{a}3 of "priority in accordance with coming-to-be and [i.e.?] time."

6

(8.1–4).[13] Similarly, matter (or the material cause) is prior in time to the compound of matter and form. But that does not entail that it existed before the compound did. For the heavens themselves are compounds of matter—primary body or ether—and form.[14] Since they are eternal, however, their matter cannot exist before they do.

What exhibits the requisite sort of priority in the case of attributes are the subjects—the underlying substances—that undergo alteration when attributes come-to-be or pass-away: "Only substances are said unqualifiedly to come-to-be. In the other cases it is evident that there must be some subject, which is the thing that comes-to-be [something]; for when a quantity, a quality, a relation, a when, or a where comes-to-be, it is of a subject, because substance is never said of any other subject, whereas the

---

[13] *Ph.* VIII 7 260^{b}29–261^{a}12: "Again it [locomotion, change of place] must be primary in time, since this is the only kind of motion [change] possible for eternal things. But [it may be objected], for each particular thing that comes-to-be, locomotion must be the last kind of motion it undergoes. For after a thing comes-to-be, first alteration *(alloiôsis)* and increase [growth] *(auxêsis)* take place, whereas locomotion *(phora)* belongs only to things already completed. There must, however, be another thing that is in the process of locomotion and prior, which will be the cause even of the coming-to-be of the things that come-to-be, but which is not itself in process of coming-to-be, as, e.g., what begets is the cause of what is begotten. It might indeed appear that coming-to-be is the primary kind of movement [change] for the simple reason that things must first come-to-be [before they can do anything else]. But though this is the case for any particular thing that comes-to-be, in general there must be something in movement prior to things that come-to-be that does not itself come-to-be [viz., the first heavens, which is in eternal circular movement], and again there must be another thing prior to this [viz., the unmoved mover, God]. And since coming-to-be cannot be the primary movement—for then all things in movement could pass-away—it is clear that none of the movements next in order is prior. By the movements next in order I mean increase, then alteration and decrease [decay] and passing-away. For all these are posterior to coming-to-be, so that if not even coming-to-be is prior to locomotion, neither is any of the other changes *(metabolôn)*."

[14] Ether is a fifth element, beyond the strictly sublunary elements—earth, water, air, and fire. It is discussed in 3.4, 7.2, and 8.2. *Sôma prôton* is Aristotle's own favored term for it, but *Cael.* I 2 269^{b}2–6, I 3 270^{b}19–25, *Mete.* I 3 339^{b}25–27 acknowledge that *aithêr*, as used by Anaxagoras and others, has the same referent. Hence, as is often done, I shall use 'ether' instead of the more cumbersome 'primary body'.

7

others are said of [substance]" (*Ph.* I 7 190ᵃ32–ᵇ1).[15] For an attribute to come-to-be, then, is for a particular substance that exists in actuality to come to have it, since "without substances it is not possible for attributes or changes to exist" (*Met.* XII 5 1071ᵃ1–2). For a particular substance to come-to-be, on the other hand, is not for an already existing attribute to come-to-be in some other subject. Substance is prior in time to attributes for this reason.[16]

Being separate entails being primary in account, knowledge, and time. But being primary in these ways also seems to entail being separate: "For neither in account nor in time nor in knowledge[17] can the attributes be prior to the substance, since they will also be separate [if they are]" (*Met.* VII 13 1038ᵇ27–29). We can see why this is so if we return to the inseparability of attributes. For attributes are inseparable from substance, in Aristotle's view, because to be an attribute just is to be something that is predicated of some substance as subject. It follows that the account or definition of what a given attribute is must capture this essential fact about it. Hence, in the context of a *de re* theory of attributes, the priority in account accorded to substances ensures their priority in substance (ontological independence).

It would be a mistake to conclude, however, that separation in general just is three-way primacy. For *chôriston* is not a technical term in Aristotle, but an intuitive one. Primarily spatial in connotation, it is amenable to metaphorical extension to cover non-spatial relations. For example, F is separate from G when their accounts are distinct, or when they are separable in thought.[18] But while the ordinary connotation of *chôriston* allows it to perform yeoman service for Aristotle, it usually does little more than gesture in the direction of the precise relations, differing from context to context, that he uses it to convey. Thus while three-way primacy is not separation, it does capture almost all of what is essential to the type of separation characteristic of substances.

---

[15] Aristotle's account of alteration and change is discussed in 5.1.

[16] I am grateful to Alan Code who, on reading an earlier version of this section, sent me a copy of his very useful "Aristotle's Metaphysics as a Science of Principles," in which a similar view is defended (354–355).

[17] Reading γνώσει with Frede and Patzig, *Aristoteles Metaphysik Z*.

[18] *Ph.* V 3 226ᵇ21–3 (place); *EN* X 5 1175ᵇ31 (time); *DA* III 9 432ᵃ20; *Met.* VII 5 1030ᵇ23–26 (account); *Ph.* II 1 193ᵇ34 (thought).

I say almost all, because one other sort of priority exhibited by substances remains to be considered, namely, priority in nature. In *Categories*
12, this is explained as follows: "Of things that reciprocate as to implication
of existence, that which is in some way the cause of the other's existence
might reasonably be called prior in nature. And that there are some such
cases is clear. For there being a man reciprocates as to implication of
existence with the true statement about it: if there is a man, the statement
whereby we say that there is a man is true, and reciprocally—since if the
statement whereby we say there is a man is true, there is a man. And
whereas the true statement is in no way the cause of the actual thing's
existence, the actual thing does seem in some way the cause of the statement's being true; for it is because the actual thing exists or does not that
the statement is called true or false" (14^b11–22). Clearly, then, natural
priority is a sort that substances enjoy. For attributes exist because substances do, but not vice versa.

In addition to this distinctive sort of natural priority, Aristotle also
recognizes an apparently different sort: "the order of coming-to-be and
that of substance are opposed. For that which is posterior in the order of
coming-to-be is prior in nature, and that which is first in nature is last in
coming-to-be" (*PA* II 1 646^a24–28).[19] Thus the actual animal is prior in
nature to the potential one that is prior in coming-to-be, though the two
do not reciprocate as to implication of existence: "there was no necessity,
given that your father came-to-be, that you should come-to-be, only that
he should have, given that you did" (*GC* II 11 338^b9–11). This sort of
natural priority, however, seems to be just the sort of priority in time
enjoyed by substances.

Since priority in time is one sort of natural priority, then, and entails the
other distinctive sort, it follows that the three types of priority explicitly
attributed to substances really do comprise *all* the forms of it, as *Met. VII 1*
1028^a31–$^b2$ claims.

At the end of the day, then, what we have discovered is this. To be a
substance is to be separate from attributes (that is, all nonsubstances), and
so to be ontologically independent of—or prior in substance to—them.
Being separate, in turn, entails being prior in nature (in both senses of the
phrase) and entails (and is entailed by) being prior in account, knowledge,
and time. Substance is thus ontologically primary and also epistemologically primary. When substance is analyzed into form and matter, however,

---

[19] Also *Ph.* VIII 7 261^a13–14.

9

the issue of which of them is the focus of the various sorts of primacy also becomes important, and with it the issue of which of them might be prior to the others in at least some of the ways in which they are prior to attributes. But that is a topic we cannot adequately discuss until Aristotle's own analysis of substance has been further explored.

1.2 Platonic Forms

Separation is the hallmark of Aristotle's substances. It is likewise the Aristotelian hallmark of Platonic forms:[20]

> *Met. XIII 4 1078ᵇ12–32* The belief in forms came about in those who spoke about them, because, in regard to truth, they were persuaded by the Heraclitean argument that all perceptibles are always in flux, so that if scientific knowledge is to be of anything, there must, in their view, be some different natures, over and above perceptibles, which are permanent; for there is no scientific knowledge of things in flux. Socrates occupied himself with the virtues of character, and in connection with them became the first to raise the problem of universal definitions. . . . It was reasonable that Socrates should seek the essence (*to ti estin*). For he was seeking to deduce, and essence (*to ti estin*) is the first principle of deductions. . . . For there are two things that may be fairly ascribed to Socrates—inductive arguments and universal definition, both of which are concerned with a first principle of scientific knowledge. But Socrates did not separate the universals or the definitions. His successors, however, did separate them, and these were the kinds of beings they called forms.

Hence, in Aristotle's view at least, separate forms are the offspring of a Heraclitean view about perceptibles (they are in flux) and a Socratic view about scientific knowledge (its first principles are definitions of universal essences). Whether he is right about this is another matter, but we needn't worry about it. Our focus is Aristotle and how he understood Plato, not in whether he was right to understand him as he did.[21]

---

[20] Platonists themselves, however, may not have explicitly advocated it as such: "Those who talk about forms do not notice that they too are doing this: they separate the objects of natural science though they are less separable than the objects of mathematics" (*Ph.* II 2 193ᵇ35–194ᵃ1).

[21] As an historian of philosophy, Aristotle enjoys a mixed reputation. My own

Just what being in flux amounts to is somewhat unclear, but for our purposes Aristotle's views are again all that matter.[22] Here is what he says: "Because they saw that all this world of nature is in movement, and that no truth is to be had about that which is in [process of alteration], it was not possible to have the truth at least about that which is in [process of] every sort of alteration. This belief blossomed into the most extreme of all the opinions we have mentioned, that of those who call themselves Heracliteans" (*Met.* IV 5 1010^{a}7−11). What is "most extreme" about this Heraclitean opinion is that it involves a denial of the principle of non-contradiction: "[from] the views of Heraclitus . . . it would follow that opposites would be predicated of the same thing" (XI 6 1063^{b}24−26).[23] For what is altering in every way, and so is always changing from F into not-F, is "no more (*ouden mallon*)" F than not-F (XII 5 1062^{b}2−7), and so is thought to be both equally.[24]

As a result, all statements made about fluxing things are on the same footing so far as truth is concerned: "the doctrine of Heraclitus, that all things are and are not, seems to make everything true" (*Met.* IV 7 1012^{a}24−26). The Platonists were right, then, to draw the conclusion that the objects of knowledge cannot be perceptibles, if these are in flux. For what is known to be F must *be F and not also not-F.* But no fluxing thing can have that feature—not even, as Aristotle perceptively notices, when F is the complex attribute G-and-not-G, since the opposite of it too must be true of them (XI 5 1062^{a}31−^{b}2).

Moreover, the Platonists were right to follow Socrates on scientific knowledge. For Aristotle himself believes that the first principles of a science are definitions of universal essences (2.1). Since universals are not identical to particulars, the Platonists were for this reason, too, on the side of the angels in treating forms as distinct from perceptibles. It was only in treating them as separate, then, that they went too far.

---

view is that he is a much more discerning student of Plato's philosophy, at least, than he is sometimes represented as being.

[22] Fine, *On Ideas,* 54−61, carefully discusses various options.

[23] Also *Met.* IV 3 1005^{b}23−25, 7 1012^{a}24−28.

[24] Compare *Republic* V 475e−480a, especially 479b9−10: "Is any one of the [perceptible] manys [e.g., the many perceptibly beautiful things] what someone says it is, then, any more (*mallon*) than it is not what he says it is?" Aristotle's own ingenious defense of the principle of non-contradiction is explored in 9.4−5.

Though *XIII 4* is a large part of Aristotle's account of the origins of Platonism, it omits a crucial chapter: "Since they [Platonists] took it to be necessary that were there to be any substances besides the ones that are perceptible and in flux they would have to be separate from them, and they had no others, they set apart these things spoken of universally, so that it followed that universals and particulars were virtually the same natures" (*Met.* XIII 10 1086^{b}7–11).[25] Initially at least, it may seem that the things described as "spoken of universally" here are the forms themselves, and that the Platonists are described as having "no others," because forms were the only substances in their ontology besides the fluxing perceptible ones. But since what is being described is the way Platonists *came to have forms in their ontology in the first place,* that cannot be right.

What Aristotle actually intends becomes clear only when we add the following text to the omitted chapter: "They [Platonists] claim that there is man-itself, and horse-itself, and health-itself, with no further qualification—a procedure like that of the people who said there are gods, but in human form. For just as the latter were positing nothing other than eternal men, so the former are positing forms as eternal perceptible substances" (*Met.* II 2 997^{b}8–12). What the Platonists began with, then, was a perceptible substance, F. And the first thing they did was attribute "no further qualification" to it, that is to say, no qualification besides F. As a result, the F-itself, as they called it, had all and only those features essential to Fs. (Recall that what the Platonists separated and Socrates did not were universal *essences.*) Second, to avoid having the F-itself be subject to flux, they made it eternal.

What drove the Platonists to proceed in this way, moreover, wasn't a lack of ontological resources, but a lack of philosophical ones: "Those who say there are forms are right in a way to separate them, since they are substances; but in another way they are wrong, because they say the one over many [i.e., a universal] is a form. The reason [they do both] is that they don't know how to characterize the indestructible substances that are over and above the particular perceptible ones. So they make the former the same in kind as the destructible ones (since we know those) [by] adding to perceptible ones the word 'itself', [e.g.] the man-itself and the horse-itself" (*Met.* VII 16 1040^{b}27–34). In having "no others," then, what the Platonists lacked were any substances besides particular perceptible ones on which to model the universals they needed as stable, non-fluxing objects of

---

[25] Also *Met.* I 6 987^{a}29–^{b}8, XIII 4 1078^{b}12–32.

knowledge. That is why, on their account, universals and particulars are "virtually the same natures." It is these perceptible substances, therefore, which are the input to Platonism, that are the "things spoken of universally," and not the forms that are its output.

As (would-be) particular substances, forms are ultimate subjects of predication that enjoy ontological priority. As (would-be) universal essences, they also enjoy epistemological priority. As both ontologically and epistemologically prior to perceptible substances, however, forms are also separate from them. And that renders them problematic: separation is "responsible for the problems that arise with the forms" (*Met.* XIII 10 1086ᵇ6–7). These problems are our next topic.

1.3 Problems with Platonic Forms

A particular is something there can be only one of, whereas a universal is "by nature such as to belong to many things" (*Met.* VII 13 1038ᵇ11–12). It follows, Aristotle claims, that universals cannot be separate from their instances: "What is one cannot be in many places at once, but what is common [a universal] exists in many places at once; so clearly no universal occurs apart from particulars and separate" (VII 16 1040ᵇ25–27). It is because of what universals essentially are, then, that they can exist only in particulars. Aristotle's *in-re*-ism about them is based on precisely that. Forms, however, as particulars themselves, can exist separately. How then can each of them also be a universal—a one over many? This problem about the nature of universals and their relation to particulars—the *one-over-many* problem, as it has come to be called—continues to be at the center of the debate between nominalists, Platonists, and Aristotelian realists about universals.[26] But for that very reason it is not a decisive objection to Platonism.

A second problem that Aristotle lays at the door of separation is presented in the famous *Third Man Argument* (*Met.* VII 13 1038ᵇ34–1039ᵃ3). In the *Peri Ideôn (On Ideas)*, preserved in Ps. Alexander, it is set out as follows:

> *On Aristotle's Metaphysics I 84.22-85.2* If *[84.22]* what is predicated truly of some plurality of things is also *[84.23a]* [some] other thing besides the thing of which it is predicated, *[84.23b]* being separated

---

[26] E.g., Lewis, "New Work for a Theory of Universals," 197–201.

from them (for this is what those who posit the ideas [i.e., forms] think they prove; for this is why, according to them, there is such a thing as man–itself, because man is predicated truly of the particular men, these being a plurality, and it is other than the particular men)— but if this is so, there will be a third man. For if the [man] being predicated is other than the things of which it is predicated and subsists on its own, and *[84.28]* [if] man is predicated both of the particulars and of the idea, then *[85.1]* there will be a third man besides the particular and the idea. In the same way, there will also be a fourth [man] predicated of this [third man], of the idea, and of the particulars, and similarly also a fifth, and so on to infinity.[27]

At the heart of this argument lie three crucial principles:

One-over-many: Whenever a plurality of things are F, they are F in virtue of having one thing, the F, predicated of them. *(84.22)*

Separation: Whenever F is predicated of a plurality of things, F is separate from the things of which it is predicated. *(84.23a)*

Self-predication: Any form of F is itself F. *(84.28)*

From *Separation,* a fourth is derived:

Non-identity: Whenever F is predicated of a plurality of things, F is non-identical to the things of which it is predicated. *(84.23b)*

These four principles generate the regress begun in *85.1* with the third man.

The *Third Man Argument* is a serious problem, then, for anyone committed to such principles. But it is one that may be solvable, even by a Platonist. For example, it is open to him to treat the F-itself as a self-subsistent particular F, which is F because it is perfectly F. Perceptible Fs, by contrast, are (imperfectly) F through resembling the paradigm F-itself to which they are non–identical.[28] The F-itself will then be F because of itself and not because of something else that it resembles. The *Third Man* is thereby defused and *One-over-many* somewhat weakened. The cost, however, is commitment to the existence of self-subsistent abstract paradigms,

---

[27] Fine, *On Ideas,* contains the Greek text of *Peri Idêon,* a translation (from which I quote), and a full philosophical commentary.

[28] Fine, *On Ideas,* 229–231.

and to explaining the resemblance that exists between them and percept-ibles. But that is a cost one might simply be willing to pay. Like *One-over-many*, therefore, the *Third Man* is a serious problem for Platonism, but not a decisive one.

A third problem raised by separate forms has received somewhat less attention than the others.[29] It concerns the question of whether the first principles are particulars or universals: "For if they are universals, they will not be substances, since nothing common signifies a this but rather a such, but substance is a this. And if we can actually posit what is predicated in common [i.e., a universal] as a [particular] this, Socrates will be several animals—himself and man and animal, since each of these signifies some this and one. If, then, the first principles are universals, these things follow. But if they are not universals, but of the nature of particulars, they will not be knowable. For the scientific knowledge of all things is universal. It follows that there must be other principles prior to the first principles, which are predicated universally of them, if indeed there is to be knowl-edge of them. [And this is absurd, since no principles are prior to first ones]" (*Met.* III 6 1003[a]7–17).[30] The first part of the problem, then, concerns definition. Socrates is a particular this—one single thing. He is also a man (species), and so an animal (genus). If man and animal are themselves particular thises, however, Socrates will not be one, but several. Thus if first principles are, like forms, particular thises that are also in some way universals, they will not be definable, since any proposed definition will fragment the supposedly unitary definiendum into all the different particulars that appear in the definiens.[31]

The second part of the problem concerns scientific knowledge, and is developed as follows:

Met. VII 6 1031[a]28–[b]14 In the case of things spoken of intrinsically *(kath' hauta)*, is it necessary that they be the same [as their essences]? E.g., if there are some substances to which no other substances or

---

[29] Though Code, "The Aporematic Approach to Primary Being in *Metaphysics* Z," recognizes its fundamental importance.

[30] Also *Met.* XI 2 1060[b]19–23: "A further problem is raised by the fact that all knowledge is of universals, i.e., of the such, but substance does not belong to universals, but is rather a this and separate, so that if there is scientific knowledge of the first principles, how are we to suppose the first principle to be substance?"

[31] Aristotle's own views on the unity of definition are discussed in 3.8.

natures are prior, as some say holds of the forms [is this true of them]? For [*a*31] if the good–itself and the essence (*to einai*) of good will be different . . . then there will be other substances and natures beyond those that were mentioned [the forms], and those others will be prior and substances,[32] if the essence (*to ti ên einai*) is substance. And [*b*3] if, on the other hand, they have been detached from one another, of the ones [forms] there will not be knowledge and [*b*4] the others [essences] will have no being (and by being detached I mean [what holds] if neither the essence of good belongs to the good–itself nor being good to it). For we have scientific knowledge of each thing when we know its essence, and the same holds in the case of the good and [of] all other things, so that if the essence of good is not good, neither is the essence of being a being, nor is the essence of one one. Similarly, either every essence is, or none is, so that if the essence of being is not a being either, neither [is] any of the others. [*b*10] Besides, that to which the essence of good does not belong is not good. Therefore [*b*11] it is necessary that the good and the essence of good be one, and beauty and the essence of beauty, and so with all things that are not spoken of coincidentally, but that are spoken of intrinsically, and are primary.

The F–itself was introduced by the Platonists to be an epistemological first principle safe from flux. Suppose, then, that the F–itself is not detached from the essence of F, so that one belongs to (or is predicated of) the other. The two will then be different, since one will be a particular subject and the other a universal attribute. The essence of F, however, is primary in scientific knowledge. Hence, since the same things must be both ontologically and epistemologically primary, it must be a substance. The primacy of the F–itself is, therefore, threatened (*a*31).

Suppose, on the other hand, that the F–itself and the essence of F are detached from one another, so that neither is predicated of the other. Each will then be a separate substance. But substances are epistemologically primary. Hence to know them is to know the essences to which they are identical. This will not now be true of the F–itself, however, since it and its essence are different substances (*a*31).

By the same token, if the essence of F is detached from the F–itself, it cannot be F, since to be F, for a Platonist, is to participate in the F–itself. It

---

[32] Omitting μᾶλλον with Frede and Patzig, *Aristoteles Metaphysik Z* and the mss.

follows that the essence of being is not a being. On the plausible assumption that all essences are on an ontological par, it follows that the essence of F does not exist ($^b4$). It also follows that the F-itself, which is supposed to be F, cannot be F. For to be F is to have something whose essence is the essence of F, and from that essence the F-itself is, by hypothesis, detached ($^b10$).

Whether or not the F-itself is detached from the essence of F, then, apparently devastating consequences ensue. Hence, in Aristotle's view at least, Platonism is epistemologically and ontologically self-defeating. But what is true of it, is equally true, apparently, of any theory that fails to identify the intrinsic beings (the substances) with their own essences ($^b11$). A general requirement of a successful theory is thereby established.

This two-part problem—the first part about definition, the second about ontology and scientific knowledge—is the Primacy Dilemma. It is the focus of the chapters that follow. For, unlike either *One-over-many* or the *Third Man,* it is as much a problem for Aristotle himself as for his Plato. For to be ontologically primary, Aristotle's own substances have to be particulars. But to be substances they must also be epistemologically primary. Therein lies the rub. For, like Socrates and Plato, Aristotle believes that it is universals, specifically universal essences, not particulars, that are primary in this way. But, apparently, nothing can be both a universal and a particular—look at the disasters that befall Platonism.

The Primacy Dilemma is a serious problem, therefore, and one whose seriousness Aristotle clearly recognizes. In fact, he describes it as the "greatest" of the problems philosophy faces (*Met.* XIII 10 1087^{a}10–13). Little wonder, then, that by following out his subtle and ingenious response to it we shall be led to the very heart of his metaphysical vision.

TWO

SCIENTIFIC KNOWLEDGE

2.1 Aristotelian Sciences

An Aristotelian science deals with a distinct, non-overlapping genus of beings that have forms or essences.[1] When appropriately regimented, it may be set out as a structure of demonstrations *(apodeixeis)*, the indemonstrable first principles of which are real (as opposed to nominal) definitions of those essences.[2] More precisely, the first principles special to a science are like this. Others that are common to all sciences, such as the principle of non-contradiction, have a somewhat different character (9.4). Since all these first principles are necessary, and demonstration is necessity preserving, scientific theorems are also necessary.

Though we cannot grasp a first principle by demonstrating it from yet more primitive principles, it must—if we are to have any unqualified scientific knowledge at all—be "better known" than any of the science's other theorems (*EN* VI 3 1139^{b}33–34). This better knowledge is provided by understanding *(nous)* and the process by which principles come within understanding's ken is induction—*epagôgê* (1139^{b}28–29, 6 1141^{a}7–8).[3] Induction begins with perception of particulars, which in turn gives rise to retention of perceptual contents, or memory. When many perceptual contents have been retained in memory, we "come to have an account out of the retention of such things" (*APo.* II 19 100^{a}1–3). Craft and science

---

[1] *APo.* I 7 75^{b}17–20, 11 77^{a}26–32, 23 84^{b}13–18, 28 87^{a}38–39, 32 88^{a}30–^{b}3; *Met.* IV 2 1003^{b}19–21.

[2] Sorabji, "Definitions: Why Necessary and in What Way?"

[3] Aristotle's canonical account of this process is given in *APo.* II 19. More compressed versions appear in *Ph.* I 1 and *Met.* I 1. Bolton, "Aristotle's Method in Natural Science: *Physics* I," carefully compares these three accounts, arguing persuasively that they use "the same unusual language . . . to say the same thing."

arise from experience, which is a unified set of such memories (100ª3–6), "when, from many notions gained by experience, one universal supposition about similar objects is produced" (*Met.* I 1 981ª1–7). Getting from particulars to universals, therefore, is a largely noninferential and epistemologically unproblematic process. If we simply attend to particular cases—perhaps to all, perhaps to just one—and have some acumen *(agchinoia)*, we will get there.[4]

The transition from experience to craft or science results in the grasp of universals, but so too does the earlier transition from memory to experience: "To have a supposition that when Callias was ill of this disease, this did him good, and similarly in the case of Socrates, and in many other such cases, is a matter of experience. But to have a supposition that it has done good to all persons of a certain sort, marked off in a class, when they were ill of this disease, e.g., phlegmatic or bilious people when burning with fever, this is a matter of craft knowledge" (*Met.* I 1 981ª7–12). For recognizing a multiplicity of people as belonging to a single class, and a single type of treatment as having benefited all of them, clearly requires some grasp of universals. What the experienced lack, therefore, is not a grasp of universals generally, but a grasp of the special sort of universals required for scientific explanation—they "know *(isasi)* the that, but they do not know the why, while others [scientists] know the why, i.e., the cause" (981ª28–30). That is why they cannot provide the sort of formal instruction typically found in a craft or science: "In general it is a sign of the one who knows that he can teach, and therefore we think that craft is scientific knowledge to a higher degree than experience is; for the former [someone who knows] can teach and the latter [someone with mere experience] cannot" (981ᵇ7–10).

The following text provides important insight into these two types of universals, and what moving from one to the other involves:

APo. II 19 100ª15–ᵇ5 When *[ª15]* one of the undifferentiated items makes a stand, then for the first time there is a universal in the soul; for although one perceives particulars, perception is of universals—e.g., of man and not of Callias the man. Next, *[ᵇ1]* a stand is made among these items, until something partless and universal makes a stand. E.g., such-and-such an animal makes a stand, until animal does; and with animal a stand is made in the same way. Thus it is clear that we

---

[4] *APr.* II 23 68ᵇ15–29 (all); *APo.* I 31 88ª12–17, II 2 90ª24–30 (one); *APo.* I 34 89ᵇ10–13 (acumen).

must get to know the first principles by induction; for this is the way in which perception instills universals.

The undifferentiated item that makes the stand referred to in *15 is "the entire *(pantos)* universal" (*APo.* II 19 100^a6–7). In *Physics* I 1, where it is called "the whole *(holon)* universal" (184^a25), it is characterized as "indeterminate" and "better known in perception" (184^a21–26). This is the sort of universal, therefore, that perception is "of" (*15). When such undifferentiated or indeterminate universals are analyzed into their "elements *(stoicheia)* and first principles," they become intrinsically clear and unqualifiedly better known than their perceptible predecessors (184^a16–21). These elements and principles are the "partless" items that make the stand referred to in *1.

It is clear from this account of induction that first principles come in two varieties: *ontological* first principles or essences, which are fundamental causal factors in the world; and *epistemic* first principles, principles of our scientific knowledge of the world, which are accounts or definitions of these essences. Aristotle is not always careful to distinguish these. For example, he speaks of Socrates as not separating "the definitions," when it is the essences that are their ontological correlates to which he is referring (*Met.* XIII 4 1078^b30–31). Such carelessness becomes at once intelligible and innocuous, however, when we recall that Aristotle is a realist about definition, as about truth, who requires a structural isomorphism between definiens and definiendum: "the definition is an account, and every account has parts, and as the account is to the thing, so the part of the account is to the part of the thing" (10 1034^b20–22).[5]

Like the step from memory to undifferentiated universals, the step from the latter to analyzed universals is itself inductive (*APo.* II 19 100^b3–4). Thus induction includes two rather different sorts of processes: the broadly perceptual (and somewhat physiologically conceived) one by which we reach unanalyzed universals from the perception of particulars, and the other, more intellectual and discursive one, by which we proceed from unanalyzed universals to analyzed ones and their definitions. When Aristotle characterizes Socrates' elenctic method as inductive (*Met.* XIII 4 1078^b28–29), it is presumably the latter process he has in mind.

The inductive path to first principles and scientific knowledge begins, then, with perception of particulars and of perceptually accessible, unanalyzed universals, and leads eventually to analyzed universals (first prin-

---

[5] Also *Cat.* 12 14^b14–22; *Met.* II 1 993^b30–31, IV 7 1011^b26–28.

ciples) and accounts (definitions) of them. Perception alone, unaided by understanding, cannot reach the end of this journey, therefore, but understanding without experience cannot so much as begin it (*APr.* I 30 46ª17–18, *DA* III 8 432ª7–9).

2.2 Dialectic and First Principles

Because the first principles proper to a science "are primary among all [the truths contained in it]," they cannot be demonstrated within that science. They can, however, be defended by dialectic. For, since it "examines," and does so by appeal not to scientific principles *per se* but to *endoxa,* dialectic "provides a way to the first principles of all lines of inquiry" (*Top.* I 2 101ª36–b4). In due course, we shall see what that way is. First, though, we need to understand what dialectic utilizes on the journey.

Endoxa are opinions that are accepted without demurral "by everyone or by the majority or by the wise, either by all of them or by most or by the most notable and reputable" (*Top.* I 1 100b21–23), so that the many do not disagree with the wise about them, nor do "one or the other of these two classes disagree among themselves" (I 10 104ª8–11). *Endoxa,* therefore, are beliefs to which there is simply no worthwhile opposition (I 11 104b19–28). Merely apparent *endoxa,* by contrast, are opinions that mistakenly appear to have this uncontested status (I 1 100b23–25, 10 104ª15–33).

Defending first principles on the basis of *endoxa* is a matter of going through the problems *(aporiai)* "on both sides of a subject" until they are solved (*Top.* I 2 101ª35). Suppose, for example, that the topic for dialectical investigation is this: Is being one and unchanging, or not? A competent dialectician will, first, follow out the consequences of each disjunct to see what problems they face. Second, he will go through the problems he has uncovered to determine which can be solved and which cannot (VIII 14 163b9–12). As a result he will be well placed to attack or defend either disjunct in the strongest possible way.

Aporematic, which is the part of philosophy that deals with such problems, is like dialectic in its methods, but differs from it in important respects. In a dialectical argument, for example, the opponent may refuse to accept a proposition that a philosopher would accept: "The premises of the philosopher's deductions or those of the one investigating by himself, though true and familiar, may be refused by . . . [an opponent] because they lie too near to the original proposition, and so he sees what will happen if he grants them. But the philosopher is unconcerned about this.

Indeed, he will presumably be eager that his axioms should be as familiar and as near to the question at hand as possible, since it is from premises of this sort that scientific deductions proceed" (*Top.* VIII 1 155^{b}10–16).[6] Since the truth may well hinge on propositions whose status is just like these premises, there is no guarantee that what a dialectician might consider most defensible for the purposes of dispute will be true.

Drawing on this new class of *endoxa,* then, the philosopher examines both the claim that being is one and unchanging, and the claim that it is not, in just the way that the dialectician does. As a result, he determines, let us suppose, that the most defensible, or least problematic, conclusion is that in some senses of the terms being is one and unchanging, in others not. To reach this conclusion, however, he will have to disambiguate and reformulate *endoxa* on both sides, partly accepting and partly rejecting them (*Top.* VIII 14 164^{b}6–7). Others he may well have to reject outright. If so, some beliefs that initially seemed to be *endoxa,* that seemed to be unproblematic, will have emerged as only apparently such (I 1 100^{b}23–25). These he will have to explain away: "We must not only state the true view, but also give the explanation for the false one, since that promotes confidence. For when we have a clear and good account of why a false view appears true, that makes us more confident of the true view" (*EN* VII 14 1154^{a}22–25). If, at the end of this process "the problems are solved and the *endoxa* are left, that," Aristotle claims, "will be an adequate proof" of the philosopher's conclusion (1 1145^{a}6–7).

But in that claim lies a problem. For while dialectic treats things "only in relation to opinion," philosophy must treat them "according to their truth" (*Top.* I 14 105^{b}30–31). *Endoxa,* however, are just opinions accepted without demurral by "everyone, or by the majority, or by the wise." Since even such unopposed beliefs may nevertheless be false, how can an argument that relies on them be guaranteed to reach the truth? The answer lies in peirastic *(peirastikê)*—in aporematic philosophy's dialectical capacity to examine (I 1 101^{b}3).

Peirastic is "a type of dialectic which has in view not the person who knows but the one who pretends to know, but does not" (*SE* I 11 171^{b}4–6). In other words, it is the type especially useful in dealing with sophists (I 1 165^{a}21). We may best understand how it operates, and what it accomplishes, however, by exploring sophistical refutations, which are its evil twin. For whereas peirastic exposes the genuine ignorance of someone

---

6 Also *APr.* I 30 46^{a}3–10; *Top.* I 14 105^{b}30–31.

who pretends to scientific knowledge, sophistical refutations give the appearance of exposing the ignorance of someone who really does have such knowledge (I 6 168ᵇ4–10).

Sophistical refutations come in two varieties: an a-type, which is "an apparent deduction or refutation rather than a real one," and a b-type, which is "a real deduction that is only apparently proper to the subject in question" (*SE* I 8 169ᵇ20–23). Thus, while a-type sophistical refutations are invalid or eristic arguments, b-type are closely akin to paralogisms (I 11 171ᵇ34–37).

The paralogisms proper to a science are those based on its first principles and conclusions (*Top.* I 11 171ᵇ36–37). For example, someone who squares the circle by means of lunes produces a geometrical paralogism, since he "proceeds from principles that are proper to geometry" and "cannot be adapted to any subject except geometry" (172ᵃ4–5).[7] But someone who uses Bryson's method of squaring the circle,[8] or who uses Zeno's argument that motion is impossible in order to refute a doctor's claim that it is better to take a walk after dinner, has produced a b-type sophistical refutation. For Bryson's and Zeno's arguments are not proper to geometry or medicine but "common" (172ᵃ8–9). Such arguments are paralogistic, moreover, even if they are sound: "Bryson's method of squaring the circle, even if the circle is thereby squared, is still sophistical because it is not in accord with the relevant subject matter" (171ᵇ16–18). Hence the difference between paralogisms and b-type sophistical refutations is that the former have premises proper to the relevant science but false, whereas the latter have premises that are not proper to it but true.

Because paralogisms depend on premises proper to a science, it is the business of the practitioner of that science to diagnose and refute them. It is not his business to deal with b-type sophistical refutations, however, since these depend on common things *(koina)*. For "it is dialecticians who study a refutation that depends on common things, i.e., do not belong to any [special] craft" (*SE* I 9 170ᵃ38–39). What these common things are, as this text suggests, are transcategorial attributes, such as being, unity, similarity, and so on, as well as such logical axioms as the principle of non-contradiction, which, because they hold of beings in all genera, cannot be the

---

[7] An argument of this sort, due to Hippocrates, is described in Heath, *A History of Greek Mathematics* Vol. 1, 183–201.

[8] It is difficult to say just what this method amounted to. See Heath, *A History of Greek Mathematics* Vol. 1, 223–225.

subject matter of a science that is, by its very nature, restricted to a single genus (2.1).[9] Since these attributes and principles are not proper to a science, *endoxa* about them cannot be proper to it either.

For the same reason dialecticians must also deal with a–type sophistical refutations, such as Antiphon's argument for squaring the circle. For this argument assumes that a circle is a polygon with a very large (but finite) number of sides. As a result, it "does away with the first principles of geometry" (*Ph.* I 2 185ª1–2)—specifically, the principle that magnitudes are divisible without limit.[10] Consequently, it cannot be discussed in a way that presupposes that principle, and so must be discussed on the basis of *endoxa* (*Top.* I 2 101ª37-ᵇ4).

Since what makes b–type sophistical refutations sophistical, then, is just the fact that they employ *endoxa* that aren't proper to a science as if they were proper to it, we should expect that peirastic arguments will differ from them simply in having *endoxa* as premises that are in fact proper to it. Aristotle's somewhat opaque characterization of peirastic deductions confirms this expectation. For these, he says, "deduce from premises that are accepted by the answerer [i.e., the one being examined], and that must be known *(eidenai)* by anyone who claims to have the [relevant] scientific knowledge *(epistêmê)*" (*SE* I 2 165ᵇ4–6). Such premises are "taken not from the things from which one knows *(oiden),*" he says, "or even from those proper to the subject in question, but from the consequences that a man can know *(eidota)* without knowing *(eidenai)* the craft in question, but which if he does not know *(eidota)*, he is necessarily ignorant of the craft" (I 11 172ª21–34). In other words, they are not first principles of the relevant science—not "things from which one knows"—or other principles proper to it, but "consequences" of them.

---

[9] When the common things are logical axioms they are sometimes referred to as "common opinions" (*Met.* III 2 996ᵇ28, 997ª21), which makes them sound like *endoxa* (as I too hastily took them to be in "Dialectic and Philosophy in Aristotle"). But *Met.* IV 3 1005ª27–28 makes it plain that these axioms are common because they hold in common of all things that share the transcategorial attribute being, and not because they are held in common by all people: "it is clear that it is qua being that these things [the logical axioms] hold of all things (since this [viz., being a being] is what is common to [all of] them)." Some people, after all, do deny even the principle of non–contradiction (9.3). Nonetheless, *koina* and *endoxa* are closely related.

[10] Heath, *A History of Greek Mathematics* Vol. 1, 221–222, citing Simplicius.

Later in the same passage these consequences are identified as *endoxa:* "everybody, including those that do not possess a craft, makes use of dialectic as peirastic; for everyone tries to use peirastic to some extent in order to test those who claim to know things. And this is where the common things come in; for the testers know *(isasin)* these things for themselves just as well as those who do possess the craft—even if they seem to say quite inaccurate things" (*SE* I 11 172ª30–34). Hence, as we were led to expect by our investigation of b-type sophistical refutations, the premises of peirastic arguments are indeed *endoxa* proper to the science that the one undergoing peirastic examination is claiming to know.

Peirastic premises can be known *(eidenai, isasin)* by someone who lacks scientific knowledge *(epistêmê),* then, and are consequences of the principles of a science. It follows that they are true, and potentially objects of scientific knowledge—a potential that would be realized if they were in fact demonstrated from first principles. Since such premises are *endoxa,* it follows that some *endoxa* also have these features. But why do *endoxa* have to have them in order to serve as peirastic premises?

A person who really does have scientific knowledge may yet be the victim of a sophistical refutation—he may find himself caught in a contradiction when he is interrogated by a clever sophist. The mere fact that someone can be bested in this way, therefore, is not enough to show that he lacks scientific knowledge. What is further required is, first, that this argument not be a sophistical refutation, that its premises be true and proper to the science in question. But even that is not enough. For, second, they must also be premises that anyone who knows that science would have to know. Otherwise, an examinee could reject them and still know the science. Third, they must be premises it is possible to know without knowing the science. Otherwise, they could not figure in arguments available to nonscientists. Thus the various features that the premises of a peirastic argument must have are entailed by the purpose such arguments are intended to serve of enabling nonscientists to unmask the ignorant pretender to scientific knowledge.

As a generally educated person, the aporematic philosopher knows what it takes to be a genuine science of whatever sort: "In every study and investigation, humbler or more honorable alike, there appear to be two kinds of competence. One can properly be called scientific knowledge of the subject, the other as it were a sort of educatedness. For it is the mark of an educated person to be able to reach a judgment based on a sound estimate of what is properly expounded and what isn't. For this in fact is what we take to be characteristic of a generally educated person. And we expect such a person to be able to judge in practically all subjects" (*PA* I 1 639ᵃ1–8). Hence an educated person will know, for example, what level of exactness a science should have, given its subject matter (*EN* I 3 1094ᵇ23–27), and "what we should and should not seek to have demonstrated" (*Met.* IV 4 1006ᵃ5–11).

Using peirastic, therefore, the philosopher can determine, whether *x* is a pretender to, for example, mathematical knowledge. If *x* passes that test, the philosopher can use his own knowledge of what a mathematical science must be like to determine whether *x*'s mathematical claims are in fact scientific. If he finds that they are, he knows—albeit nonscientifically—that the undemonstrated mathematical first principles that *x* accepts are true. If, in particular, *x* accepts as such a principle that magnitudes are divisible without limit, the philosopher knows that it is true.

When he uses his dialectical skill to draw out the consequences of this principle and of its negation, however, he sees problems and supporting arguments based on *endoxa* on both sides. Since he knows the principle is true, however, his goal will be to solve the problems it faces and undo the arguments that seem to support its negation. If he is successful, he will have refuted all dialectical objections to it, and so will have provided a "demonstration by refutation" of it (*Met.* IV 4 1006ᵃ12). Such a demonstration is dialectic's—and so aporematic philosophy's—way to a first principle, and constitutes the "adequate proof" of it to which Aristotle refers (9.4–5).

In many texts, Aristotle characterizes problems as knots in our understanding that dialectic enables us to untie, in others, he characterizes dialectic itself as enabling us to make first principles clear.[11] What aporematic philosophy offers us in regard to the first principles of the sciences, then, is no knots—no impediments to clear and exact understanding. And with such clarity comes understanding of the most excellent and unqualified sort that manifests the virtue of theoretical wisdom. For such understanding could not be "the most exact form of scientific knowledge" if aporematic philosophy could make yet clearer and more exact what it had already grasped (*EN* VI 7 1141ᵃ16–17). Aporematic philosophy, then, is what the second stage of induction—the stage that culminates in under-

---

[11] *APr.* I 30 46ᵃ17–27; *Ph.* VIII 3 253ᵃ30–32; *DA* II 2 413ᵃ11–13; *Met.* III 1 995ᵃ27–33, VII 6 1032ᵃ6–11.

standing's grasp of analyzed universals—consists in. It is patently a descendent of the Socratic elenchus.[12]

Aporematic is not, however, the whole of philosophy. There are philosophical sciences similar in structure to the other more familiar ones (9.2–3). It is the philosopher-as-scientist's job to discover the first principles of these and, as aporematic philosopher, to defend them against arguments based on *endoxa*.[13]

2.3 Natural Sciences

"If we must speak exactly and not be guided by [mere] similarities," Aristotle tells us, we will not class anything as a genuine science unless it gives us knowledge of what "does not admit of being otherwise" (*EN* VI 3 1139^{b}18–24). At the same time, he says that "scientific knowledge is of what holds always or for the most part *(hôs epi to polu)*" (*Met.* VI 2 1027^{a}19–21), and that what holds for the most part does admit of being otherwise: "nothing can happen contrary to nature considered as eternal and necessary, but only where things for the most part happen in a certain way, but may also happen in another way" (*GA* IV 4 770^{b}9–13). This problem—consistency as I shall call it—will be our major target for the remainder of the chapter.

When we say that something admits of being otherwise, there are two quite different things we may have in mind: "What admits of being otherwise is said in two ways. In one it signifies *what holds for the most part* but falls short of [unqualified] necessity. . . . In another it signifies . . . *what happens by luck,* since it is no more natural for this to happen in one way than in the opposite" (*APr.* I 13 32^{b}4–13). What happens by luck, to begin with it, must have a coincidental efficient cause. Aristotle's examples show what he has in mind: "a builder is an intrinsic cause of a house, but that which is pale or knows music is a coincidental cause [of a house]," even if what is pale and knows music is the builder (*Ph.* II 5 196^{b}26–27).[14] In other words, the fact about the builder that is the real cause of his building a

---

[12] As Bolton, "Aristotle's Account of the Socratic Elenchus," argues.

[13] The accounts of dialectic, peirastic, and general education given in this section are further developed in my "Dialectic and Philosophy in Aristotle" and "Aristotelian Education."

[14] Also *Met.* VI 2 1027^{a}3–4.

house is not his being pale, but his knowing the craft of building. Generally speaking, therefore, x's being F_1 is a *coincidental efficient cause* of y's being G_1 if and only if either of the following holds:

1. x's being F_2 is an *intrinsic (kath' hauto)* efficient cause of y's being G_1, and F_1 is a coincidental feature of x.

2. x's being F_1 is an *intrinsic* efficient cause of y's being G_2, and G_1 is a coincidental feature of y.[15]

Since "the coincidental is indeterminate in number" (*Ph.* II 5 196[b]28), so that any old attribute can play the role of F_1 in (1) or G_1 in (2), such causes are clearly not of any scientific interest.

In addition, what happens by luck must have an 'as if' final cause (*Ph.* II 5 196[b]23–31),[16] which is to be understood as follows: If y's being G is the sort of thing that might be "an outcome of [deliberative] thought" (196[b]21–22), it is a candidate final cause of action. If wish *(boulêsis)*, which is the desire that drives deliberation or deliberate choice, was indeed its intrinsic efficient cause, y's being G is a genuine final cause. But if y's being G is just a coincidental effect of x's being F, y is only x's 'as if' final cause. In that case, y's being G is the result of luck.

Unlike chance *(to automaton)*, therefore, which applies quite generally to what results from coincidental efficient causes, luck *(tuchê)* is restricted to the subclass of them that are "achievable by action" (*Ph.* II 6 197[a]36–[b]3), and so consists of all those things "whose cause is indefinite and that come about not for the sake of something, and neither always nor for the most part nor in an orderly way" (*Rh.* I 10 1369[a]32–34). But this difference has no bearing on the scientific interest of what happens by luck: it is of no such interest (*Met.* VI 2 1027[a]19–21).

So much for what holds by luck. What, then, of what holds for the most part? How does a theorem that holds in this way differ from one that holds always or universally? The natural answer for us to give is that the differ-

---

[15] Like Mellor, *The Facts of Causation,* I think that causation fundamentally links facts, the constitutive attributes or universals of which occur in laws (considered as the ontological correlates of law statements). Thus x's being F_1 (or the fact that x is F_1) on a particular occasion causes x's being G_1 (or the fact that x is G_1) on that occasion only if F_1 and G_1 occur linked in a universal law of the appropriate sort. Hence I shall also speak (more loosely) of universals being causally linked. Aristotle almost certainly has the same sort of picture of causation in mind, as we shall see.

[16] Freeland, "Accidental Causes and Real Explanations."

ence is one of quantification: the first has the universal quantifier ($\forall$), the second, the quantifier most (M).[17] But this cannot be Aristotle's answer. For, first, theorems that hold for the most part are, in his view, universally quantified. Thus some universal laws hold "for the most part" (*EN* V 10 1137^{b}14–16), and "for the most part all [crabs] have the right claw bigger and stronger than the left" (*HA* IV 3 527^{b}6–7). If such theorems had (M) as their quantifier, therefore, they would have to be of the form

$$(Mx) \ (\forall x) \ (Fx \rightarrow Gx).$$

Since nothing can have that form, we have a problem—*quantifier.*

Second, deductions with universal premises and conclusions remain valid even when these hold only for the most part: "What follows [from] a thing for the most part—and what it follows [from]—must also be taken; for in the case of problems about what holds for the most part, deductions depend on propositions that, either all or some of them, hold for the most part (for the conclusion of each deduction is similar to its first principles [premises])" (*APr.* I 27 43^{b}32–36).[18] The corresponding deductions with (M) in place of ($\forall$), on the other hand, are not always valid. This deduction is valid:

$$\frac{(\forall x) \ (Fx \rightarrow Gx)}{(\forall x) \ (Gx \rightarrow Hx)}$$
$$(\forall x) \ (Fx \rightarrow Hx).$$

This one is not:

$$\frac{(Mx) \ (Fx \rightarrow Gx)}{(Mx) \ (Gx \rightarrow Hx)}$$
$$(Mx) \ (Fx \rightarrow Hx)$$

—most centenarians are women; most women are under seventy; but no centenarians are under seventy. Thus if theorems that hold for the most

---

[17] In saying this, I mean to beg no questions about the proper way to represent Aristotle's formal logic. Approximate representation of it in the Predicate Calculus simply allows some problems to be raised in a perspicuous way. The problems would arise in any case.

[18] Also *APo.* I 30 87^{b}22–25, II 12 96^{a}8–17.

part are of the form (M*x*) (F*x* → G*x*), the logic Aristotle provides for them is inconsistent. This problem is *validity*.[19]

Finally, sciences whose theorems hold for the most part have the same structure as sciences whose theorems hold by necessity. A deduction is a demonstration "when the premises from which the deduction starts are true first principles" (*Top.* I 1 100ᵃ27–28). But "there will be immediate first principles also in the case of what holds for the most part" (*APo.* II 12 96ᵃ17–19). Holding for the most part, then, is no obstacle to being demonstrable: "There is no scientific knowledge through demonstration of what holds by luck; for what holds by luck is neither necessary nor does it hold for the most part but comes about separately from these; and demonstration is of either of the former" (*APo.* I 30 87ᵇ19–22). Since "demonstration is a necessary thing" (*Met.* V 5 1015ᵇ6–7), it follows that what holds for the most part must also hold by some sort of necessity, even if not by the "unqualified necessity" that applies to things that "owe their necessity to something other than themselves" (1015ᵇ9–11) and that neither come-to-be nor pass-away (*EN* VI 3 1139ᵇ23–24). This problem is *modality*.

Any acceptable account of what holds for the most part, then, must solve *quantifier, validity,* and *modality*—preferably without invoking error. If, in addition, it leads to a credible solution to *consistency*, that will pretty much guarantee its correctness.

Aristotle associates what holds by necessity with what holds always: "*necessary* and *always* go together (since what is necessary cannot not be)" (*GC* II 11 337ᵇ35–36). He associates what holds for the most part with what rarely fails to happen: "the contrary of what happens for the most part is always comparatively rare" (*Top.* II 6 112ᵇ10–11). Finally, since what holds coincidentally (or by luck or chance) holds neither necessarily not for the most part (*Met.* V 30 1025ᵃ16–19), he associates it with what happens rarely. Apparently, then,

$$(\forall x) (Fx \rightarrow Gx)$$
$$(Rx) (Fx \rightarrow Gx)$$
$$(Mx) (Fx \rightarrow Gx)$$

are to be understood as

---

[19] Most scholars despair of its solution. Henkinson, "Philosophy of Science," 115, is typical: "the prospects for producing a logic of 'for the most part' useful in systematizing the vaguer parts of the Aristotelian sciences looks bleak indeed."

(Always) (Fx//Gx)
(Rarely) (Fx//Gx)
(Rarely) (Fx//not-Gx)

—which are in turn to be understood as specifying the frequency with which x will be G relative to (//) its being F.[20] The first states that it will always be G relative to being F; the second, that it will rarely be G relative to its being F; the third, that it will rarely be not-G relative to its being F.

There is surely something right and important here, but it cannot lie in interpreting what holds for the most part directly in terms of relative frequencies. For that would still leave our three problems unsolved. This is obviously so in the case of *quantifier* and *modality*, but its failure in the case of *validity* is equally decisive. The argument

$$(\forall x)\ (Fx \rightarrow Gx)$$
$$\underline{(\forall x)\ (Gx \rightarrow Hx)}$$
$$(\forall x)\ (Fx \rightarrow Hx)$$

is valid when F necessitates G and G necessitates H, guaranteeing that

(Always) (Fx//Gx)
(Always) (Gx//Hx)
(Always) (Fx//Hx)

is also valid. But the argument obviously does not remain valid when not-Gx is merely rare on condition Fx. For (reverting to our earlier counterexample), on the condition that something is a centenarian, it is rare that it is not a woman; on the condition that it is a woman, it is rare that it is not under seventy; but it does not follow that, on the condition that something is a centenarian, it is merely rare that it is not under seventy.

In addition to associating what holds for the most part with a notion of relative frequency, Aristotle also associates it with what holds "provided there is no impediment" (*Ph.* II 8 199^{b}17–18). Perhaps, then, we might transform theorems that hold for the most part into theorems that hold necessarily—and so always—by incorporating an explicit reference to the conditions under which the impediments are missing. (Mx) (Fx → Gx) would then be analyzed as the universally quantified, $(\forall x)$ (Fx & C →

---

[20] Noticed and carefully explored by Judson, "Chance and 'Always or For the Most Part'," 82–99.

Gx)—where C formulates the relevant conditions in an independent and noncircular fashion.[21] The trouble with this suggestion, however, is that, while it solves *quantifier* and *modality*, it fails to solve *validity*. For the conditions under which all Fs are Gs need not be the same as those under which all Gs are Hs. And once we make this clear, the weakness of the suggested analysis of (Mx) (Fx → Gx) is apparent. For

$$(\forall x)\ (Fx\ \&\ C_1 \to Gx)$$
$$(\forall x)\ (Gx\ \&\ C_2 \to Hx)$$
$$\overline{(\forall x)\ (Fx \to Hx)}$$

is not generally valid.

Finally, Aristotle associates what holds for the most part with what holds by nature—"what holds either universally or for the most part is in accord with nature" (*PA* III 2 663^{b}28–29)[22]—and contrasts it, as we saw, with what comes about coincidentally or as a result of luck or chance. The association and the contrast are both based on causation. When Fs are by nature Gs, being F causally influences being G. When Fs are only coincidentally G, on the other hand, being F does not causally influence being G.[23] That is why what holds by nature is of interest to science. How, then, are we to explain the fact, already uncovered, that what holds by nature holds only for the most part and not always?

The first thing we must do is distinguish between a universally quantified scientific theorem and its ontological correlate, which is the relation between universals that makes it true. When this relation is a necessitation relation, N(F, G), holding between the universals F and G, x's being F necessitates x's being G, and ($\forall x$) (Fx → Gx) holds *always*. When the objective probability, (Pr:P) (F, G), that an F is a G is less than 1 but sufficiently close to it, a *snecessitation* relation N⋆ (F, G) holds between F and G, so that x's being F snecessitates x's being G.[24] In this case, ($\forall x$) (Fx → Gx) holds *for the most part*. If (Pr:P) (F, G) is not sufficiently close to 1,

---

[21] A suggestion floated in Henkinson, "Philosophy of Science," 115.

[22] Also *Ph.* II 8 198^{b}34–36; *GA* IV 8 777^{a}17–21.

[23] Except perhaps coincidentally—a complication we may safely ignore.

[24] The resulting vagueness has the advantage—desired by Aristotle (*EN* I 4 1094^{b}19–27)—of allowing different sciences to adopt the standards of explanatory adequacy or exactness appropriate to their particular subject matter.

the relation between F and G is one of coincidence. Then $(\forall x) (Fx \rightarrow Gx)$ holds *rarely*. Since N is just the special case where (Pr:P) (F, G) is 1, and N⋆ the range of cases where it is sufficiently close to 1, necessitation and snecessitation are arguably different degrees of strength of the same relation.[25] Hence *modality* is solved.

On this view, 'always', 'for the most part', and 'rarely' are not quantifiers that appear in scientific theorems themselves, but rather characterizations in terms of relative frequencies of the relations between universals that are the truth-makers or ontological correlates of these theorems. So when Aristotle says that for the most part all crabs have the right claw larger than the left, what he means is that the scientific theorem "all crabs have the right claw larger than the left" is made true by the fact that being a crab snecessitates having a right claw larger than the left. That solves *quantifier*.

Now for *validity*. The argument

$$(\forall x) (Fx \rightarrow Gx)$$
$$\underline{(\forall x) (Gx \rightarrow Hx)}$$
$$(\forall x) (Fx \rightarrow Hx)$$

is valid when the premises hold necessarily and always. Does it remain valid when the premises and conclusion hold only for the most part? To answer, we must look to the ontological correlates of its premises and conclusion and ask whether the following holds:

$$N^\star (F, G)$$
$$\underline{N^\star (G, H)}$$
$$N^\star (F, H).$$

The obvious objection to claiming that it does hold, is that the premises may be true when x is F but not G, or G but not H, so that the conclusion fails to follow. Aristotle, however, holds a *de re* theory of universals (1.1). Hence, in his view, the universals N⋆ (F, G) or N⋆ (G, H) will not be instantiated in such cases, since G or H will not. We may legitimately restrict our attention, therefore, to situations in which these universals are instantiated. Since N⋆ is arguably transitive in such situations, the universal N⋆ (F, H) will also be instantiated in them. Hence when N⋆ (F, G) and N⋆ (G, H) are both instantiated by x, so will

---

[25] This sort of view of deterministic and probabalistic causation is defended in Armstrong, *What Is a Law of Nature?*

N* (F, H) be. Aristotle is on intelligible ground, then, when he says that if the premises of a demonstration are necessary, so is the conclusion, "while if for the most part, the conclusion too is such" (*APo.* I 30 87^{b}22–25).[26]

The final point to make about what holds for the most part returns us to the fact noticed earlier that what holds—as we may now put it—by *snecessity* holds for the most part provided there is no impediment. Given that what holds for the most part rarely fails to occur, it seems that such impediments must themselves occur rarely. But this Aristotle seems to deny: "Nature tends, then, to measure the coming-to-be and passing-away of animals by the regular motions of these bodies [the sun and moon], but nature cannot bring this about exactly because of the indeterminateness of matter, and because there are many causes that hinder coming-to-be and passing-away from being according to nature, and often cause things to occur contrary to nature" (*GA* IV 10 778^{a}4–9). Notice, however, that the "indeterminateness of matter" is, as it were, a standing condition, while the "many causes that hinder" are not. Perhaps, then, we should divide things up as follows. The indeterminateness of matter explains why theorems of natural science are sneccesities whose contraries occur rarely. Impediments explain why what otherwise would occur rarely may occur often.[27] Adding a condition, C, that excludes impediments will not then change the modal status of the theorems in question. For such theorems owe their modal status to something that cannot be excluded: the indeterminateness of matter. In 3.7, we shall see what this indeterminateness is and why it has this effect.

---

[26] When I said in *Practices of Reason,* 13–17, that if ($\forall x$)(Fx → Gx) holds for the most part, being F "probabilizes" being G, I had this sort of account much less clearly in mind. Conditional probabilities, by contrast, leave *validity* unsolved. For [P(F/G)]n—i.e., the probability of x's being G on the condition that it is F is n—and [P(G/H)]n do not entail that [P(F/H)]n. The probability that x is a woman (G) given that x is a centenarian (F) may be 0.9, as may the probability that x is under 50 (H) given that x is a woman (G), but the probability that x is under 50 (H) given that x is a centenarian (F) is 0. I am grateful to Mohan Matthen for useful written comments that forced me to make all this more explicit.

[27] Presumably, the same sort of explanation can be given of *Pol.* I 5 1254^{b}27–34: "Nature tends to make the bodies of [natural] slaves and free people different . . . But the opposite often happens as well: some have the bodies of free men; others the souls."

We have solved *quantifier, modality,* and *validity,* then, but not *consistency.* For we still cannot see how Aristotle can claim that we can have scientific knowledge only of what holds necessarily and always, while at the same time allowing that we can have scientific knowledge of what holds snecessarily and only for the most part.

2.4 Natural and Theoretical Sciences

Aristotle usually works with a tripartite division of the sciences into theoretical, practical, and productive.[28] But he sometimes distinguishes sciences, which he usually classes as theoretical (*Met.* VII 1 1025^{b}25–28), from a narrower group, labeling the first natural and only the second theoretical: "What is by necessity does not belong in the same way to everything that is in accord with nature. Almost all [natural scientists] try to carry back their explanations to this, not distinguishing the several ways in which necessity is spoken of. For there is the unqualified kind [of necessity] that belongs to eternal things, and there is the hypothetical kind [of necessity] that belongs to everything that comes-to-be [by nature], just as to everything produced by the crafts, e.g., a house or anything else of that sort. For if a house or other such end is to be achieved, it is necessary that matter of such-and-such a sort be available, and first this must come-to-be and be set in motion, and then that, and so on in continuous succession, until the end—i.e., that for the sake of which each thing comes-to-be and exists—is reached. Such also are the things that come-to-be in nature. But the mode of demonstration and of necessity in the natural sciences is different than in the theoretical ones. . . . For the first principle in the latter is what is, whereas in the former it is what will be. For since health or a man is such-and-such, it is necessary for this to be or come-to-be; but not [necessary] that since this is or has come-to-be that the other is or will be. Nor is it possible to trace back the necessity of demonstrations of this sort to eternity, so as to say that since this exists therefore that does" (*PA* I 1 639^{b}21–640^{a}8). Theorems of the theoretical sciences (so identified) are unqualifiedly necessary, then, while those of the natural sciences are only hypothetically necessary. Thus the distinction between these two types of sciences might seem to promise a solution to *consistency.* For Aristotle might mean that there can be theoretical scientific knowledge only of what holds with unqualified necessity, while allowing

---

[28] E.g., *Top.* VI 6 145^{a}15–18; *Met.* XI 7 1064^{a}16–19; *EN* VI 2 1139^{a}26–28.

that there can be natural scientific knowledge of what holds for the most part. Unfortunately, the promise here will turn out to be largely illusory.

The reason unqualifiedly necessary theorems differ from hypothetically necessary ones is that the former are convertible, while the latter are not: "Granted that the earlier coming-to-be of something is necessary if a later thing is to be, e.g., if a house, then foundations, and if foundations, then clay: does it follow that if foundations have come-to-be, a house must necessarily come to be? Or can we not yet say this, unless it is unqualifiedly necessary that the latter itself come-to-be? In this case, if foundations have come-to-be, it is also necessary that a house come-to-be; for such was the relationship of the earlier thing to the later, viz., that if there is to be the latter, necessarily there will be the former, earlier, thing. If, accordingly, it is necessary for the later one to come-to-be, it is necessary also for the earlier one, and if the earlier one comes-to-be, it is accordingly necessary for the later one to do so—not because of the earlier one, however, but because it was assumed that it was necessary that it should exist. So in those cases where it is necessary for the later one to exist there is conversion, and it is always necessary if the earlier one comes-to-be that the later one should also come-to-be" (*GC* II 11 337^{b}14–25). Moreover, the reason that unqualifiedly necessary theorems are convertible has to do with their content: "If the coming-to-be of something is unqualifiedly necessary, it must come back in a circle and return on itself. . . . So there must be conversion; i.e., if this comes-to-be necessarily, then the earlier, and again, if that, then the later comes to be necessarily. . . . E.g., because the spatial movement above it is in a circle, the sun moves in this way, and since it moves in that way, the seasons, because of it, come-to-be in a circle and return upon themselves, and since these come to be in this way, the things affected by them do so in their turn" (338^{a}4–338^{b}5). It is because astronomy deals with eternal unalterable beings with fixed circular orbits, then, that its theorems are convertible. For in the case of such beings, the particular that is at place p_1 at time t_n was at p_1 earlier and will be there again later, no matter what time t_n is: "it is plain that those whose substance—that which is moved—cannot cease-to-be will be numerically the same" (338^{b}14–15). And it is this that makes conversion possible.

Now the (sublunary) elements are also cyclically transformed into one another: "water and air come-to-be in a circle, and if there is a cloud [a type of air], there must be rain and if there is rain, there must be a cloud" (*GC* II 11 338^{b}6–8). What recurs in their case, however, is not a particular but a form: "Those whose substance can cease-to-be must necessarily return on themselves in form, not numerically. That is why water from air and air from water is the same in form, not number" ($338^b16–18$). In this respect, the transformation of the elements is like the succession of human generations: "Men and animals do not return on themselves in such a way that the same one comes-to-be again (since there was no necessity, given that your father came-to-be, that you should have come to be, only that he should have, given that you did), and it seems that this coming-to-be is in a straight line" ($338^b8–11$). In both cases conversion is blocked, therefore, and with it unqualified necessity.

Conversion is also sometimes blocked, however, in sciences, such as geometry, whose theorems do hold with unqualified necessity: "The necessity in mathematics is similar in a way to the necessity in the things that come-to-be in accordance with nature: since the straight is thus and so, it is necessary that a triangle should have angles together equal to two right angles, but not conversely" (*Ph.* II 9 $200^a15–18$).[29] It follows that the contrast between convertible and nonconvertible necessities does not correspond to that between unqualified and hypothetical ones, and so does not explain why some scientific theorems hold necessarily, others only snecessarily. Hence it cannot explain either how Aristotle can consistently claim that we can have (natural) scientific knowledge of the latter, while at the same time restricting (theoretical) scientific knowledge to the former.

Nonetheless, there is an important connection between snecessity and hypothetical necessity. Unconvertible but necessary theorems are similar to hypothetically necessary ones "in a way." Presumably, this is so solely because both are unconvertible. For it is clear that they do differ in the sort of necessity they exhibit: "The unqualified sort [of necessity] belongs to eternal things, whereas the hypothetical sort belongs to everything that comes-to-be, such as in the products of craft. . . . And it is exactly the same in things that come about by nature [and so snecessarily]" (*PA* I 1

---

[29] This text suggests—as Charles, "Teleological Causation in the *Physics*," argues—that hypothetical necessity is stronger than a modal sufficient condition. For treated as such, Aristotle's conditional does convert: if a triangle has angles equal to two right angles, necessarily a straight line is thus and so. Presumably, then, hypothetical necessity is somehow sensitive to the direction of explanation. It is *because* a straight line is thus and so that necessarily a triangle has angles equal to two right angles, but it isn't *because* a triangle has angles equal to two right angles that necessarily a straight line is thus and so. For in geometry the theory of lines explanatorily precedes the theory of triangles, since a triangle is by definition a plane figure enclosed by three intersecting straight lines.

639^{b}23–30). In other words, the sort of necessity proper to what holds for the most part is indeed hypothetical necessity. But, to repeat, that does not explain why what is necessary in this way holds only for the most part.

Though our investigation of hypothetical necessity has failed to solve *consistency,* it has proved somewhat illuminating and will prove even more so later on. The same is true, oddly enough, for the initially unprepossessing contrast between theoretical and natural sciences. As heirs to Copernicus, we draw no distinction between sublunary and superlunary physics. But Aristotle does. For he thinks that the eternal and unchanging movements he finds in the superlunary realm draws superlunary physics closer to the archetypal theoretical science of mathematics, and requires a special kind of matter—ether—that is invariant and regular in a way that sublunary matter is not.[30] The result, when Aristotle is bearing all this in mind, is that superlunary physics (astronomy) becomes a theoretical science and sublunary physics merely a natural one. But that leaves sublunary physics without a place in Aristotle's normal triadic classification of sciences, since it is neither practical nor productive. From our point of view, then, it is no doubt tempting to collapse the distinction between sublunary and superlunary physics, and follow Aristotle's more common practice of treating all of natural science as theoretical science. But this would be a mistake, as we shall see in 8.1–5. Until then, however, it will do no harm to hold the distinction in reserve.

2.5 Exact and Inexact Sciences

In addition to dividing the sciences into theoretical, practical, and productive, Aristotle also distinguishes them by their degree of exactness, claiming that theoretical wisdom, which culminates in understanding, is the most exact of all: "Theoretical wisdom is the most exact form of scientific knowledge. . . . It follows that theoretical wisdom is understanding plus scientific knowledge—scientific knowledge of the most valuable things having a crown, as it were" (*EN* VI 7 1141^{a}16–20). To understand why this is so we need to understand what exactness is and why it and value go together. Exactness first:

APo. I 27 87^{a}31-35 One science is more exact than, and prior to, another if [^{a}32] it is at the same time knowledge of the that and the why, but not of the that separate from the why; and if [^{a}33] it is not

---

[30] Freudenthal, *Aristotle's Theory of Material Substance,* 74–148.

said of a subject and the other is said of a subject, e.g., arithmetic and harmonics; and if [*34*] it depends on fewer [posits], the other on an additional posit, e.g., arithmetic and geometry.

The "that" referred to in *a32* is the fact that such-and-such an essence exists, that such-and-such a first principle holds. The "why" is the scientific explanation of that fact (*Met.* VI 1 1025^{b}16–18, 9.1).

When a science S' assumes facts of this sort, while another science S explains them by identifying their causes, S' is subordinate to S: "The why differs from the that in another fashion, when each is considered by means of a different science. And such are those which are so related to one another that the one is under the other, e.g., optics to geometry, mechanics to solid geometry, harmonics to arithmetic, and star-gazing to astronomy (some of these sciences bear almost the same name—e.g., mathematical and nautical astronomy and mathematical and acoustical harmonics). For here it is for the scientists who deal with perceptibles to know the that and for the mathematical scientists to know the why. For the latter possess demonstrations which give the explanations, and often they do not know the that, just as people who have theoretical knowledge of universals often do not know some of the particulars through lack of observation" (*APo.* I 13 78^{b}34–79^{a}6). Generally speaking, then, the science that explains the first principles of another science is prior to and more exact than the one whose first principles it explains.

a33 is both a separate point and a further explication of *a32*. One reason S may be more exact than S' is that S, though it deals with the same forms or essences as S', does so in a different way: "These [sciences, e.g., S] are those which, being somewhat different in substance [i.e., essence], make use of forms. For mathematics is concerned with forms, since its objects are not said of any subject; for even if geometrical objects *are* said of some subject, still it is not qua said of a subject that they are known" (*APo.* I 13 79^{a}6–10). Thus geometry deals with lines and points in abstraction from matter, and so can achieve a kind of exactness that a science dealing with material lines and points cannot: "There will be difficulties in natural science that are not present in mathematics, for mathematical objects are spoken of in abstraction [from matter], physical ones, with an additional posit" (*Cael.* III 1 299^{a}13–17). That is why "a mathematical exactness of argument is not to be demanded in all cases, but only in the case of things that have no matter" (*Met.* II 3 995^{a}14–16). Matter, then, is the sort of thing referred to as a subject in *a33*.

*a*34 is a variation on *a*33, since positing *(prosthesis)* is the inverse of abstraction *(aphairesis)*. Hence "those [sciences] which involve fewer posits are more exact than those involving additional ones" *(Met.* I 2 982ᵃ25–27). For example, mathematics is more exact than natural science, because natural science deals with material beings that move and change, and so must posit the existence of perceptible matter, whereas mathematics, which deals with such beings "qua unchangeable and separate from matter" (VI 1 1026ᵃ9–10), need not.

Though mathematics is more exact than natural science for this reason, it is not the primary or most exact science. That accolade goes to theology, since it is the most valuable science and deals with the most valuable being, God—a being separate from matter not just (like mathematical objects) in thought, but also in reality *(Met.* I 2 983ᵃ4–11, XII 9 1074ᵇ33–35). The connection between the most exact science and the one dealing with the most valuable things is therefore made—if not as yet in a fully transparent way.

Unqualifiedly speaking, scientific knowledge deals exclusively with universals and their necessary or snecessary interrelations. Nonetheless, it also has important bearing on hylomorphic particulars: "There is no demonstration or any unqualified scientific knowledge, but only coincidental knowledge, of destructible things, because nothing holds of them universally but only at some time and in some way. When there is a demonstration, one of the premises must be non-universal and destructible—destructible because when it is the case the conclusion too will be the case, and non-universal, because its subjects will sometimes be and sometimes not be. Hence one cannot deduce that anything holds universally but only that it holds now" *(APo.* I 8 75ᵇ24–30). Something similar is also true of definition: "There is no definition of what is already a compound, e.g., *this* circle, or of any other perceptible particular. . . . These are known by perception . . . and when they depart from this actuality [i.e., when they are no longer actually being perceived] it is not clear whether they are or not" *(Met.* VII 10 1036ᵃ2–7). The problem with extending unqualified scientific knowledge to particulars, in other words, is that particulars undergo not Heraclitean flux, but ordinary change, so that "whenever they are out of our sight, we are unaware whether they are [such-and-such] or not" *(EN* VI 3 1139ᵇ21–22). It follows that Aristotle buys a weaker version of the argument that he thinks led Plato to separate forms from perceptibles. For while change sets limits to scientific knowledge of particulars, in his view, it does not altogether preclude it—we can demonstrate that some things hold of a particular *now*. Properly time-relativized knowledge of particulars, in other words, can be scientific knowledge.

The reason that hylomorphic particulars undergo change is that they involve matter, since it is one of the factors that must be present for change of any sort to occur (5.1). *Prima facie*, then, matter is as responsible for the fact that no unqualified scientific knowledge can be had of particulars as it is for the loss of exactness within the sciences of universals themselves.

Though scientific knowledge deals only coincidentally with hylomorphic particulars, there are bodies of knowledge, which Aristotle classes as sciences, that are essentially concerned with them. These include practical sciences (such as practical wisdom, household management, and political science), which deal with action *(praxis)*, and crafts (such as medicine and building), which deal with production *(poiêsis)* (*EN* VI 7–8). But these sciences are yet less exact than those that deal with universals and only coincidentally with particulars: "There is no deliberation about sciences that are exact and self-sufficient, e.g., about letters, since we are in no doubt about how to write them [in spelling a word]. . . . [Hence we deliberate] more about the crafts than about the sciences, since we have more doubts about them. Deliberation is concerned with what holds for the most part" (*EN* III 3 1112ᵃ34–ᵇ9). Notice the correlation presupposed here between the exactness of a science and the modal status of its theorems: the less exact sciences have theorems that hold for the most part, whereas the exact ones have theorems that hold always.

Aristotle recognizes a number of different kinds of sciences, then, that differ in exactness from one another because of their degree of abstraction from matter: theology's first principles are forms or essences that are separate from matter both in thought and in reality; those of mathematics are forms or essences that are separate from matter in thought but not in reality; those of natural science are forms or essences that are separate from matter neither in thought nor in reality; practical and productive sciences, whatever about their first principles, must deal with hylomorphic particulars themselves. Theology and mathematics are exact for this reason— theoretical, in the precise sense; natural science is inexact—theoretical only in being neither practical nor productive; practical and productive sciences are more inexact still.

Some essences are related by necessity, then, others by snecessity. Some theoretical sciences are exact; others inexact. Scientific theorems about universals related by snecessitation hold only for the most part. Sciences that include such theorems are less exact than those whose theorems hold

41

always. Exact sciences must deal with universals related by necessity, then, and inexact ones with universals related by snecessity. The explanation of exactness and inexactness, however, appeals to the (in)separability of the pertinent essences from matter. Given realism, the explanation of necessity must appeal to the same thing.

More remains to be said, but at least the outlines of a solution to *consistency* are now genuinely discernible: exact scientific knowledge is exclusively of what holds necessarily and always, whereas inexact scientific knowledge is of snecessities that hold only for the most part.

THREE

ESSENCE

3.1 Natural Beings

Since essences are the ontological, and their definitions the epistemological, first principles of the various Aristotelian sciences, differences in the exactness of these sciences must in the end rest on differences in essences and their definitions. Essences, then, and the pertinent ways in which they differ are our next topic.

The first principles of inexact theoretical sciences are natural essences or natures *(phuseis)*, internal sources of "change and staying unchanged, whether in respect of place, growth and decay, or alteration" (*Ph.* II 1 192^{b}13–15). The beings that have these natures are hylomorphic compounds—compounds of matter *(hulê)* and form *(morphê, eidos)*. But while natures owe something to matter and something to form, form has "a better claim than matter to be called nature" (193^{b}6–7). For natural beings can survive change in their matter—a human grows from an embryo to a mature adult—but if their form is changed, they cease to exist (*Pol.* III 3 1276^{a}34–^{b}8). Thus form and essence are commonly identified: "by form I mean the essence of each thing" (*Met.* VII 7 1032^{b}1–2).

It is also characteristic of a being with a nature to have a function *(ergon)* and an end *(telos)* that are intimately related: "the nature is the end, i.e., that for the sake of which" (*Ph.* II 2 194^{a}27–28); "each thing that exists, of which there is a function, exists for the sake of its function" (*Cael.* II 3 286^{a}8–9).[1] Hence something that cannot perform its function shares no more than a name with its functional self: "If the whole body is dead, there will no longer be a foot or a hand, except homonymously, as one might speak of a stone 'hand' (for a dead hand will be like that); but everything is defined by its function and its capacity; so that in such condition [viz., dead] they should not be said to be the same things but homonymous

---

[1] Also *EN* IX 7 1168^{a}6–9; *EE* II 1 1219^{a}13–17.

43

ones" (*Pol.* I 2 1253ª20–25).[2] Aristotle's view of natural beings is therefore teleological; he sees them as defined by their end or function, and as needing to have their behavior explained by reference to it. A being's end, essence, or function also fixes what its good is, and what its perfections, excellences, or virtues are (*Ph.* II 3 195ª23–25, *EN* I 7 1098ª7–20).

Though the nature of a being is more its form than its matter, the various types of matter of which natural beings are constituted have forms or natures of their own. Thus it is part of the nature of fire—one of the four elementary types of Aristotelian matter—to rise. Hence "Fire rises" is a theorem of a natural science, a necessary truth.[3] Other necessities, however, are based in the natures of hylomorphic compounds and are not reducible to those in their matter. Human beings necessarily have teeth of a certain sort, but they do not have them because of necessities inherent in the matter from which teeth are made, any more than the walls of a house have heavy rock foundations and light timber tops because heavy things sink and light ones rise (*Ph.* II 8 198ᵇ16–199ª8, 9 199ᵇ35–200ª11).

Despite being differently located, these two sets of necessities are also importantly related. For matter cannot constitute a hylomorphic compound unless it has a nature appropriate to achieving the end or performing the function that is definitive of the compound's own nature: "Similarly in the case of all the other things in which a that for the sake of which is present: without things that have a necessary nature it could not exist, but it does not exist because of these (except in the way that a thing exists because of its matter), but for the sake of something. E.g., why is a saw such as it is? So that this may be, i.e., for the sake of this. It is impossible, however, that the thing it is for the sake of should come-to-be unless it [the saw] is made of iron. It is necessary, then, that it should be made of iron, if there is to be a saw and the function belonging to it" (*Ph.* II 9 200ª7–13). When what is by nature F must be constituted of matter that is G, as a saw must be constituted of iron, it is *hypothetically necessary* that F be constituted of matter that is G. In other words,

Given that x is by nature F, necessarily because of this x must be constituted of matter that is G.[4]

---

[2] Also *Mete.* IV 12 390ª10–13; *PA* I 1 640ᵇ33–641ª6.

[3] *Top.* V 8 137ᵇ37; *Ph.* IV 8 214ᵇ14; *Cael.* IV 1 208ᵇ8–12.

[4] Charles, "Teleological Causation in the *Physics*," 119–121.

Or, substituting appropriately,

> Given that x must perform the function or achieve the end definitive
> of things that are by nature F, necessarily because of this x must be
> constituted of matter that, because it is G, has a nature appropriate for
> performing that function or achieving that end.

So one important area in which hypothetical necessity operates, and the
most important one for our purposes, is in the teleological relation of
matter to form.[5]

To enable a hylomorphic compound to perform its function or achieve
its end, the hypothetically necessary matter (material cause) alone is not
sufficient; it needs to be shaped or formed. Form or essence—the formal
cause—is what does the shaping: "What is only potentially flesh or bone,
before it acquires the form with which the account accords that defines the
essence of flesh and bone, does not yet have its proper nature, and does not
[yet] exist by nature" (*Ph.* II 1 193ᵃ36–ᵇ3).[6] We may represent the emergence of formed things, therefore, as the result of a sort of interaction
between the necessities definitive of the natures of matter and form, matter
resisting form to some degree depending on the extent to which it is or is
not ideally suited for achieving the end (or performing the function) for
which form is, so to speak, shaping it.

3.2 How Natural Beings Come-to-Be

To understand the nature of this interaction more fully and assess its consequences for the various sciences dealing with natural things, we need to
turn to Aristotle's most detailed example of it—the embryological theory
developed in the *Generation of Animals*. It is useful to begin, however, by
setting that theory in a somewhat broader context.

Starting with inanimate things, we find in nature an apparently continuous scale of beings that differ infinitesimally from one another: "Nature proceeds from the inanimate to the animals by such small steps that,
because of the continuity, we fail to see to which the boundary and the
middle between them belongs. For the first kind of thing after the inanimate is the plant kind, and among these one differs from another in

---

[5] Perhaps it is the only area, as Cooper, "Hypothetical Necessity and Natural
Teleology," argues.

[6] Also *GA* II 1 734ᵇ24–34; *Met.* VII 17 1041ᵇ4–9.

seeming to have a greater share of life; but the whole kind, in comparison with the other [inanimate] bodies, *appears* pretty much as animate, while in comparison with the animal kind it appears inanimate. The change from them [plants] to animals is continuous, as we said before" (*HA* VIII 1 588^{b}4–12).[7] The simplest beings on this scale, after the elements, are homoeomerous stuffs, such as water, wood, olive oil, flesh, and bone, whose parts have the same account as the whole (*GC* I 1 314^{a}20, 10 328^{a}10–12).

These stuffs are constituted out of the elements in some ratio *(logos)*, when the active capacities (hot, cold) master the corresponding passive ones (dry, moist): "We must describe the operations of the productive [capacities] and the forms taken by the passive ones. First, unqualified coming-to-be in general and natural change and the corresponding natural passing-away are the work *(ergon)* of these [productive] capacities; and these [processes] occur in plants, animals, and their parts. Unqualified natural coming-to-be is a change produced by these capacities, when present in the right ratio,[8] in the underlying matter of a natural thing, and this [ratio] is [determined by] the passive capacities we mentioned. The hot and the cold cause the thing to come-to-be when they master the matter" (*Mete.* IV 1 378^{b}28–379^{a}1). The fundamental form of such mastery is concoction *(pepsis)*, which is responsible both for producing a homoeomerous stuff in the first place and for preserving its nature subsequently: "Concoction is a completion *(teleiôsis)* effected by a thing's own natural heat from the corresponding passive capacities, these being [definitive of] the matter proper to the thing. For when a thing has been concocted it has been completed and brought into being. And the first principle of the completion is its own proper heat. . . . The end *(telos)* [of the process of concoction] is the thing's nature—but nature in the sense of form, i.e., substance. . . . Concoction,

---

[7] The *apparentness* of continuity is also emphasized in *PA* IV 5 681^{a}12–15: "Nature proceeds in a continuous way from inanimate things to animals by way of living things which are not actually animals, with the result that scarcely any difference *seems* to exist between one lot and the next because of their close proximity." Presumably there is a boundary, therefore, between inanimate and animate, plant and animal, even if it is hard to detect. See Balme, "Aristotle's Use of Division and Differentiae," especially 86, and Coles, "Animal and Childhood Cognition in Aristotle's Biology," 291–293.

[8] *DA* I 4 408^{a}14–15: "the mixture of elements that makes flesh has a different ratio [of them] from the one that makes bone."

then, is what everything undergoes when its matter, i.e., its moisture, is mastered; for this is what is given definition by the thing's natural heat, and as long as the [defining] ratio exists in it, it possesses its nature" (*Mete.* IV 2 379^b18-35). Natural heat, then, is *formative* heat—the principle in nature responsible for the coming-to-be and preservation of hylomorphic compounds.[9]

Because homoeomerous stuffs are barely formed, they have a low level of natural heat. As form is added—as homoeomerous stuffs first come to constitute the structural parts of animals (such as hands and eyes), and these in turn come to constitute whole animals of different degrees of complexity—natural heat increases: "the more complete animals are those that are hotter in nature and more fluid, i.e., not earthy" (*GA* II 1 732^b31-32). These animals also pass on their form most completely to their offspring: "The more complete and hotter animals produce their offspring in a [more] complete state as far as quality [as opposed to size] is concerned" (733^a33-^b2). Since man is the most complete animal—"of the complete, or viviparous animals, man is the first" (4 737^b26-27)— he is also the hottest: "All animals with lungs breathe. . . . The reason some have this part, and why those having it need to breathe, is that the more valuable of the animals are hottest; for at the same time their soul must have been made more valuable, since they have a more valuable nature than the fishes.[10] Hence too . . . that animal in which the blood in the lung is purest and most plentiful is the most upright, viz., man. And the reason why he alone has his upper part directed to the upper part of the universe is that he possesses such a part [viz., lungs]" (*Resp.* 13 477^a13-23). It follows that degree of heat, degree of purity of blood,[11] degree of completion, and degree of value all go together, and that they do so because of the formative role of natural heat.

Aristotle's *scala naturae*, then, is a scale whose apparent continuity is provided by that of the natural formative heat required for the coming-to-

---

[9] A conclusion convincingly defended in Freudenthal, *Aristotle's Theory of Material Substance.*

[10] Reading ἰχθύων with Biehl at $^a18$. The mss have φυτῶν (plants). Also *GA* II 6 744^a28-31.

[11] Purity of blood is particularly associated with its thinness and smoothness at *PA* II 4 650^b22-24. The general connection between the qualities of blood and the characters of animals and their perceptual capacities is discussed at 651^a13-19. See Coles, "Animal and Childhood Cognition in Aristotle's Biology," 299–310.

be and preservation of natural hylomorphic compounds. In the following text, however, such heat is characterized in a number of different ways: "The potentiality of all soul seems to be associated with a *body* different from and more divine than the so-called elements. . . . For within the seed of everything there is present that which makes the seeds be fertile, the so-called hot. This is not fire or that sort of capacity, but the *pneuma* enclosed within the seed and within the foamy part—more precisely, *the nature in the pneuma,* which is *analogous* to the element that constitutes the stars" (*GA* II 3 736^{b}29–737^{a}1). A second text goes somewhat further: "Of this [transparent] sort are air, water, and many solid bodies. For it is not qua water or qua air that these are transparent, but because there exists in them *a certain nature* which is *the same* in both and also in the eternal body above" (*DA* II 7 418^{b}6–9). Since a nature could just be a common attribute, rather than a body, this text is apparently more cautious than the first. It goes further, however, in speaking of identity rather than analogy, and in extending its scope beyond living beings to all transparent bodies. A third text goes further still: "What we call transparent is not something special to air, or water, or any other of the bodies usually called transparent, but is a common nature or potential present in these, and *in all other bodies* in a greater or lesser degree, and does not exist separately" (*Sens.* 3 439^{a}21–25). If these three characterizations are allowed to strengthen and extend each other, therefore, the formative heat present in all bodies turns out to be just ether itself. It is this doctrine, as we shall see, that many others presuppose.

If all bodies include ether as their formative principle, we need some way to refer to what is left when, in thought at least, we abstract it from them. This residue I shall call *sublunary matter.* But what gets abstracted, and so what gets left behind, is contextually determined, since what is a hylomorphic compound at one level may be matter at the next level up. When the four sublunary elements are formed into homoeomerous bone material, for example, we get those elements again if we abstract the formative ether. In this case, they are sublunary matter. When the bone material is further formed into a living tibia, however, when we abstract the formative ether, we get bone material. In this case, *it* is sublunary matter.

3.3 How Human Beings Come-to-Be

Both Socrates and Xanthippe contribute something to their offspring, *z,* but they do not contribute the same thing: Socrates contributes form but

48

no matter, Xanthippe contributes matter but no form: "The male provides both the form and the source of movement while the female provides the body, i.e., the matter" (*GA* I 20 729^{a}9–11). This is *Theorem 1* of Aristotle's embryology.

Theorem 2 tells us how the male seed *(sperma, gonê)* and the female menses *(katamênia)* combine to produce *z:* "Nothing comes away from the carpenter to the matter of the timber, nor is there any part of carpentry in the product, but the shape and the form are produced from the carpenter through the movement in the matter.[12] His soul (in which the form is) and his knowledge [of carpentry] move his hands or some other part in a movement of a particular kind—different when the product is different, the same when it is the same—the hands move the tools and the tools move the matter. Similarly, the male's nature, in those that emit seed, uses the seed as a tool containing actual movements, just as in craft productions the tools are in movement; for the movement of the craft is in a way in them" (*GA* I 22 730^{b}8–23). What Socrates' form or essence does to Xanthippe's menses through the agency of his seed, therefore, is to start a movement in it—a movement which, initially at least, is qualitatively identical to its own movement: "When it [the seed] comes into the uterus it causes the female's residue [the menses] to take shape[13] and moves it in the same movement in which it itself is actually moving" (II 3 737^{a}20–22).

In Socrates, this movement is—or is encoded in—his natural formative heat, which is present in his blood and is responsible for the preservation of his form. From there, it is transmitted to his seed, which is itself a very concentrated or concocted blood product: "In blooded animals, blood is the final form of the nourishment . . . and since seed too is a residue from nourishment, i.e., from its final form, surely it follows that seed will be

---

[12] *GA* II 3 737^{a}7–16: "But the body of the seed, in which there also comes a portion of the first principle of soul, part of which is separate from body in all those in which something divine is included (and what we call understanding is such), and part of which is not separate—this body of the seed dissolves and evaporates, having a fluid and watery nature. That is why one should not always look for it to come out again, nor to be any part of the constituted form, any more than the curdling juice that sets the milk: it too changes and is no part of the mass that is being constituted."

[13] "Cause . . . to take shape" translates *sunistêsi*. This is what rennet does to milk. It sets it, causing solid lumps to form.

either blood or something analogous to it or something constituted out of these. Every one of the parts [of the animal] is constituted out of blood as it becomes concocted and somehow divided into portions. And seed . . . has been known in some cases to have a bloodlike appearance when discharged. Therefore, it is evident that seed is a residue from that nourishment which is a form of blood—that which is finally distributed to the parts. This is why [seed] has a great capacity . . . and why it is reasonable that offspring should resemble their parents. For that which goes to all the parts [of the body, viz., the blood] resembles that which is left over [the seed]. Hence the seed of the hand or of the face or of the whole animal is in an undifferentiated way a hand, or a face, or a whole animal, i.e., what each of the latter is in actuality, such seed is potentially" (GA I 9 726^{b}1–18). From the seed the movement is transmitted by concoction to the menses, where it initiates the formation of the fetal heart. Once the heart is formed the fetus then grows of its own accord, drawing its nourishment from its mother through the umbilicus (II 1 735^{a}12–26, 5 741^{b}7–9). When Socrates' seed has communicated its own movement to Xanthippe's menses, therefore, its work is done.

Xanthippe's menses, on the other hand, while they have the potential to be moved in such a way as to become z and all its parts, cannot actually do so until they are set in movement by the actual movements in Socrates' seed (GA II 3 737^{a}18–34). *Theorem 3,* which is quite general in scope, explains why: "So far as things formed by nature or by human craft are concerned, the formation of that which is in potentiality is brought about by that which is in actuality" (1 734^{a}29–31). It is because actuality is prior to potentiality, then, that Xanthippe requires Socrates if she is to produce z.

Once the movement from Socrates' seed has been transmitted into Xanthippe's menses, a number of different things can happen to it that determine z's gender, as well as various other of his heritable characteristics. The three theorems that characterize these happenings are summed up as follows: "But it is necessary to take hold of the general principles. *[Theorem 4]* is the one just stated, that some movements are present potentially and others actually. But in addition there are two more; *[Theorem 5]* that what gets mastered departs from type, into the opposite; *[Theorem 6]* that what slackens passes into the movement that is next to it: slackening a little into a near movement; more, into one that is farther away; finally, [the movements] so run together that it [the fetus or child] doesn't resemble any of its own or kindred, rather all that's left is what is common [to all], and it is [simply] human" (GA IV 3 768^{b}5–12). To determine what these theorems amount to, we must explore in greater detail the various movements involved in reproduction.

The movements in Socrates' seed arise from the different elements in his own form or essence: "Now what is special and particular always has more force in coming-to-be. For Coriscus is both man and animal, but man is closer to what is special [to him] than animal. In coming-to-be both what is particular and what is generic are operative, but more so what is particular. For this is the substance. For indeed the offspring comes-to-be a such too, but also a this, and the latter is the substance. That is precisely why it is from all these capacities that the movements in the seed come" (GA IV 3 767^{b}29–36). Hence the very same formal elements that are exemplified as capacities in Socrates' form or essence are exemplified as movements in his seed, guaranteeing that these movements are, at least to begin with, formally identical to the capacities that transmit them to the seed. If this were not so, how could their transmission to the seed result, as we shall see it does, in the transmission of the human form to z?[14] For convenience let us say that |Socrates| is the capacity in Socrates' essence that is special and particular to it; |male|, the capacity it shares with the essences of other male human beings; |human|, the capacity it shares with the essences of either sex; |animal|, the capacity it shares with the essences of other animals; and so on. Moreover, let us use this same notation to represent the formally identical movements in Socrates' seed that correspond to these capacities, so that each of them will be a sub-movement of his seed's complex overall movement.

In addition to these actual sub-movements, Socrates' seed contains a hierarchy of merely potential movements: "Some of the movements are present actually, others potentially: actually—those of the male progenitor and of the universals such as man and animal, potentially . . . those of the ancestors" (GA IV 3 768^{a}11–14). One such potential ancestral movement (symbolized by slant lines) is /Socrates' father/; another is /Socrates' grandfather/; a third is /Socrates' great-grandfather/; and so on. These

---

[14] The best discussion is the analysis of GA I 18 722^{a}1–16 in Furth, *Substance, Form and Psyche*, 110–145. He is surely right to see as a major intellectual achievement "the certainty and clarity of Aristotle's appreciation of the fact that the biological phenomena require there to be *two different ways in which specific form occurs:* one way in which it is exemplified by specimens of the species, and a different way that figures in the copying process from forebear to offspring" (113).

actual and potential movements are among the ones to which *Theorem 4* refers.

Xanthippe's menses have a structure that is similar, yet significantly different. For the movements in her menses that correspond to those in Socrates' seed are, like those of ancestors, potential only: "Some of the movements are present . . . potentially . . . [e.g.,] those of the female" (*GA* IV 3 768^{a}11–14). Thus, corresponding to |Socrates|, |male|, |human being|, and |animal|, we have /Xanthippe/, /female/, /human being/, and /animal/. And corresponding to /Socrates' father/, /Socrates' grandfather/, and so on, we have /Xanthippe's mother/, /Xanthippe's grandmother/, and so on.

For simplicity's sake, let us focus on |Socrates| and see what happens to it during reproduction. If it is transmitted to the menses and "stands fast" (*GA* IV 3 768^{a}32), z will resemble Socrates. If it fails to do so, it may be wholly mastered, in which case it departs from type, as *Theorem 5* puts it, "into the opposite," that is to say, into an actual movement formally identical to /Xanthippe/: "for as father and mother are opposed in general, so too the particular male progenitor is opposed to the particular female progenitor" (768^{a}7–9). Alternatively, it may "slacken" or degrade in a way described in *Theorem 6:* "The movements that are crafting [the menses] slacken into ones that are near them, e.g., should the movement of the male slacken, it shifts-over first by the minimal difference into that [i.e., the movement] of his father; second, into that of the grandfather; and in this way among the females too, in fact, the [movement] of the female progenitor [shifts over first] into that of her mother, or if not, into that of her grandmother; and so on up the line" (768^{a}14–21). Thus if |Socrates| fails to master Xanthippe's menses, it may (as one possibility) slacken into |Socrates' father|—that is, into an actual movement formally identical to /Socrates' father/.

What causes |Socrates| to slacken in this way is Xanthippe's menses (*GA* IV 3 768^{b}15–23). These are very much like Socrates' seed—they are "seed that is not pure but needs working on" (I 20 728^{a}26–27). But because Xanthippe's natural heat is cooler than Socrates' she cannot complete the final stage of forming or concocting them into pure seed by herself: "The female exists in virtue of a particular incapacity, in being unable to concoct seed out of the nutriment in its last stage (which is either blood or the analogous part in the bloodless animals) owing to the coldness of her nature" (728^{a}18–21). Nonetheless, Xanthippe can concoct her menses (or the seminal residue in them) to within that last stage of being pure seed. For the potentials they contain are much closer to being actualities than those of other matter (II 1 735^{a}9–11). If (counterfactually) Xanthippe could take the final step and completely concoct her own menses, the result would be a female child that resembled Xanthippe herself. We might think of Xanthippe's menses, then, as having a complex natural tendency to form such a child by moving in the appropriate way—a tendency that Aristotle expresses by referring to it as a potential movement. It is this complex tendency that offers opposition to |Socrates| and that can (among other things) master it or cause it to slacken into |Socrates' father| or |Socrates' grandfather|, and so on.[15]

If z resembles Xanthippe rather than Socrates, therefore, this must be because /Xanthippe/ caused |Socrates| to slacken into a movement qualitatively identical to /Xanthippe/, which then produced the appropriate capacity in z's form or soul. But this seems to be inconsistent with *Theorem 1*, since we now seem to have the female contributing form rather than just matter to the fetus.[16] The solution to this problem lies in Aristotle's unjustly reviled—because misunderstood—doctrine that being female is "a sort of natural deformity" (*GA* IV 6 775^{a}15–16), so that a female is "as it were a deformed male" (II 3 737^{a}27–28).

/Xanthippe/ contains potential movements only. But when Socrates' seed acts on the menses it is in, the result is that |Socrates| is altered or deformed, as a saw may be blunted by the wood it is cutting. It is this deformed movement that is transmitted to the fetus. Hence what concocts the menses is not an actual movement contributed by Xanthippe (all the movements in her menses are potential only), but an actual movement that derives exclusively from Socrates' form. That is why, as the result of a deformation of a movement deriving from the male form, a female is a deformed male.

Generalizing, we can say that whenever a movement deriving from a male form is altered or deformed by the natural tendencies in the female menses, the resulting fetus will itself be deformed (*GA* IV 3 767^{a}36–^{b}15). But it will be deformed, as opposed to having an undeformed form contributed by its mother, precisely because it is always the father who

---

[15] Notice how close Aristotle has come to the idea of dominant and recessive genes.

[16] Furth, *Substance, Form and Psyche*, 133–141, argues that this problem is fatal to Aristotle's embryology. Though I think he is mistaken about this, his stylish book has been an inspiration.

contributes the actual movements that concoct the menses. All the menses can do is either be mastered by those movements or deform them, they cannot generate any actual movements of their own. Thus *Theorem 1* is safe: the male contributes form only; the female matter only.

Why did Aristotle adopt this theorem? Why didn't he allow both male and female to contribute formal elements to the fetus? The answer lies in the formal or teleological explanations he favors both in his embryology and elsewhere. For these explanations cannot admit partial or incomplete forms. They cannot allow that part of z's form comes from Xanthippe and part from Socrates. And the reason they can't is that in order to explain how such partial forms can unite into a single form capable of informing or animating a unified animal like z, they would have to presuppose the existence of a background unified form ensuring that they unite in the right way.[17]

It follows that whatever degree of complexity is needed to explain the facts of biological inheritance must be present in the form or essence of the male progenitor. For example, if z can inherit his mother's nose, Socrates' seed must have as one of its sub-movements, the movement |Socnose| that corresponds to the capacity in Socrates' form responsible for the existence and preservation of his distinctive snub nose. When |Socnose| tries to master /Xannose/, the corresponding potential sub-movement in /Xanthippe/, it must be caused to slacken by it (or be deformed by it) into an actual movement that is formally identical to /Xannose/.[18] In order to explain such facts as the heritability of appearances or noses, therefore, the

---

[17] Furth, *Substance, Form and Psyche*, 139–141. This problem becomes even more vivid when we turn to the craft analogy that underwrites hylomorphic analysis and that Aristotle so frequently draws on as an aid to the imagination. For suppose that M is making half a house and that F is making half a house. What could possibly explain the fact that for the most part the halves they make can be combined to form a single house? The only plausible answer seems to be that they both make their halves by following the appropriate parts of one and the same unified plan.

[18] Sub-movements of this sort are countenanced at *GA* IV 4 772^{b}31–35: "If the thing doing the working up gains the mastery, both [sets of sexual organs of the sort that are sometimes present in deformed offspring] are similar [to the male's]; if it is completely mastered, both are similar [to the female's]; but if it masters here and is mastered there, the one [set] is male and the other female. (For whether we consider the reason why the whole animal is male or female, or why the parts are so makes no difference.)"

male natural essences that are the first principles of embryology must apparently be very thick essences.

With appropriate modifications, however, the account of human embryology is a template for the generation of animals and for all other living beings. For what is distinctive about such beings is that the efficient cause of their coming-to-be is another actual being who transmits his form to them (*Met.* XII 4 1070^{b}30–34). Just as z receives his form from Socrates, who actually has that same form himself, every other natural being receives its form from an ancestor who also actually has it. It seems to follows that natural essences in general will have to be appropriately thick.[19]

3.4 The Inheritance of Understanding

It is clear how movements encoded in the formative heat of the seed can start movements in the menses that result in the formation of the fetal heart, which has the capacity—characteristic of nutritive soul—to draw in nourishment (in its case through the umbilicus). It is even to some degree clear how perceptual capacities might develop in the fetus as the movements that 'code for' the various sense organs begin to take place within it. But there is a real problem about understanding, since "bodily actuality is in no way associated with its actuality" (*GA* II 3 736^{b}28–29). For how can what is without a bodily organ develop in a fetus as a result of something on the order of physical movements or formative heat? Aristotle himself recognizes the difficulty of the problem: "We must make clear whether that which is constituted in the female takes over anything from that which enters, or nothing; concerning [e.g.,] soul, in virtue of which it is called an animal, . . . whether it is present within the seed and the fetus or not, and where it comes from. . . . It is plain enough that they [seed and fetus] have nutritive soul . . . but as they develop they also have the perceptive soul in virtue of which they are animal. For they do not become simultaneously animal and man, or animal and horse, and so on; for the end is the last thing to be produced, and the end of each animal's coming-to-be is that which is special to it. That is why, where understanding is concerned, it is a very great problem as to when and how and from where it is acquired by those

---

[19] This section draws on and modifies the Appendix to *Practices of Reason,* which in turn draws on and modifies the proposals in Cooper, "Metaphysics in Aristotle's Embryology." I am grateful to Marc Cohen and Cass Weller for perceptive comments on an earlier version.

who share this first principle, and [why] we must try hard to grasp [its solution] according to our capacities and to the extent that it is possible" (736^{a}27–^{b}8). To determine just how great that extent is, it is useful to proceed in stages.[20]

Stage 1: Understanding is no different in one regard from any other type of psychological capacity, it must be possessed potentially by both seed and fetus before it can be possessed actually: "Seeds and fetuses which are not yet separate must clearly be classed as possessing the nutritive soul potentially, but not actually, until they are drawing in their nourishment like separated fetuses, and are performing the function of this sort of soul. . . . And what we say of the perceptive and understanding souls should clearly conform to that; for all souls must be possessed potentially before actually" (*GA* II 3 736^{b}8–15). It follows that we must be able to distinguish between potential understanding and actual or active understanding, and to allow the former to be possessed before the latter (7.2–3).

Stage 2: The various ways in which the first principles of the various types of psychological capacities can be present in seed or fetus are next cataloged:

> *GA II 3 736^{b}15–20:* Either [^{b}15] they must all be produced [in the menses] without existing [there] beforehand, or they must all pre-exist, or some must, but not others; and they must be produced in the matter [i.e., the menses] either [^{b}18] without having entered in the male's seed, or having come from there; and [^{b}19] in the male they must either all be produced [in the seed] from outside [it], or none from outside, or some but not others.

Here ^{b}15 concerns the menses and what it contributes to the fetus; ^{b}18 concerns the seed and what it contributes to the fetus; and ^{b}19 concerns the male progenitor and what he contributes to the seed. For the line of descent, as we know, is from the male progenitor's blood to his seed, from seed to menses, and so to fetus. Since the first stage in this descent (that from male progenitor to seed) is the most problematic, Aristotle's attention naturally focuses on it.

Stage 3: In order to be able to describe this initial stage correctly, we need to distinguish different elements in the seed itself. On the one hand, there is the body of the seed (its matter), on the other, there are the

---

[20] I have benefited from the discussion of this problem in Balme, *Aristotle De Partibus Animalium I and De Generatione Animalium I,* 158–165.

formative movements within it: "Consider now the body of the seed *(to tês gonês sôma)*,[21] in and with which is emitted the first principle of soul, part of which is separate from the body and belongs to those beings in which something divine is included (and this is what is called understanding), while the other is not separate [from the body]" (*GA* II 3 737ᵃ7–11). When we refer to a male progenitor's contribution to the seed, then, we are really referring to his contribution to the *body* of the seed. For the seed itself, as a formative agent, already contains the first principle of the formative movements that the male progenitor has contributed to it by imbuing it with formative heat.

Stage 4: The catalog of ways in which the ontological first principles of the various types of psychological capacities can be present in the seed or can enter the body of the seed, laid out in *ᵇ19,* are next used to draw a conclusion about understanding:

> *GA* II 3 736ᵇ22–29 [ᵇ22] All first principles whose activity is bodily are clearly unable to be present without body (e.g., walking without feet). [ᵇ24] And hence they cannot enter [the body of the seed] from outside. For [ᵇ25] they can neither enter by themselves, not being separate, nor enter in as the principles of an already formed body; for the seed is a residue produced by a change in the nutriment. [ᵇ27] It remains then that understanding alone enters additionally from outside and alone is divine; for bodily activity is in no way associated with its activity.

ᵇ22 restricts our attention to first principles of psychological capacities whose activities (or activations) are bodily in that they require bodily organs, as walking requires feet and seeing, eyes. ᵇ24 tells us the two conditions under which these could enter something "from the outside." This signals, as 736ᵇ19 makes clear, that the something in question is the body of the male seed. ᵇ25 shows that the principles cannot meet either of the conditions: they cannot enter by themselves, apart from body, because they are not separate from it; they cannot enter the body of the seed as the principles of an already formed body, because seed, as a residue produced by nutriment, doesn't contain things like feet and other bodily parts. On the other hand, because bodily activity is in no way associated with the activity of understanding, understanding does enter the male seed from outside and is divine *(ᵇ27).*

---

[21] Also *GA* I 19 726ᵇ20–21, II 3 737ᵃ7 *(to sôma tou spermatos).*

Stage 5: We now seem to have two problems instead of the one with which we began: we need to know how understanding is produced in the body of the seed from outside, and how the other psychological capacities are produced in it *not* from outside. Aristotle's answer to these questions is given in the continuation of the passage discussed in Stage 4: "The potentiality of all soul seems to be associated with a body different from, and more divine than, the so-called elements; and as souls differ from each other in value and lack of value, so too this sort of nature differs. For within the seed of everything there is present that which makes the seeds be fertile, the so-called hot" (*GA* II 3 736^{b}29–35). Now the "so-called hot," as we know, is natural formative heat (3.2). Hence what psychological capacities that differ in value differ in is the quality of such heat. Since understanding is something divine, and so "surpasses everything in capacity and value" (*EN* X 7 1178^{a}1–2), it is associated with formative heat of a particularly high quality: "the highest heat in the heart is purest in man—his understanding reveals the high quality of the blend, for man is the wisest of the animals" (*GA* II 6 744^{a}28–31).

Stage 6: All psychological capacities, including understanding, are associated with a body *(sôma)*. Yet understanding's activity is in no way associated with any bodily activity *(sômatikê)*. How can that be? The answer suggested in *736^{b}29* is underwritten in the following passage: "There must be some simple and primary body *(sôma)* which by virtue of its own nature is naturally moved in a circle . . . as fire moves up and earth down towards the center [of the earth] . . . [and which is] over and above the bodies that are about us here, different and separate [from them], and having a more valuable nature the more distant they are from those here" (*Cael.* I 2 269^{b}3–17). What *736^{b}29* is stating, then, is not that the activity of understanding isn't bodily at all, but only that it isn't bodily in the weaker sense of being associated with fire, air, and the other bodies "that are about us here." Understanding is associated with *super*lunary body, in other words, but not with *sub*lunary body.

Sublunary body is what we previously called sublunary matter—earth, water, fire, air, and whatever matter is partly or wholly constituted from them. Superlunary body is ether, the matter of the stars and heavenly spheres. The matter that we have so far been calling perceptible, therefore, we should, strictly speaking, call sublunary. Nonetheless, because Aristotle's own preferred term for sublunary body is perceptible matter, we shall follow suit and avoid strict speaking except where necessary for precision.

Stage 7: What are under discussion in *736ᵇ22–29*, then, are psychological capacities associated with sublunary body. And what is being claimed about them is that they cannot enter the (sublunary) body of the seed from outside *(ᵇ24)*. *ᵇ25* explains, in the way we examined above, why this is so. *ᵇ27* then claims that understanding can enter the body of the seed from outside, because its activity, while associated with superlunary body, is not associated with sublunary body. The picture that emerges, therefore, is this. The body of the seed contains the matter that is hypothetically necessary for the various psychological capacities associated with sublunary body, such as perception and locomotion. But it does not contain any of the matter that is hypothetically necessary for understanding, which is associated with superlunary body. Hence for the seed to acquire such capacities as potentials, the superlunary body with which understanding is associated must enter the sublunary body of the seed from outside it, that is, from the male progenitor in whose blood it is contained.

The role of superlunary body in this solution is bound to strike us as somewhat disconcerting, especially given its characterization in *ᵇ27* as "divine"—though a lot depends, no doubt, on what that characterization amounts to. But there is a way in which it is also rather reassuring. For we can now see that though understanding enters the body of the male seed from outside, it does so by normal embryological processes, so that its source is just the male progenitor himself, not God or any other undisclosed and possibly mysterious agent. The inheritance of understanding, as a result, is a 'natural', intraspecies affair.

A human being's soul is his essence or form (*DA* II 1 412ª19–20). But natural science deals only with those parts of it that are parts of human nature: "it is not all soul, but [only] one or more parts of it, that is [an animal's] nature" (*PA* I 1 641ᵇ9–10). The parts with which natural science does not deal are those that are separate from (as we must now say) perceptible sublunary matter: "It is also clear that it belongs to the natural scientist in a way to provide theoretical knowledge even of the soul, i.e., of so much of it as is not without matter" (*Met.* VI 1 1026ª5–6). Thus understanding, though part of the human soul, is not part of human nature. The human is one thing, so to speak, the *merely* human another. To represent this fact about understanding in a distinctive way, I shall set it in guillemets, «understanding», when it appears in the human essence. More generally, any component of an essence so set has the following feature: theoretical knowledge of it is not provided by the science of which that essence is a first principle.

3.5 Artifactual Essences

Artifacts, such as beds and tables, are hylomorphic compounds, but they do not have natures. Neither do they come-to-be by nature. Instead, they are products of craft *(technê)*, or productive science. Yet artifact production is very like natural reproduction. In particular, both natural beings and artifacts inherit their form or essence from something else. The crucial difference is that whereas natural beings and their progenitors have the very same essences—"man begets man" (*Met.* XII 4 1070^{b}34)—artifacts and their producers do not: "From craft come the things whose form is in the soul of the producer—and by form I mean the essence of each thing and the primary substance. . . . For example, health is the account in the soul, the knowledge [of the form]. So the healthy thing comes to be when the physician reasons as follows: Since health is this, necessarily if the thing is to be healthy this must be present—e.g., a uniform state—and if the latter is to be present, there must be heat, and he goes on, always thinking like this, until he is led to a final this that he himself is able to make. Then the process from this point onward, toward health, is called production" (VII 7 1032^{a}32–^{b}10).[22] Thus, while *z* inherits his natural essence (appropriately deformed by Xanthippe's menses) from Socrates who shares it, the form of a bed first exists as an object of understanding in the soul of a carpenter, and makes its way from there, via his actions and bodily movements, into the wood. A bed comes not from a bed, then, but from the form of a bed existing in a human soul.

The major difference between craft knowledge and natural science is a result or acknowledgment of this difference between the ways in which the things they deal with come-to-be. Natural science deals with things that are necessarily a certain way, whereas craft knowledge deals with the same things as luck—hylomorphic particulars that can be manufactured or modified through human planning and action (*EN* VI 4 1140^{a}17–18). Nonetheless, there is an important similarity between the essences that are their first principles. For just as some natural essences include an element—«understanding»—of which natural science does not provide theoretical knowledge, so all artifactual essences contain an element that productive sciences do not provide theoretical knowledge about. This element is happiness *(eudaimonia)* or doing well in action *(eupraxia)*. It is a

---

[22] Also *Ph.* II 7 198^{a}21–27; *GA* I 22 730^{b}8–23; *Met.* VII 9 1034^{a}21–26, XI 7 1064^{a}10–19.

component of artifactual essences because we produce artifacts not simply for their own sakes, but for the sake of happiness: "Understanding itself moves nothing, however, but only the kind that aims at some end and is practical; for this is a first principle of production too; for every producer produces for the sake of some end, and what he produces is not the end unqualifiedly (but only as promoting something [else] and of something [in particular]), but action is [an unqualified end]; for doing well in action is an [unqualified] end, and the desire [that is a first principle of decision] is for this" (2 1139ᵃ35–ᵇ4). Thus a house has happiness as a component of its essence, since to be a house is to be something that promotes happiness in such-and-such a way. It is not the craft of building that tells us what happiness is, however, but political science *(politikê)*. For since it combines an understanding of happiness with the deliberative and executive capacities needed to ensure that whatever we do, whether as producers or agents, really will promote it, all crafts are subordinate to it.[23]

These facts about crafts, together with the close analogies between the role of the essence of a house in a builder's soul and that of the human essence in the male seed, allow us to model artifactual essences on natural ones. Hence we might think of the essence of a house, for example, as having two components, |house| and «happiness», linked as follows:

«happiness»

|house|

—where what is at the tail of the arrow is for the sake of what is at its head. For what a builder builds must promote happiness. Qua builder, however, he does not know what happiness is, since his science does not provide him with that knowledge. That is why happiness is enclosed in guillemets in the essence of a house he has in his soul. Once the builder is provided with the definition of happiness by the political scientist, however, he can design and build a house of the requisite happiness-promoting sort. That is why |house| is not in guillemets. For of *it* a builder does have knowledge.[24]

---

[23] *EN* I 1–2, VI 5 1140ᵃ25–28, 13 1144ᵃ29–36; *Pol.* VII 1 1323ᵃ14–34. Political science, however, derives its understanding of happiness from yet another science. See my *Practices of Reason,* 50–98.

[24] Sedley, "Is Aristotle's Teleology Anthropocentic?" 180, answers his own ques-

How deep are the differences between natural essences and artifactual ones? Aristotle thinks they are very deep. So, for example, he thinks that houses and bird nests are deeply different, because the latter "come-to-be and exist by nature" (*Ph.* II 8 199ª29–30), while the former are artifacts that do not.[25] To see why he thinks this, however, we must return to the notion of hypothetically necessary matter. If a builder wants to build a house, he must make it out of a type of matter that will enable it to function as a house does, providing shelter, and so on. This imposes some constraints on the type of matter he can employ, but it leaves him considerable latitude: most types of wood, metals of various sorts, stone, marble, glass, ice, and plastic are materials out of which houses can be made. Were he trying to make even a simple animal, his choices would be much more constrained. Moreover, the form a builder imposes on the material he chooses need not seep very deeply into it: he arranges the wood, nails or glues it together, saws and shapes, but his craft doesn't get down into the wood itself, so to speak. Were he making an animal, capable of self-movement, perception, and reproduction, this would not be so.

Because artifacts possess these two features, their form and matter are separately accessible, so that we can readily see where matter ends and form begins. We see the blueprint, on the one hand, and the bricks and mortar, on the other. Then we see the finished product—the blueprint realized in bricks and mortar. That is one reason why Aristotle so often uses artifacts to illustrate the distinction between matter and form, and tells us that we must grasp it by analogy with them: as the bronze is to the statue, so is matter to form (*Ph.* I 7 191ª8–12). Nonetheless, in the case of living things, the analogy is hard pressed, since the fact that they lack the two features in question makes it difficult to distinguish what is matter in them from what is form.

Part of the reason that Aristotle thinks that artifactual essences are different from natural ones, then, is that the difficulty of separating form from matter in the case of natural beings makes it difficult to see how there could be a blueprint for their manufacture of the sort that exists in the case of

---

tion as follows: "things are so arranged that the entire contents of the [Aristotelian] natural world, including not only plants and animals but perhaps even seasons and weather, exist and function primarily for the benefit of man." If he is right, natural essences will also contain happiness as a component. Moreover, if natural sciences do not provide knowledge of happiness, it will appear in guillemets in them also.

[25] Cohen, *Aristotle on Nature and Incomplete Substance*, 29–31.

artifacts. Equipped with electron microscopes and capable of genetic engineering, we are in a much better position to see what the naked eye cannot. Hence for us the distinction between natural essences and artifactual ones, like that between bird nests and houses, is bound to seem to be of little metaphysical significance. Where the difference has a tendency to remain metaphysical, however, for us as for Aristotle, is with self-conscious life.

The reason to introduce artifactual essences into our story, therefore, is perhaps more epistemological than metaphysical: they belong in it because of the presence in them of «happiness». But for the very reasons that Aristotle himself invariably uses tl.em as examples, they also provide us with insights into matter and form that it is hard to get in any other way.

3.6 Mathematical Essences

Mathematical essences too are essences of hylomorphic compounds. In their case, however, the matter in question is intelligible matter (*noêtê hulê*). Moreover, intelligible matter is present both in particular mathematical objects, such as this particular mathematical circle, and also, as we are about to see, in their universal essences. The following text may serve as our initial focus:

> *Met. VII* 10 $1035^b31–1036^a12$ Now there are parts of the form (by the form I mean the essence), and of the compound of form and matter, and of the matter itself. But [$^b33$] only the parts of the form are parts of the account, and the account is of the universal. For the essence of circle and circle, and the essence of soul and soul, are the same. But [$^a2$] there is no definition of what is already a compound, e.g., *this* circle, or of any other perceptible or intelligible particular. By intelligible circles I mean, e.g., mathematical ones, by perceptible ones I mean those made of bronze or wood. These are known by understanding or perception [respectively], and when they depart from this actuality [i.e., when they are no longer actually being understood or perceived] it is not clear whether they are or not. They are always spoken of and known by means of the universal account, for [considered] intrinsically matter is unknowable. [$^a9$] Some matter is perceptible, e.g., bronze and wood, and all changeable matter, whereas other [matter] is intelligible—i.e., what is present in perceptible things but not qua perceptible, such as the matter of mathematical objects.

*a*2 repeats some familiar doctrine—essences, not hylomorphic particulars, have definitions—and draws a conclusion that we previously expressed as follows: scientific knowledge may be coincidentally of particulars, but unqualifiedly speaking it deals exclusively with universals. It also tells us something new: particular intelligible or mathematical circles are not definable, because they are subject to the same kind of change as particular perceptible ones. It follows that even these abstract mathematical objects are only coincidentally objects of scientific knowledge.

*a*9 explains why this is so. Intelligible matter is the matter present in perceptible hylomorphic compounds, but not qua perceptible. Consequently, if a particular circle constituted of perceptible matter undergoes change, so too does the intelligible circle that shares its matter (*Met.* III 2 998*a*13–15). For the matter of the intelligible circle is just perceptible matter *considered in a certain way,* and it is in reality, not thought, that the change occurs.

According to *b*33, only the parts of a thing's form are parts of its universal account. *a*2 seems to imply, therefore, that matter, as unknowable when taken intrinsically, cannot be among these parts, since the universal account is precisely what we do know. Things are not quite so simple, however: "Some matter is intelligible, and some perceptible, and of the account always one part is the matter and the other the actuality [i.e., the form], e.g., circle is plane figure"(*Met.* VIII 6 1045*a*33–35). It follows that intelligible matter is indeed part of the universal account or essence of a mathematical circle. Presumably, then, there must be two notions of matter operative in these texts. The matter *VII 10 1036*a*2* excluded from being part of the universal account or essence is the particular bit of matter that constitutes a particular hylomorphic compound. The matter that is included, by contrast, since it is the matter of something universal, must itself be a universal of some sort: "man and horse and the things that thus apply to particulars, but universally—these are not substances, but are a sort of compound of this account and this matter taken universally" (VII 10 1035*b*27–30).[26] On the face of it, then, the matter that is part of the universal essence of circle is not this particular bit of intelligible matter, but this particular bit of intelligible matter "taken universally."

The following text explains what such common matter is and how we gain access to it: "Mathematicians produce theoretical knowledge that deals with abstractions. For in their theorizing they eliminate all percep-

---

[26] Also *Met.* VII 11 1037*a*5–10.

tible attributes, e.g., weight and lightness, hardness and its contrary, heat and cold, and all the other perceptible contraries, and leave only the quantitative and the continuous, sometimes in one, sometimes in two, sometimes in three dimensions, and the attributes of things qua quantitative and qua continuous, and do not theorize about any of their other aspects" (*Met.* XI 3 1061^{a}28–35). What gets left behind in the process of mathematical abstraction, then, are all the perceptible attributes. Hence "what is present in perceptible things but not qua perceptible" (VII 10 1036^{a}9) is perceptible matter considered in abstraction from such attributes. What gets abstracted, on the other hand, what is not left behind, is "the quantitative and the continuous." If, as seems likely, the quantitative is the formal element and the continuous, the material one, the intelligible matter taken universally that is present in the universal account of circle must just be bare spatial continuity in two dimensions. In the definition of circle as "plane figure," therefore, plane must just be two-dimensional space, while figure must be part of the quantitative—that is to say, one of the formal elements in the universal account of a mathematical essence.[27] The entire account or universal essence of circle, then, is such-and-such a form in such-and-such matter.[28]

I have focused on geometry thus far because Greek mathematics—Aristotle's included—is fundamentally geometric in nature and inspiration. Numbers (positive integers), for instance, are typically represented by lines or points, and points are often conceived of as "sections and divisions of lines" (*Met.* XI 2 1060^{b}12–17) or as quantities that have a position on a line but are "not divisible in any dimension" (V 6 1016^{b}25–26). Hence what holds of geometrical essences should also hold of arithmetical ones and whatever other mathematical essences there are. It is presumably for this reason that Aristotle speaks in *VII 10 1036^{a}9* of "the matter of mathematical objects," and not more particularly of the matter of geometrical ones only.

The bearing of all this on the separation from matter of such things as the essences of mathematical circles is no doubt evident: they are separate

---

[27] *Met.* V 25 1023^{b}20–23 tells us that in the case of a cube the formal element is "the [characteristic] angles."

[28] I was heartened to find that I had been anticipated in this interpretation by Mueller, "Aristotle on Geometrical Objects," 167, which (unaccountably) I did not read until after I had worked out my own proposal.

in thought from perceptible matter, but not from intelligible matter taken universally. For one cannot, even in thought, separate a circle's essence from its universal material constituent. Moreover, though separate *in thought* from perceptible matter, mathematical essences are not separate *in reality* from it. This is implicit in *Met. VII 10 1036ª2*, explicit elsewhere: "The mathematical sciences will not be about perceptible things just because their objects are coincidentally perceptible, though not [theorized about] as perceptible; but nor will they be about other objects separate [from] and over and above these [perceptible ones]. Many [attributes belong] intrinsically to things as being, each of them, of a certain kind—e.g., there are attributes that are special to animals qua male or qua female (yet there is no female or male separate from animal). So too there are [attributes] which belong to things merely qua lengths or qua planes" (XIII 3 1078ª3–9). Mathematical objects, after all, are just perceptible objects considered exclusively in a certain way—qua extended, or qua planar, or what have you. They are not new substances that enjoy an ontological independence of their own.[29]

This gives mathematics a rather anomalous position among the sciences, since unlike natural science and theology, it does not deal with substances.[30] Consequently, though more exact than natural science, it isn't a more exact science of substance. Indeed, since the essences that are its first principles are ontologically dependent ones, it will drop out of the ranking altogether when it is sciences of substance that are being ranked in order of priority and exactness. The reason for us to study mathematical essences, therefore, when our topic is substance, is that in addition to their intrinsic interest they provide a useful guide not only to natural essences and substances, but also to the supernatural or intelligible ones we shall eventually meet (7.3–6).

3.7 Penmattered Natural Essences and Inexact Sciences

Mathematical essences have intelligible matter taken universally in them, and so are not separate in thought from it. Natural essences or natures have a parallel feature, which we must now explore:

---

[29] Lear, "Aristotle's Philosophy of Mathematics," provides compelling defense.

[30] Though mathematical astronomy is an exception to this claim (*Met.* XII 8 1073ᵇ5–8).

Met. VI 1 1025ᵇ26-1026ᵃ6 Natural science must be theoretical science; but *[ᵇ26]* it provides theoretical knowledge only about being that admits of being moved, and only about substance that according to its account is for the most part, not being separate [from matter].[31] Now, we must not fail to notice the mode of being of the essence and of its account. For, without this, inquiry achieves nothing. *[ᵇ30]* Of things defined, i.e., the essence, some are like snub, some like concave. These differ because snub is bound up with matter (for snubness is concavity *in a nose*), while concavity is without perceptible matter. If then all natural things are like snub (e.g., nose, eye, face, flesh, bone, and, in general, animal, or leaf, root, bark, and, in general, plant; for none of these can be defined without reference to change, but always have matter), it is clear how we must seek and define the essence of a natural thing. It is also clear that it belongs to the natural scientist in a way to provide theoretical knowledge even of the soul, i.e., so much of it as is not without matter.[32]

ᵃ30 tells us that the essence of snub is not separate from something. But what? Obviously not some particular nose, such as Socrates' nose. For Socrates' nose is an indefinable particular, whereas the essence of snub is a definable universal. As in the case of mathematical essences, therefore, the matter from which natural essences are not separate must be matter taken universally, and the separation in question must be separation in thought. For matter taken universally is an abstraction, a creature of thought.

Part, then, of what *ᵃ30* says is that natural essences include a universal material element. That formulation, however, does not by itself distinguish natural essences (represented by snub) from mathematical ones (represented by concave). For the latter too contain such an element. The saving difference, as *ᵃ30* also makes clear, is that in their case that element is intelligible matter, whereas in case of natural essences it is perceptible (sublunary) matter. For convenience, then, let us say that natural essences,

---

[31] Reading καὶ περὶ οὐσίαν τὴν κατὰ τὸν λόγον ἐπὶ τὸ πολύ οὐ χωριστὴν μόνον with the mss. The OCT adds ὡς prior to ἐπὶ πολύ to give: "and only about substance that in respect of its account is for the most part not separate from matter." This saddles Aristotle with a view he does not hold. For all his natural substances are absolutely inseparable from matter.

[32] Also *Met.* VII 8 1033ᵇ24–26, 10 1035ᵇ28–31, 11 1036ᵇ21–32, 1037ᵃ5–10, ᵃ21–ᵇ7, 1039ᵇ27–31, XI 7 1064ᵃ19–28.

as not being separate from perceptible matter taken universally, are perceptually enmattered, or *penmattered*.[33]

What is important about penmattered essences is stated in $^a26$: they are the ontological correlates of accounts or definitions that hold only for the most part. The difference between them and mathematical essences, however, lies in one thing only: the type of matter involved in them. It follows that it must be because the matter involved in natural essences is perceptible sublunary matter that their definitions hold only for the most part. Our problem, then, is to explain how that can be so.

One component of the human essence, we may suppose, is the capacity responsible for the movement in male seed that codes for chin hair in males and its absence in females (*APo.* II 12 96^{a}9–11). Moreover, both capacity and movement are two different occurrences of one and the same formal element: chin-hair. Because this element is part of a nature, however, inseparable in thought from perceptible sublunary matter taken universally, it must have a material element that is the matter of chin-hair taken universally. This may be represented by a variable, m, the values of which are actual bits of perceptible matter. What we previously called chin-hair, therefore, we may now more accurately call: chin-hair-in-m. Since Socrates is a male, chin-hair-in-m is present in his essence and seed. Hence we may represent it in our usual notation as $|$ chin-hair-in-m $|$.

On two occasions, O_y and O_z, on which Socrates impregnated Xanthippe, $|$ chin-hair-in-m $|$ mastered the relevant potential movements in her menses. On a third, O_x, it slackened. The consequences for the offspring produced on these three occasions—x, y, and the familiar z—were as follows: z developed chin hair in puberty as did his sister y; his brother x

---

[33] These will be the ontological correlates of the "enmattered accounts *(logoi enuloi)*" mentioned at *DA* I 1 403^{a}25–28. Perceptible and intelligible matter taken universally may seem 'metaphysical' in the bad sense, but, because they are abstractions, they are actually quite respectable. Suppose a bronze circle consists of a certain quantity of bronze b, I(b) is b with all its properties except its spatial continuity and magnitude screened out. Similarly, if m is the quantity of matter that constitutes Socrates, P(m) is m with all its properties except its spatial continuity, magnitude, and perceptibility screened out. I(b) is b *considered as* or qua continuous magnitude; P(m) is m *considered as* or qua continuous perceptible magnitude. Intelligible matter taken universally is just the output of the "*as*-operator or qua-operator" I, therefore, and perceptible matter so taken, the output of P, and these outputs are just as intellectually respectable as the *as*-operators whose outputs they are. See Lear, "Aristotle's Philosophy of Mathematics," 168–169.

didn't. What is the cause of these differences between x, y, and z? It cannot lie in the formal elements of the movements responsible for the state of their chins, since the very same formal element, chin-hair, is present on O_x, O_y, and O_z. It must then lie in their matter—in differences between the bits of perceptible sublunary matter that m takes as its values on these three occasions. Therein lies the pertinent difference between perceptible and intelligible matter. The latter, like Euclidean space, is uniform—different bits of it all have the same (lack of) features. The former, by contrast, is "indeterminate" (*Ph.* IV 2 209^{b}9), "irregular," "not everywhere the same" (*GC* II 10 336^{b}21–22), and "capable of being otherwise than it for the most part is" (*Met.* VI 2 1027^{a}13–14).

It is a theorem of human embryology that adult male humans have hair on their chins, and another that adult female humans lack it. But these theorems do not hold necessarily and always: x is a counterexample to the first, y to the second. Instead, they hold snecessarily and for the most part (*APo.* II 12 96^{a}9–11). Chin-hair-in-m is not unique in being penmattered, however, since every element of a nature or natural essence is penmattered. We may conclude that the theorems of all natural sciences have the same status as our sample theorems of embryology—they too are snecessary and hold only for the most part. Contrariwise, the theorems of all sciences whose first principles are not penmattered—all the theorems of the theoretical sciences—hold necessarily and always. It follows that the exactness of an Aristotelian science is a function of the degree to which the essences that are its first principles are abstractable from matter. We can have exact scientific knowledge of a universal essence provided that it is not penmattered. When we turn to penmattered universal essences, however, exactness is lost (*Met.* II 3 995^{a}14–17). And the reason it is lost is that perceptible sublunary matter is variable or indeterminate. That solves our problem about the relationship between an essence's being penmattered and its definition holding only for the most part.

It is clear that a comparable story can also be told about artifactual essences—clear enough, I think, not to require elaborate rehearsal. One difference, though, merits explicit mention. Artifactual essences can be embodied or realized in very many more kinds of hypothetically necessary matter than natural ones. Hence it is likely that distinct bits of each of these kinds of matter will differ from one another in many more ways than x's matter can differ from y's or y's from z's. Whatever theorems might be thought to hold of artifacts are likely to have more exceptions, therefore, than comparable ones holding of natural beings. Perhaps, that is why

Aristotle is so confident that "nature is more exact . . . than any craft" (*EN* II 6 1106^{b}14–16).

3.8 The Definition of an Essence

If something is a natural essence—indeed an essence of any kind—it must have a definition *(horismos)*. For essences are the ontological correlates of definitions that are themselves the epistemological first principles of sciences. The fact that sciences are structures of *demonstrations,* therefore, must be reflected in these definitions, and so in the essences they define (*DA* I 1 402^{b}22–403^{a}2). One important form of such reflection is described as follows: "To proceed from primitives is to proceed from first principles; for I call the same things primitives and first principles. A first principle of a demonstration is an immediate proposition, and a proposition is immediate if there is no other proposition prior to it. A proposition is one part of a contradictory pair[34]—one thing said of one" (*APo.* I 2 72^{a}5–9). Thus if 'F is G' is a definition, both F and G must, in the appropriate way be "one"— one intrinsic being. But because a definition is perforce complex, there is a problem here: "that whose account we call a definition, why is it one? E.g., man is twofooted animal—let this be its account. Why then is this one and not many, animal *and* twofooted?" (*Met.* VII 12 1037^{b}10–14). Since this problem concerns the unity of a genus (animal) and its differentia (two-footed), let us call it *genus.*

Genus would be solved, Aristotle claims, if genera participated in their differentiae, so that the genus and the differentiated genus were one and the same. For then being twofooted, for example, would be part of being an animal and not some further thing in addition to it. If genera participated in their differentiae, however, "the same thing [the genus] would have to participate in opposites at the same time, since the differentiae by which the genus is differentiated are opposites" (*Met.* VII 12 1037^{b}19–21). Moreover—and this gives rise to a second problem—"even if [the genus] does participate in the differentiae, the argument is the same—at least if there is more than one differentia: e.g., footed-twofooted-featherless. For why are *these* one and not many?" (1037^{b}21–23). This new problem concerns the unity of the differentiae themselves. It has two quite different components. The first of these is *vertical differentia*. It asks why differentiae at different levels in the same division—such as footed and twofooted—

---

[34] Reading ἀντιφάσεως with Barnes.

are one rather than many. The second is *horizontal differentia*. It asks why differentia at the same level in different divisions—such as, footed and featherless (supposing these to be at the same level)—are one rather than many.

If the following text is to be our guide, these three problems admit of a single solution:

Met. VII 12 1037ᵇ27–1038ᵃ26 First we must examine definitions that are by divisions. For [ᵇ29] there is nothing in [such] definitions except the genus that is mentioned first and the differentiae; the other genera are the first one plus the differentiae combined with it, e.g., first animal, next twofooted animal, and then featherless, twofooted animal; and similarly even if it is formulated through further differentiae. In general it makes no difference whether it's formulated through many or though few—nor therefore whether through few or through two (of the two one is differentia and the other genus, e.g., of twofooted animal, animal is genus and the other differentia). [ᵃ5] If, then, the genus isn't unqualifiedly anything apart from the species [taken] generically or if it is [something apart from them], but only as matter (for sound is genus and matter, and the differentiae make the species—i.e., the letters—out of sound), it's evident that the definition is the account [constructed] out of the differentiae. [ᵃ9] But further, [the genus] must be divided by the differentia of the differentia[35]: e.g., a differentia of animal is footed; again, the differentia of footed has to be [of animal] qua footed. Hence we must not say of what's footed that one [division] is feathered and the other featherless—not, at any rate, if we are to formulate correctly (rather it's through incapacity that we'd do that). Instead, [we should say] that one [division] is cloven-footed and the other noncloven-footed. For these are differentiae of foot, since cloven-footedness is a type of footedness. And we aim always to proceed in this way until we get to what is undifferentiable. [ᵃ17] At this point there will be exactly as many species of foot as there are differentiae, and the [species of] footed animal will be equal in number to the differentiae. If, then, these things are so, it's evident that the ultimate differentia will be the substance of the thing and the definition . . . [and] one differentia—the ultimate one—will be the form, i.e., the substance.

---

[35] Reading τῇ τῆς διαφορᾶς διαφορᾷ with Joachim and Irwin.

It is easy to see how *genus* is solved here. For $^b29$ shows that only one genus is involved in a definition, and $^a5$ shows that this one genus is nothing besides a set or collection of species taken generically (*DA* I 1 402^{b}5–8, II 3 414^{b}20–28). Thus a twofooted animal isn't a generic animal plus something else as well. Rather, being twofooted is a way of being an animal, and there is no way of being an animal other than some such specific way.

Similarly, $^a9$ offers an equally intelligible solution to *vertical differentia:* the ultimate differentia is a differentia of all its predecessors in the same division, so that they constitute a sort of determinate-determinable chain. Hence just as there are no generic animals, there are no simply footed ones. Rather, to be a footed animal is to be either a footed$_1$, a footed$_2$, or a footed$_3$ animal—where the numerical subscripts signify the ultimate differentiae of footedness (webbed, toed, and so on). Finally, in $^a17$ it is argued that the (definition of the) species, form, or substance is identical to the (definition of the) ultimate differentia. Hence, if being twofooted were an ultimate differentia of man, being a man would be a case of being just *one thing,* namely, twofooted.

The solution to *horizontal differentia,* on the other hand, is harder to discern. It could be readily solved if each species had only one ultimate differentia, as $^a17$ seems to be assuming, but this is not so: "One should try to take the animals by genera in the way already shown by the popular distinction between bird genus and fish genus. Each of these has already been marked off by many differentiae, not dichotomously. For by dichotomy either one cannot obtain them at all (for the same one falls into more than one division, and opposites fall into the same) or there will be only one differentia and this, either as a simple one or as a compound, will be the ultimate species. If, on the other hand, one does not take the differentia of a differentia, one can only make the division continuous in the way that one unifies speech by a conjunction. I mean the sort of thing that comes about if one divides off the featherless and the feathered, and among the feathered the tame and the wild or the white and the black; for tame or white is not a differentiation of feathered but begins another differentiation and is coincidental here. This is why one should divide off the one genus straight away by many differentiae in the way that we say" (*PA* I 3 643^{b}10–24). Species have many ultimate differentiae, then, not just one. Since these are not all differentiae of a differentia, why are they one? Why is being a featherless, twofooted animal being one thing?

What $^b19$ suggests is that differentiae at the same level in different divisions, such as different ultimate differentiae, are united—made into one thing—by being differentiae of the same genus, namely, animal. The problem is that the genus, since it is just the species taken generically, seems poorly suited to play this unifying role. The threat of circularity, indeed, is palpable: the species is one thing because its differentiae are a horizontal unity; its differentiae are such a unity because they are differentiae of one thing—the species taken generically. The following text, however, seems to offer the beginning of an explanation of how such circularity may be avoided:

> Pol. IV 4 1290^{b}25–37 If we wanted to grasp the species of animal, [^{b}25] we would first determine what it is that every animal must have, e.g., some of the sense-organs, something with which to masticate and absorb food, such as a mouth and a stomach, and also parts by which it moves. If these were the only [necessary] parts, but [^{b}29] they were differentiated (I mean, e.g., if there were several types (genê) of mouths, stomachs, and sense-organs, and also of locomotive parts in addition), then the number of ways of combining these will necessarily produce several types (genê) of animals. For [^{b}33] the same [species of] animal cannot have multiple differentiated [types] of mouths, nor of ears either. Hence, when these have been grasped, [^{b}34] all the possible ways of pairing them together will produce species of animals, and as many species of animals as there are combinations of the necessary parts.

What is described here is, so to speak, a way of conceptually constructing the various species of animals out of the necessary parts of an animal. But what is the mode of construction?

One thought is that it is moriological (or mereological), that species are defined in terms of their parts (moria) in such a way that the latter are prior in definition to the former. The result would be that the essences of the parts of animals, rather than the essences of whole animals, would be scientific first principles and, as such, substances.[36] But while we do indeed "say that animals and plants and their parts are substances" (Met. VII 2 1028^{b}9–10), what we say provides only the starting point for an investigation into the problem of whether what we say is true. Hence it leaves open the possibility that "only some of these things" or "none of them, but only

---

[36] A view of this sort is defended in Pellegrin, "Aristotle: A Zoology without Species," 106: "in Aristotelian biology the ousiai [substances], in the primary and strong sense, are the moria [parts] and . . . this biology is primarily a 'moriology'."

some others" are substances (1028^b13-15). The outcome of the investigation, however, makes it plain that animal parts are not substances at all: "It is evident that even of the things thought to be substances most are potentialities—e.g., the parts of animals (for none of these is separate, and when they are separated [from the whole functioning animal], they all exist as matter)" (16 1040^b5-8). It follows that *Pol. IV 4* cannot be advocating moriology at all.

What it is advocating is in fact a quite different doctrine. To identify the necessary parts of an animal, we must already have a grasp of what a generic whole animal—an animal of any species—needs in the way of such parts ($^b25$).[37] We are able to achieve this, without having already defined the animal species, because our pre-theoretical observation allows us to develop a sufficiently rich conception of what capacities an animal of any species requires in order to live a characteristically animal life: perception, absorption of nourishment, movement, and so on.[38] If these parts were differentiated (something that biological research would reveal), different combinations of them will give rise to different species ($^b29$). For the ultimate differentiae—which are the ultimate differentiae of the necessary parts—just are the species, form, or substance (*Met. VII 12 1038^a17*). That is why animals of the same species cannot have multiply differentiated types of mouths ($^b33$).

To understand $^b34$ we need to develop the picture sketched in *Pol. IV 4* as a whole in a little more detail. Let us suppose that mouth, stomach, sense-organ, and locomotive part are the only necessary parts of an animal, that each species of animal has exactly one of each of these parts, and that each of the parts comes in exactly three differentiated types, $mouth_1$, $mouth_2$, $mouth_3$, $stomach_1$, $stomach_2$, $stomach_3$, and so on for the others. How many species of animals will there then be? If $^b34$ were proposing a moriological account of species, in which a species is just a logical sum or conjunction of necessary parts, the answer would seem to be: *eighty-one* (3^4).[39] For the general recipe for an animal species would then be:

---

[37] *HA I 1–6* might be taken as exhibiting precisely such a grasp.

[38] Aristotle's reference at *PA I 4 644^b1-2* to "genera that have been correctly marked off by common usage," perhaps suggests this idea. A constructivist approach, which avoids circularity in this way, is described in Grice, "Method in Philosophical Psychology," especially §5.

[39] This is the sort of account embraced by Pellegrin in his resourceful and

mouth+stomach+sense−organ+locomotive part

and each species of animal can have exactly one of the three different types of each of these four parts. Aristotle, however, is not proposing such an account.

Look again at *Met. VII 12*. It says that the species of footed animal will be equal in number to the ultimate differentiae of foot (*a*17). In the case we are imagining, therefore, it seems that there are just *three* species of animal, corresponding to the three types of locomotive part. *b*29 makes it very likely, however, that Aristotle is assuming for the sake of simplicity that a species has just one necessary part, or one ultimate differentia in just one division, since he claims that the number of differentiae is irrelevant to the argument. For he is explicit elsewhere that an ultimate differentia of this sort is not the one to which the species is identical: "Clearly there cannot be more than one such differentia [i.e., an ultimate differentia within a division]; for by proceeding continuously [i.e., taking a differentia of the differentia at each stage] one reaches the ultimate differentia (though not the ultimate differentia which is the species). And this is either the toed alone, or the whole compound, if one divides off, e.g., man, putting footed with biped or toed. If man were merely a thing with toes, this method would have shown it to be his one [ultimate] differentia. But since in fact he is not, he must necessarily have many differentiae not under one division" (*PA* I 3 644ª1−8). Presumably, then, the ultimate differentia that is identical to the species is some sort of combination of the ultimate differentiae of the necessary parts that determine the species. But what sort?

The necessary parts of an animal do not constitute a unified species simply "by being conjoined, as the *Iliad* [might be made into a single sentence in this way]" (*Met.* VIII 6 1045ª12−14). Rather, they must constitute a teleologically organized system. Thus, for example, "the matter [made] of the elements must exist for the sake of the homoeomerous parts

---

stimulating book, *Aristotle's Classification of Animals,* 156: "Only rational zoology, the only real zoology (for Aristotle, too, everything that is rational is real), can construct *a priori,* by the combination of the various species of each part, the entire animal world. It is this ideal zoology that appears, as a project, in the passage from the *Politics* [IV 4] . . . referring to biology only for comparison, Aristotle is not there tangling with the ultimate unpredictables of the real. Because of the ineradicable margin of contingency that he meets in *physis,* the naturalist should also have recourse to empirical investigations."

[e.g., flesh and bone] . . . and those [for the sake of] the non-homoeomerous ones [e.g., face and hands]" (*PA* II 1 646^{b}5–8), while "the genus
of bone," which is homoeomerous, must exist "for the sake of the flesh" (9
654^{b}27–29), which is also homoeomerous. The parts are not the system
they constitute, however, rather they stand to it as matter to form: "We
have postulated four causes: the that for the sake of which as end and the
account of the substance [essence] (these should be taken pretty much as
one thing), and third and fourth the matter and that from which comes the
first principle of the movement. . . . The matter for animals is their parts
(the non-homoeomerous parts for every whole animal, the homoeomerous parts for the non-homoeomerous ones, and those bodies that are
called elements for the homoeomerous ones)" (*GA* I 1 715^{a}1–11). The
ultimate end of this entire teleological system, then, is the realization of an
animal's distinctive essence, which is also its end. This is what the variously
differentiated necessary parts must promote and subserve: "[As with blood]
so too with the other such [homoeomerous] parts and also with the
nonhomoeomerous ones. For here too it must be supposed that such
differentiations as occur either promote the functions, i.e., the substance
[essence], of each [species of] animal or promote what is better or worse"
(*PA* II 1 648^{a}13–16). The essence or final cause, therefore, as contained in
ether or vital heat, is what determines how the various necessary parts
must be interrelated, and what their various differentiae must be: "the
cause of the relations between them [the homoeomerous and non-
homoeomerous parts] is, of course, a final cause" (*PA* II 1 646^{b}27–28).

Species of animals are not, then, mere moriological sums of their necessary parts. Moreover, they do they live in featureless, abstract environ-
ments. Hence their necessary parts must not just be teleologically organized, they must be so teleologically organized as to adapt the resulting
species to some available natural habitat: "There are many species of food
too. Hence the lives of both animals and of human beings are also many.
For it is impossible to live without food, so that differentiations in diet have
produced differentiated ways of life among the animals. For some beasts
live in herds and others live scattered about, whichever is advantageous for
getting their food, because some of them are carnivorous, some her-
bivorous, and some omnivorous. So, in order to make it easier for them to
get hold of these foods, nature has made their ways of life different. And
since the same things are not naturally pleasant to each, but rather different
things to different ones, among the carnivores and herbivores themselves

the ways of life are different" (*Pol.* I 8 1256^{a}19–29). Not every type of mouth, stomach, sense-organ, and locomotive part, therefore, will go together to constitute a viable species of animal. A mouth and teeth suitable for grazing, for example, cannot be paired with a stomach that cannot digest grass—and similarly in the cases of the other necessary parts. Hence we ought not to consider "the possible ways of pairing" mentioned in *Pol. IV 4 1290^{b}24* as merely logical possibilities, knowable a priori, but as real biological ones.[40]

The number of species in the scenario we imagined earlier isn't likely to be three, then, since the ultimate differentia of just one of an animal's necessary parts isn't the ultimate differentia to which the species is identical. But neither is it likely to be eighty-one, since not all logically possible combinations of types of necessary parts are likely to be real biological possibilities.

Since the unity among the horizontal differentia of a genuine species is unity of a biologically significant sort, it seems reasonable to grant that Aristotle is on intelligible ground in claiming in *Met. VII 12 1037^{b}29* that the solution he provides for *genus* also solves *horizontal differentia*. For if the essence of man is something like featherless, twofooted animal (if *that* is man's ultimate differentia, substance, and species), its essence *is* one thing, and so is sufficiently a unity to be a first principle of a science.

The very structure of animal essences is reflected, moreover, in the interrelations of the various sciences that deal with animals: "We have

---

[40] I agree with Charles, "Aristotle on Substance, Essence, and Biological Kinds," 233, that "in grasping a definition one needs to be able to explain why the kind defined is a unity: i.e., to show that it possesses necessarily certain properties in virtue of some basic property it necessarily possesses." But I see no reason to exclude a biologically possible combination of ultimate differentiae of the necessary parts of an animal from being such a basic property. Charles excludes it (254–258) because he thinks that such a property must succumb to *horizontal differentia,* and so cannot itself be one thing. For the reasons given in the text I think he is mistaken about this. Gill, "Comments On Charles," reaches the same conclusion, by an alternate, but compatible route: "the organism's various necessary features, for instance, its nutritive, reproductive, and locomotive organs, are explained by different soul functions that together make up its distinctive form" (267). Charles is right, nonetheless, to press the question of how we are to ensure that essences don't become a bloated combination of "all properties which a common nature needs to survive" (258).

discussed the other three causes, for the account and that for the sake of which as end are the same, and the matter for animals is their parts. . . . It remains for us to discuss the parts in animals that contribute to their coming-to-be, about which nothing has so far been determined, and about what the cause of movement is. And the investigation of the latter and of the cause of coming-to-be are in a way the same. That is why our discussion has brought them together, putting those parts at the end of our account of the parts [of animals] and the beginning of our account of coming-to-be immediately after them" (GA I 1 715^{a}7–18). This text refers to De Partibus Animalium and De Generatione Animalium, and explains why the former precedes the latter. It also refers to a discussion of the essence or final cause, but does not make explicit in what treatise it occurs, or whether that treatise is prior or posterior to De Partibus. The following text, however, provides the information we need to fill this gap:

> HA I 6 491^{a}4–19 This, too, is why [^{a}4] we must get theoretical knowledge [of the various species of animals] by taking each of them separately. What has in that manner been said, then, is at this point regarded as an outline sketch, a foretaste of the objects and attributes about which we must gain theoretical knowledge. But in what follows we shall deal with them exactly, in order to grasp, first, the differentiae and coincidental attributes of all [the animals]. After that, we should try to discover the causes. For [^{a}11] this is the natural line of inquiry—to begin with investigations of each [species of animal], since from these will become evident the things about which and from which there are demonstrations. So [^{a}14] first of all we must consider the parts from which animals are constituted; for it is most of all and primarily with respect to these that whole [animals] are differentiated—some of them having and others not having [a certain part], or with respect to the position [of a part], or with respect to the organization [of the parts], or with respect to the differentiations mentioned earlier, viz., those of species, excess or deficiency, analogy, and opposite attributes.

Focus first on ^{a}11. It tells us that the investigation described in the previous sentences will result in definitions of essences (since these are the first principles *from which* demonstrations proceed), and in knowledge of coincidental attributes (since demonstrations are *about* the intrinsic ones of these and not about the others). ^{a}14 tells us how the investigation described in ^{a}4 should proceed: it should focus on the parts of animals.

This seems to suggest that the investigations detailed in *Historia Animalium* are not investigations into the distinct animal species at all, even though that is what *ᵃ4* leads us to believe.[41] But, as *ᵃ14* makes clear, the apparent suggestion to the contrary is apparent only. For the parts of animals are the focus simply because "it is most of all and primarily with respect to these that whole [animals] are differentiated." In other words, an investigation into parts is an investigation into species, because what the latter reveals is that species can be differentiated and defined by appeal to their parts.

Historia Animalium is, then, an investigation of the various species that will in the end lead to definitions of their essences. Hence it is a treatise on formal and final causes. As such, it must precede *De Partibus*. For the parts of an animal are its matter (*GA* I 1 715ᵃ9), and matter is posterior to form: "What relates to coming-to-be is the opposite of what relates to substance [essence], since what is posterior in coming-to-be is prior in nature, and what is prior in coming-to-be is posterior in nature. For a house does not exist for the sake of the bricks and stones, but these for the house, and the same holds for other matter. This is evident not alone from induction, but also from the account. For all coming-to-be is a coming-to-be from something to something, i.e., from a first principle to a first principle—from the primary cause of movement, which already possesses a certain nature, to a certain form *(morphê)* or other such end. For a man begets a man and a plant a plant, in each case out of the underlying matter. In time, then, the matter and the coming-to-be must be prior, but in account the substance [essence], i.e., the form of each thing, [is primary]. This is clear if we state the account of the coming-to-be, since the account of house-building includes that of house, but that of house does not include that of house-building. And the same holds in [all] other cases [of coming-to-be]. Hence the matter [made] of the elements must exist for the sake of the homoeomerous parts [of an animal], since these are posterior to it in coming-to-be, and those [for the sake of] the nonhomoeomerous ones" (*PA* II 1 646ᵃ24–ᵇ8). Just as a whole is prior to its parts, in other words, so the sciences of the whole are prior to the sciences of the parts. Granted Aristotle's realism, it could be no other way.

---

[41] E.g., Pellegrin, *Aristotle's Classification of Animals,* 141: "the sketch [mentioned in *HA I 6 491ᵃ4*] is not the study undertaken in the *History of Animals,* for no one could argue that this book is a collection of studies of individual kinds [i.e., species] of animals."

3.9 The Parts of an Essence

Also of great importance to the question of how essences are to be defined is the problem of what their parts are: "Since the definition is an account, and every account has parts, and as the account is to the thing so the part of the account is to the part of the thing, the problem already arises: must the account of the parts be present in the account of the whole, or not?" (*Met.* VII 10 1034^{b}20–24). This problem, in turn, leads to another: "Not surprisingly, a further problem arises: what parts are parts of the form and what are not [parts of the form] but of the combined thing? And if this is not clear, we cannot define anything, since definition is of the universal, i.e., of the form. If, then, it is not evident which parts are [parts] as matter and which are not, it will not be evident either what the account of the thing is" (*Met.* VII 11 1036^{a}26–31). At stake, then, is the integrity of the notion of a definition or essence, and so of Aristotelian science as a whole.

We may begin, as Aristotle does, by looking at the problem as it arises in the case of mathematical essences: "Some people raise the problem [of what parts are parts of the form] already even in the case of the circle and the triangle, [saying that] it's not appropriate to define [these] in terms of lines and the continuous, but rather all these [lines, etc.] too are [to circle and triangle] as flesh and bones are to man, and bronze and stone to statue. And [thus] they reduce everything to numbers, and say that the account of line is that of the two. . . . It follows that there is a single form of many things whose forms are evidently different . . . and it then becomes plausible to make this form the one form of all things, and to make nothing else a form. Thus all things will be one" (*Met.* VII 11 1036^{b}8–20). The mistake made by these thinkers (Platonists and Pythagoreans) is to think that one cannot define circle in terms of line and continuous two dimensional space, but must rather say that circle is constituted out of these as matter. Circle, triangle, and the rest won't differ in form, then, but only in matter. The result is that there is only one form, which, when realized in different matter, results in the variety of beings.

To avoid this untenable conclusion, we need to be able to say that line and the continuous are parts of the essence of circle, and are not simply its matter. And this is something Aristotle can say without threatening the unity of definition and essence, because the elements that appear in his definitions are not separate substances, as they are for the Platonists, and because the definitions themselves are tightly unified. The trouble is that he now faces the opposite problem of how to delimit what is simply matter in these cases. This is where intelligible matter comes in: "Where mathematical objects are concerned, why is it that the accounts of the parts (e.g., the semicircles) are not parts of the accounts of the whole (e.g., the circle)? For these objects are not perceptible ones. But in fact there is no difference, for some nonperceptible objects also have matter. Indeed everything that is not an essence has matter of some sort, I mean [what is not] itself intrinsically a form. Accordingly, these [the semicircles] won't be [parts] of the universal [circle], but will be parts of the particular ones, as was said before, for one kind of matter is perceptible, another, intelligible" (*Met.* VII 11 1036^{b}32–1037^{a}5). If the perceptible matter were the only kind, mathematical circles, as nonperceptible, would not be hylomorphic compounds. Hence they would be intrinsically forms—not, as we saw to be the case, such-and-such a form in such-and-such matter. All the parts of the universal circle, therefore, would have to be parts of its form or essence, and so their accounts would have to be parts of its account. Hence the problem. In fact, however, the accounts of the parts are not parts of the account of the universal circle itself, since it is constituted not just by a formal element, but also by a material one, namely, intelligible matter taken universally.

How does this solve the problem of what things are parts of the universal circle? In the case of the universal circle, intelligible matter taken universally is bare spatial continuity in two dimensions. So the universal circle constituted of such matter does not consist of two semicircular parts. Particular circles, on the other hand, whether intelligible or perceptible, do contain two semicircular parts. For the former can be split in two by a diameter, the latter by a diametrical cut.

Turning to natural essences, we find a similar problematic, and a similar—but not an exactly similar—solution proposed. Here it is useful, from the expository point of view, to begin with the solution and work backwards: "It is also clear that [in the case of man] the soul is the primary substance, and the body is matter, and man and animal is what arises out of the two taken universally. As for Socrates or Coriscus, if soul is Socrates too, he is spoken of it two ways; for some speak of him as soul, some as the compound [of soul and body], but if [spoken of] unqualifiedly, [he is] this soul and this body, then as the universal so also the particular" (*Met.* VII 11 1037^{a}5–10). A particular man or animal consists of a particular soul (formal element, primary substance), and a particular body (material element). Hence a particular soul is a this in this. The universal man or animal, like the universal circle, arises out of these two elements taken universally.

Hence it, too, has a universal formal element (this soul taken universally) and a material element (this body taken universally).[42] That is why, if Socrates is spoken of unqualifiedly, which he is when he is spoken of as a this in this, he is similar in structure to the universal man. For the latter, too, is a this (taken universally) in this (taken universally).

So much for the solution, now for the problem: "The reduction of all things [to forms] in this way and the taking away of matter is wasted labor. For some things are surely this [form] in this [matter] or these [parts] in this condition [i.e., with this form]. And [so] the comparison that Socrates the Younger used to make in the case of animal is not sound, for it leads away from the truth and makes one suppose it possible that man can exist without his parts, in the way that circle can without bronze. But the case is not similar. For animal is a perceptible thing, and cannot be defined without [reference to] movement and therefore not without the parts in a certain condition. For it is not a hand in any condition that is part of man, but one capable of fulfilling its function, hence, one that is ensouled [or alive, i.e., that has the appropriate form]; but one that is not ensouled is not a part" (Met. VII 11 1036^{b}22–32). What Socrates the Younger thought, then, is, first, that the parts of the universal circle stand to it as matter to form. Hence, because the universal circle can exist in other matter, and so separate from bronze, he thought that it can exist without even the parts of its form (1036^{a}31–^{b}3). Moreover, because he thought that the universal man is analogous to the universal circle, he concluded that it, too, could exist without the parts of its form. He was wrong on both counts.

The universal circle would be separate in thought from bronze, even if all circles were made of bronze, but the universal man is not separate in thought from "flesh and bones and parts of this kind" (Met. VII 11 1036^{b}1–4)—parts, which include hands. For man is a "perceptible thing, and cannot be defined without [reference to] movement, and therefore not without the parts in a certain condition." In other words, the difference between the universal man and the universal circle that Socrates the Younger failed to grasp is, to put it crudely, that men are essentially alive and moving, whereas circles are not.

Are flesh, bones, hands, and so on then parts of the formal element of the universal man? No. For like man itself, these things too are ensouled

---

[42] Met. VII 10 1035^{b}27–30: "Man and horse and anything else that applies in this way to particulars, but universally, is not a substance, but a sort of compound of this account [form] and this matter taken universally."

and functional—that is to say, since soul is a formal element, they too are hylomorphic compounds. Thus the universal definition of hand, like that of man, will be: a this (taken universally) in a this (taken universally). That is why man can be defined either as this soul (taken universally) in this flesh, bones, and so on (taken universally) or as these parts (taken universally) in the (functional) condition of being informed by soul. In other words, it is the formal elements in the definitions of its parts that are parts of the form of man, and not their material elements.

The importance of these problems about the parts of definitions, and so of intelligible and perceptible matter, which play a vital part in their solution, is readily appreciated when we consider the role of essences as first principles of sciences. For if G is part of F's essence, "All Fs are Gs" will be a theorem of the science of Fs—but a theorem that is, so to speak, true by definition. That means, in effect, that the theorem is somewhat less informative, and so somewhat less explanatory, than it would be if held for some other reason. Intelligible and perceptible matter taken universally help keep mathematical and natural essences from becoming bloated, therefore, and so increase the number of theorems that, because they employ thinner essences, are more genuinely informative and explanatory.

3.10 The Formal Element of an Essence

On the account developed so far, Socrates' ultimate differentia is the ultimate differentia of the human species. For "it is evident that the ultimate differentia will be the substance of the thing and the definition" (*Met.* VII 12 1038^{a}19–20), and "substances are the last species, and these are undifferentiated in form [essence], like Socrates and Coriscus" (*PA* I 4 644^{a}23–25). Socrates' essence, then, is the same as that of any other human being, and so is the human species essence. Using '+' now to symbolize the relation that guarantees the requisite sort of teleological unity, we may represent it as:

$$|\text{animal}| + |\text{twofooted}| + |\text{featherless}|$$

But this as we know from our investigation of | chin-hair | is really only the representation of the formal element of Socrates' essence. The entire essence also contains a material element. Making that explicit, we get:

$$|\text{animal--in--}m_1| + \text{twofooted--in--}m_2| + |\text{featherless--in--}m_3|$$

Notice what follows. Socrates' form—the formal element of his essence—is just the human species form: "once we have the whole thing, such and such a form in this flesh and in these bones, this is Callias or Socrates; and they are different because of their matter (since [their matters] are different), but the same in form; for the form is indivisible" (*Met.* VII 8 1034^{a}5–8).

Therein, as will no doubt be evident, lies another difficult problem. For a species form seems far too thin to explain the inheritance of specific traits, such as those coded for by |Socrates| or |Socnose|, which are obviously not entailed by the ultimate differentiae of the human species. That explanatory task seems to require a much thicker form, one which includes all of a particular individual's heritable traits. Drawing on our earlier investigations, and assuming that |Socnose| and the like are components of |Socrates|, we may represent this thicker individualized form as:

|animal| + |human being| + |male| + |Socrates|+/Socrates'

father/ + Socrates' grandfather/+Socrates' great-grandfather/

Embryology seems to require thick individual forms, then, while the doctrine of the unity of essence seems to give us only thin species ones. This problem, since it has to do with how thick or thin is the formal element in an essence, we may call *thickness*.

The various parts—including the various necessary parts—of different creatures can differ from one another in a number of importantly different ways:

HA I 1 486^{a}14–^{b}22 Of the animals, some have all their parts mutually identical, whereas some have different ones. Some parts are identical [^{a}16] in form [or species] *(eidei),* e.g., one man's nose and eye are identical to another man's nose and eye, one's flesh to the other's flesh, one's bone to the other's bone; and the same applies to the parts of a horse and of such other animals as we say are identical in form [species]. For as the whole is to the whole, so each part is to each part. [^{a}21] In other cases—those whose genus is the same—they are indeed identical [in form], but they differ in excess or deficiency. By genus I mean, e.g., bird and fish, for each of these has differentiations with respect to its genus, i.e., there are numerous species both of fish and of birds. Now the differences of most of the parts in animals lie in [^{b}5] the oppositions of their attributes, e.g., of colors and shapes, in that some have the same things to a greater, others to a lesser degree, and additionally in greater or fewer number, and larger or smaller size, i.e., to put it generally, in excess or deficiency. Thus in some the texture of the flesh is soft, in others firm; some have a long bill, others a short one; some have many feathers, others few. Furthermore, even in the cases we are considering, it happens that different ones have different parts, e.g., some have spurs, others don't, some have crests and others don't. But *[b14]* as a general rule most of the parts and those out of which the bulk of the body is constituted, are either identical [in species or form] or differ by way of opposition, i.e., of excess or deficiency—for greater or lesser [degree] may be taken to be a sort of excess or deficiency.[43] Some animals, however, do have parts that are neither identical in species nor [different] in excess or deficiency, but *[b19]* that are [merely] analogous, e.g., as bone is to fishspine, nail to hoof, hand to claw, feather to scale. For what the feather is in a bird, the scale is in a fish.

Focus first on the parts described in *a21*. They differ, but because they differ only in excess or deficiency, they are genuinely identical in form, not, like those in *b19*, merely analogous. Why so? Why is this sort of difference compatible with identity, while that between feathers and scales is not?

The answer seems to be that differences in excess and deficiency are due to differences in matter: "The wet, the dry, the hot, and the cold are the matter of composite bodies; and the other differences follow after these, e.g., heaviness and lightness, firmness and looseness, roughness and smoothness, and any other such attributes of bodies as there may be" (*PA* II 1 646[a]16–20). Presumably, then, crane feathers are sufficiently similar in function to sparrow feathers that their forms are the same, even though, because of differences in their matter, they differ in other ways. This does not hold, however, of scales and feathers. Their functions, though analogous, are sufficiently different that their forms are different.

Though *HA I 1* is not perhaps entirely clear on the question, Aristotle is explicit elsewhere that the differences described in *b5*, such as those of color and shape, are also differences in excess or deficiency. Witness, for example, the following discussion of nose shape: "A straight nose is the most beautiful, but one that deviates from being straight and tends towards

---

[43] Opposition (contrariety) is the greatest degree of difference between things (*Met.* V 10 1018[a]25–31).

being hooked or snub can nevertheless still be beautiful to look at. Yet if it is tightened still more towards the extreme, the part will first be thrown out of due proportion, and in the end it will cease to look like a nose at all, because of an excess or deficiency of these opposites" (*Pol.* V 9 1309^{b}23–29). Here the difference between straight, hooked, and snub noses is a matter of excess or deficiency in opposites. The same is true in the case of colors. For while many colors are constituted out of white and black in some definite ratio, others are constituted in "some incommensurable ratio of excess or deficiency" (*Sens.* 3 439^{a}19–^{b}30). Presumably, then, differences in color too must be explained in terms of differences in matter, so that however finely shades of blue are discriminated, the very same shade may differ in sheen or velvetiness when exemplified by the same type of feather in different blue jays.[44]

The parts described in ^{a}16 have the same universal account or definition—the same form—because they are the parts of animals that belong to the same species. But if things belong to the same species, they also belong to the same genus. Hence these parts must be a sub-set of the parts described in ^{a}21. It follows that though Socrates' parts have the same account or definition—the same form—as Coriscus', they too may differ in excess or deficiency from his. Take twofooted, for example, and suppose that it is an ultimate differentia of man. Socrates and Coriscus will then both be twofooted animals. But their feet may, and almost certainly will, differ in size (Socrates' are larger, Coriscus' smaller), in consistency (Socrates' are softer, Coriscus' harder), in texture (Socrates' are smoother, Coriscus' rougher), in shape (Socrates' are broader, Coriscus' narrower), in color (Socrates' are paler, Coriscus' darker), and so on. But these differences are not further differentiae of twofooted—by hypothesis, twofooted is *ultimate*. Rather, like the differences in the chins of *x, y,* and *z,* they result from differences in the actual matter in which the very same differentia is realized.

What holds of twofooted, however, also holds of all the other ultimate differentiae of the species—that is, of the differentiae of its other necessary parts. Hence it holds of the form as a whole, which is identical to a biologically possible combination of these ultimate differentiae. Whatever differences there may be between Socrates' form and Coriscus', therefore, must be differences in excess or deficiency that are due to differences in the

---

[44] To capture such differences, heraldry distinguishes three types of colors: tinctures, metals, and furs.

matter in which they are realized. That is to say, they must be differences between these forms considered as realized in actual matter. For "as number does not admit of greater or lesser degree, neither does the substance in respect of the form, but if indeed any substance does, it is the one that involves matter" (*Met.* VIII 3 1044ᵃ9–11).

For simplicity, then, let us focus on just one component of the human species essence, namely, | twofooted-in-m_2 |. In all human beings its formal element, | two-footed |, is the same. But because m_2 takes different values in different human beings, because perceptible sublunary matter is indeterminate, | twofooted-in-m_2 | will almost certainly be different in different human beings, or even in the same one at different times. What applies to | chin-hair-in-m |, in other words, also applies to it. The very same formal element, therefore, that results in Socrates having large, soft, smooth, broad, pale feet, results in Coriscus having small, hard, rough, narrow, dark ones. For what explains these differences isn't form as such, but form as realized in particular matter. It is, as Aristotle says, "the ultimate differentia in the matter that is the species" (*PA* I 3 643ᵃ24). Hence differences in the matter in which that differentia is realized can explain why it has different effects. Once that is made explicit, however, *thickness* ceases to be a problem.

Here is a thought experiment which may help to drive the point home, though it is not Aristotelian and will not bear too much scrutiny. Imagine that Socrates is the first human being, as Adam and Eve are in the Bible story. Imagine that his form is just species form, and that he reproduces hermaproditically by producing menses of his own. Let different quantities of these menses differ only by excess or deficiency. Bear in mind that the natures of offspring are affected by such things as winds, seasons, and the age and general physical condition of their progenitors (*Pol.* VII 16). Allow reproduction to begin. If it continues long enough, there will be human beings who differ as much as Socrates and Coriscus or as Coriscus and Xanthippe. Yet only species form will have been ultimately involved in their generation.

Collapsing the no longer needed distinction between Socrates' thick form and his species form, then, we may represent his natural form *tout court* as follows:

| animal | + | twofooted | + | featherless |

and his natural essence as

$$|\text{animal-in-}m_1| \ + \ |\text{twofooted-in-}m_2| \ + \ |\text{featherless-in-}m_3|$$

But Socrates' natural essence or nature is only a part of his essence as a whole—the penmattered part. If we wanted to represent his essence as a whole, we would have to include «understanding» in it.

It is worth noticing that the solution to *thickness* draws on the very same feature of natural essences—penmatteredness—as the solution offered in 3.7 to the problem of explaining why the theorems of natural science hold only for the most part. This should increase our confidence that it is on the right track.

3.11 Other Essences

Artifactual, mathematical, natural essences cannot exist in reality separate from actual quantities of matter. In thought, none can exist separate from some sort of matter taken universally. But there are also essences that are like these natural essences, except that their matter is of a special unchangeable sort. These include the essences of the heavens. Moreover, there are essences that both in thought and in reality can exist apart from matter of any kind, taken in any way—essences that are entirely matterless—for example, God's essence. Eventually, we will need accounts of them also.

FOUR

BEING AS SUBSTANCE

4.1 Intrinsic Being

Our investigation of the exact and the inexact sciences led us to investigate the various kinds of essences—penmattered, intelligibly mattered, and matterless—that are their ontological first principles. Our route was from epistemology to metaphysics. Now we begin to travel in the opposite direction, investigating being and substance so as to arrive at an understanding of one science in particular, namely, the science of being qua being (9.1).

Of the various types of being Aristotle recognizes, one of the most important is *kath' hauto* or *per se* being—intrinsic being, as I have been calling it. This sort of being is divided into four different types, the first two of which are defined as follows:

> *APo.* I 4 73^a34-^b4 G belongs to F intrinsically if [$^a34$] G is in F's essence—e.g., as line belongs to triangle and point to line (for here the substance of F is composed of G and G belongs in the account which states F's essence)—or [$^a37$] if G belongs to F and F belongs in the account that makes clear G's essence—e.g., straight and curved belong [in this way] to line, and odd and even, prime and compound, equilateral and oblong to number, since either line or number belongs in the accounts that state their essences. [$^b3$] Similarly, in other cases too, this is what I mean when I say that G belongs to F intrinsically.

If G is part of F's essence, GF is an intrinsic$_1$ being ($^a34$). In this case, it is demonstrable within some science that all Fs are necessarily or snecessarily Gs. Consequently, intrinsic beings of this type are of interest to Aristotelian science.

Is this also true of the intrinsic$_2$ beings defined in $^a37$? One might think not, on the grounds that if F is part of G's essence, it is not demonstrable that all Fs are Gs: being a number is part of the essence of being odd (to be odd is to be an odd number) but one cannot demonstrate in any science that all numbers are odd (*Top.* I 13 173^{b}8). To be sure, some things are demonstrable in this case, such as that all numbers are odd or even or that some numbers are odd. But since scientific theorems must be universally quantified propositions, in which one thing is predicated of one thing, neither of these can be what Aristotle intends (*APo.* I 2 72^{a}8–9, 4 73^{b}26–74^{a}3).[1] What he actually has in mind is revealed in the following text:

> *APo.* I 4 73^{b}16–24 In the case of what is an object of unqualified scientific knowledge, whatever is said to hold of things intrinsically, in the sense of belonging in what is predicated [i.e., intrinsic$_1$] or of being belonged in [i.e., intrinsic$_2$], holds of them both because of themselves and by necessity. For it is not possible for them not to hold, either [^{b}19a] unqualifiedly *(haplôs)* or [^{b}19b] [as regards] the opposites *(ta antikeimena)*—i.e., as straight or bent belongs to line and odd or even to number. [^{b}21] For a contrary is either a privation or a contradiction in the same genus, e.g., as even is what is not odd *in numbers,* in so far as it follows [from a number's being not odd that it is even]. Hence [^{b}23] if to assert or deny is necessary, it is also necessary for what is intrinsic to belong.

^{b}19b says that it is necessary for G to hold of F "[as regards] the opposites." ^{b}19a contrasts this with the case in which it is necessary for G to hold "unqualifiedly," or simply, of F. What is the difference? Since in both cases G holds necessarily of F, it cannot be a modal one. Perhaps, then, it has to do with what G holds of: in the case of intrinsic$_1$ beings, G holds of what is unqualifiedly F, whereas in the case of intrinsic$_2$ beings, it holds of what is F, but not unqualifiedly so. If this right, "[as regards] the opposites" presumably states the needed qualification. So if F is number, say, and the opposites are odd and even (*^{b}21*), then the newly qualified subject would be either odd number or even number.

If odd number, or more generally φF, is the new subject, what is being predicated of it? That is what ^{b}23 tells us. It says that if asserting or denying *any* predicate G of φF results in something necessary (a theorem), φF must be an intrinsic$_2$ being—it must be in the appropriate way one thing. In

---

[1] Disjunctive attributes do however occasionally appear in Aristotle's syllogisms. Barnes, *Aristotle Posterior Analytics,* 113, lists the following as the only ones he has found: *APr.* I 31 46^{b}3–19, 46^{b}30–35, 46 51^{b}39–41, 52^{a}34–37, II 22 68^{a}3–16.

other words, the theorems that involve intrinsic$_2$ beings are theorems about complex subjects—complexes that really are subjects or substances and not, for example, a combination of a substance and an attribute that holds of it only coincidentally. The theorem that holds in these cases is not $(\forall x)(Fx \to Gx)$, therefore, but rather $(\forall x)(\varphi Fx \to Gx)$. That is why 73^b3 is able to characterize both intrinsic$_1$ and intrinsic$_2$ beings as cases in which G belongs intrinsically to F. Since odd numbers and straight lines are perfectly good beings for science to investigate, it is hardly surprising that there are such theorems. Aristotelian science would be hopelessly impoverished if there weren't.[2]

Despite Aristotle's characterization in $^b23$, not all values of φ for which φF is an intrinsic$_2$ being are pairs of opposites. For example, acute angle, right angle, obtuse angle, and perfect number are all intrinsic$_2$ beings, but angle, right, and obtuse are a triple not a pair, and perfect has no opposite.[3] Neither is φ restricted to differentiae,[4] even though in some cases φ may be a differentia of F, as odd and even are differentiae of the genus number (*Top.* IV 2 122^{b}19–24): male animal is an intrinsic$_2$ being, but male is not a differentia of animal (*Met.* VII 5 1030^{b}25–26).[5] It is not clear, indeed, that the values of φ need constitute any easily specified natural class, besides, of course, the class of beings such that G is part of the essence of φF.

The third type of intrinsic being is that exemplified by the already familiar subjects, the primary examples of which are substances: "Certain items are not said of any other subject: e.g., whereas the walking [thing] is something else [that happens to be] walking (and similarly for the white [thing]), substances and whatever signifies a this, are not just what they are in virtue of being something different. Things that are not [said] of a subject I call intrinsic beings" (*APo.* I 4 73^{b}5–9). Subjects, then, are intrinsic$_3$ beings. They are what they are in virtue of being themselves, in virtue

---

[2] McKirahan, *Principles and Proofs*, 92–93, argues on different grounds for a similar conclusion.

[3] Aristotle's use of the term 'opposites *(enantia)*' to characterize the values of φ is, therefore, "a hasty generalization" (McKirahan, *Principles and Proofs*, 89–90).

[4] Pace Ferejohn, *The Origins of Aristotelian Science*, 96–99.

[5] Other examples are given in McKirahan, *Principles and Proofs*, 91, who notes that "if odd and even are differentiae of number, then prime and composite are not, nor are square and oblong." Yet prime number, composite number, square number, and oblong number are all intrinsic$_2$ beings.

of their own essences—as, for example, a man is a man in virtue of his own essence, since there is nothing *else* he must be in order to be a man. Here, as one might say, G belongs intrinsically$_3$ to F, because G is what F essentially is. If G is an attribute, such as walking or white, on the other hand, G belongs to F not in virtue of F itself, but in virtue of something else, namely, how it happens to be related to G.

The three sorts of intrinsic being we have so far encountered are all cases of predicative being, cases of F being G, or G holding of F. The fourth and final sort of intrinsic being seems on the surface to be quite different: "What holds of something because of itself holds of it intrinsically, and what does not hold because of itself is coincidental, e.g., if there was lightning while someone was walking, that was coincidental, since it was not because of his walking that there was lightning—that, we say, was coincidental. But what holds because of itself holds intrinsically—e.g., if something died while being sacrificed, and died in virtue of the sacrifice, [we say] that it died because of being sacrificed, and that it was not coincidental that it died while being sacrificed" (*APo.* I 4 73^{b}10–16). What is at issue here is the distinction between intrinsic and coincidental causes. The idea is, therefore, that if x's being F is an intrinsic cause of x's being G, so that x is G in virtue of being F, then GF is an intrinsic$_4$ being. As before, so here too $(\forall x)$ (Fx → Gx) will be a theorem of some Aristotelian science—a necessary or snecessary truth.

What all four types of intrinsic being have in common, therefore, what makes them worth the metaphysician's attention, is that they are the ontological correlates or truth-makers for scientific theorems. For if F is intrinsically$_1$ G (G is part of F's essence), or intrinsically$_2$ G (F is part of G's essence), or intrinsically$_3$ G (G just is F's essence), or intrinsically$_4$ G (being F is an intrinsic cause of being G), then $(\forall x)$ (φFx → Gx) is a theorem of some science (where φ may be empty). Moreover, it looks as if these are the only types of being that can play this role, since they seem to constitute an exhaustive catalog of the necessary or snecessary relations that can hold between a subject (F) and something (G) predicated of it. It remains to be seen whether this is what Aristotle thinks.

4.2 Coincidental Being

Because intrinsic beings are the ontological correlates of scientific theorems, we might be inclined to think that what is metaphysically interesting about coincidental beings is that they are *not* the ontological correlates of such theorems. And this seems to be Aristotle's own view: "it is evident that no science deals with coincidental beings, since every science deals either with what holds always or with what holds for the most part" (*Met.* VI 2 1027ᵃ19–21). Yet there is a type of coincidental being—so called *per se* accidents or intrinsic coincidentals—whose status seems incompatible with this view: "There are three things in demonstrations: one, the thing being demonstrated, the conclusion (this is what belongs intrinsically to some genus); another, the axioms (axioms are the things on which the demonstration depends); third the subject genus of which the demonstration makes clear the attributes and the intrinsic coincidentals" (*APo.* I 7 75ᵃ39–ᵇ1). A triangle is by the definition of its essence a plane figure bounded by three straight lines. It follows, but is not part of its essence, that its interior angles are equal to two right angles (*PA* I 3 643ᵃ27–31). Similarly, to revert to an earlier example, it is not part of the essence of a circle that it consists of two semicircles, though it is a theorem of geometry that all circles so consist. Intrinsic coincidentals, then, *are* the ontological correlates of theorems: "Every demonstrative science provides theoretical knowledge of the intrinsic coincidental attributes of some subject" (*Met.* III 2 997ᵃ19–20).⁶

The scientifically interesting classification of beings seems, as a result, to cut across the metaphysically interesting classification of them into intrinsic and coincidental. We could rectify this, of course, by the simple expedient of including intrinsic coincidentals among the intrinsic beings. But the fact of the matter is that they are already there. For if intrinsic₄ beings are a distinct class, different from the other three, they must be the class of intrinsic coincidentals. Apparently, then, intrinsic coincidentals are sometimes classed as intrinsic beings and sometimes as coincidental ones. That, presumably, is why Aristotle dithers occasionally on their scientific relevance. In future, therefore, I shall follow his usual practice, rather than the letter of some of his laws, and class them as intrinsic beings. As a result, all intrinsic beings, including intrinsic coincidentals, will be the ontological correlates of scientific theorems, and all the rest—all coincidental beings—will fail to be such.

What makes an intrinsic being the ontological correlate of a theorem, to repeat, is its form or essence. It should follow, therefore, that matter has a distinctive part to play in the ontological correlates of coincidentally true

---

⁶ Also *APo.* I 6 75ᵃ18–19, 22 83ᵇ19–20; *Ph.* II 2 193ᵇ26–28, III 4 203ᵇ33; *Met.* III 1 995ᵇ20, 25–26, XI 4 1061ᵇ4–6, XIII 3 1078ᵃ5–9.

propositions. This is precisely what Aristotle claims: "Since not all beings come-to-be by necessity and always, but the majority of things hold for the most part, there must of necessity be coincidental being; e.g., a pale man is not always or for the most part musical, but since this sometimes happens, it must be coincidental (if not, everything will be from necessity). The matter, therefore, which is capable of being otherwise than it for the most part is, is the cause of the coincidental" (*Met.* VI 2 1027^{a}8–15). We may infer that the sort of systematic role that perceptible matter plays in connection with what holds for the most part, it also plays in connection with what holds coincidentally.

4.3 Categories of Intrinsic Being

Intrinsic$_2$ beings, we discovered, are complex subjects. Why, then, aren't coincidental beings also such subjects? If male human is a complex subject, why isn't pale human, or musical human? Aristotle's answer is that only one being is involved in the first case: male human is just one single subject, since to be a human male just is to be a φ-human.[7] Pale humans, by contrast, are coincidental beings because no modal bond of this sort holds between being human and being pale. As a result, being a pale human is being not one thing, but two, since in such a subject two distinct beings coincide—being pale and being human.

The beings that do such coinciding, however, are all themselves intrinsic beings: "The kinds of intrinsic beings are precisely those that are signified by the types of predication *(katêgorias);* for they [intrinsic beings] are said to be in as many ways as there are ways of signifying being. Since among things predicated, some signify what-it-is, some quality, some quantity, some relative, some affecting or being affected, some where, some when, therefore being signifies the same as each of these. For there is no difference between 'a man *is* keeping healthy' and 'a man keeps healthy' or between 'a man *is* cutting or walking' and 'a man cuts or walk'; and similarly in all the other cases" (*Met.* V 7 1017^{a}22–30). Without prejudice, as the lawyers say, let us call these kinds *categories.*

The beings in categories are intrinsic beings, but what sorts of things are these beings? Here is the beginning of an answer:

---

[7] Our discussion in 3.3 suggests that possible values of φ in this case would be seed-emitting or form-transmitting.

Top. I 8–9 103^{b}7–27 Anything that is predicated of something must either be . . . [^{b}9] a definition . . . if it signifies the essence . . . or, if it does not, [^{b}10] a special property *(idion)* . . . or [^{b}13] one of the terms in the definition, or [^{b}14a] not; and if it is one of the terms in the definition, it must [signify] [^{b}14b] the genus or [^{b}15] the differentiae, since the definition is composed of genus and differentiae. If, however, it is not one of the terms in the definition, evidently [^{b}17] it must be a coincidental attribute; for a coincidental attribute was said to be that which a thing has, but is neither a definition nor a genus nor a special property. Next we must determine the different kinds of predication in which one will find the four kinds [of predication] mentioned above. These are ten in number: what–it–is, quantity, quality, relative, when, where, position, having, affecting, and being affected. For the coincidental attributes, the genus [i.e., the differentia], the special properties, and the definition will always be in one of these categories. For all the [dialectical] premises that involve these four things signify either what–it–is, or quantity, or quality, or one of the other categories.

The beings mentioned include intrinsic$_1$ beings (^{b}13, ^{b}14a, ^{b}14b), intrinsic$_2$ beings (^{b}10), intrinsic$_3$ beings (^{b}9), and intrinsic$_4$ beings (^{b}17). Thus the entire complex apparatus of definition, essence, genus, differentiae, special property, and coincidental attribute can be brought to bear on any intrinsic being, whatever category it is in: "The what–it–is, taken in one way, signifies the substance and the this, but taken in another way, [it signifies] each of the other things predicated, quantity, quality, and the like. For just as being *(to estin)* too belongs to all, not in the same way, however, but rather to one primarily and to the others derivatively, so too the what–it–is belongs unqualifiedly to substance, and to the others in a [derivative] way. For we may ask what it is even of a quality, so that quality too is a what–it–is" (*Met.* VII 4 1030^{a}17–24). Thus the accounts of beings in any category are definitions of their essences.

Strictly speaking, however, only the accounts of substances have this feature: "If there are definitions of these things too [e.g., odd, even, male, female], either they have them in another way, or . . . definition and essence must be said in many ways, so that in one way only substances have definitions and essences but in another way non-substances also have them. Clearly, then, definition is the account of the essence, and the essence is either of substances alone or of them most of all and primarily and unqualifiedly" (*Met.* VII 5 1031ª7–14). With that proviso, however, our conclusion stands: in at least a derivative sense the accounts of beings in any category are definitions of their essences.

Suppose, then, that F is an intrinsic being—a being with an essence. What is F? The answer will be a definition (though perhaps in a derivative sense) whose terms signify the genus and differentiae of F, or (equivalently) its ultimate differentia or essence. And this essence will place F in one of the categories, depending on what sort of essence it is. Other features of F will be either special properties of it or coincidental attributes.

Intrinsic beings, then, are beings that are definable by genus and differentia—beings that in some sense have essences. But what kinds of beings are these? Are they universals, particulars, or something else? In the following two sections we shall investigate these questions, first, in the case of non-substantial intrinsic beings, then, of substantial ones.

4.4 Non-Substantial Intrinsic Beings

Suppose F is *spale,* the pallor of Socrates. What is its essence? Aristotle's answer is that its genus is quality, its species, color, and its differentia, such and such ratio of black to white (*Sens.* 3 440ª31–ᵇ25). Like Socrates' own essence, therefore, the essence of spale will not differ from the essence of Coriscus' pallor, provided that the same definition applies to both. Moreover, just as Socrates himself has both matter and form, so does spale:

> *Met.* XIV 1089ᵇ24–28 In the case of categories other [than substance], another thing to give us pause is [ᵇ25] how they can be many. Because they are not separate, it is through subjects coming-to-be and being many that qualities and quantities are many. [ᵇ27] And yet there ought at any rate to be a type of matter for each [category], except that [ᵇ28] it cannot be separate from the substances.[8]

The matter of spale is surface: "in the case of color they [i.e., the form, the privation, and the matter] are white, black, and surface" (*Met.* XII 4 1070ᵇ20–21).[9] What it is in the case of the other categories, we need not worry about. Nevertheless, we should note that a variety of distinct types

---

[8] Also *Met.* VII 3 1029ᵇ22–27, XII 5 1071ª24–29.

[9] In 6.3 we shall see that the matter of color is not just surface, but the surface boundary of the transparent in a delimited body.

of matter will be needed in addition to the types needed by substances themselves.

Continuing to take spale as our representative non-substantial intrinsic being, then, let us use our conventional notation to represent its essence as:

|such and such ratio of black to white in surface|

Since this essence is manifestly penmattered, it will not be separate in thought from surface taken universally: there are no unextended colors. Like Socrates' own essence, moreover, the essence of spale is a universal, present in Socrates' surface and in the surfaces of any other particulars that are spale. Unlike it, the essence of spale is not that of a substance. $^b28$ explains why. The matter of spale—surface—cannot exist separate from substance, since a surface must be the surface of something, and so cannot exist just by itself. For the universal essence of spale to exist, therefore, is for it to be in the surface of some substance. For example, spale exists if the essence of the color in Socrates', or Coriscus', or something else's surface is that of spale.

Now focus on $^b25$. It answers the question of how things in, for example, the category of quality can be many. The answer it proposes is "through their subjects' coming-to-be and being many." $^b27$ adds that in addition to the subject—the substance—a distinctive kind of matter is needed. It seems clear, therefore, that the question is not how there can be different qualities, such as colors and smells or vermilion and spale, but how there can be different *particular instances* of the very same quality. For change or coming-to-be does not have any bearing on differences between universals as such, but it does have obvious and immediate bearing on their particular instances. If Socrates alone is spale, there is just one instance of spale; if Coriscus and lots of other spale people come-to-be, there will be many instances of it; if all the spale things pass-away, spale will no longer exist. The spale in Socrates' surface, therefore, (or the spale in his surface at time t, or throughout time t_1 to t_n) is a particular instance.

The answer to the controversial question of whether Aristotle's ontology includes non-substantial particulars, then, is that it does.[10] Every instance of spale—and so presumably every instance of every other intrinsic being in a category other than substance—is such a being. That is why

---

[10] Ackrill, *Aristotle Categories and De Interpretatione,* 74–76, Owen, "Inherence," and Frede, "Individuals in Aristotle."

97

we find Aristotle claiming that when someone is seeing the color spale (or knowing the letter A), the object he sees (or knows) is a particular—a this (*Met.* XIII 10 1087ª15–21).[11] Presumably, then, *to ti leukon* and *hê tis grammatikê* referred to in *Categories* 1 are such entities—the particular (instance of) pale and the particular (instance of) knowledge-of-grammar (1ª27, 1ᵇ8).

4.5 Substantial Intrinsic Beings

On general principles alone, what is true of spale and other non-substantial intrinsic beings should also be true of substance itself. But is it? In other words, are there, in addition to the universal human species essence, particular instances of it, and if so, what are they? To try to answer this question fully would, in effect, be to presuppose results that have yet to be established. What we have already discovered, however, allows us to conclude—at least tentatively—that the human species essence is an intrinsic being pretty much like spale. Obviously, it itself is a universal of some sort that has instances. But are these instances hylomorphic compounds, such as Socrates and Coriscus, or the particular formal components of such compounds? That is the hard question.

A few texts, some of them already familiar, will help us to see at least a good part of the answer. First, the formal component of a particular human being is itself a this: "Substance is spoken of in two ways, [it is both] the ultimate subject, which is no longer said of anything else, and a this *(tode ti)*, i.e., separate—and such is the shape, i.e., the form of a particular thing" (*Met.* V 8 1017ᵇ23–26).[12] Second, this formal element is not identical—or not unqualifiedly identical—to the hylomorphic particular whose formal element it is: "As for Socrates or Coriscus, if soul is Socrates too, he is spoken of it two ways; for some speak of him as soul, some as the compound [of soul and body], but if [spoken of] unqualifiedly, [he is] this soul and this body" (VII 11 1037ª7–9). Hence we do seem to have a choice to make: either the particular instances of the human species es-

---

[11] I assume that if *x* is a this *(tode ti)*, it is a particular. But we cannot be fully confident that such an assumption is justified until we have shown that it also carries this implication when applied to forms (*Met.* IX 7 1049ª35) or natures (*Met.* XII 3 1070ª11).

[12] Also *Met.* VII 10 1035ᵇ27–30, 11 1037ª5–10, VIII 1 1042ª29, IX 7 1049ª35, XIII 3 1070ª13–14.

sence are hylomorphic compounds or they are the formal elements of such compounds, but not both.

From the fact that the formal element of a particular compound is a this, it might seem simply to follow that, like the compound itself, it is a particular. But it doesn't. For when Aristotle calls something *tode ti,* he might mean that it is an *individual* not a *particular.* The pertinent difference is this. An individual, such as an ultimate differentia, is something that is one in number, in the sense that, as fully determinate, it cannot be further differentiated or divided. Nonetheless, as repeatable and definable, it is a universal. A particular, by contrast, is a *kath' hekaston*—a particular instance of some individual.[13] To be confident that Aristotle intends the formal component of a compound to be a particular, therefore, we need, as a first step, to find him referring to it not just as *tode ti* but as *kath' hekaston.*

The following passage, which we have already looked at for other purposes, is a case in point. The topic under discussion is how the form, which exists in the male human progenitor as a structure of capacities, gets transmitted, via movements in his seed, to the menses of the female, and so to the offspring. And what is crucial for present purposes is that this form contains as a component the element, man, which is explicitly referred to as *kath' hekaston:* "Now what is special and particular *(to kath' hekaston)* always has more force in coming-to-be. For Coriscus is both man and animal, but man is closer to what is special [to him] than animal. In coming-to-be, both what is particular *(to kath' hekaston)* [i.e., man] and what is genus [i.e., animal] are operative, but more so what is particular *(to kath' hekaston).* For this is the substance. For indeed the offspring comes to be a such too, but also a this *(tode ti),* and the latter is the substance. That is precisely why it is from all these capacities that the movements in the seed come" (*GA* IV 3 767^{b}29–36). Thus man—that is to say, the human form or essence, as it exists in Coriscus, his seed, and his offspring—is a *kath' hekaston.* Notice too that *tode ti* and *kath' hekaston* are treated as equivalent, so that Aristotle slides effortlessly from describing substance as *kath' hekaston* to describing it as *tode ti.* We should expect, therefore, that he will also associate being one in number with being *kath' hekaston,* and not exclusively or differentially with being *tode ti.* In the following text, he does just this: "There is no difference between speaking of something as one in number and as particular *(kath' hekaston).* For this is just what we mean by what is particular—what is one in number, and by the universal

---

[13] E.g., Whiting, "Metasubstance," 609 n. 4.

we mean what is set over these" (*Met.* III 3 999^{b}33–1000^{a}1). If a *kath' hekaston* is a particular, therefore, the formal element of a particular hylomorphic compound is itself a particular.

But are we entitled to the antecedent of this conditional? Mightn't it be argued, on parallel grounds, that *kath' hekaston* is just as ambiguous as *tode ti,* that it too as often and appropriately designates an individual as a particular?[14] We may seem to have reached an impasse. In fact, we have reached a solution. Witness again the following text: "It is only [coincidentally] that sight sees universal color, because this color *(tode to chrôma)* which it sees is *a* color, and this A *(tode to alpha),* which is the object the grammarian has [actual] theoretical knowledge of, is *an* A" (*Met.* XIII 10 1087^{a}19–21). In other words, the color spale (a nonsubstance) and the letter A can be looked at either as universals (determinate individuals) or as particulars (instances of those individuals). Presumably, then, *tade tina* and *kath' hekasta* can also be looked at in these ways—either as individuals (universals) or as particulars (instances of universals).

Socrates' universal essence, as an ultimate differentia, is an individual—a wholly determinate or not further divisible universal. Is his formal element, which is a *tode ti* and a *kath' hekaston,* identical to that individual or to a particular instance of it? No, on both counts. For that individual, as a penmattered essence, also has a formal element and a material element. So what we ought to say is that the formal element of a particular compound is a particular instance of the individual formal element of the pertinent penmattered individual essence, whereas its material element is an instance of the individual material element of that essence. Thus it is the hylomorphic compound, not its formal element, that is a particular instance of the individual essence as a whole. The structure of the particular compound, remember, is similar to that of the individual essence (*Met.* VII 11 1037^{a}9–10, 3.9). Taken universally, then, intrinsic beings of this sort are universal individual essences; taken as particular instances of those essences, they are particular hylomorphic compounds.

4.6 The Structure of Intrinsic Being

According to *Categories* 2, the intrinsic beings in the various categories are related in four importantly different ways:

---

[14] Cooper, *Reason and Human Good in Aristotle,* 28–29, and Gill, *Aristotle on Substance,* 31–34.

1. Some are *said-of* a subject but are not *in* any subject. For example, man is said-of a particular man, but is not in him or any other subject.

2. Some are *in* a subject but are not *said-of* any subject. For example, spale is in a body, but is not said-of any subject, where something is in something just in case it is "in something, not as a part, and cannot exist separately from what it is in" (1^a24-25).

3. Some are both *said-of* and *in* a subject. For example, knowledge is in the soul and is also said-of a subject, for we can say-of knowledge-of-grammar that it is grammar.

4. Some are neither *said-of* nor *in* a subject, for example, a particular man or a particular horse.[15]

Beings in (4) are by definition members of a category called substance$_c$. In fact, they are examples of *primary* substance$_c$—substance in the strictest sense (*Cat.* 5 2^a11-14). Those in (1), which are the species and genera to which primary substances belong, are examples of secondary substance$_c$ (2^a14-16).

The distinguishing feature of being said-of something, amounting to at least a partial definition of it, is that if G is said-of F, both of the following are true:

1. F is G

2. F is H

—where H is the definition of G. Aristotle's examples illustrate why this should be so. When G is the genus or species of F, as animal and man are the genus and species of Socrates, and knowledge the genus of knowledge-of-grammar, G is part of the definition of F's essence or ultimate differentia. That is why secondary substances "make clear the primary substance" (*Cat.* 2 2^b30-31).

The distinguishing feature of being in something, on the other hand, again amounting to at least a partial definition, is that when it is true that F is in G, it is also true that:

1. F is G

2. G is not a part of F

---

[15] Question: If G is said-of F, is GF an intrinsic being, and vice versa? If G is in F, is F coincidentally G, and vice versa? Ask instead: why the change of terminology? Said-of and in are part of the vocabulary of a new theory within which the structure of intrinsic being will be analyzed.

3. G is not separate from F

4. Not (F is H)

—where H, as before, is the definition of G. Again, Aristotle's examples reveal what he has in mind. If Socrates is spale, an instance of spale *(spaleinst)* must inhere in his surface. But spaleinst, though a particular, is not identical to Socrates himself. That is why the definition of its essence is not predicable of him. On the other hand, spaleinst is not a separate particular, since it cannot exist separate from surface, and surface cannot exist separate from some substance.

It remains to discuss (2), and in that regard we naturally turn for enlightenment to the following text, where the various ways in which one thing can be part of another are cataloged: "We call a part, in one sense, the result of any kind of division of a quantity . . . in another sense, only those among such parts as give the measure of a thing. . . . Again the results of any non-quantitative division of a form *(eidos)* . . . (that is why species *(eidê)* are parts of their genus); again anything into which a whole, whether a form or something that possesses a form, is divided, or out of which it is composed, e.g., . . . both the bronze (i.e., the matter in which the form is) and the [characteristic] angles are parts of a bronze cube. Again, whatever is in the account that makes clear each thing is also a part of the whole; that is why a genus is also called part of its species, although in a different way the species is part of the genus" (*Met.* V 25 1023^{b}12–25). Clearly, spaleinst is not a part of Socrates in any of these senses. For Socrates is not a quantity and spaleinst is neither his matter, nor his form, nor an element in the account that makes clear his essence.

The point of classifying the items in (4) as primary substance$_c$, and of introducing said-of and in, which relate intrinsic beings to one another in asymmetrical ways, is ontological. For intrinsic beings said-of or in other intrinsic beings are ontologically dependent on them. Consequently, if there is a type of intrinsic being on which all other types are asymmetrically dependent, it will be ontologically primary. It is to signal the special status of such beings that Aristotle introduces primary substance$_c$: "if the primary substances did not exist, it would be impossible for any of the others to exist" (*Cat.* 5 2^{b}5–6). And it is because there are primary substances, beings on which all other beings are ontologically dependent, that the question "What is being?" just is the question "What is substance?" (*Met.* VII 1 1028^{b}2–4).

The next task is to search through all the intrinsic beings, which have already been defined by genus and differentiae, to determine how they are related by said-of and in. Having carried it out, Aristotle reports that all the other intrinsic beings are either said-of or in particular men (Socrates), or particular horses (Bellerophon), or other such particulars (*Cat.* 5 2ª35–36). *Prima facie,* then, these particulars are the primary substances. To reflect this fact, the categories—now organized, as they were not before, to capture part of the structure of intrinsic being—are listed as follows:

substance$_c$: Socrates, Bellerophon, man, horse

quantity: four-foot, five-foot

quality: white, grammatical

relative: double, half, larger

where: in the Lyceum, in the marketplace

when: yesterday, last year

position: is-lying, is-sitting

having: has-shoes-on, has-armor-on

affecting: cutting, burning

being affected: being-cut, being-burned (*Cat.* 4 1ᵇ25–2ª4).

The manifest difference between this list and the similar one examined in 4.4 (*Top.* I 8–9) seems at first blush to be merely terminological: where the latter has what-it-is, this one has substance. We can now appreciate, at least to some degree, that the difference is actually substantial: the old list was just a list; the new one is a partial map. Subscript 'c', silently in use since the beginning of this section, reflects the change: it signals that substance is a concept belonging to metaphysics—more particularly to the metaphysics of the *Categories*—and keeps us aware of the purposes and operations of that somewhat strange subject.

Consider spale's universal essence. Earlier we represented it as:

1. |such and such ratio of black to white in surface|

But this does not reflect the ontological dependence of spale on primary substance$_c$. To do that it would have to have a further layer of complexity added:

2. |such and such ratio of black to white in surface of primary substance$_c$|

But even this essence is not yet complete, since it doesn't make clear the specific category of being that spale belongs to. Adding that content to the essence, we get:

3. |such and such ratio of black to white in surface of primary substance$_c$ as quality|

What (3) is, therefore, is (1) analyzed in the metaphysician's favored idiom. Contrariwise, (1) is (3) before the metaphysician has set to work on it. It is the essence of spale that the natural scientist takes as a first principle of his science of color. Strictly speaking, therefore, if we are to observe our earlier conventions, we should represent (1) as:

1'. |such and such ratio of black to white| «in» surface of «primary substance$_c$» as «quality»

—where, as before, the guillemets symbolize an element in an essence of which the science that has the essence as a first principle does not provide theoretical knowledge. Another way to say what (3) is, therefore, is that it is (1') without the guillemets—their absence symbolizing that metaphysics does provide such knowledge of in, said-of, primary substance$_c$, and quality, telling us what each of them is.

Similarly, Socrates' natural essence, which we earlier represented as:

1. |animal| + |twofooted| + |featherless| + «understanding»

should now be represented as:

2. |animal| + |twofooted| + |featherless| + «understanding» «said-of» «primary substance$_c$» as «secondary substance$_c$»|

This essence is a first principle of natural science. But it is metaphysics, not natural science that, by explaining primary substance$_c$, secondary substance$_c$, said-of, and understanding, removes the guillemets, bringing into the full light of theoretical knowledge what had previously been in shadow. In the case of said-of, in, and secondary substance$_c$, that task has already been accomplished. In a moment it will have been accomplished for quality and, in part at least, for primary substance$_c$ too.

We can now more fully appreciate why the category of what-it-is should not be confused with the category of substance$_c$, and why it is the former, rather than one of the other categories, that is replaced by the latter. For it is in specifying the *what-it-is* of a being in *any* category that one inevitably finds oneself dealing with primary substance$_c$, since it alone is a component of the essences of all of them.

4.7 *The Task of* Categories

If Aristotle is to be confident on the basis of "an examination of cases" (*Cat.* 5 2^{a}35–36) that *all* other intrinsic beings are either said-of or in Socrates, Bellerophon, and the like, his examination must be systematic—by category. But that raises problems of its own. For, first, though we know how to define beings—such as spale—that belong in categories, we do not yet know how to define the different categories—such as quality—in which they belong. Second, we do not know how to define what a category itself is, how to determine membership in the list of categories, or how to determine whether any list we come up with is complete. One part of the enterprise of the *Categories* is to fill these lacunae in our knowledge. We shall begin, therefore, with the definition of the individual categories, limiting attention to just two, substance$_c$ and quantity—the first because it is the focus of our interest, the second to provide a fuller picture of the nature of the enterprise as a whole.

Here, then, is the dossier on substance$_c$ from *Categories* 5:

1. No primary substance$_c$ is either said-of or in any subject (2^{a}11–14).

2. All the other intrinsic beings are either said-of or in primary substances$_c$, and so depend for their being or existence on them (2^{a}34–^{b}6).

3. Every primary substance$_c$ is a "this" (3^{b}10), something "individual *(atomon)* and one in number" (3^{b}12–13).

4. "It seems most distinctive" of substances$_c$ "to be numerically one and the same and to be able to receive opposites" (4^{a}10–11)—to be capable of undergoing change over time. For "nothing like this is apparent in any other case" (4^{a}21–22).

5. Substances$_c$, like quantities, have no contraries (3^{b}24–32).

6. Substance$_c$ "does not admit of the more and the less," even though a particular is more a substance than a species and a species more a substance than a genus (3^{b}33–5). For "one man is not more a man than another" and no man is more a man at one time than at another (3^{b}35–4^{a}8).

7. The definitions of the predicates formed from secondary substances$_c$ (e.g., 'animal' and 'man') apply to everything to which the predicates apply: "the primary substances admit the definitions of the species and genera, and the species admits that of the genus" (3^b2-4).

8. Secondary substances$_c$ do not signify a this but "a sort of thing" (3^b15-16). For "man and animal are said of many things" (3^b17-18).

(1)–(4) characterize primary substance$_c$ only; (5) and (6) *may* characterize it; (7) and (8) don't characterize it.

Categories 6 provides a similar dossier on quantity:

1. Some quantities are discrete (numbers, spoken words); others continuous (lines, surfaces, bodies, time, place) (4^b20-25).

2. Some quantities are composed of parts which have position in relation to one another (the parts of a line or a plane); others are not composed of such parts (the parts of time have an order but not a position, since no two of them can exist simultaneously) (5^a15-37).

3. A quantity (for example, four-foot or five-foot) has no contrary (5^b11-14). Many and few, large and small, which might seem to be counterexamples, are actually relatives, since "nothing is called intrinsically large or small but in relation to something else" (5^b16-18).

4. Quantities do not admit of the more and the less: "one thing is not more four-foot than another" (6^a19-25).

5. What is most distinctive of quantities is that they are either equal or unequal (6^a26-35).

Like its predecessor, this dossier too is readily recognizable for what it is—a partial conceptual analysis, providing broadly logical criteria for distinguishing quantities from other categories of intrinsic beings.

So much for the problem of how to define the individual categories. We see more or less how it is to be done, and that the *Categories* helps us do it. What about our second question? How are we to determine what is or isn't a category, and whether any list of categories is complete? We may begin with a marginally easier question. What problem would you have to be trying to solve in order to generate a list like Aristotle's as part of the solution? The answer I want to defend is this: You would have to be involved in the aporematic (dialectical) project of determining what a genuine problem *(aporia)* is. For it is by making his way through these that the aporematic philosopher discovers the knowledge of first principles he seeks: "If we want to make progress [in philosophy], our first task is to explore the problems well. For we will be in a position to make progress later on only if we loosen the knots these problems cause by solving them; but we can't untie the knots if we don't know that we are tied up. When our understanding *(dianoias)* has a problem, that points to a knot in the subject matter. For having a problem is like being tied up: in both cases we are unable to go forward. We must then complete a study of all the difficulties beforehand. For (in addition to the reasons just mentioned) those who do not go through the problems before they begin their search are like people who do not know where they have to go; moreover, they do not even know whether or not they have found what they were searching for. For the end or goal [of the search] is unclear to them, but clear to someone who has gone through the problems in advance. Moreover, one is bound to be better equipped to make a judgment [as to where the truth lies] if one has previously listened to all the disputing arguments, like different sides presenting their cases" (*Met.* III 1 995^{a}27–^{b}4). The Problem-problem, therefore—the problem of what a problem is—is something metaphysics needs to address.

We have seen Aristotle's own schematic answer to it in 2.2. A problem is a difficulty of the following general form:

There are compelling *endoxa* supporting GF (all Fs are Gs)

There are compelling *endoxa* supporting HF (all Fs are Hs)

G and H are opposed (no F is both G and H).

An aporematic philosopher will be interested, therefore, in any general features of F and G which either ensure or preclude their genuine opposition.[16] As a first approximation, then, we may think of a category as a maximal class of intrinsic beings, the predicates formed from which are opposed (*Cat.* 5 3^{a}33–^{b}9): 'man' and 'dog' are opposed (nothing can be both a man and a dog), so man and dog go in the same category; 'man' and 'white', on the other hand, are not opposed, so they go in different categories. An aporematic philosopher will be interested in categories, then, because they will help him to diagnose—and so to solve—genuine problems. Hence we can now also see a further reason for him to be

---

[16] Notice that opposition has now come within the metaphysician's purview, and with it the principle of non-contradiction.

interested in said-of and in. For if G is said-of F, F and G must belong to the same category, but if G is in F, F and G must belong to different categories.

Given that the Problem-problem is a major reason to distinguish categories from one another, an aporematic philosopher will often want to work with as rich a list of them as possible. For the richer the list, the easier it will be for him to determine whether he is dealing with genuine opposites and a genuine problem or apparent opposites and an apparent problem. For similar reasons, he might want to utilize a logic rich in rules of inference, since it will make fallacies easier to detect. By contrast, a systematic philosopher, striving for insight into the nature of being, will want to reduce the list of categories to more manageable proportions, so as to be able to determine its fundamental structure and philosophical basis. For similar reasons, he might want to reduce his rules of inference to a few basic ones. Presumably, that is why, when Aristotle replaces his aporematic hat with his systematic one, he becomes interested in reduction. In the *Prior Analytics,* for example, in order to prove the completeness and consistency of his logic, he shows how to reduce the fourteen valid moods of the syllogism to four: Barbara, Celarent, Darii, and Ferio. Similarly, in the *Metaphysics,* he shows how to reduce some categories to others: "Relatives are least of all something natural or a substance, being posterior to quality and quantity. . . . An indication that relatives are least of all a kind of substance or being is this: they alone are not generated or destroyed or changed in the way that in quantity there is increase and diminution, in quality, alteration, in where, locomotion, and in substance, coming-into-being and passing-away. There is none of this with relatives. For a thing will be greater or less or equal without itself changing if *another* thing changes in quantity" (*Met.* XIV 1 1088^{a}22–35). In order to constitute a genuine category of intrinsic beings, then, it seems that Fs must pass the following test: if x is F at t_1 and not-F at t_2, it must have *undergone change* between t_1 and t_2. Relatives do not pass this test, so strictly speaking there is no such category. (Notice that change must now be included in the metaphysician's bag of analytical devices, and so will need to be defined and defended by him.)

Categories 15 seems to be a contribution to this same reductive task: "Having is spoken of in a number of ways: having as a state and condition or some other quality (for we are said to *have* knowledge and virtue); or as a quantity, like the height someone may *have* (he is said to have a height of five or six feet); or as things *on* the body, like a cloak or tunic; or as *on* a part, like a ring on a hand; or as a part, like a hand or foot; or as in a container, as with the measure of wheat or the jar of wine (for the jar is said to *have* wine [in it] and the measure wheat, so that these are said to *have* as in a container); or as a possession (for we are said to *have* a house or a field). One is also said to *have* a wife, and a wife a husband, but this seems to be a very strange way of having, since by [someone's] having a wife we signify nothing other than that he is married to her" ($15^{b}17$–30). It seems, then, that some havings are qualities (having knowledge of virtue) or quantities (having a height of six feet), and that all the others are relatives. For example, Socrates has-shoes-on, is a canonical example of having (*Cat.* 4 $2^{a}3$). Yet, ignoring the fact that Socrates has two feet, it may be analyzed as:

$$(\exists x)\ (\exists y)\ [(\text{has}_1\ (\text{Socrates},\ x)\ \&\ \text{has}_2\ (x,\ y)\ \&\ \text{foot}\ (x)\ \&\ \text{shoe}\ (y)]$$

—where both has$_1$ (which is an example of having as a part) and has$_2$ (which is an example of having on a part) are relatives. Since the category of relatives has already been eliminated, having will follow suit. Perhaps that is why it is usually omitted from Aristotle's lists.[17] No doubt, one can also see how position might succumb to one or other of these eliminative strategies. Perhaps that is why it too disappears from such lists. But, to reiterate, there is no point in eliminating categories if one's purposes are primarily aporematic. It is when one turns from problem solving to theory construction that reduction becomes attractive—not that one should over-sharpen the boundary between these two activities.

To a second approximation, then, a category might be partially defined as follows:

1. *Existence Condition:* If F is a focus of change, there is a category C_1 such that F is in C_1

2. *Identity Condition:* If F is in C_1 and G is in C_2, and F and G are opposites, then $C_1 = C_2$

—where F is a focus of change just in case Fx at t_1 and not-F x at t_2 entails that x has undergone change between t_1 and t_2. With this partial definition, we can begin to construct categories. But how will we know when we have finished? There seems to be no *a priori* closure guarantee: if we find a class of this sort and it is disjoint from each of the categories on Aristotle's list, we simply add it on. Aristotle is trying to produce a complete list, and thinks he has succeeded, but, unlike Kant, he is not pretending to have a

---

[17] *APo.* I 22 $83^{a}21$–23; *Ph.* V 1 $225^{b}5$–9; *Met.* V 7 $1017^{a}24$–27.

transcendental deduction to show that he is right. The final sentence of the *Categories* might well be adapted, indeed, to express what I take to be his view of the matter: "Some further ways of having might perhaps come to light, but we have made a pretty complete enumeration of those commonly spoken of" (*Cat.* 15 15^{b}30–32).

Given his interest in problems and hence in categories thus characterized, an aporematic philosopher must also be interested in *types* of intracategorial opposition. No surprise, therefore, that *Categories* 10 and 11 are devoted to this very topic. For they catalog what seem to be the only ways in which members of the same category may be opposed:

1. as relatives: double, half

2. as contraries: good, bad

3. as privation and possession: blindness, sight

4. as affirmation and negation: he is sitting, he is not sitting

If any of (1)–(4) hold between G and H, therefore, nothing can possibly be both. Consequently, if there are *endoxa* to support the claim that GF and *endoxa* to support the claim that HF, there is indeed a genuine problem about F.

What then about *Categories* 12–14? Do they also deal with matters of aporematic import? *Categories* 12–13 is devoted to cataloging and distinguishing the different varieties of priority and posteriority, on the one hand, and simultaneity, on the other. In the case of the former, five varieties are distinguished: G is prior to H (H is posterior to G)

1. in time: when Gs are older or more ancient than Fs

2. in reciprocity of being: when being G entails being H, but not vice versa, as happens e.g., when H is a genus of which G is a species

3. in order: e.g., when F is a science that is prior to G

4. in value: when Fs are more valued or more esteemed than Gs

5. in nature: when being F entails being G and vice versa and being F is the cause of being G, but not vice versa[18]

---

[18] Priority in reciprocity of being is usually called priority in definition (*Met.* VII 1 1028^{a}35–36).

In the case of simultaneity, there are three varieties: F and G are simultaneous

1. in time: when F and G come into being at the same time

2. in nature$_1$: when being F entails being G and vice versa, but being F is not the cause of being G and vice versa

3. in nature$_2$: when F and G are coordinate species of the same genus, i.e., if they result from the same division of the genus

These relations are of interest to the aporematic philosopher because, in the context of problem solving, an interest in the ontological priority and posteriority presupposed by the theory of categories must be an interest in priority and posteriority *in general,* and so in simultaneity, which is a way of not being either prior or posterior. For failure to distinguish the various types of these can only lead to pseudo problems and shallow philosophy.

Many of the deepest problems studied by Aristotle and his predecessors involve change—consider, for example, its role in the argument that led Plato to separate the forms. Besides, as we saw, change is involved in the very definition of the categories themselves. Hence *Categories* 14 discusses types of change and the relations of opposition that exist between them. The six types it distinguishes are as follows:

1. coming-into-being

2. passing-away

3. increase

4. diminution

5. alteration

6. change of place

These are coordinate with the categories in an obvious way: coming-into-being and passing-away are substantial changes (birth, death); increase and diminution are quantitative (expanding, shrinking); alterations are qualitative (pale to suntanned); change of place is a change in where something is.[19] The genuinely opposed members on the list are (1) and (2), on the one

---

[19] The fact that no change is listed corresponding to relatives, when, position, and having suggests that the so-called Cambridge change that x undergoes when, without having altered in height himself, he becomes shorter than y, because y has grown taller, is being excluded from consideration.

hand, and (3) and (4), on the other. Change in place is "most opposed to staying in the same place—and perhaps to change towards the contrary place (upward change of place, e.g., being opposed to downward and downward to upward)" (15^b3-6). Change in quality is likewise opposed to "staying the same in qualification or change towards the contrary qualification (e.g., becoming white is opposed to becoming black)" (15^b12-16).

The various and apparently heterogeneous issues discussed in the *Categories* form an intelligible unity, then, when we see them as all being connected to the single task of determining the analytical machinery needed to gain a philosophically accurate view of intrinsic beings in general through cataloging, so as to solve, the genuine problems to which they give rise. And that fact proves to be a solution to a problem of another kind altogether. For it has long been acknowledged that the unity and even the title of the work we call the *Categories* are problematic.[20] If we are right about its unity, however, we are also in a position to say something about its title. For one of its best-attested ancient titles is *Pro tôn topôn*—"Prolog to the *Topics*," as we might translate it.[21] And that, if we are right, is just what it is—a prolog to the consideration of the actual problems and dialectical arguments explored in the *Topics* itself.[22]

4.8 Primary Substance$_c$

The examples given of primary substance$_c$ in *Categories* 5 are a particular man (such as Socrates) and a particular horse (such as Bellerophon). How should we extrapolate from these examples to determine what the primary substances$_c$ in general are? Consider an analogous problem. The examples given of intrinsic beings in the category when are all past times (yesterday, last year). How should we extrapolate from these examples to determine what the whens in general are? In the latter case, the solution is easy: focus on the fact that they are times and ignore the fact that they are past times. It

---

[20] Frede, "The Title, Unity, and Authenticity of the Aristotelian Categories."

[21] Porphyry, Andronicus, Simplicius, Boethius, Olypiodorus, Elias, Adrastus, Herminus, and others refer to it by this title. Frede, "The Title, Unity, and Authenticity of the Aristotelian Categories," 19 nn. 44–57 provides the exact references.

[22] I am grateful to Stephen Menn who, on reading this section, sent me a copy of his "Metaphysics, Dialectic and the *Categories*," which reaches a similar conclusion in a different but largely compatible way.

is easy, because it is obvious that there are times other than past ones, and that the category of whens is supposed to include all of them. In the case of primary substance$_c$, it is not so easy. Should we focus on the fact that Socrates and Bellerophon are primary particulars and ignore the fact that they are hylomorphic? Or is the fact that they are hylomorphic crucial? The answer depends on whether or not there are non-hylomorphic substantial particulars in the category of primary substance$_c$.

In the *Metaphysics,* God is a substantial particular, separate from matter both in reality and in thought.[23] Is God such a substance in the *Categories?* Surely, he is. For the *Categories* is part of the so-called *Organon*—the book of tools or instruments—and the God of the *Organon* is "an intelligible living being" (*Top.* V 6 136^{b}7)—a non-hylomorphic particular.[24] What category, then, is God in? Look back to the dossier on substance$_c$. Here are the entries that may apply to primary substance$_c$:

1. No primary substance$_c$ is either in or said-of any subject.

2. All the other intrinsic beings are either said-of or in primary substances$_c$.

3. Every primary substance$_c$ is a this, a numerically distinct particular.

4. "It seems *(dokei)* most distinctive of [primary] substance to be numerically one and the same and to be able to receive opposites" (*Cat.* 5 4^{a}10–11).

5. Substances$_c$, like quantities, have no contraries.

6. Substance$_c$ "does not admit of the more and the less."

This dossier is a close but imperfect fit for Aristotle's God. The first three entries and the final two fit him, but (4) seems problematic, since God does

---

[23] As is conventional, I use the male pronoun to refer to Aristotle's God *(ho theos)*, even though as a form he is sexless.

[24] Some scholars have been so impressed by the fact that matter is not mentioned in the *Organon* that they have inferred that Aristotle had not yet discovered hylomorphic analysis when he wrote it. They have been unaccountably less impressed, or have simply failed to notice, the presence of pure forms there. But these presuppose hylomorphic analysis as assuredly as matter itself does. Moreover, Aristotle is already aware in the *Analytics* that some theorems hold universally and necessarily and others hold only for the most part and snecessarily. And matter, as we saw, is crucial to that distinction.

not undergo change of any kind. Problematic or not, however, that is where Aristotle thought God belonged. Here—again from the *Organon*—is a proof text: "Some things are actualities without potentiality (e.g., the primary substances)" (*Int.* 13 23ª23–24). It is a proof text, because God is such an actuality. Presumably, then, we should take the *dokei* in (4) seriously. It *seems* to be distinctive of primary substances, in general, that they can undergo change, because it is genuinely distinctive of the most familiar primary substances—hylomorphic particulars. But it is not a feature of all primary substances, since it is not a feature of those that, as "actualities without potentiality," are pure forms.

The particulars in the category of primary substance$_c$, then, need not be hylomorphic. If they are ontologically primary particulars, that is enough. Nonetheless, a question remains to be answered. If non-hylomorphic particulars are included in the category of primary substance$_c$, why didn't Aristotle provide such a substance as an example? The best answer is suggested by Aristotle himself, and has already been implicitly drawn on. It is this. Perceptible hylomorphic substances are more familiar to us than intelligible ones, and are agreed by everyone to be substances (*DA* II 1 412ª11–12; *Met* VII 3 1029ª33–ᵇ12). They better convey what Aristotle has in mind by primary substance$_c$, therefore, than a more *recherché* intelligible particular would. That point aside, it remains the case that the category of primary substance$_c$ is—and is for Aristotle himself—a category of substantial particulars in general, not of hylomorphic ones alone. At least in aspiration, therefore, the *Categories* is universal in scope.

FIVE

PERCEPTIBLE SUBSTANCE

5.1 Perceptible Substance and Change

In the *Categories,* the crown of ontological primacy is conferred indiscriminately on primary particulars, whether hylomorphic compounds (Socrates and Bellerophon) or pure forms (God). In the *Metaphysics,* these two types of substance$_c$ are distinguished from one another and also from a third type: "There are three types of substances—one that is perceptible (of which one type is eternal, another passes-away (and is recognized by all), like plants and animals—of this we must grasp the elements, whether one or many; and another that is unmoving . . . the former [two] belong to natural science (for they involve movement), but the latter belongs to a different one [viz., theology], if there is no first principle common to it and the other kinds of substance" (*Met.* XII 1 1069^{a}30–^{b}2). Thus Socrates, previously a substance$_c$, is now a *perceptible* substance$_m$ (notice the new subscript), and God, an *intelligible* substance$_m$.

The difference between substances that are perceptible and eternal and those that are perceptible and pass-away reveals a second layer of complexity in substance$_m$ that was also missing from substance$_c$. Primary substance$_c$ is presented as unanalyzed or incomposite, but perceptible substance$_m$ is analyzed into matter and form. As a result, it can be divided into two kinds, which differ from one another solely in their material component. The matter of the eternal ones is ether, so that they move in circular orbits but are otherwise unchanging (*Cael.* I 2 269^{b}2–6, 8.1–2). The matter of the ones that pass-away is indeterminate sublunary matter (ultimately some combination of earth, water, fire, and air, on the one hand, and ether, on the other), so that they are both moving and changing. Our focus in this chapter is on substances of the latter sort, substances whose essences are penmattered.

Socrates' essence, which appeared after one round of metaphysical analysis in the *Categories* as

| animal | + | twofooted | + | featherless | + «understanding» said-of

«primary substance$_c$»

appears in the *Metaphysics* as

| animal | + | twofooted | + | featherless | + «understanding» said-of

«compound of perceptible sublunary matter and form»

Further metaphysical analysis will need to remove the guillemets by defining their contents. Before we start removing guillemets, however, we need a clearer understanding of how the items they enclose got to be part of Socrates' essence in the first place. The answer, in a nutshell, is *change*.

Consider the proposition that x has an attribute F at time t_1 and y has a different attribute G at time t_2. In symbols,

$$F x \text{ at } t_1 \ \& \ G y \text{ at } t_2$$

If x and y are one and the same and F and G are opposites, this proposition reports a change (*Ph*. I 5). Making it explicit that these conditions are met, gives us:

$$F x \text{ at } t_1 \ \& \ G y \text{ at } t_2 \ \& \ (x = y) \ \& \ \text{Opposites (F, G)}$$

Let us call this our *canonical recipe* for change, and call changes that fit it *canonical changes*.

Of the six types of changes cataloged in *Categories* 14, the following are canonical: alterations, changes of place, increases and diminutions (4.7). For in these cases x is a substance that lasts through the change: "Only substances are said unqualifiedly to come-to-be. In the other cases it is evident that there must be some subject, which is the thing that comes-to-be [something]; for when a quantity, a quality, a relation, a when, or a where comes-to-be, it is of a subject, because substance is never said of any other subject, whereas the others are said of [substance]" (*Ph*. I 7 190^{a}32–^{b}1). Call canonical changes of this sort *attribute* changes. Being capable of lasting through them seems, as we know, to be "most distinctive" of primary substances$_c$ (*Cat*. 5 4^{a}10–21).

Suppose, then, that we substitute does-not-exist (not-E) for F, and does-exist (E) for G. Does

Not-Ex at t_1 & Ey at t_2 & ($x = y$)

represent a canonical change? It seems not. For because x has no referent at t_1, neither the first conjunct nor the entire proposition of which it is a part can be true (*Cat.* 10 13^{b}14–27). Nonetheless, x did exist at t_2 and did not exist at t_1. This is what we may call an *existence* change. Apparently, it is not a canonical one.

Next consider a variation on existence change. Socrates' essence is the human species essence. Hence for him to exist is for him to be a man: "One-man, man-that-is, and man are the same thing; and nothing different is signified by the reduplication in wording of 'he is one man' and 'he is one man that is'" (*Met.* IV 2 1003^{b}26–29). Socrates wasn't a man at t_1, however, since he hadn't been born then. But he was a man at t_2. This is a case of coming-to-be or *substantial* change (passing-away is also such a change). For the same reason that existence change seems not to be canonical, substantial change seems not to be so. Nonetheless, substantial changes do occur.

Making a virtue of necessity, one might conclude that the difference between such changes and attribute ones is precisely that they are non-canonical, so that Socrates comes-to-be at t_1 just in case nothing was Socrates prior to t_1 and something was Socrates after t_1. The problem with this idea is that if a man can come-to-be from nothing, anything can come-to-be from anything. And that undermines science. For it leaves substantial change ungrounded in being or reality, and so precludes its scientific explanation. That is why "our first point must be that nothing whatever is by nature such as to affect or be affected by any chance thing, nor does anything come-to-be from just anything, unless you take a case of coincidental [causation]" (*Ph.* I 5 188^{a}31–34).[1] Parmenidean animadversions against not-being, and a thing's coming-to-be from nothing, probably have a similar basis. The scientific demand that change be grounded in being, therefore, is what in the end must guide our analysis of it—an analysis that the *Categories* presupposes but does not provide.

There is good reason, then, for Aristotle to try to model substantial changes on canonical ones, since that will insure their scientific intelligibility. Hence what he needs is something that stands to Socrates as he stands to his coincidental attributes—something that can underlie his substantial change in much the way that he underlies an attribute change:

---

[1] Also *Met.* XII 7 1072^{a}19–21.

"But that substances, i.e., whatever things unqualifiedly are, also come-to-be out of a subject, will be evident on examination. . . . It is clear, then, that whatever comes-to-be is always compound: there is something that comes-to-be and another that comes-to-be it. The latter is of two sorts: either the subject or the opposite. By the opposite, I mean, in one case [attribute change], the unmusical, and by the subject, the man, and in the other [substance change], the absence of shape or form or order [are the opposites] and the bronze, stone, or gold is the subject" (*Ph.* I 7 190^{b}1–17). Without prejudice, let us call the subject that underlies the coming-into-being of Socrates his *matter (m)*. Omitting the redundant identity clause, the canonical recipe for such change will then be:

Not-Sm at t_1 & Sm at t_2

Call this the *substance recipe*.

Is it a good recipe for substantial change? Perhaps. But there are some problems to be gone through before we can be sure. The first is the *artifact problem*. Suppose m is a quantity of bronze, and that S is a statue of Socrates. Why does the substance recipe report S's undergoing a substantial change rather than an attribute change in m? Aristotle's answer is that when we state things accurately, we see that m does not really become S at all: "As for that out of which as matter things come-to-be, some, after they have come-to-be, are said to be not that, but that*en*, e.g., the statue is not stone but ston*en*, and the man, i.e., the healthy man, is not said to be that out of which [he came to be]. The reason is that he comes-to-be out of both the privation and the subject, which we call the matter (e.g., it's both the man and the sick [thing] that come to be healthy), but he is more [correctly] said to come-to-be out of the privation—e.g., out of what is sick, what is healthy [comes], rather than out of what is a man. Hence what is healthy isn't called sick, but is called a man, and the man is called healthy. But in the case of things where the privation is unclear or has no name, e.g., in [the case of] bronze, [the privation] of whatever form, or in [the case of] bricks and timbers [the privation of] house—out of these they [the statue, the house] seem to come-to-be in the way that in the other case [what is healthy comes-to-be from what is sick]. Hence just as in the latter case the thing [that comes-to-be] is not called that out of which [it comes-to-be, i.e., sick], so here the statue is not called wood, but takes on a derived form, wood*en,* and braz*en* but not bronze, and ston*en* but not stone, and a house is brick*en* (but not bricks); since it also isn't the case that out of wood a statue comes-to-be, or out of bricks a house, if one were to look closely, one would not say this unqualifiedly, because coming-to-be requires a change in that out of which [it comes-to-be], rather than that it remain [the same]. This, then, it why it is put in this way" (*Met.* VII 7 1033ᵃ5–23). What comes-to-be S, therefore, isn't *m*, but rather non-S-formed *m*, or what is not S-formed. But what is not S-formed does not persist through the change that takes place in *m*, anymore than what is sick persists when a man changes from being sick to being healthy. Moreover, no quantity of bronze could play the role in relation to S (the statue of Socrates) that Socrates plays in attribute change, since none shares S's existence and identity conditions. For example, as a result of a long sequence of gradual repairs to S, wholly distinct quantities of bronze, *m* and *m'*, can constitute it at different times. It follows that S cannot be an attribute of *m*. For attributes are ontologically dependent on their subjects and cannot float free of them, as S, by coming-to-be constituted by *m'*, can float free of *m*.

A moral of the artifact problem, then, is that the appearance of a new artifactual substance in the world is the appearance there of something that employs already existing matter for ends of its own, so to speak, and that does not usually depend for its existence or identity on any particular quantity of matter. It can gain new matter or lose old matter, much as Socrates can change from being unmusical to being musical, without threat of passing-away.

The second problem faced by the substance recipe is the BODY-*body* problem.[2] In the case of Socrates' statue, as with any artifact, it is easy to specify what its matter is, since it is just whatever parcel of bronze happens to constitute it. Moreover, it is easy to say what its matter was at some time in the past (it was made of *this*), and what matter will be its before it comes into existence (it will be made of *this bronze here*). But what is Socrates' own matter? If S is Socrates, what is *m*? It is his body. But what is *that*? Is it his flesh and bones, what he, so to speak, passes-away into? No, it can't be. For his body is functionally defined all the way down to its "homoeomerous parts" (*PA* II 1 646ᵃ14–24). If you cut off a hand, it is no longer a hand, because it is no longer alive, no longer able to perform its function. The same is true of a piece of bone (*Mete.* IV 12 390ᵃ10–13; *PA* I 1 640ᵇ33–641ᵃ6). By parity of reasoning, Socrates' corpse, since it survives his death,

---

[2] This problem was first formulated by Ackrill, "Aristotle's Definitions of *Psuchê*." It is further explored in Williams, "Hylomorphism," and Cohen, "Hylomorphism and Functionalism."

isn't what constitutes him when he is alive. Is what constitutes him, his living body, then? No, because that is both his form and his matter (*DA* II 1).

Though we cannot, for these reasons, pick out Socrates' matter in the way that we can pick out the bronze of the statue, we can grasp it by analogy with the bronze (*Met.* IX 6 1048^{a}35–^{b}9). Socrates' corpse isn't his matter, any more than the hair, fingernail parings, and flakes of skin that he loses regularly are his matter. But by seeing his actually functioning matter as potentially such things, we grasp what stands to him as the bronze does to his statue: "Potentially, the half line is prior to the whole one, and the part to the whole, and matter to substance; but actually they are posterior; for it is only when the others [the wholes] are dissolved that they [the parts] will actually be" (V 11 1019^{a}8–11). What we thereby grasp is Socrates' BODY. And grasp it we must, if we are to ground substantial change in being by modeling natural beings on artifacts, their reproduction on artifact production, and both of these on attribute change. The alternative is ungrounded substantial change and the crippling of science. How to grasp it, though, is another question altogether—one to which we shall soon be in a position to return.

One final kind of change seems particularly problematic, namely, *elemental* substantial change. The elements earth, water, air, and fire are the most primitive types of sublunary matter. Yet, they can change into one another: "[the elements] cannot come-to-be from something incorporeal nor from a body which is not an element, what remains is that they come-to-be from one another" (*Cael.* III 6 305^{a}31–32). Suppose, therefore, that earth (E) is transformed into water (W), then into air (A), then into fire (F). If this is a canonical change, we may represent it by means of the following *element recipe:*

$$\text{E}m \text{ at } t_1 \ \& \ \text{W}m \text{ at } t_2 \ \& \ \text{A}m \text{ at } t_3 \ \& \ \text{F}m \text{ at } t_4$$

The problem as before, only sharper, is, what is *m?* It cannot be one of the elements, since that would lead to contradiction: nothing can be both fire and air simultaneously. It cannot be a fifth kind of matter more primitive than they: *ex hypothesi,* there is no such thing.

If there is a solution to this dilemma, it seems that it must be similar to the one proposed to the BODY-body problem. Suppose, then, that there is a kind of stuff, call it *prime matter,* and let *m* be a quantity of it. Like Socrates' body, *m* cannot actually exist separate from some quantity of some element. But unlike Socrates' body, which dies to become a corpse, *m*'s death as one element is, in good Heraclitean fashion, always its birth as another: "the death of fire is birth for air, and the death of air is birth for water" (B76). A BODY decays into a body, then, an element into another element.

Does it follow that prime matter is the bare featureless potentiality lacking all positive determinations that tradition represents it as being? Suppose it does. Then prime matter could impose no constraints whatsoever on element transformation: any element could be transformed into any other without either rhyme or reason. In other words, at the elemental level (and so on up) anything could come from anything. Naturally enough, that is something Aristotle rejects. In his view, each of the four elements has two differentiae drawn from a list of four: hot, cold, wet, dry. Once duplications (hot and hot) and impossible combinations of these (hot and cold) are eliminated, the remaining ones define the elements: earth is cold and dry; water cold and wet; air hot and wet; fire hot and dry (GC II 2 329^b7-10, 3 330^a30-^b7). It is these differentiae that determine what transformations are permissible. If the elements involved are adjacent (if, like earth and water, they share a differentia), transformation is a matter of one opposed differentia or capacity 'mastering' the other: "air will result from fire if the dry is mastered by the wet," whereas "water will result from air, if the hot is mastered by the cold" (4 331^a27-30). If one differentia in each element is actually destroyed, however, "because either the same or opposite ones are left, in neither case does a body result, as happens e.g., if the dry of the fire and the wet of the air are destroyed, since the hot in both is left" (331^b26-32).[3] Since elemental substantial change is in this way scientifically scrutable, prime matter, as traditionally conceived, cannot underlie it.[4]

Should we conceive of prime matter, then, as having a nature of its own? If it were a body separate from the elements, we would have to do so, since it would of necessity be either "light or heavy, hot or cold" (GC II 1 329^a9-12). But since it isn't separate from them, we don't (329^a24-26). Instead, we should grasp it *by analogy*. But that will be possible only if it has an analog that we already grasp. Is there such a thing? Consider again the element recipe:

E*m* at t_1 & W*m* at t_2 & A*m* at t_3 & F*m* at t_4

---

[3] The account of element transformation is similar to that of the generation of animals. In particular, the fact that mastery can either lead to an opposite or to destruction has an exact analog there (GA IV 1 766^b15-16).

[4] My discussion of the mechanisms of element transformation is indebted to the fuller one in Gill, *Aristotle on Substance*, 41–82.

Since m has no nature of its own, it must be the existence of the relevant causal relations between the differentiae of E, W, A, and F—or between events that have those differentiae as components—that are the ontological correlates or truth-makers of the element recipe, not the existence of a more primitive intrinsic being, Gm, that underlies element transformation by persisting through it. If the element recipe is true, however, so is its existential generalization:

$$(\exists x) \ (Ex \text{ at } t_1 \ \& \ Wx \text{ at } t_2 \ \& \ Ax \text{ at } t_3 \ \& \ Fx \text{ at } t_4)$$

And it is that generalization which, for us at least, constitutes the requisite analog of matter.[5] For in grasping the notion of a variable bindable by a quantifier, we are grasping just what Aristotle is trying to grasp by m—the matter that underlies element transformation.[6] The scientific intelligibility of element transformation is thereby preserved and prime matter—as a real but featureless stuff—is avoided.[7]

Because element transformation has to be understood in terms of causal relations between differentiae (or between events that have them as constituents), the same must hold in the case of the BODY-body problem. For the BODY is not an intrinsic being that is there before the living body arrives on the scene, remains while it does, and continues to be after it is gone. Rather, by grasping the causal relations between actually moving menses (M), embryo (E), infant (I), adult (A), and corpse (C), we have grasped the value of x that makes it true that

$$(\exists x) \ (Mx \text{ at } t_1 \ \& \ Ex \text{ at } t_2 \ \& \ Ix \text{ at } t_3 \ \& \ Ax \text{ at } t_4 \ \& \ Cx \text{ at } t_5),$$

---

[5] Needless to say, the quantifier need not be a first-order one.

[6] This idea is based on a more-or-less equivalent one suggested by Cohen, "Aristotle and Individuation," 59 n. 26: "There is an obvious connection between *matter* and *thisness* for Aristotle. The unknowability (cf. 1036^{a}8) and indefiniteness (cf. 1037^{a}27) of matter, and its banishment from proper definitions (cf. 1035^{b}33, 1036^{b}5–6) that we find in Z 10 and 11 may . . . be due more to its indexical role than to anything else."

[7] I agree with Charlton, "Did Aristotle Believe in Prime Matter?" therefore, that the answer to his question is no. Cohen, *Aristotle on Nature and Incomplete Substance,* 55–100, resourcefully argues for the same answer on somewhat different grounds.

and so have grasped BODY.

Since the BODY-body problem is just a special case of the general problem raised by substantial change, we should suspect that the latter will also be solved by finding the right sort of causal relations between appropriate events, and not by finding an intrinsic being that persists through substantial change.[8] For while some intrinsic being, such as a quantity of bronze, may last through the coming-into-being and passing-away of a substance in the way that Socrates lasts through his attribute changes, none need do so. For example, the quantity of bronze that bridges the gap between the last moment before the statue exists and the first moment afterwards need not persist along with the statue for the rest of its existence. Indeed, the quantity of bronze that bridges the gap between the last moment of the statue's existence and the first moment of its nonexistence may, like the m and m' encountered earlier, be wholly distinct from the one that bridged the gap between the last moment prior to its existence and the first moment afterwards. Substances are not quite Heraclitean patterns in a flow of matter, as eddies are patterns in a flow of water, but they are sometimes helpfully seen as such.

The substance recipe has proved its worth: *all* changes can it seems be represented as canonical changes, provided the substances that undergo them are hylomorphic compounds. That is why Socrates—generable, changeable, destructible—must be such a compound, and why his essence is enmattered.

5.2 Primary Substance$_m$

Because "it is agreed that there are some substances among perceptible things," the search for primary substance$_m$ "should first be made among them," since they are better known to us than any others (*Met.* VII 3 1029^{a}33–^{b}12). Since perceptible substances are hylomorphic compounds, there are, then, three candidates to consider: the compound itself, its matter, and its form.

Now a primary substance$_m$ has three principal and familiar characteristics:[9]

---

[8] Shoemaker, "Identity, Properties, and Causality," shows how to develop an account of identity through time of this sort.

[9] Two others have a somewhat secondary status: (4) A primary substance must be an intrinsic or *natural unity,* continuous by nature, whose change is indivisible

1. It is "most of all" a primary *subject,* or "that of which all the others are said" (*Met.* VII 3 1028^{b}36–1029^{a}2).

2. It is *separate*—primary in account or definition, in nature, in scientific knowledge, and in time.[10]

3. It is a *this.*[11]

Prima facie, then, anything that possesses these characteristics will be primary substance$_m$.

Though this new dossier has much in common with the one provided in the *Categories* for primary substance$_c$, there are two noteworthy differences. First, the new dossier is general in a way that the older one is not. For the fourth entry in the old dossier claims that "it seems" characteristic of primary substance$_c$ to be able to last through change. But that characteristic, we now know, is peculiar to perceptible substance$_m$. Hence it is omitted. Second, the new dossier integrates epistemology with metaphysics in a way that the older one does not. For the requirement that primary substance be primary, not just in definition, nature, and time, but also in scientific knowledge, has no precedent in the *Categories.* Thus the investigation of substance in the *Metaphysics* is richer—metaphysically more probing—in at least two ways than its predecessor. Whether it also comes to different conclusions about what the primary substances are remains to be seen.

With the new dossier to hand, in any case, we are ready to search for primary substance$_m$. But it is a search that seems fated to be short lived: "I call matter that which is not intrinsically anything, or any quantity, or anything else by which being is determined. For there is something of which each of these is predicated, so that its essence *(to einai)* is different from that of each of the other things that are predicated [of it] (for the others are predicated of the substance, but it of the matter). Therefore, the

---

(*Met.* V 6 1015^{b}36–1016^{a}9, X 1 1052^{a}19–^{b}1); (5) it cannot be composed of substances, and cannot have parts that can exist separate from it except as matter (*Met.* VII 16 1041^{a}3–5).

[10] *Met.* VII 1 1028^{a}23–24, 3 1029^{a}27–28, VIII 1 1042^{a}28–29 (separate), VII 4 1030^{b}4–7 (account), V 11 1019^{a}1–3 (nature), VII 1 1028^{a}32–33 (knowledge, time).

[11] *Met.* III 6 1003^{a}9, V 8 1017^{b}24–25, VII 3 1029^{a}27–28, 4 1030^{a}5–6, XI 2 1060^{b}21–22.

last [subject of predication] is not intrinsically some [substance] or some quantity, or anything else; nor is it [intrinsically] the negations [of these], since they too will belong [to it] coincidentally. And so, for those who theorize about [substance] in this way, the result is that matter is substance. But this is impossible. For being separate and being a this seem to belong to substance most of all. Hence the form and what's [compounded] out of the two would seem to be substance rather than the matter. Moreover, the substance that is [compounded] out of the two—I mean the one that is [compounded] out of the matter and the form *(morphê)*—should be set aside, for it is posterior [to the other two] and clear; and the matter is also evident in a way. But the third has to be investigated, for it is most problematic" (*Met.* VII 3 1029ª20–34). It seems, then, that the matter of a perceptible hylomorphic compound and the compound itself are no longer genuine contenders in the primacy stakes, since neither has the kind of definitional or epistemological primacy required of a separate this. Does that mean that the form of a hylomorphic compound wins these stakes, as it were, by default—that Socrates' form, rather than Socrates himself, is primary substance$_m$?

Let us suppose for a moment that the answer is yes, so that Socrates' form *is* primary substance$_m$. How has the Primacy Dilemma been avoided? After all, if Socrates' form is a particular, it cannot be primary in scientific knowledge, and if it is a universal, it cannot be a subject or separate or a this. Presumably, we will find the answer, if one exists, by discovering more about what the form of a hylomorphic compound is.

5.3 Form

Aristotle identifies form with primary substance$_m$, and both of these with essence: "by the form I mean the essence of each thing, i.e., the primary substance" (*Met.* VII 7 1032ᵇ1–2).[12] It seems, then, that Socrates' form must just be his familiar penmattered essence. That is why, once the claims of matter and compound to primacy have been dismissed, Aristotle turns not to form as such, but to essence. For essences, because of their role as first principles of sciences, are already familiar when metaphysics begins its work, whereas substance$_m$ or form is not: "Since at the start we went through how many ways we define substance, and of these one seems to be the essence, we ought to get theoretical knowledge of it. For it is useful to

---

[12] Also *Met.* VII 7 1032ᵇ14, 10 1035ᵇ32, VIII 4 1044ª36.

advance toward what is better known—since this is how anyone succeeds in learning—by advancing through what is less well known by nature to what is better known" (VII 4 1029^{b}1–5).[13] Essence, then, is to be our guide to substance$_m$ and form.

Since the fundamental role of penmattered essences—indeed of essences of any sort—is to serve as the ontological correlate of definitions, let us take up Aristotle's discussion of such essences at the point where the problem of their definability is raised: "If someone says that an account with an additional posit is not a definition, a problem arises as to which things that are not simple but coupled have definitions; for they [coupled things] can only be explained as with an additional posit. I mean, e.g., that as well as nose and concavity, there is also snubness, which is a compound of the two, and is said to be this in this; and it is not coincidentally that either concavity or snubness is an attribute of the nose, but intrinsically, nor is it in the way that pale belongs to Callias or to man . . . but instead as male to animal, or as equal to quantity, and as all things [are] which are said to belong intrinsically" (*Met.* VII 5 1030^{b}14–26). Pale man and snub nose (or female animal) are coupled things. But there is a difference between them: pale man is a coincidental being; snub nose, an intrinsic one. We might think, then, that while coincidentally coupled beings will lack definitions, intrinsically coupled ones will possess them. But this is not so. Intrinsically coupled beings also lack definitions.

The argument that leads Aristotle to this conclusion follows immediately, though it takes some unpacking before its relevance becomes fully apparent:

Met. VII 5 1030^{b}28–1031^{a}3 [^{b}28] If snub nose and concave nose are the same, snub and concave will be the same. But [^{b}30a] if not (because [^{b}30b] we cannot speak of snub without the thing of which it is an intrinsic affection, since snubness is concavity in a nose), then either [^{b}32a] it is impossible to speak of a snub nose or else [^{b}32b] the same thing will have been said twice: concave nose nose (since snub nose will be concave nose nose). [^{b}34] It is absurd, then, for such a thing to have an essence. [^{b}35] But if not [i.e., if it is not impossible to speak of snub noses], it [the supposed definition of snubness] will go on indefinitely: for in snub nose nose yet another [nose] will be

---

[13] I follow the text of the mss, rather than the transposition proposed in the OCT, and take all of the transposed material (1029^{b}3–12) as a methodological reflection.

present. *[ª1]* Clearly, then, only substance has a [strict] definition. For *[ª2]* if the other [intrinsic] beings that are predicated have them, it is by addition.[14]

Either snub nose and concave nose are the same *(ᵇ28)* or they aren't *(ᵇ30a)*. If they are the same, snubness, which is a coupled thing, must be the same as concavity, which is a simple one. That possibility is excluded, however, because snub is a being the definition of which includes a reference to the substance (nose) of which it is an attribute, whereas concavity is not such a being *(ᵇ30b, Met.* VII 11 1037ª25–33 below). Hence snub nose and concave nose are not the same. But if they are not the same, either we cannot speak of snub noses *(ᵇ32a)* or we will say the same thing twice *(ᵇ32b)*. For the account of snub (concave nose) and snub itself signify the same thing, and so may be substituted for one another (VII 4 1030ª6–7). Performing the substitution in snub nose gives us concave nose nose. Either we cannot speak of snub noses, therefore, or snub has no essence, and so no definition, since concave nose nose is incoherent "babble *(adolescheia)*" *(ᵇ34)*. For when an account repeats the same thing a number of times, that's babbling.[15]

If we *can* speak of snub noses, however, the supposed essence or defini-tion of snub will go on indefinitely *(ᵇ35)*. For "we cannot speak of snub without the thing [nose] of which it is an intrinsic affection" *(ᵇ30b)*. Hence from snub nose we get snub nose nose, and so on, by repeatedly substitut-ing snub nose for snub. The result is yet more chronic babbling than before. Since such babbling definitions are unacceptable, snub is indefinable. But all intrinsic beings in categories other than substance are like snubness, since each of them is a this in this *(ª1)*. Hence only substances are strictly definable *(ª2)*.

---

[14] The overall form of the argument in this text is disputed. I agree with Balme, "The Snub," and Frede and Patzig, *Aristoteles Metaphysik Z*, that it is a dilemma. A different proposal is developed in Bostock, *Aristotle Metaphysics Books Z and H*, 97–100.

[15] *SE* 13 173ª32–ᵇ11: "As for making someone babble. . . . This is the aim in all arguments of the following kind: if uttering a name and uttering its account are the same, double [name] and double of half [account] are the same; if then double is double of half, it will be double of half of half. . . . [And so on.] All arguments of this kind occur . . . in dealing with any terms which . . . also have their sub-stance—i.e., the things of which they are states or attributes or the like—exhibited in their accounts . . . e.g., if the snub is concavity of the nose, and there is a concave nose, then there is a concave nose nose." Also 3 165ᵇ12–22.

We can now see why intrinsic beings that are not substances cannot have definitions and essences, or not, at any rate, in the primary and unqualified way in which substances have them (*Met.* VII 5 1031ª7–14). But it seems that penmattered essences—Aristotle's favorite *döppelganger* for which is snub—are subject to the very same criticism. For a penmattered essence is also a this (taken universally) in this (taken universally). Not surprisingly, then, Aristotle claims that penmattered essences, too, lack definitions (remember that form is essence and primary substance$_m$):

> *Met.* VII 11 1037ª25–33 The compound substance has an account in one way, but in another it hasn't. For [ª27] of it with its matter there is no account, since it [matter] is indefinite, but [ª28] with respect to the primary substance, there is one, e.g., in the case of man, the account of his soul. For [ª29a] the [primary] substance is the form present in the thing, and [ª29b] the compound substance is said to be [composed] of it and the matter. Concavity is an example, for a snub nose and snubness are composed of it and nose (for nose will be present twice in these). And in the compound substance, e.g., snub nose and Callias, matter will also be present.

ª27 claims that compound substances are not definable, because matter is indefinite; ª28 that the formal elements of such substances suffer no such liability—they are strictly definable. ª29a identifies form as primary substance$_m$. ª29b excludes from the ranks of the definable not just hylomorphic particulars, such as Callias, but their penmattered essences as well. Only the formal elements of penmattered essences are definable, then, not the essences as a whole.

A similar conclusion is drawn on rather different grounds in the following passage:

> *Met.* VII 11 1037ª33–*b*5 We have also said that [ª33] in some cases, a thing and its essence are the same, i.e., in the case of primary substances (e.g., curvature is the same as the essence of curvature, if it is primary). [*b*3] By primary substance I mean one that does not imply the presence of something in something else, i.e., in a subject-as-matter. But [*b*4] if a thing [is a substance] by being matter or composed of matter, it is not the same [as its essence].[16]

---

[16] Also *DA* III 4 429*b*10–15; *Met.* VII 6 1031*b*11–14, 1032ª4–11.

128

At issue is the requirement that whatever is primary substance$_m$ must be identical to its essence, on pain either of being unknowable or of not being primary in scientific knowledge. $^b3$ identifies the substances that have this feature as those that do not imply the presence of something in something else. $^a33$ states that curvature (an analog of concavity rather than of snubness) would be an example if it were primary. Since penmattered essences do seem to imply the presence of something (their formal elements) in something else (their material elements), they seem not to fall into the class that $^b3$ characterizes as being identical to their essences. Indeed, since they are composed of matter, they seem rather to fall into the class that $^b4$ characterizes as not being identical to their essences. If form is essence, in other words, penmattered essences, as also containing a material element, are not essences—at least not in the strictest sense.

So much for the doctrine, what now of its cogency and its message about the nature of form? Let us return to | chin-hair-in-m |. m is the hypothetically necessary matter of chin-hair taken universally. But what sort of thing is that? As in the case of elemental substantial change, the best way for us to grasp it is as the ontological correlate of a variable bindable by a quantifier. Consider the open sentence or predicate chin-hair (x). The ontological correlate of x is not some strange entity, rather it is a range of ordinary entities, namely, all those that are in the extension of the predicate. The role of m in | chin-hair-in-m |, therefore, is simply to serve as a place holder for anything in that extension. Since when one defines | chinhair | one doesn't define any of those things, what one defines, put in Aristotelian terms, is just the formal element in | chin-hair-in-m |. That, I think, and for something like these reasons, is the conclusion that Aristotle comes to about penmattered essences. Since the role of essences is to serve as the ontological correlates of definitions, he also concludes that essences, unqualifiedly speaking, just are forms.

The bearing of this conclusion on an apparent problem with the inexact sciences merits brief discussion. The problem is this. The formal element, | chin-hair |, of a penmattered essence, | chin-hair-in-m |, is itself matterless. If it is the ontological correlate of a definition, D, that is the first principle of an inexact science, S, | chin-hair | must be an ontological first principle of S. But how is that possible without changing the modal status of S's theorems—turning them, in effect, into theorems that hold always and necessarily rather than snecessarily and for the most part? The answer should now be evident. | chin-hair | may be what is defined by D, but it is

|chin-hair| *as realized in some particular bit of matter,* some particular instance of *m,* that is causally efficacious, and that bit of matter is partly determinative of what |chin-hair|'s efficacy will be on a given occasion. Think again of Socrates' three children and the different states of their chins.

What is of greater immediate relevance to us, however, is that we are now at liberty to re-file much of our lengthy dossier on essence under the new heading: form.

5.4 Suniversals

Our discussion of form, though heartening in one way, since it shows how much we already know about it, may seem to leave us pretty badly off where the Primacy Dilemma is concerned. For definition, as Aristotle always resolutely maintains, is "of the universal" (*Met.* VII 11 1036ª7–8). If Socrates' form is a universal, however, how can it be separate and a this? And if it isn't separate and a this, or if it isn't primary in definition and knowledge, how can it possibly be primary substance$_m$? Aristotle's response to this challenge, though not by itself a rebuttal of it, nonetheless constitutes the first important step in its solution.

What Aristotle does, in effect, is to uncover a concealed complexity within the apparently exclusive distinction between particulars and universals:[17]

> *Met. IX 7 1049ª27–36* That of which [something is said], i.e., the subject, is differentiated in this way: either [ª28] in being a this or [ª29] in not being a this; e.g., the subject for attributes is a man, i.e., a body and a soul, whereas musical or pale is the attribute. . . . Whenever this is so, the ultimate [subject] is a substance; but whenever this is not so, but the predicate is a form and a this, the ultimate [subject] is matter and material substance.[18]

In ª28, the subject is Socrates (or the like) and what is predicated of him is a universal. In ª29, the subject is Socrates' matter (or the like), and what is predicated of it is a form or essence. Thus, while ª28 involves universals, ª29 involves what we may call *suniversals.*

---

[17] Noticed by Code, "Aristotle: Essence and Accident," and Driscoll, "EIΔH in Aristotle's Earlier and Later Theories of Substance."

[18] Also *Met.* VII 13 1038ᵇ5–6.

Universals are things that are (wholly) present in *many* particulars—"what is said universally is by nature such as to belong to many things" (*Met.* VII 13 1038^{b}11–12). Particulars, by contrast, are things that are severally *one* and jointly many, things that can be counted, that have an arithmetic—"this is just what we mean by particulars: what are numerically one" (III 4 999^{b}34–1000^{a}1). Matter and form seem, as a result, to belong in neither camp. For form is what particularizes matter, and matter is what, prior to being formed, is not a particular, not a this: "We speak of one kind of being as substance, but of this one thing, the one that is not intrinsically a this, [we speak of] as matter, another, that in virtue of which it is then said to be a this, [we speak of] as form or shape" (*DA* II 1 412^{a}6–9). Just as we can think of matter as pre-particular,[19] then, we can think of form as pre-universal. Thus suniversal forms carve up or individuate the world into particular objects of singular reference, whereas universals characterize bits of the world that are already individuated. Submit Socrates to a metaphysical striptease, therefore, in which you remove all the things that are predicated of him, and you don't get Locke's something we know not what, or a bare particular, but a particular with a suniversal form.[20] When what Socrates *has* is (so to speak) gone, what he *is* is left.

We can now see more clearly why matter is excluded as a candidate primary substance$_m$. Matter is pre-particular. Hence, while it is the ultimate subject of suniversals, it is not the sort of subject that a primary substance is, since it is not a subject of universal attributes and is not a this (*Met.* IX 7 1049^{a}27–36). Moreover, because it isn't "intrinsically anything, or any quantity, or anything else by which being is determined" (VII 3 1029^{a}20–21), it cannot exist separate from the suniversal forms that particularize it (1029^{a}26–28). By the same token, when taken intrinsically, it is undefinable and unknowable (VII 10 1036^{a}8–9). Hence it fails all three of the primacy tests and cannot be primary substance$_m$.

---

[19] This idea reappears in Strawson, *Individuals*, 214–225, and in Quine, *Word and Object*, 90–95.

[20] I agree with Gill, *Aristotle on Substance*, 26–31, that the 'striptease' Aristotle imagines at *Met.* VII 3 1029^{a}10–19, in which a hylomorphic compound has its "attributes, products, and potentials" stripped away, until there is literally "nothing remaining," is one whose real possibility he does not himself countenance. Since, "for those who investigate in this way matter must evidently be the only substance" (1029^{a}18–19).

When we turn to the compound, however, things are much less clear cut. On the negative side, the compound inherits some of matter's failings. For, first, as a hylomorphic particular constituted of matter that isn't definable, it isn't definable either: "there is no definition of what is already a compound, e.g., this circle, or of any other perceptible or intelligible particular" (*Met.* VII 10 1036^{a}2–3). Second, as a particular, not identical to its essence, it cannot be epistemologically primary (VII 6 1031^{a}28–^{b}14). Third, because it is a compound of matter and form, it seems to be posterior to these more primitive elements. On the positive side, however, the compound is a subject of universal attributes, and so is both unqualifiedly separate, and a this.[21]

One is bound to be struck, at this point, by the thought that compound and form have the strengths of each other's weaknesses, that form is primary in definition and scientific knowledge, whereas the compound is primary in time. But that thought is defeatist, since it amounts to holding that nothing can be primary substance$_m$.

5.5 Winners and Losers

But perhaps defeatism is the only legitimate posture remaining. For although the story about forms as suniversals is an attractive one that goes a long way toward legitimating the distinction between suniversals and universals, it is clear that it does not, by itself, resolve the Primacy Dilemma in form's favor. For Socrates' form is his species form. Call that a suniversal, as perhaps we should, but it still isn't a particular, is it? Epistemologically primary it may be, but if particulars are primary substances$_m$, as they are primary substances$_c$, it cannot be ontologically primary. Unless of course the rules have changed, so that particulars are no longer ontologically primary. If so, the Primacy Dilemma has forced Aristotle to become a kind of Platonist. Why? Because suniversal forms, rather than particulars, have become the primary substances$_m$, the ontologically most basic things.

The resulting doctrinal change would be a huge *volte-face*. It would be a bit like Descartes becoming a Hobbesian materialist. It happens, but it usually happens with fanfare and elaborate justifications of the change of heart: think of Kant when Hume wakened him from his dogmatic slumbers, or Hilary Putnam when Kant wakened him from his. In Aristotle,

---

[21] *Met.* IX 7 1049^{a}27–36 (subject), VIII 1 1042^{a}29–3 (separate), VII 8 1033^{b}24 (this).

there is no fanfare, no explicit recantation, no recantatory argument adver-tised as such. This proves very little, but it is surely surprising. Moreover, recantation in this area, if it occurred, would also be philosophically disturbing. Why? Because the argument for the ontological primacy of particulars is so good.

Nonetheless, if we are restricted to hylomorphic compounds and their elements, whether material or formal, it is hard to see how we can honor the compelling claims of that argument and the equally compelling ones that have their origins in science. But maybe Aristotle can yet show us a way.

SIX

SUBSTANCE as FORM

6.1 Potentiality and Actuality

The next steps in Aristotle's attempt to solve the Primacy Dilemma are taken in *Metaphysics* VIII–IX, where matter is identified with potential being, form with actual being. Potentiality and actuality, however, represent definitional bedrock—the place where explicit definition gives out, and analogy takes its place: "What we mean to say will be clear by induction from particular cases: we must not seek a definition of everything, but must get a view of some of them by analogy. In this case: as what is building is to what can build, and as what is awake is to what is asleep, as what is seeing is to what has its eyes shut but has sight, and as what has been shaped out of matter is to the matter, and as the finished work is to what is unworked—let actuality be defined by the first part of this contrast, and potentiality by the second" (*Met.* IX 6 1048^{a}36–^{b}6). Whether or not potentiality and actuality can bear the weight thus placed on them remains to be seen. No doubt, it will depend on how well illuminated they are by the inductive base of the analogy, how well they illuminate other metaphysical notions, how compatible they are with Aristotelian science, and how much help they provide with the Primacy Dilemma. It is with the inductive base that we must begin, in any case, if we are to test their merits. We shall explore it, as Aristotle implicitly does, in five stages.

Stage 1: Suppose that S is a bronze statue of Socrates. At t_1 it hasn't yet been painted spale (the color of Socrates' skin), though it could be painted spale. At t_1 S is potentially spale. At t_2 Polyclitus has finished painting S. S is then actually spale. What is it that becomes actual at t_2? Aristotle's answer is this: "The matter and the form always have to exist beforehand. This is true for what-it-is [i.e., substance] and for each of the other categories, such as quality and quantity; for what comes-to-be is not a quality, but the qualified wood, not a quantity, but the quantified wood or animal" (*Met.* VII 9 1034^{b}12–16). What happens at t_2, then, is that two intrinsic beings—S and spale, or being S and being spale—come to coincide, with the result that a new coincidental being comes-to-be: spale-S. And what causes it to come-to-be, what actualizes S's potential to be spale, is Polyclitus, who need not himself be spale.

This story is the basis of our analogical understanding of the forms of intrinsic beings in non-substance categories. What it shows is that such forms are actualizations of potentials, which are themselves ways that actual substantial particulars might be. Since many different particulars might be these ways, such potentials are universals. Their actualizations, however, are not universals, but (dependent) hylomorphic particulars. Consequently, this story is also the basis of our analogical understanding of universals: they are potentials, like the potential S has at t_1 to be spale—ways, to repeat, that substances might be.

Stage 2: m is a quantity of bronze. At t_1 it hasn't acquired S-form, but could do so. Hence it is potentially S-formed. At t_2 *m* acquires S-form and so becomes actually S-formed. What becomes actual at t_2 is neither *m* nor S-form, however, but S, the brazen statue, the compound of *m* and S-form: "the brazen sphere comes-to-be, but not sphere or bronze; and the same is true of bronze if it comes-to-be" (*Met.* VII 9 1034^{b}10–12). Hence two actual beings, *m* and S-form, come to coincide at t_2, with the result that a third, S, comes-to-be. And what causes them to coincide is Polyclitus, who has S-form already existing in his understanding. Similarly, if S-form were Socrates' own form, rather than that of his statue, it would pre-exist in Socrates' male progenitor: "A unique feature of substance may be grasped from these cases [of production and animal reproduction], that it must be preceded by another actual substance, which makes it, e.g., an animal if an animal comes-to-be; whereas for a quality or quantity this is not necessary, but a potential alone will do" (1034^{b}16–19). Contrast this with Stage 1. When a spale S comes-to-be, an actual being, S, which is potentially spale, comes-to-be actually spale. When S itself comes-to-be, on the other hand, an actual being (S-form) is transmitted to an actual being (a quantity of bronze) that has the potential to receive it.

If S-form is substantial form, therefore, nothing can have it potentially unless something else has it actually: if nothing is actually a human being, nothing is potentially a human being; if nothing is actually a statue, nothing is potentially one. This is easier to see in the case of human beings than in that of statues, since human beings come from actual human beings that pre-exist them. But S-form, existing in Polyclitus' understanding, seems not to be a statue, but some sort of universal or suniversal. As a potential object of understanding, it is just that. But when Polyclitus is actively understanding it, as he is when it is guiding the hand movements that transmit S-form to the bronze, things are different: "Scientific knowledge, like knowing scientifically, is of two kinds, one potential, one actual. The potential—being (as matter) universal and indefinite—is of what is universal and indefinite, but the actual, being a this, is of a this" (*Met.* XIII 10 1087ª15–18). Thus the statue Polyclitus is understanding, like the one he makes, is a particular. Indeed, it is a hylomorphic compound, though its matter is neither bronze nor bronze taken universally (7.4). For the essence of an artifact, like that of a natural being, is itself penmattered—not separate from perceptible matter even in thought.

One of the things we grasp in grasping this part of the analogy is that anything can be matter if it is potentially something it actually isn't. In other words, matter just is whatever could be some way: "The substance [that serves] as subject, i.e., the matter, is agreed: it is what is potentially [something]" (*Met.* VIII 2 1042ᵇ9–10). This is matter's account. It tells us what it is to be matter. It isn't the specification of a new kind of stuff—prime matter as traditionally conceived—that is pure potential (VII 3 1029ª20–21, 10 1036ª8–9). Consider an analogy. Suppose something is a particular just in case it is an occupier of a space-time region. That's what it is to be a particular. It isn't a new etiolated type of particular—a bare particular—that just is such an occupier and nothing else.

In grasping the differences between Stages 1 and 2, we begin to grasp more fully what substantial form—specifically the substantial form of a hylomorphic particular—itself is. For while non-substantial forms are actualizations of potentials that are universals, ways actual substantial particulars might be, substantial forms are not actualizations of potentials of this sort. They are suniversals, actualizations of potentials that exist in matter. The crucial consequence is that whereas a universal cannot be actualized by itself, and wouldn't be a particular if, *per impossibile,* it could be, a suniversal actualized is a particular, and is, as it were, the offspring of such particulars. What the discovery of suniversals reveals, therefore, is a duality in substantial forms: qua potentials, they are suniversals; qua actualities, they are particulars.

Stage 3: At t₁ Polyclitus doesn't know how to make S, neither does Callias. But, unlike Callias, Polyclitus has the potential to learn sculpting, "he has the right sort of genus and matter" (*DA* II 5 417ª27). As a result, Polyclitus has a *first potential* that Callias lacks. At t₂ Polyclitus knows how to make S, since he has learned sculpting in the meantime, though he isn't actually doing any sculpting then. At t_2 Polyclitus has a *second potential (first actuality)* that he lacked at t_1. At t_3 he is actualizing this potential in actually sculpting S. He then has a *second actuality* that he lacked at t_2 (1 412^{a}3–28, 5 417^{a}21–^{b}2).

If everyone were like Callias at t_1, the potential to sculpt wouldn't be actual to any degree; it would have no toe-hold in being. Because of how Polyclitus is, however, the potential to sculpt has a minimal toe-hold in being at t_1, a still greater one at t_2, and a maximally great one at t_3. Since the potential to sculpt is an analog of form, and an animal's form is its soul, soul too is something that can be actual to these different degrees. When Socrates is asleep, his soul is analogous to Polyclitus' potential to sculpt at t_1. When he awakens, it is analogous to Polyclitus' potential to sculpt at t_2: that is why it "is the first actuality of what has life potentially" (*DA* II 1 412^{a}27–28). As form is to matter, so actuality is to potentiality; as actuality is to potentiality so (among other things) "what is awake is to what is asleep" (*Met.* IX 6 1048^{b}1–2).

Polyclitus and Callias do not differ in form or essence at t_1, yet they do differ in potentiality. Since matter just is whatever is potentially anything, this difference must lie in their matter. Once matter has received substantial form, moreover, the resulting hylomorphic compound has the potential to receive the forms of intrinsic beings in the other categories. This potential too is due to matter, since "matter is the cause of the coincidental" (*Met.* VI 2 1027^{a}13–14). If Socrates' essence were not penmattered, in other words, it would be impossible for him either to sleep or, when awake, to learn anything.

Stage 4: The defining marks of a movement or process *(kinêsis)* are as follows:

1. It takes time (*EN* X 4 1174^{a}19).

2. Like the time that measures it, it is infinitely divisible (*Ph.* III 7 207^{b}21–25; *Met.* V 13 1020^{a}26–32).

3. It has a definite limit, t_n, and cannot go on once that limit is reached. By the same token, it is incomplete at every time prior to t_n (*EN* X 4 1174^{a}21–23).

4. It consists of sub-processes that are different in form from the whole process and from each other (1174^{a}23–^{b}2).

We can see these five features exemplified in the process, P, that Polyclitus goes through in sculpting S.

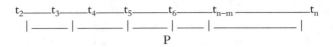

t_2 to t_3: Polyclitus carves out the mold for the body of S. t_3 to t_4: he carves out the mold for the head and arms. t_4 to t_5: he smelts the copper and tin. t_5 to t_6: he pours the bronze into the molds. t_6 to t_{n-m}: he assembles the statue out of the molded parts. t_{n-m} to t_n: he fine-finishes the statue and paints it spale. At t_n he completes the process and produces S. P is this entire process of production.

Even at t_2, therefore, when it is a second actuality, part of Polyclitus' potential to sculpt is not fully actual, since it still contains unactualized potential that won't be actualized until some later time in P. Moreover, at t_n, when P is complete, the earlier stages no longer exist. And immediately after t_n the potential to sculpt collapses back into a second potential. It is impossible, therefore, for all of the parts of P to be fully actualized—to be second actualities—simultaneously. That is why processes *take time*.

What Stage 4 tells us about form and matter becomes apparent when we look at Socrates' soul. If Socrates is asleep at t_2, his soul is a second potential that is partly like his potential to sculpt. Hence, when he wakes up at t_3, a process begins. For Socrates' soul is still not fully actual then, since part of it, just like Polyclitus' potential to build at t_2, is still unactualized potential.

Stage 5: Not all second actualities are processes, however, some are activities *(energeiai):*[1] "Since of the actions that have a limit none is an end but all are in relation to the end—e.g., as slimming is to slimness. For the bodily parts themselves, when they are slimming, in that respect are in the process of changing, but those things the process is for the sake of do not yet belong to them—and such things are not actions or at least not complete ones (for they are not an end). But the sort in which the end is contained is a [canonical] action. E.g., in the same instant one is seeing and has seen, is being practically wise and has been practically wise, is understanding and has understood. But if you are learning, it is not the case that in the same instant you have learned, nor if you are being cured, that in the same instant you have been cured. However, someone who is living well at the same time has lived well and someone who is happy at the same instant

---

[1] *Energeia* as it contrasts with *dunamis* (potential) is usually translated 'actuality'. As it contrasts with *kinêsis* (process, movement, change) it is often, as here, translated as 'activity'.

has been happy. If that were not so, these things [living well, being happy] would have to come to an end at some time, as is the case with slimming. Of these, then, one group should be called processes and the other activities. For every process is incomplete, e.g., slimming, learning, walking, building; these are processes and are incomplete. For one cannot in the same instant be walking and have walked, nor be house-building and have built a house, nor be coming-to-be and have come-to-be, nor be in process and have been in process; they're different, as [in general] are being in process and having been in process" (*Met.* IX 6 1048^{b}18–33). The defining mark of an activity, φ, therefore, is:

1. φ is complete, in the sense of containing its end, at every instant: if someone is φ-ing at t_1, he has φ-ed at t_1.

As a result, φ also possesses five other features:

2. It doesn't occur in stages, and so can't be incomplete.

3. It is temporally point-like (*DA* I 4 409^{a}1–3; *EN* X 4 1174^{b}12–13).

4. It does not take time to occur, and so does not really occur "in time" (*Ph.* VIII 8 262^{b}20–21).

5. It has no set limit, and so can go on indefinitely: φ-ing can stop, but it need never finish.

6. It has no heteroform sub-parts: the parts of φ-ings are themselves φ-ings.

In 6.2, we shall submit activities to scrutiny. For the moment, however, we may take them simply on trust.[2]

Suppose, then, that understanding really is an activity. Since Socrates engages in it, his soul or form, in addition to containing potentials that are actualized as processes, contains some that are actualized as activities. In the case of the latter, therefore, there is no unactualized potential left behind to be actualized later. For unlike the potential to build a house, the potential to understand is fully actualized even at an instant. It follows that understanding, since it involves no unactualized potential, involves no matter—"bodily activity is in no way associated with its activity" (*GA* II 3 736^{b}28–

---

[2] My account of Stages 4 and 5 is especially indebted to the lucid discussion in Heineman, "Activity and Change in Aristotle," which also provides a useful guide to the vast literature on this topic.

29). Hence it must be pure actuality, pure form. Socrates' soul taken as a whole is not pure form. But if there were a soul that was a pure or matterless form, it would be in essence an activity.

The picture of form and matter that emerges at the end of Aristotle's five-stage analogical account of it, then, is this: Form, unqualifiedly speaking, is activity—complete actuality. Matter, unqualifiedly speaking, is complete potentiality—complete absence of actuality or form. If form is primary substance$_m$, therefore, primary substance$_m$ must be complete actuality. Between matter at one end of the scale of actuality and form at the other, there are beings that are neither complete actualities nor complete potentialities. They are the hylomorphic compounds. Just what category they belong in remains to be seen.

Notice that this picture is pretty much the same as the one in which form was portrayed as shaping hypothetically necessary matter to the extent that the necessities inherent in it allowed. How actualized a form can be depends, then, on what sort of matter is hypothetically necessary in order to actualize it. If none is needed, a form can be completely actualized. If some is needed, its actualization will be a matter of degree—a degree determined, as we shall see, by how earthy (or unclear) the ether in its hypothetically necessary matter has to be (7.2).

6.2 Activities and Their Ends

The initial four stages in Aristotle's account of form are sufficiently uncontroversial and commonsensical not to require extended defense. But activities are another kettle of fish. Are they really different from processes? Is the distinction between the two well-founded? To answer we need to explore Aristotle's dossier on them in greater detail, focusing especially on the first entry (if someone is φ-ing at t_1, he has φ-ed at t_1), since it is the base on which the others rest.

Aristotle claims that walking is a process not an activity. Yet if someone *is* walking at t_1, isn't it also true that he *has* walked at t_1?[3] Now consider acting in a practically-wise way, which is an activity. Suppose that Pericles is continuously engaged in it, and so is continuously activating the state that is his practical wisdom, while he is giving his famous funeral oration. Nonetheless, at t_1 he is describing the Athenian way of life, at t_2 he is

---

[3] I borrow the question from Ackrill's seminal paper, "Aristotle's Distinction between *Energeia* and *Kinêsis.*"

speaking of the dead, at t_3 he is addressing women, and so on. Arguably, then, his activity has heteroform parts, just as a walk does. Moreover, it seems to have as an end something that it does not contain at every instant: "Practical wisdom is, as it were, a kind of steward of theoretical wisdom, procuring leisure for it and its function [understanding], by subduing and moderating the passions" (*MM* I 34 1198^{b}16–20).[4] It could happen, then, that though Pericles is being practically wise, he is yet failing to procure the leisure needed for theoretical activity. Hence, though he is φ-ing at t_1, it is not true that he has (successfully) φ-ed at t_1.

Since practical wisdom is "the same state of the soul" as political science (*EN* VI 8 1141^{b}23–24), this problem also emerges in the following text: "From the virtues concerned with action we try to a greater or lesser extent to gain something over and above the action itself. . . . But the action of the politician is unleisurely also, and aims—over and above political action itself—at mastership and honors, or at any rate at happiness—which is something different from political action, and is clearly sought as being different. Hence, among actions expressing the virtues, those in politics and war are preeminently fine and great, but are unleisurely and aim at some [further] end, and are not chosen [solely] because of themselves" (X 7 1177^{b}2–18). The activity of being practically wise is one thing, then, happiness is another, different thing—an end that may fail to be achieved, and so cannot be being achieved at every instant at which that activity is taking place.

This pincer-like attack on activities appears pretty devastating. Can it be resisted? I think it can. But since not all ways of resisting it are equally instructive, it will prove useful to proceed in stages, focusing first on processes and then turning back again to activities. Walking is a kind of locomotion, or spatial movement—a way, like swimming or hopping, of getting from one place to another. x has done some walking, therefore, just in case he has, in walking fashion, moved from place p_1 to place p_2, and then from p_2 to p_3, and so on. Arguably, then, each bit of walking is different in form from every other: "The production of the temple is a complete production, since it needs nothing further to achieve the proposed goal; but the production of the foundation or the triglyph is an incomplete production, since it is [the production] of a part. Hence they differ in form [from the complete production]; and we cannot find a process complete in form at any time, but, if at all, in the whole time. The

---

[4] Also *EN* VI 13 1145^{a}6–11; *EE* VII 15 1249^{b}9–21; *Pol.* VII 14 1333^{a}16–30.

same is true of walking and the other [processes]. For if spatial movement is a process [of moving] from one place to another, it includes movements differing in form—flying, walking, jumping, and so on. And besides these differences there are differences in walking itself. For the place from which and the place to which are not the same in the whole racecourse as they are in a part of it, or the same in one part as in another; nor is traveling along one path the same as traveling along another, since what we cover is not just a path, but a path in a [particular] place, and this path and that path are in different places" (*EN* X 4 1174^{a}25–^{b}2). Walking is a process, therefore, at least in part because parts of walks have different starting points and ending points from each other, and from the walk as a whole, and take paths that are in different places. By the same token, suppose that x is at the spatio-temporal starting point, p_1t_1, of his walk. At $t_{\tilde{1}}$, keeping his left foot at p_1, he raises his right foot. At t_2 his right foot is in the air.[5] The movement he makes between t_1 and t_2 is part of his walk, but it is not itself a walk, or a bit of walking, since it is not itself a case of x's having moved from p_1 to another place. For this reason too walking is a process not an activity.

So blunt a response to a subtle criticism, though not without some force, is bound to leave one dissatisfied. For it might well seem that in defining walking as we did, and as Aristotle does in the text just quoted, we have made things too easy for ourselves. Perhaps, x's lifting of his foot *is* a bit of walking. One would be hard pressed to argue the case either way without begging the question. Better, then, to set this objection aside and see if we can do better.

Since x's walking is an intentional activity, part of it consists in the causation of his bodily movements in the appropriate ways by his beliefs, desires, and intentions. If x's movements weren't so caused, if they weren't controlled by his intention to walk, what x was doing at t_1 might not be walking, but rather some sort of spasm or fit. These beliefs, desires, and intentions can be active as causes, however, and yet be ineffective in producing movement of the legs. In such cases, x *tries* to move his legs in walking fashion, but because, unknown to him, his spinal cord is severed,

---

[5] Samuel Beckett's famous description in *Watt* makes the point yet more vividly: "Watt's way of advancing due east, for example, was to turn his bust as far as possible towards the north and at the same time to fling out his right leg as far as possible towards the south, and then to turn his bust as far as possible towards the south and at the same time to fling out his left leg as far as possible towards the north . . . and so on, over and over again, many many times, until he reached his destination."

he fails. What such failure reveals is that walking does have an end—the appropriate movement of the limbs—that it does not contain at every instant, and so may fail, as in the case of paralysis, to contain at all. x has begun to walk at the instant, t_0, at which his intention is put into effect. But he has not yet walked, or succeeded in walking then.

This way of looking at walking represents it as being just like building a temple. The form of the walk, existing as the content of an intention in the soul of the walker, is like the form of the temple as a whole existing in the soul of the builder. The first stage or step of the walk, which is for x to lift his right foot, is like the production of the foundation, the second, which is for him to bring his right foot down at p_2, is like the production of the triglyph, and so on, until x lands at p_n, and the walk as a whole is completed.

Can we generalize this defense of Aristotle's conception of a process from intentional actions, such as walking, to non-intentional spatial movements, which are the paradigm cases of processes? The natural thought is that if we can, it must be by looking into their causes. And this seems to be Aristotle's own thought. For he claims that processes fail to contain their ends at every instant because of the nature of the potentials of which they are the actualizations: "A process of movement seems to be an activity of a sort, but an incomplete one—the reason is that the potential whose activation it is, is incomplete" (*Ph.* III 2 201^{b}31–33). What he means, I think, is this: x's potential to φ is incomplete if its actualization at t_1 is compatible with x's not actually φ-ing at t_1, which in turn is made possible by the existence of opposite potentials.

If x is to move in a certain way, then, it must have the passive potential to do so, and something (typically something else), which has the requisite active potential, must actualize that passive potential: "One sort [of potential] is a potential to be affected, [it is] the first principle, in the thing itself that is being acted upon, of undergoing change, by the agency of another or of [itself] qua other" (*Met.* IX 1 1046^{a}11–13). Moreover, these passive potentials may be potentials to move in somewhat different directions. If so, the result of their being simultaneously actualized will be some third kind of movement. This is what happens, for example, when a fiery body's natural potential to move upwards is actualized at the same time as its passive potential to move downwards: "The movement is most often sideways because it is a combination of two movements, an imposed one downwards, and a natural one upwards, and bodies under these conditions move obliquely" (*Mete.* I 4 342^{a}24–26). More dramatically, it is what happens when a body, which has had its potential to move actualized, fails to move at all because a wholly opposite potential is actualized at the same time: "A sign that the movement from p_1 to p_2 is the opposite of the one from p_1 to p_3 is that they arrest or stop one another if they happen to occur simultaneously" (*Ph.* VIII 8 262^{a}6–8). Since no actual movement occurs at all in such a case, we can see why the potential to move from p_1 to p_2 is incomplete as compared with a (second) potential whose actualization is an activity. For if this potential is actualized at the same time as the potential to move from p_1 to p_3, it cannot contain its end at that time, since no movement from p_1 to p_2 occurs.[6] What the case reveals is of quite general application: a potential that can be actualized and simultaneously prevented from attaining its end is incomplete, so that its actualization is a process—an incomplete activity.

Generally speaking, then, all processes, whether walking or building a temple or moving in space, fail to contain their ends at every instant because the potentials of which they are the actualizations are incomplete in this sense: they can be actualized at a time but prevented from achieving their ends at that time. The problem we now face is to explain why the same isn't true of an activity, such as being practically wise, given that activities too can have ends that are different from the activities themselves.

To solve this problem we need to look at two sorts of ends that Aristotle distinguishes, namely, *internal* ends and *external* ends. Suppose that the end of φ-ing is e. If the following biconditional is true, e is an internal end of φ-ing:

Necessarily [the φ-ing that results in e is going on at t) ↔ (e exists at t)]

---

[6] The need to invoke *dunameis* (potentials or capacities), rather than actual movements, in these sorts of cases is recognized by Hussey, "Aristotle's Mathematical Physics," 222: "if there is only one object, being moved in two different ways at once, the compounded motion seems to be the only actual one. If this is right, then how is this motion to be explained? It cannot be done by reference to the component motions, if these do not exist. In this case it seems that we must invoke the capacities of the two agents. These agents, to be explanatory, must both be actually acting on the object. Instead of speaking of the composition of changes, we should in these cases more correctly speak of the composition of agents or capacities to produce a change. This is in line with the talk of changes' 'stopping', 'overcoming', or even 'destroying' other changes." Hussey focuses on the active potentials. But the same point applies to passive potentials as well.

But if instead the following conditional is true, e is an external end of φ-ing:

> Necessarily [the φ-ing that results in e is going on at t) → (e does not exist at t)]

—where an external end is one that is "over-and-above *(para)*" what results in it, whereas an internal one is "other than *(allo)*" what results in it, but not over and above it (*EN* I 1 1094ª3–5, III 3 1112ᵇ32–33). A product, then, is a paradigm external end, since it comes into existence only when the production that results in it is complete and does not exist while the production is still going on.

Though Aristotle sometimes uses the term *praxis* to refer to any intentional action, he also uses it in a stricter, canonical sense to refer exclusively to what results from deliberate choice *(proairesis)*.[7] Understood canonically, actions are activities, whereas productions (though actions more loosely understood) are processes. It is actions in the strict sense, then, that are at issue here, and it is their ends, the ends of activities, that are internal ends.

In the following compressed text, Aristotle attempts to explain what such ends are:

> *Met.* IX 8 1050ª21–23 *[ª21]* The result *(ergon)* is the end, *[ª22a]* the activity is the result, and *[ª22b]* this is why the term activity is said with relation to the result and *[ª23]* is extended to the actualization *(entelecheia)*.

The actualization referred to in *ª23* is the actualization of a second potential. But this actualization must be distinguished from the activity that is its end *(ª21)* or result *(ª22a)*. Consider the following case: John laughed a hollow laugh. The hollow laugh is the result, we may suppose, of John's actualization of his acquired second potential to laugh such laughs. It is an activity in the primary or nonextended sense of the term. Hence *ª22b*. His laughing of it is an activity in a secondary or extended sense, because what he is doing would not be laughing if it did not result in a laugh.[8] Hence *ª23*.

---

[7] *EN* III 1 1111ª25–26 (loose), VI 2 1139ª20 (canonical).

[8] Compare Thomas Nagel's witty riposte to those who say that it is the process of dying they fear, not death: "I should not really object to dying if it were not followed by death."

Since laughing a hollow laugh must, for this reason, result in a hollow laugh, the latter is the internal and logically necessary result of laughing. The distinction is easy to miss, because we almost always use the same word for both the activation and its result. But this is not always so. For example, we strike blows and sing notes, and we can distinguish the blow from the striking of it, and the note from the singing of it. Likewise, we need to distinguish the act from the doing of it—the activity as result from the activity as activation of a second potential.

It is the distinction between act and result that Aristotle marks by referring to the latter as "other than *(allo)*" the act whose end it is. Hence the internal end of activating a second potential is precisely the activity that is its result. Unlike an external end, it is not something over and above that activation: the note lasts only as long as it is sung; the blow, only while being struck. Likewise an action or a thought lasts only as long as the doing or thinking of it.[9]

The ends of processes are paradigmatic external ends. Not all such ends are the ends of processes, however, since some actions or activities also have external ends. But how can that be true? How can actions or activities, which are not productions, possibly have external ends? The question, as we can now see, gets things somewhat the wrong way around. There is no real problem with activities having external ends (John might laugh the hollow laugh in order to irritate) so long as processes can't have internal ones. But we have already seen why they can't. For a process is the actualization of a potential that can be actualized and simultaneously prevented from attaining its end. And an internal end, as a logically necessary result of actualizing a potential, cannot possibly fill this bill.

Since an activity (A_1) contains its ends at every instant, it might be represented schematically as follows:

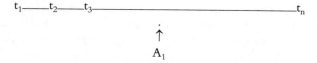

$$t_1\text{———}t_2\text{———}t_3\text{———————————————}t_n$$
$$\uparrow$$
$$A_1$$

This representation makes vivid the sense in which an activity is not in time—it does not take any time to complete. Now consider a somewhat different schematic representation of an activity:

---

[9] I have benefited in this and the preceding paragraph from the subtle discussion in Charles, "Aristotle: Ontology and Moral Reasoning."

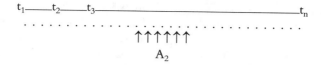

$$A_2$$

Both A_1 and A_2 are equally complete: "the good itself will not be to a higher degree good by being eternal. For a white thing is no whiter if it lasts a long time than if it lasts a day" (*EN* I 6 1096^{b}3–5). Nonetheless, A_2 goes on longer than A_1. Hence, even though an activity does not take time to complete, and is not in time in that strong way, it can be in time in another weaker way—it can be temporally extended. Indeed, it can be indefinitely or eternally extended. For, unlike in the case of a process, where achieving the end marks the process' own necessary termination, an activity can only stop, it cannot finish: we can go on actively seeing or understanding the same thing without end. Hence, while it is true that happiness is an activity, and so is complete at any instant, it is not true that a life is made happy by one instant of happiness: "for one swallow does not make a summer, nor does one day; nor, similarly, does one day or a short time make us blessed and happy" (7 1098^{a}18–20). That is one reason God is happier than we are: he is always and eternally in the happy condition that we are only sometimes in (*Met.* XII 7 1072^{b}20–28, 8.1).[10]

6.3 Activity as Primary Substance$_m$?

Aristotle is trying to show that substantial form—something on the order of a suniversal essence (albeit not a penmattered one), something that could plausibly function as the first principle of a science—can enjoy the ontological primacy that the *Categories* assigns to particulars. What he has done so far is to argue that a form, at its most actual, is an analog of activity, and that, when existing in the understanding, is qua potential a universal and qua activity a particular. What he has not done, however, is show us how to exploit all this to solve the Primacy Dilemma. He has not shown us how to represent the first principle of a science, which is qua potential a suniversal essence, as qua actuality a separate substantial particular.

---

[10] We need to distinguish, therefore, as is not often enough done, between happiness (an activity) and a happy life. See *EE* I 2 especially 1214^{b}26–27, my *Practices of Reason,* 149–159, and *Aristotle: Politics,* xlii–xlviii.

The particular content of an act of understanding, after all, seems to be ontologically dependent on that act, and so to be not a separate substance. Moreover, the act itself seems to be ontologically dependent on the performer of it—a substantial understander. *Prima facie,* then, it is the understander that is the substance, not the suniversal essence he particularizes in his act of understanding. But if that is so, the Primacy Dilemma returns with a vengeance. For it is the understander not the understood that enjoys ontological primacy, and the understood not the understander that is primary in scientific knowledge.

SEVEN

INTELLIGIBLE SUBSTANCE

7.1 Sight as a Model for Understanding

The next phase in our account of Aristotle's attack on the Primacy Dilemma focuses on one activity in particular, human understanding, since it will turn out to hold part of the key to the problem of the ontological primacy of form. We begin, however, with a discussion of sight, since Aristotle models his account of understanding very closely on it.

To understand sight, or any other psychological faculty or potential, one must first understand its activity, and prior to that, its object: "If one must say what each of them is, e.g., what the potential for understanding is, or for perception, or for nutrition, we must first say what understanding and perceiving are; for activities and actions are prior to potentials in account [or definition]. And if this is so, and if again, prior to them, we should have considered their correlative objects, then we should for the same reason determine them first, e.g., food, perceptible objects, and intelligible objects" (*DA* II 4 415^{a}16–22). We cannot understand the potential to see, in other words, unless we know what it is a potential to do. And we cannot understand what it is a potential to do unless we know what a visible object is. For visible objects cause seeing, and effects are understood through their causes: "Perceiving is certainly not of itself; but there is also something else over and above the perceiving, and this must necessarily be prior to the perceiving. For what brings about a change is naturally prior to what is changed, and this is no less true when they are spoken of in relation to one another" (*Met.* IV 5 1010^{b}35–1011^{a}2). We should expect, then, that Aristotle's account of vision will depend significantly on his account of visible objects.

In addition to such objects, however, sight also involves an organ of perception—the eye—the form (essence, function) of which is seeing and the matter, eye-jelly *(korê)*: "If the eye were an animal, seeing would be its soul; for this is the eye's substance [or essence]—that which corresponds to its account . . . and as an eye is the eye-jelly plus sight, so an animal is soul plus body" (*DA* II 1 412^{b}18–413^{a}3). The eye-jelly, which is the transparent part of the eye, is the part affected by the visible object, color, which is the special object of seeing, the one that sight alone can perceive. It is Aristotle's account of color, then, that will reveal what seeing and sight are. We shall explore it in five stages.

Stage 1: The nature of color is determined by its connection with light, and light's nature, in turn, by its connection with transparency:

> *DA* II 7 418^{a}29–^{b}13 [^{a}29] What is visible is color, and it is on top of what is intrinsically visible—intrinsically visible not in account, but because it has in itself the cause of its own visibility. [^{a}31] Every color has the capacity to produce a change in what is in actuality transparent—that is the nature of color. For this reason it is not visible without light, but the color of each thing is seen only in light. Hence we must first say what light is. [^{b}3] There is, surely, something transparent. And I call transparent what is visible—not intrinsically and unqualifiedly visible, but [visible] because of the color of something else. Of this sort are air, water, and many solid bodies. For it is not qua water or qua air that these are transparent, but because there exists in them a certain nature which is the same in both and which also exists in the eternal body above. Light is the activity of this—of the transparent qua transparent. And wherever this is, [^{b}10] potentially there is dark also. [^{b}11] Light is a sort of color of the transparent, when it is made actually transparent by fire or something such as the body above.

Part of ^{a}29 is a more-or-less terminological claim, but part is substantive. For light is not intrinsically visible by any kind of terminological fiat, but rather because it "produces seeing" (*Sens.* 6 447^{a}11).[1]

Light, however, is itself a sort of color (^{b}11)—it is "coincidentally the color of the transparent" (*Sens.* 3 439^{a}18–19).[2] That is to say, it isn't an intrinsic property of what is transparent as such (^{b}s.s.), since what is transparent may be dark rather than light (^{b}10), but a property of what happens to be actually transparent: "for wherever there is a fiery element in the

---

[1] As the author of *Col.* 1 791^{b}8–9 correctly sees: "light . . . alone is visible because of itself, while [all] other things are visible because of it."

[2] Compare *Col.* 1 791^{b}6–7: "light is clearly the color of fire."

transparent, light is present, and in its absence, dark" (439^{a}19–21). For reasons that will become clear, I shall call light and dark *proto-colors,* and others, simply colors.

^{b}3 identifies the transparent as what is found it "the eternal body above," namely, ether (3.2). It is present in transparent materials, but also "in all other bodies in a greater or lesser degree" (*Sens.* 3 439^{a}24–25).[3] If it weren't, opaque bodies could not be colored. Hence ether is crucial to color: "The nature of light is to be in the transparent [ether] as indefinite. But it is clear that the transparent [ether] in bodies must have an ultimate boundary, and it is evident from the facts that this is color. . . . For it [color] is *in* the limit of the body, but is not a limit of the body, rather we must suppose that the same nature [i.e., the transparent ether] which, when existing outside, is colored also exists inside. So both air and water are plainly colored; for their sheen is such. . . . Hence color is the limit of the transparent [ether] in a determinately bounded body" (439^{a}26–^{b}12). Colors, then, are the limits of the ether in a body with a determinate boundary. Light and dark, however, are not like that, they are proto-colors of the (interior of the) ether itself.

Stage 2: What is light or dark in the transparent ether as indefinite is white or black, when it is the limit of the ether in a determinately bounded body: "That which, when present in air [i.e., a nondelimited or indefinite body], is the very thing that produces light. It may be present in the transparent [ether], or it may not be, but may be missing. Accordingly, the same conditions that in air produce light and dark in [delimited] bodies produce white and black" (*Sens.* 3 439^{b}14–18). Hence for the surface of an object to be white (black) is just for the ether that is present in it, as in all visible objects, to be actualized (light) or unactualized (dark). For the "same nature is sometimes dark and sometimes light" (*DA* II 7 418^{b}31–419^{a}1).

Stage 3: With white and black thus defined in terms of light and dark, a way is outlined in which all other colors may be defined in terms of them: "It is possible that the white and the black should be so juxtaposed that each is invisible because it is very small, but that what is composed of both is visible. This can appear neither as white nor as black. But since it must have some color, and cannot have either of these, it must be some kind of mixture, i.e., some other kind of color. Such then is a possible way of

---

[3] Moreover, in the sublunary world at least, it "is not found separate [from bodies]" (*Sens.* 3 439^{a}23).

conceiving of the existence of a plurality of colors besides white and black, but which are a plurality because of the ratio [of white to black that constitutes them]; for they [white and black] may be juxtaposed in the ratio 3:2 or 3:4, or in ratios expressible by other numbers, or they may be in no numerically expressible ratio, but in some incommensurable relation of excess or deficiency" (*Sens.* 3 439^b19-30). Modulo this hypothesis, then, all colors are ratios of white to black (white and black themselves being the limiting cases of such ratios). It follows that for the surface of an object to be colored is just for the ether within it to be proto-colored. Thus, while the visible form of a color is some ratio of white to black, its matter is the surface boundary of the actually transparent ether in a delimited body.[4]

Stage 4: Every color can produce a change in what is actually transparent (*$^a31$*). Having this potential, indeed, is the very essence of color: "this is just what it is to be a color, to have the potential to change what is actually transparent" (*DA* II 7 419^a9-11).[5] Thus color can effect a change in all transparent objects, not just in eye-jelly. The change effected in the latter, however, is that it comes to take on the visible form of the color without its matter, "as wax receives the imprint of the ring without the iron or gold" (12 424^a17-20). That is to say, what the eye-jelly does *not* take on is the limit (surface) of the transparent ether in the determinately bounded body whose color is being seen, while what it does take on is white and black in some ratio. More exactly, that is what the *surface* of the eye-jelly takes on, and it does so because its transparent interior takes on a mixture of light and dark in that ratio.

It is in order that an animal can detect color, indeed, that its eye-jelly is transparent. For because colors are ratios of white to black, the eye-jelly must receive light and dark in some ratio if an animal is to detect them. Consequently, it must be transparent, or in a mean or intermediate state between light and dark: "[A sense] is a sort of mean between the opposites present in perceptible objects. That is why it discriminates objects of

---

[4] Contra Silverman, "Color and Color-Perception in Aristotle's *De Anima*," who identifies black and white as the material element, and the ratio between them as the formal element.

[5] Aristotle is forgetting that light and dark are colors when he gives this account. For light just is the activity of the transparent, and dark its merely potential condition. Neither, therefore, is a qualitative change in what is already actively transparent.

perception. For the mean is capable of discriminating, since it becomes to each extreme in turn the opposite extreme. And just as what is to perceive white and black must be neither of them actually, although both potentially (and similarly too for the other senses), so in the case of touch that which is to perceive hot and cold must be neither" (*DA* II 11 424ª4–10).[6] For if the eye-jelly itself were intrinsically light or dark, it wouldn't be able to take on all ratios of light to dark. By the same token, if it were already somewhat white, because of glaucoma, for example, it would not be able to discriminate between colors correctly.[7]

The result of taking on a ratio of white to black is that the eye-jelly becomes in "a way colored" (*DA* III 2 425ᵇ22–23), namely, proto-colored. Moreover, it can retain its proto-color even when color itself is no longer being seen: "Each sense-organ is receptive of the perceptible object without its matter. That is why perceptions and appearances remain in the sense-organ even when the perceptible objects are gone" (1 425ᵇ23–25). There is no question, then, of the eye-jelly's being colored simply in this sense, that a color can be seen through it, as through a lens or windowpane.[8] The resulting similarity between the eye-jelly and the colored object is what Aristotle has in mind when he says that the parts of the soul (including understanding) have knowledge of their objects by virtue of "a certain similarity or kinship" with them (*EN* VI 1 1139ª10–11).

Stage 5: The question (call it *eye-jelly*) that we must now pursue is what the relationship is between a person's eye-jelly becoming proto-colored and the person himself seeing a color, such as vermilion, with his eye. We may begin with the relationship between proto-color and color. Light is the activity of the transparent qua transparent (*DA* II 7 418ᵇ3). It is present, therefore, when the ether is activated or actualized by a fiery body (ᵇ11). Consequently, it does not have to be perceived in order to be present. The same applies to dark, since it is just the transparent ether unactualized. What applies to light and dark, however, must also apply to ratios of light

---

[6] Also *DA* III 2 426ª27–ᵇ7.

[7] *Met.* IV 5 1010ᵇ3–11, XI 6 1062ᵇ33–1063ª5; *EN* X 5 1176ª13–16. Glaucoma (*glaukôma*)—from *glaukos,* meaning bluish-green or grey—was originally the disease we now know as cataracts.

[8] Contra Burnyeat, "Is an Aristotelian Philosophy of Mind Still Credible? A Draft." The relevance of *DA* III 1 425ᵇ23–25 to Burnyeat's claim is noted by Cohen, "Hylomorphism and Functionalism," 66.

to dark: when the transparent ether takes on the right ratio by being illuminated by fire or the sun, its surface takes on the corresponding ratio of white to black. As a consequence (and this is the new stage in the account), it—or the determinately bounded object it is in—acquires a second potential, namely, the potential to be seen as vermilion by a person with an appropriately situated functioning eye.[9] For such a person has from birth a correlative second potential to see vermilion when (1) his eye-jelly is rendered actually transparent by fire or the sun, and (2) an object with the correct ratio of white to black on its surface is appropriately situated in his visual field.

These two potentials, the one of the visible object and the other of the person to see it, have a single actualization: "The actualization [activity] *(energeia)* of the perceptible object and of the sense is one and the same, although their being [essence] is not the same. I mean, e.g., actual sounding and actual hearing; for it is possible to have hearing and not to be [actually] hearing, and what has sound is not always sounding. But when what can hear is actualized and when what can sound is [actually] sounding, the actual hearing takes place at the same time as the actual sound, and one might call these, the one listening, the other sounding. If then change, i.e., affecting and being affected, is in that which is affected, both the actual sound and hearing must be in what is potentially hearing; for the actualization of that which can affect, i.e., produce change, takes place in that which is affected. . . . The same account applies also to the other senses and perceptible objects. . . . But in some cases they [i.e., the actualization of the object and that of the sense] have a name, while in others one or the other has no name; for the actualization of sight is called seeing, but that of color has no name" (*DA* III 2 425^{b}26–426^{a}13). If change, then, is in what is changed or affected, the actualization of a person's potential to see and of an object's to be seen must both be located in the person. Suppose that what underwrites this inference is that the actualization and the change are one and the same. We would then have an answer to *eye-jelly*. For the change that occurs in the eye is that the eye-jelly comes to take on the visible form of vermilion (a pattern of proto-colors), and the actual seeing

---

[9] *Met.* IV 5 1010^{b}30–1011^{a}2: "It is presumably true that [if there were no animate things] there would be neither perceptible objects nor perceptions (since they are affections of what can perceive), but it is impossible that the things that underlie [perceptible objects], those that produce the perceiving, should not exist without perception." The things that underlie colors are clearly proto-colors.

of vermilion—the actualization of the second potential to see vermilion—would be identical to that change. On this hypothesis, then, the eye-jelly's becoming appropriately proto-colored just is the seeing of vermilion.

To see why the hypothesis fails, we need to explore a peculiarity of light, which will initially seem to lend it some support: "Light is due to the presence of something, but is not a movement *(kinêsis)*. Indeed, a qualitative change *(alloiôsis)* is generally different from a movement [from one place to another] *(phora)*. For movements [from one place to another] naturally arrive first at a mid-point (and sound is held to be the movement of something moving), but with things that undergo qualitative change it is not the same. For qualitative change can occur in a thing all at once, and not in half of it first. . . . Naturally, then, the parts of a medium between an organ of perception and its object are not all affected at once—*except in the case of light,* for the reason given, *and of seeing too* for the same reason; for light produces seeing" (*Sens.* 6 446^{b}27–447^{a}11). At the same instant that an object is affected by being actually illuminated, then, all the air between it and the eye-jelly, as well as the eye-jelly itself, are simultaneously affected. Consequently, there is no transmission of light of the sort that we think is involved in vision.[10] By the same token, there is no process that is the bit-by-bit proto-coloring of the eye-jelly, since the whole of it becomes proto-colored simultaneously. Finally, there is no process of seeing. For at the very moment that light activates the second potential color of an object, it also activates the eye's second potential to see that color. It seems, then, that the eye-jelly's becoming proto-colored is an activity, just as the person's seeing vermilion is. *Prima facie,* then, they are one and the same activity.

Fortunately for Aristotle's theory of vision, matters are not so simple: "Being affected is not a single thing: it may be a sort of destruction of something by its opposite, or it may be the preservation of that which is so potentially by that which is so actually, and is like it in the way that a potentiality may be like an actuality. For that which possesses scientific knowledge becomes an actual theoretical knower, and this is either not a

---

[10] It must be admitted, however, that Aristotle is not always careful to remember this. For example, he explains keen-sightedness as the result of a thin-skin on the eye-jelly, which allows "the movement coming from without may pass straight through it" (*GA* V 1 780^{a}25–^{b}2). Similarly, the explanations he gives of various phenomena (such as haloes and rainbows) in terms of reflection of light, suggests a dynamical conception of it (*Mete.* III).

qualitative change, since the development of the thing is into itself or into actuality, or a different kind of qualitative change . . . one a change to conditions of privation, the other to a thing's state and its nature" (*DA* II 5 417^{b}2–16). Now the change that occurs when the second-potential to see vermilion is actualized is clearly the development of the thing into itself or into actuality—a *pseudo-attribute* change. What occurs in the eye-jelly, however, is not like that: it is a change from being dark to being (a ratio of) light (to dark)—a change that is the (partial) destruction of dark by its opposite. What we ought to say, then, is that whereas coming to see vermilion is an activity, a pseudo-qualitative change, the eye-jelly's taking on the visible form of vermilion (a ratio of proto-colors) is a real qualitative change, even if an instantaneous one.[11]

Our proposed solution to *eye-jelly*, then, is something like this: Just as a visual object has the second-potential to appear vermilion in virtue of having the appropriate ratio of light to dark in the transparent ether within it, so a person has the second potential to see vermilion in virtue of having an eye whose transparent jelly can undergo the qualitative change of taking on that ratio, or taking on that proto-color. In other words, eye-jelly is the hypothetically necessary matter of an organ whose form is seeing, and its taking on a proto-color constitutes, but is not identical to, seeing.[12]

Resourceful as this six-stage account of color and seeing is, it leaves us with an overwhelming question. If the eye-jelly's taking on the visible form of vermilion constitutes seeing vermilion, why doesn't the intervening air (or any other transparent material) also see vermilion, since it too takes on that form? Put another way, what is it about the eye-jelly that explains why its taking on a visible form constitutes seeing? It is a problem of which Aristotle himself is all too aware:

> *DA* II 12 424^{b}3–18 Someone might raise the problem of whether what cannot smell might be affected by a smell, or what cannot see by a color; and similarly in the other cases. [^{b}5] If the object of smell is a smell, a smell must produce, if anything, smelling; hence nothing that is unable to smell can be affected by a smell (and the same account applies to the other cases), nor [^{b}8] can any of those things that can

---

[11] *Ph.* VII 2 244^{b}10–12: "The senses also undergo a sort of qualitative change, since actual perception is a change through the body in the course of which the sense is affected in a certain way."

[12] A conclusion reached by a different (and somewhat less satisfactory) route in Sorabji's justly influential "Body and Soul in Aristotle."

perceive [something] be so affected except qua possessing the potential [to smell]. This is clear at the same time from the following too. *[ᵇ10]* Light and dark, sound and smell do not do anything to bodies, but rather the things they are in [do so], e.g., it is the air accompanying the thunderclap that splits the wood. But *[ᵇ12]* tangible objects and flavors do affect bodies; for otherwise by what could inanimate things be affected and altered? *[ᵇ14a]* Must we not, then, admit that those other objects also affect them? Or *[ᵇ14b]* is it the case that not every body is affected by smell and sound, and those which are affected are indeterminate and unstable, like air (for air smells, as if it had been affected)? *[ᵇ16]* What then is smelling apart from being affected? Or *[ᵇ17]* is smelling perceiving,[13] whereas *[ᵇ18]* air when affected quickly becomes a perceptible object?

What is under discussion here is color and the like as second potentials. That is why *ᵇ5* is an obvious and uncontroversial Aristotelian truth: actualize a color (smell) and you must, and can only, actualize the potential to see (smell). For these actualizations, as we saw, are one and the same. *ᵇ10–ᵇ18* then offers a second argument for the same conclusion, which focuses on perceptible objects considered as the equivalent of ratios of light to dark— that is to say, on those non-perception-relative states of things (proto-colors, proto-sounds, and so on) that guarantee the possession of the sort of second potentials considered in *ᵇ5–ᵇ8*. Notice that it is precisely "light and dark" not black and white that are mentioned in *ᵇ10*.

ᵇ14b suggests that what is at issue is whether certain proto-perceptibles affect bodies in general. And what *ᵇ10* says on this score is that proto-color (light and dark), proto-sound, and proto-smell do not affect bodies in general, although what they are in, namely, air (in the case of proto-sound and proto-smell) or transparent material (in the case of light and dark) may do so. The example makes clear what Aristotle means. Proto-sound "is a particular movement of air" (*DA* II 8 420ᵇ11). So it cannot affect wood. But the moving air, which is one body, can affect wood, which is another. Similarly, in the case of light. It is not light (dark) as such that heats (non-transparent) earth, but the fire that the light is in.

Tangible objects and flavors are conjoined in *ᵇ12* because, in Aristotle's view, "taste is a sort of touch" (*Sens.* 4 441ᵃ3)—a sense whose proper objects are (proto-perceptible) "hot and cold, dry and wet, rough and

---

[13] Reading ὀσμᾶσθαι αἰσθάνεσθαι with the mss. See Kosman, "Perceiving that we Perceive: *On the Soul* III, 2."

smooth, and [all] the others like that" (*DA* II 11 422^{b}26–27). So what $^b12$ is asking is this: if bodies—"soulless things"—aren't affected by these objects, what is there left for them to be affected by?

Consistency, or the desire to have a uniform theory of proto-perceptibles as a whole, might lead us to conclude that all bodies are affected not just by proto-tangibles and proto-flavors, but by proto-colors, proto-sounds, and the rest (*^b14a*). But that would be a mistake (*^b14b*). For just as proto-color affects only transparent material, proto-smell and proto-sound affect only air or other similarly indeterminate and unstable materials. Proto-smell, however, does genuinely affect air—it makes it smell. Hence we face a problem. For it seemed that what smell produces can only be smelling—a kind of perception (*$^b5$, $^b8$*). That is why $^b16$ asks what smelling as a perception is, if it isn't being affected by proto-smell, in the way that air is affected by it.

$^b17$–$^b18$ provides the answer. The reception by our nasal tissues (the analog of the eye-jelly) of the perceptible form of a proto-smell results in our smelling a smell. $^b5$ explains why, and $^b17$ appeals to that explanation again. The reception of the perceptible-form of a proto-smell by those tissues results in our smelling a smell because we have the potential to smell a smell in such circumstances. When air receives that very same form, however, it undergoes a qualitative change which results in its acquiring a second potential to smell not smells, but smelly (*$^b18$*). For, unlike us, it lacks the potential to smell smells.

We are bound to find this explanation disappointing, since it leaves the possession of our potential to perceive unexplained. But we had better be clear about the precise focus of our disappointment. For Aristotle can, of course, point out that we have the potential in question in virtue (and now I focus once again on sight) not just of having eye-jelly, but of having eye-jelly that is functionally integrated into the perceptual system of the soul of a living animal. For, strictly speaking, it is not the eye-jelly that sees, or even the soul, but the entire functioning human being: "To say that the soul is angry is as if one were to say that the soul weaves or builds. For it is surely better not to say that the soul pities, learns, or understands, but that a human being does these things by virtue of his soul" (*DA* I 4 408^{b}11–15). This difference in functional integration between eye-jelly and air, then, might be what grounds the difference in their potentials, just as failing to have matter that is a mean of the appropriate sort is part of the reason why a plant lacks the potential to perceive heat, even though it can be warmed by the sun.[14] In this respect, therefore, Aristotle may be no worse off than a contemporary physiologist who must explain the capacity of the eye to see by appealing to its connections to the central nervous system and the brain.[15]

The real focus of our disappointment should be the account of color and the nature of the constraints that it imposes (or fails to impose) on the material constitution of the eye-jelly. In a nutshell, the problem is this: proto-colors are themselves colors of a sort, and so the eye-jelly must be structurelessly transparent in order to detect them. As such, however, it all but disappears, theoretically speaking, since it contributes next to nothing to the theory of how colors are perceived. Alternatively, and in a more theory-laden idiom, we might say that because proto-colors are what cause color perception, but are themselves a sort of color, we cannot expect the same sort of explanatory riches to flow from Aristotle's theory of vision as do so from a theory in which proto-colors are not color-like, but 'primary qualities' of an entirely different sort. For when proto-colors cease to be color-like, when what plays their role in a theory of vision is something unlike color, the question of how the eye must be structured to detect color—to be affected by these primary qualities—offers the possibility of genuine insight into vision.

It would be wrong, however, not to give Aristotle enormous credit for constructing a theory of vision that recognizes the need for something like proto-colors, and that responds to that need with great ingenuity. That should not blind us, however, to the fact that his theory of vision is almost exclusively a theory of visible objects—a theory of color. His theory of the psychological side of vision, by contrast, is, as I've said, almost as theoretically invisible as the eye-jelly itself is transparent. This too will prove important—and oddly more of a benefit than a liability—when we turn to understanding.

---

[14] *DA* II 12 424ª32–ᵇ3: "It is also clear why plants do not perceive, although they have a part of the soul [i.e., nutritive soul] and are affected by tangible objects; for they are cooled and warmed. The reason is that they do not have a mean, nor a first principle of the kind such as to receive the forms of perceptible objects [without the matter]; rather they are affected by the matter as well." A plant becomes hot by taking in new matter that is already hot. See Hicks, *Aristotle De Anima,* ad loc.

[15] Everson, *Aristotle on Perception,* especially Chapter 4.

Though it will not have any analog in the case of understanding, it is worth adding, if only to avoid giving the false impression that there is no more to Aristotle's theory of vision than his account of seeing colors, that color perception—perception of the special objects of sight—is no more than the first stage in all seeing. A second stage is seeing that a given color array is, for example, a man. A third is seeing common-objects: motion, rest, number, figure, size. Second- and third-stage perception involve common sense, which is not a faculty or sense organ distinct from the five special senses, but one that comes into play when they (or some of them) act simultaneously. It is a point of their common convergence, located near the heart, and connected to it by the circulatory system.[16]

Because seeing colors is presupposed by all other seeing, suniversal forms cannot be seen, since they are not colored (*APo.* I 31 87^{b}27–39). That is one reason for the sharp divide between the visible (and indeed the perceptible in general), on the one hand, and the intelligible, on the other.

7.2 Passive Understanding

A human being has understanding *(nous)* and so can understand *(noein)*. When he is engaged in the activity of understanding *(noêsis)*, what he is understanding is an intelligible object *(noêma)*. Understanding, then, is similar in structure to perceiving. Hence "it must be unaffected, but capable of receiving the form, and be potentially such as it [the intelligible object], although not identical to it; and as that which is capable of perceiving is to perceptible objects, so must the understanding be to intelligible ones" (*DA* III 4 429^{a}13–18).[17] Now the understanding that receives the intelligible form is like the eye-jelly. For just as the latter must take on the perceptible form of whatever is seen, so some element in the understanding must take on the intelligible form of whatever is understood, and must be potentially similar or akin, but not identical, to it. For, as in the case of seeing, what this element takes on is the form of the intelligible object without its matter: "understanding is a potential for being such things without their matter" (430^{a}7–8).

The element in question is "passive understanding *(pathêtikos nous)*" (*DA*

---

[16] *DA* II 6 418^{a}17–20, III 1 425^{a}31–^{b}3, 2 426^{b}17–427^{a}14, 3 428^{b}17–24.

[17] Also *Met.* XII 7 1072^{b}19–24.

III 5 430ª24–25). It "serves as matter for each kind of thing,"[18] and this is "what is potentially each of them." In addition "there is also something else that is its [understanding's] cause and that is productive, in that it produces it—the two being related as, e.g., a craft to its matter [materials]" (430ª10–13). This second element is productive understanding *(nous poiêtikos)*.[19]

Because understanding has these two components, it will be convenient to treat them separately, beginning in this section with passive understanding. All psychological potentials, as we know, including understanding, are associated with superlunary-body or ether, and have degrees of value that are themselves determined by differences in it (*GA* II 3 736ᵇ29–737ª1)— specifically, in its thinness and clarity: "Some animals whose [vital fluid] [20] is very subtle [or smooth] have a very subtle understanding *(dianoia)*. This is due not to the coldness of their blood,[21] but rather to its greater thinness and clarity. For what is earthy has neither of these characteristics. For the thinner and purer is [an animal's vital fluid], the more easily changed is its [organ of] perception" (*PA* II 4 650ᵇ18–24). Since human understanding is of very high value,[22] the ether with which it is associated, must be especially thin and clear.

Since understanding is based in ether of this sort, it is hardly surprising that its level or quality is determined by the latter's degree of thinness and clarity. What *is* surprising, however, is the number of other things that Aristotle also attributes to the same cause:

> *PA IV 10 686ª25–687ª2* Instead of having forelegs and forefeet, man has arms and so-called hands. For [ª27] man is the only animal that stands upright, and this is because his nature, i.e., his substance [essence], is divine. Now [ª28] the function of that which is most divine is

---

[18] Hence it is called *nous hulikos* (matter-like understanding) by Ps. Alexander.

[19] Brentano, "*Nous Poiêtikos*" provides a succinct review of ancient, medieval, and more recent discussions.

[20] In 3.3–4, we saw that ether is contained in the vital fluid or blood.

[21] As was suggested earlier by a less precise formulation at *PA* II 2 648ª2–4: "The thicker [i.e., earthier] the blood is, the more it is conducive to strength; the subtler and colder, the more conducive to perception and understanding."

[22] *EE* VII 14 1248ª28–29: "what could be superior in quality to scientific knowledge and understanding besides God?"

to understand *(noein)* and to exercise wisdom *(phronein);* and this would not be easy if there were a great deal of the body at the top weighing it down, for weight hampers the movement [or change] of understanding *(dianoia)* and of the common sense. Thus when the weight, i.e., the body-like quality [of the soul], becomes too great, the body itself must lurch forward toward the ground; and then, for pres-ervation's sake, nature provides forefeet instead of arms and hands—as has happened in quadrupeds . . . because their soul could not sustain the weight bearing it down. . . . In fact, compared with man, all other animals are dwarf-like [i.e., top-heavy]. . . . That is why all animals are less wise *(aphronestera)* than man. *[ᵇ23]* Even among human beings, indeed, children . . . though possessing some other exceptional capacity, are inferior in the possession of understanding *(nous)* as compared to adults. *[ᵇ26]* The reason . . . is that in many of them²³ the first principle of the soul is movement-hampered and body-like in quality. And *[ᵇ28]* if the heat that raises the organism upright wanes still further and the earthly matter waxes, then the animals' bodies also wane, and they will be many footed; and *[ᵇ30]* finally they lose their feet altogether and lie full length on the ground. Proceeding a little further in this way, they actually have their first principle down below, and finally the head part comes to have neither movement nor sensa-tion and what you have is a plant, which has its upper parts below and its lower parts above; for in plants the roots have the capacity of mouth and head, whereas the seed counts as the opposite, being produced in the upper part of the plant on the ends of the twigs.

ᵃ27 connects man's upright stance with his possessing a divine nature or essence. ᵃ28 explains the connection: too much weight in the upper body not only bends it over, so that it cannot walk upright on two feet, but makes understanding difficult. ᵇ28 gives the reason for this: the heat—that is to say, the formative heat or ether—that makes the body upright is overcome by the earthy matter. ᵇ30 extends the explanation from quad-rupeds to snakes and plants (which are, so to speak, upside-down humans) to give us a version of part of the familiar *scala naturae.* Continued further, it would lead to the elements themselves.

ᵇ23 explains why children have less understanding than adults, and why the acquisition of understanding is a process of maturation: "spirit, wish,

---

²³ Reading πολλοῖς δὴ with Peck.

and also appetite are present in children right from birth, whereas reasoning *(logismos)* and understanding *(nous)* naturally develop as they grow older" (*Pol.* VII 15 1334^{b}22–25). But the base of passive understanding is of course present in the developing fetus from conception, having entered as ether (natural formative heat) from the male progenitor's seed (3.4). Where children are deficient, as ^{a}28 makes clear, is in their capacity for the active productive understanding that is the truly divine element in us.[24]

The reason for this deficiency is that children have not acquired the scientific knowledge, or engaged in the aporematic clarification of first principles, that alone results in understanding's actively grasping its objects.[25] The material explanation of their deficiency, on the other hand, is given in ^{b}26: the ether in which their passive understanding is based is earthier, and so less clear, than in upright adults. Since this results in their being top-heavy, it also explains why they are dwarf-like, and why, almost as if they were quadrupeds, they crawl around on all fours (*PA* IV 10 686^{b}8–14). Clarity in ether, therefore, accompanies the intellectual clarity effected by scientific training and dialectic as its basis in matter.

It is not just between species, then, but within them as well, that differences in the clarity (or earthiness) of ether are associated with the possession of different psychological potentials, or with the same one (in this instance, understanding) possessed or developed to different degrees. Moreover, in both cases, what is gradualist at the level of ether may be saltatory (or step-like) at the level of psychological potentials themselves: "Even the other animals mostly possess traces of the characteristics having to do with soul, such as present more evident differences in the case of

---

[24] *Met.* XII 7 1072^{b}22–23: "[active or productive understanding] rather than the former [passive understanding] seems to be the divine element that understanding possesses."

[25] *Pr.* XXX 5 955^{b}25–956^{a}6: "Understanding is one of the things that are in us by nature as a tool, i.e., whereas the other sciences and crafts are among the things made by us, understanding is one of those things we have by nature. . . . Understanding is of most assistance to us not in early life but when we get older, and is then most of all complete, unless it become disabled by something, as may happen also to the other things we have by nature. [Completed] understanding comes to us later than the potential to use our hands, because the tools used by the understanding are posterior to those used by the hands. For scientific knowledge is a tool . . . [Completed] understanding . . . comes to us when we are older, but we learn more quickly when we are young because we do not yet have any scientific knowledge."

human beings. For tameness and wildness, gentleness and roughness, courage and cowardice, timidity and boldness, temper and mischievousness are
present in many of them together with semblances of intelligent understanding *(dianoian suneseôs)*, like those we spoke of in the case of the bodily
parts. For some [characteristics] differ to a greater or lesser degree compared
with man, as does man compared with a majority of the animals (for certain
characteristics of this kind are present to a greater degree in man, certain
others to a greater degree in the other animals), while others differ by
analogy: for corresponding to craft knowledge, theoretical wisdom, and
understanding *(sunesis)* in man, certain animals possess another natural
capacity of a similar sort. This sort of thing is most evident if we look at the
period of childhood; for in children, though one can see traces and seeds of
the states they will have later, yet their soul at this period has practically no
difference from that of wild beasts, so that it is not unreasonable that some
characteristics are the same in the other animals [as in man], while others are
very similar, and still others [only] analogous" (*HA* VIII 1 588^{a}18–^{b}4).[26]
There are, then, three classes of psychological potentials or characteristics:
those that are the same in humans and other animals; those that humans
have to one degree, other animals to other degrees; and those of which
other animals possess only semblances or analogs—as fish, in possessing
scales, possess only an analog of feathers. Since craft knowledge, theoretical
wisdom, and understanding are included in the third class, when Aristotle
says that the wren is "endowed with craft knowledge" (IX 11 615^{a}19) or
that the elephant "is superior in understanding *(sunesei)* to the other animals" (IX 46 630^{b}21), he is speaking analogically. Literally speaking, what
these animals have is "another natural capacity of a similar sort."

With respect to these psychological potentials, then, the difference between humans and other animals is saltatory, not gradualist. Even in their
case, however, traces or seeds of them do exist in both children and other
animals, and can be more developed in some species—or in some members of the same species—than in others.[27] Thus the saltatory change from

---

[26] I have benefited from the discussion of this passage in Coles, "Animal and
Childhood Cognition in Aristotle's Biology," 311–317.

[27] Aristotle very freely attributes an analog of *phronêsis* (practical wisdom, wisdom, intelligence) to the other animals, e.g., *HA* I 2 488^{b}15 (deer, hare), IX 5
611^{a}15–16 (deer), IX 10 614^{b}18 (cranes); *PA* II 2 648^{a}5–8 (bees and others with
thin, cold blood or similar fluid), II 4 650^{b}18–27 (ants); *GA* III 2 753^{a}10–17; *Met.* I

having no scientific knowledge, or active understanding, to having some is based in a gradual change in the clarity of the ether in which those psychological potentials are based.

Failure to distinguish these two levels (and the correlative failure adequately to distinguish passive from productive understanding) easily leads to confusion, and can make even someone sympathetic to a gradualist reading of Aristotle's *scala naturae* reluctant to include human beings (or human understanding, at any rate) on it. If we bear this distinction of level in mind, however, our gradualism at the level of ether, at least, should be uncompromising, and we should see it extending all the way from the homoeomerous stuffs to human understanding itself (and perhaps beyond). For when Aristotle tells us that all living things "have by nature something divine in them" (*EN* VII 13 1153^{b}32), or when he agrees with Heraclitus that even in a humble kitchen "divinities are present" (*PA* I 5 645^{a}20–21), he has his eye on the fact that every being, simply in virtue of having some formal element, or some psychological potential (even one as rudimentary as the potential for nutrition and growth), contains divine ether of some quality. On the other hand, when he makes saltatory claims to the effect that "nature is daemonic but not divine" (*Div. Somn.* 2 463^{b}14–15), or that "understanding alone . . . is divine" (*GA* II 3 736^{b}28) and that "other animals . . . are completely deprived of this activity" (*EN* X 8 1178^{b}24–25), or that children and beasts can be harmed by their natural virtues, because "without understanding" these "are evidently harmful" (VI 13 1144^{b}8–9), he has his eye on the psychological potentials themselves, often in their most developed or completed forms. The following texts, which to some extent combine the gradualist and the saltatory, recognize this: "of the animals known to us, man alone shares in the divine, or he most of all of them" (*PA* II 10 656^{a}7–8); all living things reproduce "in order that they may partake of the eternal and the divine in so far as they can" (*DA* II 4 415^{b}3–4); understanding, "whether or not it is itself divine," is certainly "the most divine thing in us" (*EN* X 7 1177^{a}15–16).

How should we interpret these results? Are human beings on the *scala naturae* or not? Is the scale itself saltatory or gradualist? The answer is not simple, although, given what we have established so far, there is nothing

---

1 980^{b}22–25 (bees and others). Generally speaking, though, *phronêsis* has a quite limited focus in these animals as, e.g., *HA* IX 6 makes clear. The same is true of the *dianoia akribeia* (exact understanding) attributed to swallows in *HA* IX 7 612^{b}18–22.

conceptually complex about it. Look back to our discussion of theoretical and natural sciences (2.4). The impression given there is that the latter deal with the natural, sublunary realm, the former with the superlunary. This impression is not wrong, exactly, coinciding as it does with some of the ways in which Aristotle draws the distinction himself—as, for example, when he contrasts "the bodies that are about us here" with those that have "a more valuable nature the more distant they are from those here" (*Cael.* I 2 269ᵇ13–17). But the impression is misleading, nonetheless, in that it fails to acknowledge the degree to which the superlunary, in the shape of divine ether or formative heat, penetrates the natural, and so unites the natural and the superlunary into a single realm: "God has the first seat in the highest place, and for this reason is called supreme, since, according to the poet, it is on 'the loftiest peak' of the whole heavens that he dwells. His capacity is experienced most by the body that is closest to him [i.e., the primary heaven], less by the next, and so on down to the regions inhabited by us. So earth and the things that are on earth, being at the first remove from God's help, seem to be feeble and discordant and full of confusion and diversity. Nevertheless, since it is the nature of the divine to penetrate everything, it is the same in the case of the things around us as with those above, each having a greater or smaller share of God's help in proportion to its distance from him" (*Mu.* 6 397ᵇ24–398ᵃ1).²⁸ The *scala naturae,* then, is that part of the larger scale of beings, both natural and supernatural, consisting of those beings constituted from matter containing some admixture of the natural elements—beings whose essences are penmattered. The supernatural part consists of those beings whose matter (if any) contains no such admixture—beings whose essences are not penmattered.

To the degree that the human soul is penmattered, therefore, it is a natural phenomenon studied by natural science. But the matter in which a mature human understanding is based is very clear ether—ether that is not "movement-hampered and body-like in quality." When understanding is based wholly in such ether, therefore, it is not a natural phenomenon, but a supernatural one. That is why Aristotle can allow that there are parts of the

---

²⁸ *Mu.* is now universally agreed not to be a genuine work of Aristotle's, but this passage expresses doctrines that we have already seen to be genuinely Aristotelian. I cite it, therefore, as a summary of independently established conclusions, rather than as a proof text in its own right. The location attributed to God in the opening sentence is attested in *Ph.* VIII 10 267ᵇ1–9 (discussed in 8.2). The poet is Homer, *Iliad* 1 449.

human soul that will not be studied by natural, but—like God and the stars—by theoretical science (*Met.* VI 1 1026ª5–6).

7.3 Productive Understanding

Passive understanding is sufficiently straightforward in operation, I think, not to raise our philosophical hackles too high, even if its basis is rather peculiar. Productive understanding is another kettle of fish altogether. Its very name, indeed, is problematic, since just what it produces and just how it does so are unclear: "And to the understanding, so characterized, that becomes all things there corresponds the understanding that makes all of them, as some kind of state, like light, does; for in a way light too makes potential colors into actual ones" (*DA* III 5 430ª14–17). For how could productive understanding make cows, for example, in the way that light makes potential colors actual?

If an object is actually proto-colored in the appropriate way, which involves its being lighted or illuminated, it has a second potential (first actuality) to appear vermilion to a normally sighted person. Thus light is part of what makes second potential vermilion into second actuality (or actually seen) vermilion, and so *in a way* makes potential colors into actual ones. Now intelligible forms are present in passive understanding precisely as second potentials (*DA* III 4 429ᵇ5–9), and productive understanding is analogous to light. What the latter does, therefore, must just be this: it must make second potentials into second actualities.[29] Passive understanding must be able to take on all intelligible forms, therefore, and productive understanding must be able to actualize all of them by actively understanding them.

Among the colors, light has a special status. For, as "the activity of the transparent qua transparent," it is a condition of any of the other colors being visible. Since productive understanding is analogous to light, it ought to have a similar status. And so it does. For just as colors can produce changes in transparent material only when it is activated by a light source, so intelligible forms can produce changes in a passive understanding only when it is activated by productive understanding: "without this [produc-

---

[29] The "Standard View"—as Kosman, "What does the Maker Mind Make?" 347, calls it—holds that productive understanding makes *first* potentials into *first* actualities. Kosman's criticisms of this view (348–352) and his own positive suggestions (352–358) to some extent anticipate my own.

tive understanding] it [passive understanding] understands nothing" (*DA* III 5 430^{a}25).

A second special feature of light is that, as a proto-color, it is itself a visible object. By parity of reasoning, productive understanding must be an intelligible one. Hence reflexive self-understanding must be possible: "When the [passive] understanding has become each thing [i.e., has taken on its intelligible form] in the way that someone who actually has scientific knowledge is said to do so [i.e., as a second potential] and this happens when he can actualize [that second potential] by himself), it exists potentially even then in a way, although not in the same way as before it was learned or discovered [i.e., as a first potential]; and then it can understand itself" (*DA* III 4 429^{b}5–9).[30] But though the transparent is visible once activated, it is not self-activating. It has to be activated—made actually transparent—by something else that is already actively transparent, such as fire or the sun. A vicious regress immediately threatens. Moreover, it is one that cannot be stopped by appeal to a chain of actually transparent beings extending infinitely backwards in time. For that appeal simply postpones the question of why there are any such beings in the first place, or why their potential transparency is ever activated at all. Something stronger is apparently needed, then, to escape these incipient regresses. In the case of transparency, it takes the form of an appeal to a being that is eternally and in essence actively transparent (fire, the sun). We should expect, therefore, that the parallel regress that threatens in the case of understanding will be cut off by an appeal to the existence of an understanding that is eternally and in essence actively understanding.

Are our expectations justified? The following text, which will be our principal target for the remainder of the section, suggests that they are:

DA III 5 430^{a}17–25 And this [productive] understanding is [*17*] separate, impassive, and unmixed, being [*18*] in substance [or essence] an activity. For what makes is always more valuable than what is affected, i.e., the first principle of the matter. . . . [*22a*] And it is not the case that it is sometimes understanding and at other times not. [*22b*] And when separated it is just what it is, and [*23*] it alone [of the components of the human soul] is immortal and eternal. [*24*] We do not remember because this [productive understanding] is unaffected, whereas the passive understanding passes–away, and [*25*] without this

---

[30] Reading δὲ αὐτον with the mss.

[productive understanding] it [passive understanding] understands nothing.

We may begin with the somewhat mysterious $^a24$, and with the theory of memory it presupposes. Memory, like understanding, has a lot in common with perception: "A problem might be raised as to how, when the affection is present but the thing [producing it] is absent, what is not present is ever remembered. For it is clear that one must understand the affection, which is produced by means of perception in the soul, and in that part of the body in which it is, as being like a sort of picture, the having of which we say is memory. For the change *(kinêsis)* that occurs stamps a sort of imprint, as it were, of the perceptible object, as people do who seal things with a signet ring. That is also why memory does not occur in those who are subject to a lot of change, because of some affection or because of their age, just as if the change and the seal were falling on running water. In others, because of wearing down, as in the old parts of buildings, and because of the hardness of what receives the affection, the imprint is not produced" (*Mem.* 1 450^a25-^b5). Thus *passive memory*, as we call it, is stamped with the perceptible form, but not the matter, and as a result the soul acquires a second potential to remember the thing responsible for the stamping.

As a psychological potential, however, passive memory must be based in ether (*GA* II 3 $736^b29-737^a1$). But this ether must be mixed with sublunary matter if memory is to (mal)function in the requisite way. For what makes it malfunction is a disproportionate admixture in its base of the earthy matter that also impairs understanding: "Those whose upper parts are especially large, i.e., those who are dwarf-like, have poorer memories than their opposites because they have a great weight resting on their perceptive faculty, and neither from the start are the changes [produced by the perceptible object] able to persist in such people and avoid being dispersed, nor during recollection do they easily take a straight course" (*Mem.* 2 453^a31-^b4). The right admixture of sublunary matter in the ether, then, is crucial if passive memory is to hold the imprint of the perceptible object in such a way as to enable recollection to function correctly.

A second reason sublunary matter must be present in passive memory brings us closer to $^a24$. In $^a22b-^a23$ we have just been told that the productive understanding is separate, immortal, and eternal. We inherit it as a potential from our male progenitor. This makes it natural to wonder why we have to learn science again rather than inheriting our knowledge of it. $^a24$ explains why. Memory is one step in the inductive process that leads from perception to understanding's grasp of suniversal essences. But passive memory, because it is partly based in sublunary matter, passes-away when its possessor dies (DA I 4 408^{b}27–29). And when it does, the understanding's second potential to grasp its contents passes-away too, since it cannot actualize a second potential that is no longer available to be actualized (III 4 429^{b}5–10). That, in a nutshell, is why we have to relearn whatever science our fathers had already learned when we were conceived, and why we do not remember their experiences.[31]

^{a}22b is next. Some terminology will help us analyze it succinctly and effectively. A substance is separate, if and only if it is primary in definition, knowledge, and time. Separation, therefore, is an all-or-nothing matter and is not time-relative: if a substance is separate at any time, it is separate at all times. x is separated from y, however, if x (or its base) is unmixed with y (or its base). This sort of separation is a matter of degree (x can be mixed with no y or very little y or a lot of y) and is time-relative (x can be mixed with y at t_1 and not at t_2). When ether is mixed with sublunary matter, then, as it is in the case of passive memory, it is not separated from it. When passive understanding is mixed with sublunary matter, neither it nor productive understanding is separated from it. But if productive understanding is separate, it is always so.

^{a}22b tells us that productive understanding is "just what it is (hoper esti)" when "separate (chôristheis)." Implicitly, it is contrasting the condition of productive understanding at one time with its condition at another. It must, then, be speaking of productive understanding as separated from some y, rather than as timelessly separate. But separated from what y? There seem to be just two possibilities: sublunary matter and ether. That it can be separated from the first is plain: "bodily actuality is in no way associated with its actuality" (GA II 3 736^{b}28–29).[32] Whether it can also be separated from ether remains to be seen.

F is just what G is, if and only if G is in essence what F is (Top. III 1 116^{a}23–28).[33] Since productive understanding is in essence an activity (^{a}18), it follows that, when separated from the relevant y, productive understanding is an activity. This would not be so, however, if productive

---

[31] This account of ^{a}24 replaced the inadequate one given in Practices of Reason, 146 n. 11.

[32] Also DA I 1 403^{a}3–16.

[33] Barnes, Aristotle Posterior Analytics, 176.

understanding were not then separated from *all* unactualized potential. Hence, if the ether base of passive understanding is a repository of such potential, productive understanding must also be separated from it, even when passive understanding is actualized.

^{a}22a tells us that there is no time at which productive understanding is not active. Is the understanding always understanding, then, as a Cartesian ego is always thinking? Aristotle's views on sleep show us that the answer is no: "Sleep is not every incapacity of the perceptual faculty, but rather this affection arises from the evaporation that attends eating food. For that which is vaporized must be driven on to a given point and then must turn back and change just like the tide in a narrow strait. In every animal the hot naturally rises, but when it has reached the upper parts, it turns back, and moves downward in a mass. That is why sleepiness mostly occurs after eating food, for then a large watery and earthy mass is carried upward. When this comes to a stop, therefore, it weighs a person down and makes him nod off; but when it has actually sunk downward, and by its return has driven back the hot, then sleepiness comes on and the animal falls asleep" (*Somn.* 3 456^{b}17–28). Sleep, then, affects the faculty of perception. But it also affects the understanding: an understanding that is "understanding nothing . . . would be just like someone asleep" (*Met.* XII 9 1074^{b}17–18). For an understanding that is understanding nothing, that is not in contact with any intelligible object, is *ipso facto* not active (7 1072^{b}20–23).

Given its mode of operation, however, sleep can affect the understanding only though operating on a passive understanding that is not separated from sublunary matter. For what puts understanding to sleep is the presence of too much vaporized food (a type of sublunary matter) in its base: "When someone changes from drunkenness, sleep, or disease we do not say that he has acquired scientific knowledge again—even though he was unable to use his knowledge [while drunk etc.] . . . For it is due to the soul's stopping its natural restlessness that something becomes practical wisdom or scientific knowledge. . . . In some cases nature itself causes the soul to settle down and come to a state of rest, while in other cases other things do so. But in either case *the result is brought about through the alteration of something in the body,* as we see in the case of the use and activity [of practical wisdom or scientific knowledge], when someone becomes sober or wakes from sleep" (*Ph.* VII 3 247^{b}13–248^{a}6).[34] It seems, then, that sleep

---

[34] I owe notice of this passage to van der Eijk, "The Matter of Mind: Aristotle on the Biology of 'Psychic' Processes," 242–243.

constitutes "the reason why it [understanding] is not always understanding *(noein)*" (*DA* III 4 430ª5–6) that Aristotle promises to consider in *De Anima* but never explicitly does.

Because sleep operates in the way it does, it cannot affect an understanding the base of which is not mixed with sublunary matter. Since only an understanding that has survived the passing-away of its associated compound, and so is out of causal contact with all such matter, is in that condition, it is to such an understanding that ª22a must refer. Notice, however, that even before the compound passes away, being mixed with sublunary matter is, as it were, a pathological condition of the understanding, associated with immaturity and drowsiness.

Returning now to the question we left hanging a few paragraphs back, what we should say about productive understanding's separation from the base of passive understanding is this: Productive understanding, as an activity, would have to be separated from this base if the latter were the repository of potentials other than the one actualized in productive understanding itself. When the base is mixed with sublunary matter, the resulting mixture is such a repository, since sublunary matter is never an activity. But the base itself, as separated from sublunary matter, is not one. Productive understanding, then, though separated from sublunary matter, is not separate from the ether that is the base of passive understanding, since it just is that base activated.

This brings us to ª23. Productive understanding is "immortal and eternal." Does this mean that a particular productive understanding, such as Socrates', has always existed and will always exist? No: "The understanding seems to be born in us as a sort of substance, and not to pass-away. For it would be destroyed most of all by the feebleness of old age, while as things are what happens is similar to what happens in the case of the organs of perception. For if an old man acquired an eye of a certain kind, he would see even as well as a young man. Hence old age is not due to the soul's being affected in a certain way, but to this happening to what the soul is in, as in the case of drunkenness and disease. Understanding, then, and in particular theoretical understanding, are extinguished because something else within passes-away, but it itself is unaffected" (*DA* I 4 408ᵇ18–25). There is no suggestion, notice, that the birth of understanding in us might simply be the incarnation or re-incarnation of something preexisting. Nonetheless, once born, understanding seems to be immortal. It is extinguished *in our bodies* at our death, because something else passes-away at that point, namely, the mixture of ether and sublunary matter that is the base of passive understanding. But it itself remains unaffected.[35]

The immortality thus attributed to productive understanding, though less philosophically unappealing than actual eternity or backwards immortality would be, has a clear liability which the latter lacks. It is this: a merely immortal productive understanding cannot halt the vicious regress we looked at earlier. True, each human being inherits his understanding from his male progenitor. True also that the chain of such progenitors stretches infinitely backwards in time, and so has no first member. But the existence of any active, productive understandings on the chain remains to be explained. Why aren't they all just passive and inactive? That question, to the degree that it is truly pressing, is an as yet unmet challenge.

$^a17$ remains for analysis. That productive understanding is impassive we know, since it is only passive understanding that is affected and changed by taking on an intelligible form. That it is unmixed (with sublunary matter) we also know. For again it is passive understanding (or, more precisely, its base) that is mixed with such matter. But what about separation? Is $^a17$, like ^a22b, telling us that productive understanding is separated from something-or-other? No. For given that productive understanding is "born in us as a sort of substance," it is reasonable to suppose that the separation attributed to it in $^a17$ is not time-relative. It should follow, therefore, that productive understanding is a separate substance even when passive understanding is not separated from sublunary matter. And this seems to be Aristotle's view: "Since the virtues of the compound are human virtues, the life and happiness expressing them is also human. The [happiness] of understanding, however, is separate" (*EN* X 8 1178^{a}20–22). In any case, if productive understanding is to be a separate substance, that is what he must hold.

---

[35] It is noteworthy that in *Met.* XII 3 1070^{a}22–26 Aristotle is much more tentative even about the immortality of productive understanding: "When a human being is healthy, then health exists too, and the form of a bronze sphere exists at the same time as the bronze sphere. But we must investigate whether any [form] survives afterwards. For in some cases there is nothing to prevent this, e.g., the soul may be like this—not all soul, but understanding; for presumably it is impossible that all soul should survive." All he claims here is that *there is nothing to prevent* a productive understanding from being immortal and eternal. For understanding, as an activity, has no built in terminus, and so need never stop.

7.4 Self-Understanding

In this section and the next, we shall be examining a series of problems that stand in the way of treating productive understanding as a separate substance. The first of these, which is our principal focus here, is *content*. Productive understanding is a separate substance that is in essence an activity. Understanding is an activity only when it is actually in contact with an intelligible object. Hence there must be some intelligible object that understanding can be in contact with even when passive understanding is separated from sublunary matter. The problem is that the way understanding operates seems to preclude this possibility. Intelligible forms taken on by passive understanding have their origins in perceptible forms taken on by eye-jelly and the like, and are reached from them by induction, abstraction, and aporematic clarification. But when passive understanding is separated from sublunary matter, so that it is no longer in functional contact with a human animal's perceptual apparatus and memory, how is it to gain access to any forms at all? It seems to follow that productive understanding cannot be a separate substance. For if passive understanding were separated from sublunary matter, productive understanding would have no intelligible object to understand—no content. But without content, it cannot be an activity.

Content is a difficult problem, but Aristotle has an ingenious solution to it—one that relies on a fact about understanding that we have thus far noted only in passing, namely, that it is reflexive (*DA* III 4 429^{b}9–10). The problem is to explain how this is possible. In the following extended text Aristotle raises the problem and attempts to solve it—as before the analogy with sight bears the brunt of the explanatory burden:

> *DA* III 4 429^{a}18– 430^{a}7 [Understanding], since [^{a}18] it understands all things, must be unmixed . . . and hence [^{a}21] it must have no other nature than this—that it is potentially [something]. That part of the soul, then, called understanding (and I mean by understanding that by which the soul understands and grasps [things]) is in actuality none of the beings [i.e., none of the intelligible forms] before it is [actually] understanding [one of them]. Hence too, [^{a}24] it is reasonable that it should not be mixed with the body; for in that case it would come to be of a certain kind, either hot or cold, or it would have an organ as perception does; but as things stand it has none. Those who say, then, that [^{a}27] the soul is a place of forms speak well, except that it is not

the whole soul [that is so], but that [part of it] which can understand, and it is not actually but potentially the forms. . . . [*b*22] Given, then, that the understanding is something pure [i.e., unmixed] and un-affected, and that it has nothing in common with anything else, as Anaxagoras says, someone might raise these problems: [*b*24] how will it understand, if understanding is being affected in some way (for it is insofar as two things have something in common that the one is held to affect and the other to be affected)? And [*b*26] can it itself also be understood?. . . . [*b*29] Being affected in virtue of something com-mon has been discussed before—to the effect that [*b*30] the under-standing is somehow potentially the intelligible objects, although it is nothing in actuality before it understands [them]; potentially in the same way as there is writing on a wax tablet on which there is nothing actually written; that is precisely how it is in the case of the under-standing. [30*a*2a] And it is an intelligible object in just the way its [other] objects are. For, [30*a*2b] in the case of those things that have no matter, that which understands and that which is understood are the same, since [30*a*4] theoretical scientific knowledge and what is known in that way are the same. . . . [30*a*6] In those that have matter each of the intelligible objects is present potentially.

Some general claims are made here about what features the understanding must have (*a*18–*a*27). Then two problems are raised about how it can possess these features (*b*24–*b*26), which the remainder of the text tries to solve (*b*30–30*a*6).

The understanding is the place of intelligible forms (*a*27), which are the special-objects of understanding—the analogs of colors in the case of sight. Since the understanding can understand all such forms (*a*18), the only nature its passive component can have is that of being potentially each of them (*a*21)—a potential it has in virtue of being based in very clear ether. For if the passive understanding actually had one of the intelligible forms as its own, it wouldn't be able to take it on, or to take on any other form incompatible with it. (Compare the argument that leads Aristotle to con-clude that the eye-jelly must be transparent.)

For essentially the same reason, understanding cannot be mixed with (sublunary) body (*a*24). For such a body must, for example, have some degree of heat, and so must have within it the essence that is the intelligible form of heat. Consequently, if the (passive component of) the understand-ing were mixed with it, it would have the intelligible form of heat as its own. As a result, it could not take on that form or any others incompatible with it. Another way in which the understanding could be mixed with the body, however, is by having a bodily organ, an analog of the eye. But it has no such organ (ᵃ24).

Now for the problems and their solution. If (passive) understanding is a pure potentiality, how can it be affected by intelligible forms? For what is affected must have something in common with what affects it, since affecting and being affected are the same event (the same actuality) described from two different perspectives (ᵇ24). ᵇ30 answers that although (passive) understanding has nothing in common with an intelligible object before being affected by it, at the moment it is affected and becomes active, it does have something in common with that object, since it shares its intelligible form. The case of seeing is exactly analogous: the eye-jelly has nothing in common with the visible object until, through being affected by it, it comes to share its visible form.

If passive understanding is a pure potentiality, however, without any determinate nature of its own (ᵃ21), how can it be an intelligible object (ᵇ26)? This problem is analogous to the following one about seeing: how can a perfectly transparent object be visible? Not surprisingly, it receives an analogous solution: just as the latter is visible "because of the color of something else" (*DA* II 7 418ᵇ4–6), so the passive understanding becomes an intelligible object through taking on the intelligible form of something else: "Understanding understands itself in partaking of the intelligible object; for it becomes an intelligible object in coming into contact with and understanding its objects, so that understanding and the intelligible object are the same. For that which can receive the intelligible object, i.e., the substance, is understanding. And it is an activity when it possesses it" (*Met.* XII 7 1072ᵇ20–23). If what passive understanding takes on is the intelligible form of something *else*, however, how can understanding it amount to *self*-understanding? In general, it can't. But in some cases, productive understanding is identical to the intelligible object it is grasping (30ᵃ2b). Let us call this the *Identity Thesis*.

30ᵃ4 tells us that the theoretical scientific knowledge of F is identical to F itself. But the theoretical sciences, as we know, are those the ontological first principles of which are nonpenmattered essences or forms. This suggests that the class referred to in 30ᵃ2b consists more particularly of those things that have no sublunary matter. It follows that Socrates' essence, as penmattered, should not satisfy the Identity Thesis. But is this true?

Socrates' essence is his soul, which is "the first actuality of a natural body that has life potentially" (*DA* II 1 412ª27–28). When passive understanding takes on that essence, however, so that productive understanding is actively understanding it, it is no longer a first but a second actuality—just as a second-potential color, when actually seen, is a second actuality. That is why the intelligible object, the object of productive understanding, is "present potentially" in a hylomorphic compound *(30ᶦ6)*. The bearing of the fact on the Identity Thesis will become clear in a moment.

A penmattered essence, $|F|$, present in passive understanding, is a second potential—a suniversal. When actualized in productive understanding, however, it is an intelligible particular, $|F|^\star$. Here again is the proof text: "Scientific knowledge, like knowing scientifically, is of two kinds, one potential, one actual. The potential—being (as matter) universal and indefinite—is of what is universal and indefinite, but the actual, being a this, is of a this. It is only [coincidentally] that sight sees universal color, because this color which it sees is *a* color, and this A, which is the object the grammarian has [actual] theoretical knowledge of, is *an* A" (*Met.* XIII 10 1087ª15–21). But because $|F|$ is penmattered, it contains a universal material component $|m|$. If this were not so, F could, for all its essence would show to the contrary, be an unchanging mathematical object. For matter is a first principle of change, and $|m|$ is its representative in F's essence. Because $|F|$ contains $|m|$, $|F|^\star$ must contain its actualization, $|m|^\star$. Now $|m|^\star$ cannot be a piece of perceptible matter, since it is part of an intelligible object, and it cannot be such matter taken universally, since it is part of a particular. Instead, it is the material component of $|F|^\star$, of *this* intelligible object—the intelligible analog of the perceptible matter of *this* hylomorphic compound.[36]

So the question we want to answer is as follows: is $|F|$, when actualized in productive understanding, identical to the productive understanding of F? Is $|F|^\star$ identical to $U|F|$? And the answer is obviously no. For $U|F|$ is an activity; it contains no mere potential, no matter. But $|F|^\star$ contains $|m|^\star$, and so cannot be an activity. It follows that the Identity Thesis does not hold in the case of penmattered essences, and for the very reason that *30ᶦ6* states.

What, then, of the following suggestion to the contrary? "In some cases, isn't the scientific knowledge the object? *In productions, isn't it the substance,*

---

[36] The italicized pronoun thus effects what Aquinas calls a *demonstratio ad intellectum*—an indexical reference to the content of a particular thought. See Geach, *Mental Acts,* 74, 118.

i.e., the essence, without the matter? In theoretical sciences, isn't it the account, the object, and the [productive] understanding?" (*Met.* XII 9 1074^{b}38–1075^{a}3).[37] As in a few other texts, the division of the sciences into productive and theoretical is here implicitly exhaustive.[38] Thus the productive sciences are not being singled out; they are simply standing proxy for all non-theoretical sciences. What is being claimed about such sciences, moreover, cannot be that their objects satisfy the Identity Thesis, but simply that their objects are essences without matter—that is, without the actual matter of the hylomorphic compound whose essences they are. For if the objects of productive sciences did satisfy the Identity Thesis, the same would have to hold of the penmattered essences that are the first principles of the natural sciences—and so of all essences. But if the Identity Thesis were as broad in scope as that, *30^{e}6* would be unintelligible. For it seems to be describing cases in which the Identity Thesis does not hold. Moreover, we would be left wondering why the Identity Thesis is argued for by appeal to theoretical science alone in *30^{d}4,* or why that text is so insistent that it is things known "in that way" to which it applies.

The Identity Thesis does not hold—and is not being claimed to hold—of penmattered essences. But does it hold of $|G|$, which is the matterless first principle of a theoretical science? Is $|G|^\star$ identical to $U|G|$? Because $|G|$ is matterless, $|G|^\star$ has no material component, no unactualized potential. Hence $|G|^\star$ is an activity just like $U|G|$. Indeed, they are one and the same activity, since $U|G| - |G|$ actualized in the productive understanding—just is $|G|^\star$. Thus *30^{d}4* correctly specifies the scope of the Identity Thesis: it holds of only those essences that are the objects of theoretical scientific knowledge.

With the Identity Thesis now restricted to matterless essences, a solution to *content* seems within reach. When productive understanding is actually separate even from the base of passive understanding, it has no access to remembered penmattered essences, or to those reached by abstraction from them. Hence, like a Cartesian ego with nothing to think, its existence seems threatened by vacuity. Productive understanding is a separate substance, however, and so in essence an activity. Hence its essence is matterless. Hence the science that has its essence as a first principle is a theoretical science falling within the scope of the Identity Thesis. Hence

---

[37] The best mss of this text are untidy. Brunschwig, "Lambda 9: A Short-Lived Thought-Experiment" includes a careful discussion of the problems.

[38] *EE* I 5 1216^{b}6–21, II 3 1221^{b}5–6, 11 1227^{b}29–30.

$$U \,|\text{productive understanding}| \; = \; |\text{productive understanding}|\,\star$$

It follows that there is one thing that seemingly can serve as productive understanding's intelligible object, even when the compound with which productive understanding is associated has passed-away, namely, itself. Thus the threat of vacuity is at least postponed, and *content* partly solved.

One reason *content* is only partly solved has to do with the role of appearances in understanding. All animal perception involves imagination *(phantasia, to phantastikon)* and its objects, which are appearances *(phantasmata)*. These are "like sense-perceptions *(aisthêmata)*" (*DA* III 8 432ª9), but can persist after the perception that gives rise to them has ceased (III 3 428ᵇ25–429ª5). As retainable contents, appearances are crucial to memory (*Mem.* 1 451ª15–16), but they are also crucial to understanding, since "to the understanding soul appearances serve as perceptions" (*DA* III 7 431ª14–15). Consequently, "when someone has theoretical knowledge *(theôrein)* [of something] he must at the same time have theoretical knowledge of an appearance" (8 432ª8–9).[39] As a result, it seems that productive understanding cannot have itself as its content, if it cannot have an appearance of itself as its content at the same time. Appearances, however, seem available only to an understanding that is part of a hylomorphic compound equipped with a functioning perceptual system, imagination, and memory: "Understanding seems to be most of all special to the soul. But if it too is a sort of imagination, or does not exist without imagination, it would not be possible even for it to exist without the body" (I 1 403ª8–10). *Prima facie*, then, even self-understanding is impossible for a productive understanding whose base is separated from sublunary body.

The solution to this problem lies in the distinction between perceptual imagination and deliberative imagination: "Perceptual imagination *(aisthêtikê phantasia)* . . . is found in the other animals, but deliberative *(bouleutikê)* [imagination is found] in the ones that rationally calculate.[40] For whether to do this or that is already a task for rational calculation, and so it is necessary to measure by a single [standard], since one pursues what is superior. Hence one has the ability to make one appearance out of many" (*DA* III 11 434ª5–10). Rational calculation, then, involves comparing things to see which is superior, and so requires that they be mea-

---

[39] Also *DA* III 7 431ª16–17, 431ᵇ2; *Sens.* 6 445ᵇ16–17.

[40] Also *DA* III 10 433ᵇ29–30: "all imagination is either rationally calculative *(logistikê)* or perceptual. In the latter, then, the other animals share."

sured by a single standard, and this, in turn, involves being able to make one appearance out of many. For the single standard is a *universal* proposition to the effect that "such-and-such a man should do such-and-such a thing" (434ª16–19), and universals (such-and-suches) arise from experiences, which themselves arise when from many appearances retained in memory a single one is formed (*APo.* II 19 100ª6–7). It follows that the "one appearance" referred to is a universal. Moreover, since this universal is articulate enough to guide action, it is presumably an analyzed universal rather than an unanalyzed one of the sort accessible by perception. If it were not, the contrast drawn between the two kinds of imagination would begin to erode. Analyzed universals, however, can be grasped only by animals that possess understanding. Hence, rational calculation can take place only in them. That is why deliberative imagination is not shared, as perceptual imagination is, by nonhumans.

Since psychological potentials are in part defined by their proper objects, we may infer at once that appearances come in two different varieties—perceptual and deliberative. But we do not need to have recourse to that special doctrine to see why this should be so. For deliberative universals are suniversal essences, and the like—intelligible objects, not any sort of perceptual ones. And therein lies the resolution of our problem. Productive self-understanding does need to have an appearance of productive understanding as its object. But that is just to say that it needs to have its own analyzed suniversal essence as its object. As being actively understood, however, that suniversal essence is simply the activity of productive understanding itself.[41]

The second reason that *content* is only partly resolved is that there is still an air of mystery about what Aristotle's account of productive self-understanding really amounts to—an air which we can thicken appreciably, and then somewhat dissipate, by resorting once more to the analogy with sight. According to *ᵇ30*, passive understanding is like "a wax tablet on which there is nothing actually written." Productive self-understanding, therefore, is its active correlate. But what is that? Isn't it just activated blankness? Is Aristotle's solution to *content* to turn absence of content itself

---

[41] I agree with Schofield, "Aristotle on the Imagination," 256, that "Aristotle's phantasia is a loose-knit, family concept." Though I take the metaphor rather literally: deliberative appearances are offspring of perceptual ones. See D. Frede, "The Cognitive Role of *Phantasia*."

into a sort of content?[42] No. Passive understanding is an analog of the transparent eye-jelly. When a blank passive understanding is activated, therefore, the result is not blankness, but an analog of light. And just as light is a visible object (a proto-color), so its analog is an intelligible object. Understanding is a reflexive process that always involves self-under-standing, then, for the same reason that seeing always involves seeing light. Consequently, once productive understanding has been activated by some 'ordinary' intelligible object, there is nothing to prevent its being kept in activity by that other intelligible object, which became its object "as a by-product" (*Met.* XII 9 1074[b]36) of the first's becoming so, namely, produc-tive understanding itself. But there, I think, explanation comes to a stop. As grasping the analogies laid out in 6.1 are the best we can do by way of understanding matter and form, so grasping the analogy with light is the best we can do by way of grasping what the content of productive self-understanding is, when it is separated from sublunary matter.

The structural analogy between sight and the understanding, then, is the very nerve of Aristotle's theory of the understanding. Since the major component of the former is the account of visible objects, it is no surprise that the account of intelligible objects is the major component of the latter. After all, the passive understanding, as pure potentiality, is just such as to be able to take on any intelligible object without distortion. This is a serious weakness if what we want or expect is a 'computational' theory of under-standing, since it is clear that any kind of computation that uses the very same intelligible forms that we use in order to understand will be too much like understanding to provide much independent insight into it.

On the other hand, there is a compensating strength here. For it means that the mechanics of understanding gains most of its explanatory power from the vastly more credible theory of science and dialectic. Consider the case of clarity, for example. We know from the account of science that clarity of understanding is achieved, in our case at least, by the hard work of solving aporematic problems. Hence clarity of understanding is just what one achieves when all such problems have been solved. To the extent that we understand what a problem is, therefore, we grasp what it is that

---

[42] The author of *Col.* 1 791[a]12–[b]6 seems to be attempting an analog of this illegitimate move in the case of color perception, when he claims that one of the conditions under which we see black is "when no light at all passes to the eyes from the object." On this account, when one closes one's eyes one sees what Robert Nozick has allegedly called "the big black sense-datum."

clarity of understanding really amounts to. That grasp is not much tight-ened, however, when we learn that such clarity is based in clarity of ether. For the latter notion borrows much of its own explanatory power from the former—which, in turn, borrows its explanatory power from the analogy with sight, and the requirement that the eye-jelly be transparent. "God kindled our understanding to be a light in our souls" is a metaphor, Aristotle says, whose literal basis is that understanding and light "make something clear" (*Rh.* III 10 1411^{b}12–13).

7.5 Human Beings as Their Self-Understandings

A second problem for Aristotle's account of productive understanding, which we may call *essence,* will not come into sharp focus until the end of this section, but in rough form it is this: If a human being's productive understanding is a substance distinct from the compound that is the rest of him, what sort of entity is he?

Unlike minds as we conceive of them, which are found only in the upper reaches of the phylogenetic scale, Aristotelian souls are found wher-ever there is life and movement: souls are animators. Thus all plants and animals, however primitive or simple, have some sort of soul, some portion of divine ether. Moreover, unlike Cartesian or Christian souls, Aristotelian souls (productive understanding aside) are tightly tied to the bodies whose souls they are. The very account of soul as "the first actuality of a natural body that has organs" (*DA* II 1 412^{b}5–6) makes this apparent.

While the various types of soul or psychological potentials are found separated from one another in other living things, however, they are also found, hierarchically organized, within the human soul, with higher ones presupposing lower ones (*EN* I 13). On the lowest rung in the hierarchy is the potential for nutrition, and so for growth. It is the only psychological potential possessed by plants. The next rung up includes the perception, emotion, and appetite responsible for sensory awareness of the world and spatial movement. Together with nutrition these potentials are found in all animals. In human beings, they are constituents of the nonrational part of the soul. The third type of psychological potential, found only in human beings, is reason, which comprises wish *(boulêsis)*, or rational desire for the good, practical wisdom, and understanding.[43]

---

[43] *DA* III 9 432^{b}5–6; *Rh.* I 10 1369^{a}1–4 (wish); *EN* VI 2 (practical wisdom, understanding).

Looked at from the bottom up rather than from the top down, this hierarchy is teleological: lower parts and their functions are for the sake of higher ones. For example, the homoeomerous parts and their functions exist for the sake of the nonhomoeomerous or structured parts and their functions. Among the latter parts, the sense organs are particularly important with regard to survival, which is essential for all other functioning (*DA* III 12 434ª22–ᵇ27). In animals with practical wisdom, however, the senses (especially, smell, hearing, and sight) "inform us of many distinctions from which arise practical wisdom about intelligible objects as well as those of action," and so also exist "for the sake of doing well" or being happy (*Sens.* 1 436ᵇ10–437ª3). Finally, practical wisdom itself, though it exists for its own sake, also exists for the sake of understanding.[44] Understanding, then, is at the teleological peak of the organization, and so is the final or teleological cause of everything else in it.

Resorting again to our standard way of representing essences, we may sum up what Aristotle's psychology has to tell us about the human soul (form, essence) as follows:

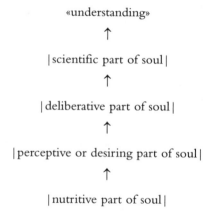

«understanding»

↑

|scientific part of soul|

↑

|deliberative part of soul|

↑

|perceptive or desiring part of soul|

↑

|nutritive part of soul|

Since understanding, like all functionally characterized things, exists for the sake of its function, «understanding», as the ultimate element in this teleological system, must be productive understanding.

Though this entire teleological system is in the human soul, the human being whose soul it is stands in a special relation to his understanding:

---

[44] See 6.2 and my *Practices of Reason*, 99–106, 139–189.

EN X 7 1178^{a}2–8 *[^{a}2]* Each [human being] seems to be this [his understanding], since he is his supreme and better part. It would be absurd, therefore, if he were to choose not his own life, but something else's. And what we have said before will also apply now. For what is proper to each thing's nature is supremely best and pleasantest for it; and hence for a human being the life expressing understanding will be supremely best and pleasantest, *[^{a}7]* if indeed this [i.e., understanding] most of all is the human being. This life, then, will also be happiest.[45]

Focus first on ^{a}7. It claims that a human being is most of all his best and most supreme part. But this, apparently, is a general feature of all teleological systems: "Just as a city and every other system seems to be most of all its most supreme part,[46] the same is true of a human being" (*EN* IX 8 1168^{b}31–32). It makes no difference, we may infer, whether we say that a soul is most of all its most supreme part or that the human being whose soul it is has this feature, since the same system incorporates both.

Before turning to the rest of *EN* X 7, we need some analytical terminology. Aristotle uses the term *anthrôpos* in the usual way to designate a being—Human, as we may call him—whose soul is a teleological system with «understanding» at its apex. But he also uses the term to designate two other quite different things: "A human being's complete happiness will be this activity [i.e., the activity of productive understanding], if it receives a complete span of life, since nothing incomplete is proper to happiness. But such a life would be superior to that expressing the human element. For someone will live it not qua human being, but qua possessing a divine element [understanding]. And the activity of this divine element is as much superior to the activity expressing the other virtue [virtue of character] as this element is superior to the compound [animal]" (8 1177^{b}24–29). The *anthrôpos* qua which someone lives an inferior life, then, lacks understanding, and so is not Human (he has one), but Human-minus-understanding. The *anthrôpos* referred to in *EN* X 7, by contrast, whose own proper life is a life expressing understanding alone, is what, without prejudice, we may call Person. He is not Human, since Human's proper life also expresses humanity-minus-understanding. Just what Person's essence is remains unsettled.

---

[45] Also *EN* IX 4 1166^{a}16–17, *Prt.* B62, 65, and my *Practices of Reason*, 133–137.

[46] *Pol.* III 6 1278^{b}11: "the governing class is the constitution."

The most natural way to interpret $^a2$, then, is as advocating the identity of either Person or Human with his productive understanding, so that either

1. Human = his productive understanding

or

2. Person = his productive understanding.

$^a2$ cannot mean (1), however, since Human has parts that his productive understanding lacks, and also has different persistence conditions (Human is mortal, his productive understanding is immortal). It must, then, mean (2).[47]

$^a2$ and $^a7$ are treated as equivalent. Hence if the former is understood as (2), the latter must be understood as:

3. Most of all (Person = his productive understanding).

Like (1), however, (3) can be decisively excluded. For numerical identity is an all or nothing relation and *malista* ('most of all') is an adverb of degree. Either $^a2$ isn't an identity statement, therefore, or it isn't equivalent to $^a7$. Since neither alternative is acceptable, we have a problem.

To solve it, we must, it seems, take (3) as stating that a certain relation, R, which does admit of degree, holds to the maximum degree (max-R) between Person and his productive understanding, with the result that $^a2$ and $^a7$ are equivalent. In other words, we have to accept:

4. Max-R (Person, his productive understanding) $\leftrightarrow$ (Person = his productive understanding).

Our task, then, is to say what R is. Taking our clue from recent work on personal identity,[48] we might suppose that it is the sort of psychological continuity that holds between Person and his productive understanding to the highest degree if and only if the two are psychologically continuous to the highest degree, so that the latter remembers all Person's experiences and carries out all his intentions. But, though suggestive, this precise value of R is unavailable to Aristotle. For Person's productive understanding cannot remember anything once Human (or Human-minus-understand-

---

[47] Notice that the objections to (1) leave (2) unscathed, since it is not settled what parts Person has or what his persistence conditions are.

[48] E.g., Parfit, *Reasons and Persons*, Part III.

ing) has passed-away, and cannot (except by chance) carry out any of Person's intentions, since all memory of these is inaccessible to it.

What is most important to Person in his own survival, however, is his own continued happiness—he wants to survive because he wants to continue living the happiest life. For Person, like all rational beings, in Aristotle's view, sets the highest value on his own happiness, since it is his greatest good. The happiest life for Person, however, is the life consisting in productive understanding (^{a}7). But this is an activity which, even when Human is still alive, is performed by his productive understanding alone: "Since the virtues of the compound are human virtues, the life and happiness expressing them is also human. That [i.e., the happiness] of understanding, however, is separate" (*EN* X 8 1178^{a}20-22). His productive understanding not only preserves what is most valuable to Person in his own survival, then, but is the self-same thing that is responsible for the happiness he calls his own when both he and Human are unquestionably still on the scene. The identity of such understanding over time, then, guarantees not only the kind of psychological continuity that is most important to Person's survival, but does so by being its normal cause. Arguably, such continuity is sufficient to make Person identical to his productive understanding.

Max-R, then, is to be interpreted as follows: Person stands in max-R to his productive understanding because he stands more in R to it than to Human-minus-understanding (or any of his other parts). He stands more in R to his productive understanding than to Human-minus-understanding (or any of his other parts) because it better guarantees that he continues to live the happiest life than does the survival of Human-minus-understanding (or any of his other parts). The degree element in max-R stems, therefore, from an implicit comparison with Human-minus-understanding and these other parts, and does not (illegitimately) modify the identity relation itself.[49]

---

[49] Suppose that though the survival of his productive understanding better guarantees that Person continues to live the happiest life than does the survival of his other parts, it is not the only thing that does so. Perhaps there is something else, not identical to understanding, which provides an equally good guarantee. If so, R even in the highest degree, will not be a one-one relation. Identity, however, is a one-one relation. Hence (4) "max-R (Person, his productive understanding) ↔ (Person = his productive understanding)" will be false. What commends it to Aristotle, we may infer, is his belief that productive understanding has no competitors, that Person can stand in max-R only to that one understanding that is

It is a weakness of this account of R, to be sure, that it offers us no explanation of why teleological systems in general should be most of all their ends, since happiness is not something that such systems can be assumed to have as their goal—other animals, for example, whose souls are also such systems, have no share in happiness.[50] But it is a weakness that is easily remedied. For, though not all teleological systems can be assumed to have happiness as their goal, it might well be thought that they do all have some sort of good as their goal. In any case, this is a feature that Aristotle's teleological systems can be safely taken to have. Hence happiness, as the supreme human good, will just be a special case of something quite general. It should not be difficult, therefore, to recast our analysis of R in general terms. For the supreme element in any teleological system will be the one that plays more of a role in promoting the good of the system than any other, and the system as a whole will therefore stand in a relation that is an analog of max-R to it.

We are now in a position to specify *essence* more precisely as follows: Human has his productive understanding as a part, yet he seems to have an essence, namely, the teleological system discussed earlier. That productive understanding is also a substance, however, so it too has an essence. Yet its essence is different from that of Human. How then can Human's essence have the tight unity requisite in an essence? Moreover, which is perhaps the same problem phrased somewhat differently, "no substance is composed of substances" (*Met.* VII 16 1041^{a}3–5). Yet Human has his productive under-

---

responsible for his happiness while Human yet lives. But the fact that productive understanding has no competitors is still not enough to guarantee that (4) is true. For though it ensures that max-R is not a many-one relation, it does not ensure that it is not a one-many relation, satisfied by many different persons. Still, it is reasonable to suppose that it is not. To see why, suppose that understanding' stands to Person' and Human' just as understanding does to Person and Human, and that Person and Person' and Human and Human' are numerically distinct, while understanding and understanding' are identical. When Human' dies but Human does not, understanding can be grasping a penmattered essence at the very time at which understanding' cannot. Yet understanding and understanding' were supposed to be identical. It seems safe to conclude that max-R is no more one-many than it is many-one, and so must, like identity, be one-one.

[50] E.g., *EN* X 8 1178^{b}24–25: "The other animals have no share in happiness, being completely deprived of this activity [i.e., understanding]."

standing as a part. How then can Human and his productive understanding both be substances?

There is, I think, only one way to solve these intractable problems, which seem to threaten the cogency of much of Aristotle's account of substance and essence. We must deny that Human is strictly speaking a substance. For the same reason, he does not have either an essence or a definition in the strict sense in which only a substance has these things. Nonetheless, even though he is not a strict substance, because passive understanding is involved in such psychological functions as perception, memory, and the understanding of penmattered essences, he is at least a tightly organized functional unity. Person, by contrast, since it is identical to Human's productive understanding, is a substance in the strict sense. For productive understanding has no substantial parts. But Person, we should now recall, is an *anthrôpos*—a human being—of a sort, namely, the sort that we beings like Socrates most of all are.

The result, therefore, is a kind of supernaturalism about human beings, since these have emerged as most of all divine or supernatural productive understandings: "man is the only animal that stands upright, and this is because his nature, i.e., his substance [essence], is divine" (*PA* IV 10 686^{a}27–28).

7.6 Self-Understanding as Primary Substance$_m$?

With *content* and *essence* at least deprived of some of their bite, our way is clear to accepting that productive self-understanding is "a sort of substance" (*DA* I 4 408^{b}19). But what sort? Productive self-understanding, as a matterless activity, satisfies the Identity Thesis, and so is identical to its own essence. And a substance identical to its own essence is a primary substance$_m$: "in some cases, a thing and its essence are the same, i.e., in the case of primary substances" (*Met.* VII 11 1037^{a}33–^{b}2). *Prima facie,* then, productive self-understanding is primary substance$_m$.

If this is true, however, productive self-understanding must constitute a solution to the Primacy Dilemma. But does it? In two respects, at least, it is certainly a better candidate than any we have seen so far. First, productive self-understanding is both a suniversal essence and a particular. For, in the case of matterless essences, these are not two things, but the same thing considered in two different ways. Considered as a potential, productive understanding is a suniversal essence that is a first principle of potential scientific knowledge; considered as an activity, it is a particular, a first principle of actual scientific knowledge. Hence it combines the particularity required in an ontological first principle with the suniversality required in an epistemological one.

Second, and of related significance, its definition or account has the same feature. Here yet again is the text that makes this explicit: "In some cases, isn't the scientific knowledge the object? . . . In theoretical sciences, isn't it the account, the object, and the [productive] understanding?" (*Met.* XII 9 1074^{b}38–1075^{a}3). Thus the account of a suniversal essence, which is a definition in the strict sense, is a suniversal when it is the object of potential scientific knowledge, but is a particular when it is the object of actual scientific knowledge. The requirement that primary substance$_m$ be primary in definition, therefore, is no immediate threat to the candidacy of productive self-understanding.

Nonetheless, it remains hard to see how human productive self-understanding can be primary substance$_m$. For, first, since it is not eternal, it is hard to see how it can it can be prior to everything else in definition, knowledge, and time. Surely, as something that can come-to-be, it owes its actuality to something that is eternally actual. Second, it is hard to see how can it be prior in these ways to all other non-eternal beings, such as the penmattered essences of the animal species. The perplexing nature of these problems shows just how much bite the Primacy Dilemma retains, even if we grant that human productive understanding *is* a separate substance of some sort.

EIGHT

DIVINE SUBSTANCE

8.1 God as Unmoved Mover

Even though human productive self-understanding fails to solve the Primacy Dilemma, it suggests that a solution may lie in the special features of matterless essences and reflexive self-understanding. In *Metaphysics* XII 6–10, which deals with one intelligible substance in particular, God, Aristotle attempts to show that this is indeed the case. In the present chapter, we shall be following closely in his footsteps as he explains what sort of cause of movement God is, what it is he directly moves, what sort of being he is, and what his special role is in "the nature of the whole" (10 1075^{a}11).

One major obstacle to treating human productive self-understanding as primary substance$_m$, as we saw, is that it is not eternal, since it comes-into-being in us as a potential based in a mixture of ether and sublunary matter. Because it is a substance of some sort, however, it must have its origin in something actual that shares its form, namely, a male progenitor. His productive understanding, in turn, has a similar origin, and so on forever backwards in time. Hence just as sleep poses a metaphysical threat to the existence of a Cartesian ego, which needs to be averted by appeal to essence (the ego is essentially a thinking thing and so cannot not think), so it also poses an analogous threat to human productive self-understanding. For sleep is a condition in which psychological capacities exist as second potentials. It is, "as it were, a border-land between living and not-living, and the sleeper someone neither completely not-being nor completely being" (*GA* V I 778^{b}29–31). If our male progenitors were forever asleep, therefore, they could still transmit passive understanding to their offspring through somnambulatory intercourse. But since actual understanding must precede potential understanding, they could not, it seems, pass on productive understanding in this or any other way. How, then, are we to explain the fact that productive understandings exist at all? In its more

general form, this problem is Aristotle's principal focus in *Metaphysics* XII
6–7. We shall analyze his discussion of it in eight stages.

Stage 1: In the following text Aristotle introduces our problem and
offers the beginning of a solution:

> *Met. XII 6 1071^{b}5–22* [^{b}5] Substances are primary among beings, and
> so if they can pass-away, all things can pass-away. But it is impossible
> that movement *(kinêsis)* comes-to-be or passes-away (since it has
> always existed), or that time does so (since there could not be a before
> or an after if time did not exist). Movement is continuous, therefore,
> just as time is, since time is either the same as movement or an
> attribute of movement. But there is no continuous movement except
> movement with respect to place, and of it only that which is circular is
> so. If, however, [^{b}12] there is something potentially moving or pro-
> ducing, but not actually so, there will be no movement; for it is
> possible to have the potential and not to actualize it. . . . [^{b}19] There
> must, then, be a first principle [of movement] of this sort, the sub-
> stance [essence] of which is activity. Moreover, [^{b}20] these substances[1]
> must be without matter, since they must be eternal, at least if anything
> else is to be eternal. They must, therefore, be activities.

^{b}5 argues for the existence of a substance that moves continuously in a
circular orbit. It presupposes that time and movement cannot come-into-
being, that time is (or is an attribute of) movement, and that only circular
movement in place is continuous. But these presuppositions, which Aristotle argues for elsewhere, need not detain us. It is enough for our purposes
to see how this part of the argument goes.

^{b}12 claims that a substance with the mere potential to cause movement is
not sufficient to explain the existence of actual movement, since a potential need not be actualized. (Eternally sleeping male progenitors cannot
explain the existence of productive understanding in their offspring.) A
few lines later, Aristotle elaborates on the point: "How will there be
movement if there is no actual cause? For matter will surely not move itself,
but the craft of carpentry [must move it] ; nor will the menses or earth
[move themselves], but the semen, i.e., the seed [must move them] " (*Met.*
XII 6 1071^{b}28–31). ^{b}19 concludes that the substance needed to explain the
existence of movement must be in essence an activity. (This is the Aristotelian equivalent of the Cartesian claim that the ego is in essence a thinking

---

[1] The plural is explained in 8.2.

thing.) [b]20 draws the further conclusion that, since movement and time are eternal, this substance must also be eternal, and so must be matterless. This matterless substance should not be confused, however, with the substance argued for in [b]5, which moves in a circle.

Stage 2: The actual, eternal, and continuous circular movement of a substance (or group of substances) can explain the existence of some sorts of sublunary movements or changes, but it cannot explain all of them: "Since it has been proved that movement with respect to place is eternal, it follows from this that coming-to-be must also occur continuously . . . [However,] it is obvious that it will not be possible for both [coming-to-be and passing-away] to occur, because they are opposites. For it is the nature of that which is the same and remains in the same condition always to produce the same, so that either coming-to-be will always occur or passing-away will [but not both] " (*GC* II 10 336[a]15–28). If both coming-to-be and passing-away are to exist, therefore, something else is needed in addition to the substance moving in circle: "If, then, there is cyclical change, something must always remain in activity in the same way. But if coming-to-be and passing-away are to exist, there must be something else that is always in activity now in one way, now in another" (*Met.* XII 6 1072[a]9–12). The substance that always remains in activity is the primary heaven—a transparent ethereal sphere to which the stars are affixed. It is always parallel to the equator, and so remains in an unchanging relation to the earth. The "something else" is the sphere to which the sun is affixed, which moves yearly along the ecliptic (the apparent path of the sun among the stars), and daily, parallel to the equator (*GC* II 10 336[a]28–337[a]33).

Together, these two causes apparently explain why there is always movement and change, and why, at the same time, there are always opposite movements and changes—not just eternal coming-to-be, but also eternal passing-away. But to explain the irregularities that occur in these sublunary movements and changes, a third factor is required: "The times of the coming-to-be and passing-away that occur in nature are equal. Often, however, it happens that things pass-away in a shorter time [than is natural] on account of the mingling of things with one another. For matter being irregular and not everywhere the same, the comings-to-be of things are also necessarily irregular, some faster, some slower" (*GC* II 10 336[b]18–23). The question arises, then, as to whether these two types of substances (together with perceptible sublunary matter) are indeed sufficient to explain "the character which movements in fact exhibit" (*Met.* XII 6 1072[a]17–18).

Stage 3: Having argued in *1071^{b}5* for the existence of a substance that is moving eternally in a circle, Aristotle's next task is to determine whether that substance too must be moved by something else, and, if so, by what sort of thing:

> *Met. XII 7 1072^{a}21–26* There is, then, something that is always moved in an unceasing movement, and in a circle (this is clear not from argument alone but also from the facts); therefore, [^{a}23a] the primary heaven must be eternal. Hence [^{a}23b] there is also something that moves it. And [^{a}24] since what is moved and moves [something] is in the middle, there is, in addition, a mover that moves without being moved, being [^{a}25a] eternal, and [^{a}25b] a substance, and [^{a}25c] an activity.

^{a}23a identifies the substance whose existence is argued for in *1071^{b}5* with the primary heaven—the outermost sphere of the fixed stars. ^{a}23b claims that there must be something that moves this sphere. This is so for two reasons. First, a movement is always the actualization of a potential.[2] So the primary heaven has a potential to move in a circle. Second, it is possible to have a potential and not to actualize it *(1071^{b}12)*. Hence, even though the primary heaven is always moving in a circle, the fact that it is actually (rather than just potentially) doing so requires explanation. With future needs in mind, let us call what explains its movement, *the primary mover—* PM.

If PM is itself moved, the argument just given will also apply to it, so that it will be between something moved (the primary heaven) and a new mover (whatever moves it). To cut off the emerging regress of movers at the first step, therefore, PM must be a mover that is not itself moved—in other words, it must be an unmoved mover *(^{a}24).* Since substance is prior to all the other beings, PM must be a substance *(^{a}25b).* Since the primary heaven, which PM moves, is eternally in movement, PM must also be eternal *(^{a}25a).* Since it is eternal, it must be an activity *(^{a}25c, 1071^{b}20).*

Stage 4: PM cannot itself be moved on pain of being just another moved mover in a never ending and nonexplanatory chain of them. But if it is not moved, it cannot be moving. For if it were, it would have to have a potential to move that some actually moving thing would have to actualize. But if it is not actually moving, how does it move anything else? The

---

[2] *Ph.* III 1 201^{a}10–11: "the actuality *(entelecheia)* of the potential as such is movement."

following difficult text, which will occupy us for some time, provides the answer:

> *Met. XII 7 1072ᵃ26–ᵇ1* *[ᵃ26a]* Objects of desire and *[ᵃ26b]* intelligible objects move [things] in this way: they move [them] without being moved. *[ᵃ27a]* Of these objects, the primary ones are the same. For *[ᵃ27b]* the [primary] object of appetite is the apparent good, and *[ᵃ28]* the primary object of wish is the real good.³ But *[ᵃ29]* we desire something because it seems [good] rather than its seeming [good] because we desire it; for *[ᵃ30a]* the first principle is [active] understanding *(noêsis)*. And *[ᵃ30b]* understanding *(nous)* is moved by intelligible objects, *[ᵃ30c]* and intrinsically intelligible objects are in one of the two columns [of opposites], and in this [column] substance is primary, and in this [sub-column], the simple one and an activity [is primary]. (Unity and simplicity are not the same; for unity signifies a measure while simplicity signifies that the thing itself is a certain way.) But *[ᵃ34]* the good too, i.e., what is choiceworthy because of itself, is in the same column, in that a best thing is always analogous to a first one.

If this argument is to explain how PM moves the primary heaven, the former must be an intelligible object *(ᵃ30b)*, and the latter must have desires or understanding or both *(ᵃ26a–ᵃ26b)*. If understanding is a cognitive state, however, the sole function of which is to grasp suniversal essences, the primary heaven, in possessing it alone, will lack all desire. But if the primary heaven lacks all desire, how can an intelligible object possibly move it? For, Aristotle is explicit, that both conative and cognitive factors are required to explain movement: "all things have the same causes, because without substances it is not possible for attributes or changes [movements] to exist. Furthermore, these will surely be soul and body, or understanding and desire and body" (*Met. XII 5 1071ᵃ2–3*). That is one problem with ᵃ26b.

The phenomenon of self-control, however, suggests that it may be specious: "Self-controlled people, even when they desire and have an appetite for things, do not do those things for which they have the desire, but they follow understanding. But it appears, at any rate, that these two cause movement, either desire or understanding" (*DA III 9–10 433ᵃ7–9*). If self-controlled people can follow their understanding against their

---

³ Also *EN III 4 1113ᵃ22–24*; *Rh. I 10 1369ᵃ2–4.*

desire, however, it seems that understanding alone *can* produce movement without the aid of desire, which is just the idea suggested by *^a26b*.

There is a measure of truth in this suggestion, but it rests on an ambiguity: "Both of these, therefore, can produce movement with respect to place, understanding and desire, but understanding which rationally calculates for the sake of something and is practical; and it differs from theoretical [understanding] with respect to its end" (*DA* III 10 433^{a}13–15). We may infer, then, that the understanding involved in *1072^{a}6–^{b}1* is not the familiar theoretical understanding, but practical understanding.

Now the end of theoretical understanding *(theôrêtikê dianoia)* is just to be "true or false," whereas that of practical understanding is "truth agreeing with correct desire" (*EN* VI 2 1139^{a}27–31). Since desire is for what appears good (*$^a29$*), *correct* desire must be for what correctly so appears, namely, the real good that is the primary object of wish (*$^a28$*). But the primary object of wish is the same as the primary object of theoretical understanding (*^a27a*). *Prima facie*, then, the function of theoretical understanding is the exclusively cognitive one of grasping the truth about the real good, as formulated in its definition, so as to bring it effectively within the ambit of the movement-producing wish: "That which produces movement will be one in kind, the desiring part qua desiring—and the first [mover] of all is the object of desire. For this produces movement without being moved, by being understood" (*DA* III 10 433^{b}10–12). It is theoretical understanding and wish that together produce movement, then, not the former alone: "understanding does not appear to produce movement without desire, since wish is a kind of desire" (433^{a}22–23). It follows that the primary heaven must possess both understanding and wish if it is to be moved by PM.

The primary heaven would still not be moved by PM, however, unless its understanding and its desire were also moved (*^a30b*): "desire and the desiring part cause movement by being moved" (*MA* 6 700^{b}35–701^{a}1). So, unless, understanding itself includes an element of desire (or desire, an element of understanding), we seem to be back where we started, with something being moved that has only a cognitive or only a conative component. That certainly would be our predicament, if understanding and desire were spatially moved by their objects. But we know this is not so: the change that occurs in a second-potential understanding or desire when it is activated is neither a spatial movement nor a qualitative change, but a pseudo-attribute change (*DA* II 5 417^{b}2–16, 7.1). Hence, it does not need to be explained in the way that the spatial movement of the primary heaven does by reference to both cognitive and conative elements. If it did, PM would need to have both wish and understanding, and so would not be simple.[4] Not all the movers in the chain characterized in $1072^a26–{}^b1$, therefore, move in the same way. The primary unmoved intelligible and desired object, PM, moves the primary heaven by producing a pseudo-attribute change in its understanding and wish, and these produce circular movement in it.

It follows that the primary heaven (and whatever else is moved by PM) must have both understanding and wish. Therein lies another problem. For we—together with some of Aristotle's predecessors—think of the heavens "as bodies only—as units having an order, indeed, but wholly inanimate" (*Cael.* II 12 292^a18–20). If Aristotle is right, however, it is only if the heavens "have a share in life and actions," that their movement by PM isn't "wholly inexplicable" (292^a20–22). By inference to the best explanation, it follows that "the heavens are alive and possess a first principle of movement" (2 285^a29–30). Consequently, they *are* the sorts of beings that can wish and understand.

According to $^a27b–{}^a28$, appetite and wish have different objects. $^a29$–^a30b suggests, however, that understanding plays the same role in relation to both of them. But this is not, strictly speaking, true. In the case of the other animals, it is perceptual imagination not understanding that brings objects effectively within the ambit of their desires. Similarly, when human beings, out of weakness of will, "follow their imaginations against their scientific knowledge" (*DA* III 10 433^a10–11), the same phenomenon occurs—it is imagination's object, not understanding's, that effectively engages their desire. Nonetheless, just because perceptual imagination plays a role analogous to that played by understanding, Aristotle sometimes allows it to be "set down as understanding *of a sort*" (433^a9–10). And that, presumably, is just what he is doing in $^a29–{}^a30b$. Appetite is an analog of wish, imagination is an analog of divine understanding, the apparent good is an analog of the real good,[5] and that is enough, in Aristotle's view, to make animal movement (or human weak-willed action) fit into the general

---

[4] For that matter, the productive understanding would not be the only part of a human soul to survive the demise of the body. For, without wish, the understanding could not be moved by an intelligible object, and so could not be an activity.

[5] *MA* 6 700^b28–29: "We must suppose that the apparent good may take the place of the [real] good, and so may pleasure, which is itself an apparent good."

explanatory schema *1072ᵃ26–ᵇ1* proposes. For the sake of simplicity, therefore, I shall ignore these analogs and give the remainder of the account exclusively in terms of wish, understanding, and the real good.

Of the two columns referred to in *ᵃ30c,* one consists of the intrinsic beings in the categories, the other of privations, the accounts of which make reference to those beings.[6] Thus dark, for example, is in the second column, since it is the privation of light, which is in the first column. Located in the column of intrinsic beings is the sub-column of substances, which is further divided into substances of different degrees of primacy, with unqualified primacy assigned to a substance that is both simple and an activity.[7] *ᵃ34* locates the real good in the same place, on the grounds that what is best has the sort of primacy among objects of choice that the most primary substance has among intelligible objects. *ᵃ27a* is (implicitly) taken to be thereby established. We can see why. For the primary object of wish is the real good, which is identical to PM. But PM is a substance, an activity, an intelligible object, and the *primary* mover. *Prima facie,* then, it is the primary object of understanding—the very thing *ᵃ30c* identifies as the most primary of primary substances. Hence the primary object of desire and the primary intelligible object are one and the same.

The identification of PM as the real good, however, gives rise to a problem that threatens the entire argument of *1072ᵃ26–ᵇ1:* "How can a first principle of movement—specifically, the natural good—be found among unmoving things, if indeed everything that is intrinsically (or because of its own nature) a good is an end, and is such a cause that for its sake the other things come-to-be and are, and if the end (or that for the sake of which) is the end of some action, and all actions are accompanied by movements? [For if these things are true it seems to follow] that this principle could not possibly be found among unmoving things, and there could not be an intrinsic good. And that is why in mathematics nothing is proved by means of this kind of cause, nor is there any demonstration [taking the form] 'because it is better (or worse)'—indeed, no one ever mentions anything of this sort" (*Met.* III 2 996ᵃ22–32).[8] It seems, then, that PM cannot be present in the class of unmoving things, since, as a good choiceworthy because of

---

[6] *Met.* I 5 986ᵃ22–ᵇ8, IV 2 1004ᵇ27–1005ᵃ2, XI 9 1066ᵃ13–26. The relation of the columns to the categories is briefly discussed in *GC* I 3 319ᵃ11–17.

[7] Set out in tabular form in 9.9.

[8] Also *Met.* XI 1 1059ᵃ34–38.

itself *(ª34)*, it is an intrinsic good.[9] But if that is true, PM cannot be an unmoved mover, and so cannot be the primary mover.

To rescue the argument, therefore, we need to recognize the ambiguity on which the problem trades: "A distinction makes it clear that that for the sake of which *is* found among unmoving things: for that for the sake of which is both the one *for* whom and that *towards* which, and of these the latter is unmoving and the former is not. Thus it [the latter] produces movement by being loved, and it moves the others" *(Met.* XII 7 1072ᵇ1– 4).[10] When, for example, a person does something (such as buying a house) for the sake of his own happiness, there is a sense in which he himself is the thing for the sake of which he acts—his act, if successful, is self-benefiting. Hence he must be a moving or changing thing. If he weren't, he couldn't be benefited or improved by such an act. The end towards which he is moving, however, is not shown to be moving by this argument. Indeed, since it produces movement by being desired, wished for, or loved, it may be unmoving *(ª26a–ª26b)*. Hence PM's status as the best good does not threaten its status as unmoved.

Stage 5: The conclusion reached at the end of Stage 4 is that PM, being the primary intelligible object, and so the primary object of desire, moves the primary heaven by being the object of both its understanding and its wish. The remainder of the argument elaborates on this conclusion, fur- ther distinguishing PM from the primary heaven:

Met. XII 7 1072ᵇ4–13 [ᵇ4] If something is moved, it admits of being otherwise than it is, so that if something's activity is the primary movement,[11] qua being moved, it admits of being otherwise—with respect to place, even if not with respect to substance [essence]. But *[ᵇ7]* since there is something that moves without being moved, and it is in activity, it can in no way admit of being otherwise. For *[ᵇ8]* movement with respect to place is primary among the [types of] movements, and of these, movement in a circle [is primary] ; and *[ᵇ9]* this it [PM] produces. Therefore, *[ᵇ10a]* it is necessarily [such as it is] ; and *[ᵇ10b]* qua necessary, it is good, *[ᵇ11a]* in that *(kai)* it is as such [i.e., good] that it is a first principle [of movement]. For *[ᵇ11b]* something

---

[9] *APo.* I 4 73ᵇ10–11: "what belongs to something because of itself belongs to it intrinsically."

[10] Also *Ph.* II 2 194ª35–36; *DA* II 4 415ᵇ2–3.

[11] Reading ἡ φορὰ πρώτε ἡ ἐνέργειά ἐστίν.

is said to be necessary in a number of ways—as that which is compelled against natural impulse, as that without which what is good does not exist, and as that which does not admit of being otherwise, but is unqualifiedly [necessary] .

$^b8$ is supported as follows: "It is clear that among spatial movements circular movement is primary. For all spatial movements . . . are either circular or linear or a compound [of the two]. And the former must be prior to the latter, since it is constituted out of them. And of the former, the circular [is prior], since it is simpler and more complete. For an object cannot have a linear movement that is infinite, since there isn't an infinite [path] of that sort—but even if there were, no object could move in it, since what is impossible cannot happen, and it is impossible to traverse an infinite [path]. On the other hand, if it turns back, it is composite, i.e., two movements, whereas if it doesn't turn back it is incomplete and passes-away. But what is complete is prior in nature and in account and in time to what is incomplete, and what cannot pass-away to what can pass-away. Moreover, what admits of being eternal is prior to what does not admit of it, and movement in a circle admits of being eternal, but none of the others, whether spatial movement or any other sort, does. For each of them must come to a stop, and if they stop, the movement passes-away" (*Ph.* VIII 9 265^{a}13–27). Compelling or not, the upshot is clear. Beings, such as the primary heaven, that move eternally in a circle are undergoing minimal movement or change, because they do not come-to-be or pass-away, or undergo change in substance or essence (*$^b4$*). Since PM causes this sort of primary movement, it cannot, on pain of regress, be undergoing such movement itself. Hence, since there is no more minimal or more primitive movement or change available for it to undergo, it cannot be moving or changing at all, and so cannot admit of being otherwise and is necessarily such as it is (*$^b7$, ^b10a*). Moreover, because PM does not admit of being otherwise, of the three kinds of necessity mentioned in ^b11b, it enjoys unqualified necessity.[12] Since PM causes the movement of the primary heaven (*$^b9$*), and does so in that it is good and so an object of wish (*^b11a*), it follows that, qua being unqualifiedly necessary, PM is good (*^b10b*).[13]

---

[12] As Ross, *Aristotle's Metaphysics,* ad loc., argues.

[13] In my view, then, ^b10b is derived within $1074^b4–13$ itself, so that the *kai* in ^b11a is explanatory (epexegetic) rather than copulative. Ross, *Aristotle's Metaphysics,* ad loc., who treats it as copulative, has to go for a dubious justification to *Met.* V 5

Stage 6: We know what PM does and how it does it. But what more precisely is it? Here is part of the answer:

Met. XII 7 1072^{b}13–30 This [PM], then, is the sort of first principle on which the heavens and the [world of] nature depend. And /^{b}14/ its activity *(diagôgê)* has the same character as ours has for the short time it is at its best (for it is always in this state [of activity], whereas we cannot be), since its activity too is pleasure (that is why perceiving and understanding are most pleasant, and expectation and memory because of them). /^{b}18/ Understanding is intrinsically of what is intrinsically best, and so /^{b}19a/ the kind that is in the highest degree [best] is of what is in the highest degree [best]. And /^{b}19b/ understanding *(nous)* understands itself in partaking of the intelligible object; for it becomes an intelligible object in coming into contact with and understanding its objects, so that understanding and the intelligible object are the same. For that which can receive the intelligible object (i.e., the substance) is the understanding. And it is an activity when it possesses it, so that this [active understanding] rather than the former [passive understanding] seems to be the divine element that understanding possesses, and theoretical understanding seems to be /^{b}24a/ most pleasant and /^{b}24b/ best. If, then, /^{b}24c/ that good state [of activity], which we are sometimes in, God is always in, that is a marvelous thing; but if /^{b}25/ [he is in it] to a higher degree, that is still more marvelous. But that *is* his state. And /^{b}26/ life too certainly belongs to him. For the activity of understanding is life, and he is that activity; and his activity is intrinsically life that is best and eternal. We say, then, that God is a living being that is eternal and best, so that continuous, eternal life and duration belong to God, since it *is* God.

The precise inferential structure of this text is a bit difficult to discern, in part because it is elliptical and condensed. Its goal, however, is plainly to identify PM (in the guise of the best good) with God, in order to draw some conclusions about him.

In Stages 4 and 5, PM emerged as an intelligible substance that is at once the best intrinsic good and the primary object of theoretical understand-

---

1015^{b}14–15: "if, then, there are certain eternal and unmoving things, nothing compulsory or against nature can happen to them." The justification is dubious, because mathematical objects are eternal and unmoving, but they are neither teleological causes nor good.

ing. This underwrites the claim that understanding is intrinsically of what is intrinsically best (*18). For understanding, as moved or activated by an intelligible object, is intrinsically of something. And if it is intrinsically of something, its primary object must be that thing. *19a concludes that the best kind of understanding has this best good as its object. The following principle licenses the inference: "If what is unqualifiedly F is a special property of what is unqualifiedly G, then what is more F will be a special property of what is more G, what is less of what is less, what is to the least degree of what is to the least degree, and what is to the highest degree of what is to the highest degree. Thus [e.g.] a natural tendency to move upwards is a special property of fire, and so also a greater natural tendency to move upwards will be a special property of what is more fiery" (*Top.* V 8 137^{b}33–138^{a}2).[14] It should follow, then, that having the best good as its object is a special property of the best kind of understanding. But that would entail that nothing else could have that good as the object of its understanding. This apparently threatening consequence will eventually turn out to be not a liability, but a boon (8.2).

Once *19a is taken as established, in any case, *19b can draw on the Identity Thesis to support the (implicit) claim that the understanding of PM is identical to PM itself. For PM is matterless, and so meets the requirements of that thesis. *24b concludes that theoretical understanding is the best thing. If we ask why it is precisely self-understanding that is mentioned in *19b, however, we are asking to have made explicit what Aristotle wants to hold in reserve until *Metaphysics* XII 9, namely, an argument to show that the only possible object of PM's understanding is PM itself (8.3).

On Aristotle's account, which is presupposed in *14, pleasure is either unimpeded activity or what completes such activity[15]—in my view, by being its internal end (6.2). In either event, since the best good is an activity, it follows that it has the same pleasant character as our own unimpeded activities. It is a further clause in the account of pleasure, however, that "the most pleasant activity is the most complete, and the most complete is of that which is in good condition in relation to the best of its objects" (*EN* X 4 1174^{b}21–23). Granted *19a–b, then, *24a follows directly.

---

[14] *Met.* XII 9 1074^{b}18–21, discussed in 8.3, implies that the value of understanding an object is determined by the value of the object understood.

[15] *EN* VII 12 1153^{a}12–15, X 4 1174^{b}23–33.

At ^b24c, God is mentioned for the first time. We naturally want to know what has legitimated his introduction at just this point in the discussion. Any answer is bound to be somewhat conjectural, but the following is sure to be at least part of it. Thus far, Aristotle has not said that the best good is a living being (though *we* perforce have had to notice that the primary heaven is such). He could hardly justify calling the best good by the name God, however, unless he were within a breath of declaring it alive. But once he has done so, the best good's cosmological role, its status as a substance, and its immense value must make the terminological shift seem not simply justified, but inevitable. From now on, therefore, PM is God.

^b24c claims that God is always doing what we are doing only sometimes. But what does $^b25$ mean by saying that God is in the good state of understanding to a "higher degree" than we are? Does it repeat the same contrast as ^b24c in other terms? The following implies that it does not: "the good itself will not be to a higher degree *(mallon)* good by being eternal. For a white thing is no whiter if it lasts a long time than if it lasts a day" (*EN* I 6 1096^{b}3–5).[16] But if God's being in the state of understanding to a higher degree than we are is not a matter of his being in it longer, what is it a matter of? A plausible answer is suggested by *Top.* V 8 137^{b}33–138^{a}2 (quoted above): God is to a higher degree in the state of understanding because it is a special property of his understanding to have the *highest* good as its object.

A somewhat different, though clearly related, route to $^b25$ may also prove illuminating: "We say that something is F to a higher degree than *(mallon)* something else, when the same word, 'F', applies to both, not only when it is more excessively F, but when it is prior and the other posterior, e.g., we say that health is a good to a higher degree, and similarly that which is by nature intrinsically worthy of choice in relation to that which produces it; yet we see that the same word is predicated of both, though not unqualifiedly. For both useful things and virtues are said to be good" (*Prt.* B82). God is in the state of understanding to a higher degree than we are, therefore, because his understanding is prior to ours. Since God is the most primary of the primary substances, this is sure to be so. The following clinches the matter: "What is the first principle of change in the soul? It is now clear: in the very way that in the whole universe it is God, so too it is in the soul. For in a sense the divine element in us moves everything. But the first principle of reason is not reason, but something superior. And

---

[16] Also *EE* 1218^{a}13–14. Wedin, *Mind and Imagination in Aristotle,* 233–234.

what, then, could be superior to scientific knowledge and understanding except God?" (*EE* VIII 2 1248^{a}24–29). Our understanding is dependent on God's, and for that very reason he is more in the state of understanding than we are, since less dependently so.[17]

^{b}26 introduces life into the argument for the first time. God is the understanding of the best good; understanding is an activity of soul; what is or has a soul is alive; so God is a living being. The remainder of ^{b}26 sums up in an obvious way.

Crucial to the entire argument of *1072^{b}13–30*, as we can now see, is the claim that God, as a substance identical to PM, is the best good.[18] But "the best good is happiness" (*EN* I 7 1097^{b}22), an activity of the soul that "expresses virtue" (1098^{a}17) and is "the highest of all goods achievable in action" (I 4 1095^{a}16–17). The problem is that it is hard to see how God can have these features. For, first, his activity, like the activities of other divine beings, expresses none of the virtues of character: "We traditionally suppose that divine beings are most of all blessed and happy. But what sorts of actions should we ascribe to them? Just actions? Surely they will appear ridiculous making contracts, returning deposits, and doing things of that sort. Brave actions, rather? Do they endure frightening things and dangerous ones because it is noble? Generous action? To whom will they give? Surely it would be absurd for them to have money or something of that sort. And what would their temperate actions be? Surely it is vulgar praise to say that they do not have base appetites. When we go through them all, anything that has to do with actions seems insignificant and unworthy of the gods" (X 8 1178^{b}8–18). Second, the very objection that Aristotle uses to criticize the Platonic form of the good, seems to apply to his own case: "even if the good . . . is some single thing, or separate, itself a thing intrinsically itself, clearly it is not something a human being can pursue in action or possess" (I 6 1096^{b}33–35). For what would it be to pursue or possess God?

---

[17] The explanation of ^{b}25 offered in Ross, *Aristotle's Metaphysics,* ad loc., is that God is more in the state of understanding than we are because his understanding, unlike ours, is not dependent on sense and imagination. The problem is that our productive understanding, when it is separate from our bodies, is not dependent on these things either.

[18] *EN* I 6 1096^{a}23–25: "good . . . [in the category of] what-it-is [substance] is called God, i.e., the understanding."

The same solution applies to both these problems. "If there are many virtues," human happiness is the activity of the soul that "expresses the best and most complete of them" (*EN* I 6 1098^{a}17–18). Since there *are* many human virtues, the consequent of this conditional comes into effect. The highest form of human happiness, however, lies in the activity of understanding. It follows that theoretical wisdom, which completes or perfects that activity, must be the best and most complete (or most perfect) virtue.[19] But theoretical wisdom is expressed in the most exact and most divine scientific knowing. Hence it is a virtue that God's activity also expresses. It follows that God just is happiness. Therein, lies the solution to the second problem. For to pursue God is just to pursue the happiness that he is. And we possess him to the degree that we can, when, by engaging in the activity that he is, we "immortalize" ourselves to the extent that we can (X 7 1177^{b}31–33).

A third problem now comes into focus. Because the primary heaven is an animate being, possessing wish and understanding, it can be moved by God. But is God enough to explain its movement? It seems not: "Suppose someone were to say that what everyone desires is the apparent good, and does not control how it appears; but rather the end appears to him in accordance with the kind of person he is" (*EN* III 5 1114^{a}31–^{b}1). Hence if God (the real good) may not appear good to the primary heaven, there is no guarantee that the latter will be moved by him. The primary heaven is not just a living thing, however, it is "the most divine of visible things" (*Ph.* II 4 196^{a}33–34), a "valuable and divine" substance (*PA* I 5 644^{b}25). As such, it doesn't need the virtues of character, because it does not have the base appetites that "produce false views" about "the best good" (*EN* VI 12 1144^{a}29–36). *Its* one desire is a wish whose object is God. Once understanding brings God within its wish's ambit, therefore, the primary heaven will necessarily be moved by him. We, by contrast, do have base appetites, which is why "the real good is apparent [as such] only to the good person" (1144^{a}34). Nonetheless, when we possess the virtues of character, our actions will flow from our understanding of the real good not from our non-rational desires for the merely apparent good: "the good is what . . . anyone would choose if he could acquire understanding and practical wisdom" (*Rh.* I 7 1363^{b}12–15).[20]

---

[19] My *Practices of Reason*, 128–131.

[20] *Practices of Reason*, 79–84.

Stage 7: With $^b26$ to hand, the argument pauses to consider an objection: "Some, however, e.g., the Pythagoreans and Speussipus, suppose that the finest or best good is not present in a first principle, on the grounds that the first principles of plants and animals are causes, but what is good and complete is found in what results from these" (*Met.* XII 7 1072^{b}30–34). If such thinkers are correct, God, as a first principle, could not be the best good, and the argument in *1072^{b}13–30* would, once again, be in jeopardy. But for reasons that we have already seen, they are not correct: "The seed comes from other things that are prior and complete, and the primary thing is not the seed, but the complete [organism], e.g., we must say that the man is prior to the seed—not the one that comes-to-be from the seed but another one from whom the seed comes" (1072^{b}35–1073^{a}3). *1072^{b}13–30* is safe—God is the best good.

Stage 8: 1072^{a}30c claims that God (PM), as the most primary of primary substances, is simple because it has "a certain nature." Now one significant way in which a thing can have a simple nature is by having no spatial magnitude, and so no spatial parts to be divided into or constituted out of (*Met.* V 3 1014^{b}5; *Cael.* II 4 286^{b}17). It seems likely, then, that, in turning at the end of the argument to issues pertaining to God's spatial magnitude and parts, the topic of his simplicity is being taken up again in greater detail:[21]

> *Met. VII 7 1073^{a}3–13* It is evident, then, from what has been said that there is an eternal, unmoving substance that is separate from perceptible things. It has also been shown *[^{a}5]* that this substance cannot have any magnitude, but is without parts and indivisible. For *[^{a}7a]* it causes movement for an infinite time, but *[^{a}7b]* nothing finite has infinite capacity. But since *[^{a}8]* every magnitude is either infinite or finite, it cannot, for this reason, have a finite magnitude, and *[^{a}10]* it cannot have an infinite one, because there is no infinite magnitude at all. Moreover, *[^{a}11]* it is impassive and unalterable, since all other movements (changes) are posterior to spatial movement. It is clear, then, why it is this way.

^{a}5 is somewhat misleading, since it has not been explicitly shown that God has neither parts nor magnitude. What has been shown, however, is something from which that conclusion supposedly follows, namely, that God must be eternal because he eternally moves the primary heaven (*^{a}8*). ^{a}7b–

---

[21] As it will be again at *Met.* XII 9 1075^{a}5–10.

$^a10$ covertly acknowledges this by providing the missing argument. The argument it provides is elliptical, however, and must be filled out before it can be analyzed.

^a7b claims that no finite capacity can cause movement for an infinite time. Here is the defense: "There are three things: the mover, the moved, and third that in which the movement takes place—the time. And these are either all infinite or all finite or some finite and some infinite (i.e., two of them or one of them). Let A be the [finite] mover, B the [finite] moved, and t the infinite time. Now let A_1 [part of A] move B_1, which is part of B. Then the time [t_1] in which [this movement takes place] is not equal to t, for the bigger [the thing moved] the bigger the time in which [the movement takes place]. Hence, t_1 is not infinite. Now by continuing to add to A_1 [other finite parts from A], I shall use up A, and by doing likewise to B_1, I shall use up B; but I shall not use up t by subtracting parts on the order of [t_1], since it is infinite; so that all of A will move the whole of B in a finite part of t. It follows, therefore, that a finite thing cannot produce an infinite movement in anything. Evidently, then, nothing finite can produce movement for an infinite time. It is clear from what comes next that it is altogether impossible for an infinite capacity to be present in a finite magnitude. Let a greater capacity be that which always produces an equal [result] in less time, e.g., heating, sweetening, throwing, or—in general—moving. Of necessity, therefore, that which can be affected [by what has some such capacity] must also be affected by a finite [magnitude] that has an infinite capacity, and more by this than by any other, since an infinite capacity is greater [than any other]. But then there cannot be any time at all in which this [movement, i.e., the affecting] takes place. For if t is the time in which an infinite capacity has heated or pushed something, and t_1 that in which a finite one did so, then, when I increase the latter by repeatedly adding one finite capacity after another, I shall eventually reach a finite [capacity] which will cause the movement performed in t [by the infinite capacity]. For, by continually adding a finite [magnitude] to a finite one, I must exceed any assigned limit. By continually subtracting in the same manner, too, I must eventually fall below any assigned limit. But then a finite capacity [can be found] that in the same amount of time will cause the movement caused by an infinite capacity. But that is impossible. Therefore, no finite [magnitude] can have an infinite capacity" (*Ph.* VIII 10 266^a13-^b6). Now what is initially most disturbing about this resourceful argument is that it seems simply irrelevant to establishing that God has an infinite capacity. For God doesn't move the primary heaven by pushing it for an infinite time, or by being so big that his capacity to move it is never exhausted. It is the primary heaven's love or desire for God that should have the infinite capacity, it seems, not God himself. We shall return to this point in a moment.

10 is next. Aristotle has many different arguments to offer in support of it (*Ph.* III 5), but since God, or whatever plays the role of PM, must be a substance, one in particular has special relevance here:

> *Ph. III 5 204ª20–31* It is evident that it is not possible for what is infinite to exist as an actual being and as a substance and a first principle. For [*ª22*] any part of it that may be taken will be infinite, if it is divisible into parts (for [*ª23*] the essence of what is infinite and what is infinite are the same, if indeed it is a substance, i.e., not said of a subject), so that either it is indivisible or divisible into infinites. But [*ª25*] the same thing cannot be many infinites (yet, just as a part of air is air, so a part of what is infinite is infinite—at any rate, if it is a substance and a first principle). Therefore, [*ª27*] it is not divisible into parts, i.e., it is indivisible. But [*ª28*] it is impossible that what is actually infinite should be so, since it must be a quantity. Therefore, [*ª29*] what is infinite is present in things coincidentally. But if so, we have said that [*ª30*] it is not possible to call it a first principle, but rather what it is a coincidental attribute of [should be so called] .

To be a first principle the infinite must be a primary substance, and so must be a matterless form identical to its essence and not said of any subject (*ª23*). Suppose, then, that p_1 is one of the parts into which the infinite is divisible. Since the infinite is not said of a subject, p_1 cannot be said of one either. Hence p_1 and the infinite cannot differ by being said of different subjects. But neither can they differ in form or essence. For suppose they did. Then, since the parts of the infinite will be prior to it (it depends on them, not them on it), the infinite will not be a primary substance. Whatever parts the infinite has, therefore, must, like those of air, share its essence. Hence they too must be infinite (*ª22*). Finally, if p_2 is also a part of the infinite, p_2 cannot differ from p_1 by being said of a different subject. But it cannot differ from p_1 in form or essence either, since all of the infinite's parts have the same essence as the infinite itself. Hence it cannot differ from p_1 at all. *ª27* follows immediately.[22]

---

[22] This resolves the difficulty noticed by Hussey, *Aristotle: Physics Books III and IV,* 79: "It is unclear why the same thing cannot be, in the sense of 'be composed of', many infinites."

28 draws on the account of quantities given in *Categories* 6. For what is actually infinite, as what must be either equal or unequal to any other quantity, must have parts. Since this contradicts *27*, what is infinite cannot be a substance. It must, then, be present in some substance as a coincidental attribute (*29*). But then it is the underlying substance and not the infinite itself that is the first principle, since substances are prior to their attributes (*30*).

With *1073ᵃ7b* and *10* defended in these ways, Aristotle's argument that God has no magnitude, and so no (spatial) parts, is complete. If God has no magnitude, however, whatever his capacity to move is, it cannot be one he possesses in virtue of being in movement himself, since "what is without magnitude cannot be in movement" (*Ph.* VIII 10 267ᵃ22–23). The impression created by *7a–ᵃ7b*, therefore, that God has some sort of infinite capacity to cause movement, if true at all, must be so because he has another sort of infinite capacity altogether. And so he does. For God, as an eternal substance, is temporally infinite. But equally important, as an activity, he can be an eternal object of desire. What I mean is this. If the object of one's desire is a process, such as to build a house, when the house is built, the desire will be fully satisfied, and so will cease being a cause of one's actions or movements. But if one's desire is for an activity, such as God, though it will be satisfied at every moment at which one is engaged in the activity, it can continue to cause one's actions or movements. For God, like Cleopatra, can make hungry where most he satisfies. Having engaged in (understanding) him, one wants to continue doing so—for he is happiness, the best good. But as an activity, God has no built-in terminus. Hence one can continue to be engaged in (understanding) him without end.

1073ᵃ11 is something of an after-thought. God is prior to the eternal circular movement of the primary heaven and so cannot be changing in that way himself. But that movement is the primary sort of movement or change to which all others are posterior. Hence God cannot be moving or changing in those ways either. Hence he is impassive and unalterable.

To sum up: God is the primary intelligible substance—a simple, impassive, and unalterable living being, who is in essence an activity, and who, as the best good or happiness, is the primary unmoved mover, who moves the primary heaven by being at once the intelligible object of its understanding and wish. The reason we are not always asleep, therefore, the reason that our understandings are sometimes productive or active, is that there is an understanding that never sleeps: God.

8.2 God and the Heavens

God moves the primary heaven directly. But what about other things? Are they moved by the primary heaven, and whatever other intermediate movers there are in between? Or are some or all of them also moved directly by God? How broad, in other words, is God's direct sphere of influence? This question is the central topic of *Metaphysics* XII 8. The discussion opens, however, with an apparently strange question: "Should we posit one such substance [i.e., one eternal unmoved mover separate from perceptible things] or more than one, and [if the latter], how many?" (1073ª14–15). The question appears strange, because we naturally think that it has already been answered: there is only one God, so there is only one eternal unmoved mover. But what is natural to us is not so to Aristotle. And by seeing why, we shall come more fully to understand the argument we have just gone through. For this is an area in which, as it seems to me, almost everyone has been led astray.

The question posed, in any case, Aristotle proceeds to attempt an answer:

Met. XII 8 1073ª22–ᵇ3 We should discuss this problem by starting from the assumptions and distinctions we have mentioned.[23] *[ª23]* The first principle, i.e., the primary being, is both intrinsically and coincidentally unmoving, but produces the single primary and eternal movement [i.e., that of the primary heaven]. And since what is moved must be moved by something, and the prime mover must be intrinsically unmoving, and an eternal movement must be produced by something eternal, and *[ª28]* a single one by a single thing, and since we see that *[ª29]* besides the simple spatial movement of the universe, which we say the first and unmoving substance produces, there are other spatial movements—those of the planets—that are eternal (for the body with a circular motion is eternal and unresting . . .), each of *these* movements must also be caused by a substance that is intrinsically unmoving and eternal. For the nature of the stars is eternal, being a kind of substance, and the mover is eternal and prior to the moved, and that which is prior to a substance must be a substance. Evidently, then, *[ª36]* there must be as many naturally eternal and intrinsically unmoving substances as there are [eternal]

---

[23] Viz., those operative in the argument of 8.1.

movements. . . . Hence it is evident that the movers are substances, and that one of them is primary and another secondary, in the same order as the movements of the stars.

The crucial premise here is $^a28,$ and what makes it particularly controversial is the mechanism by which unmoved movers, such as God, operate. For they cause movement, as we know, by being objects of wish or desire. Why is it, then, that the same one can't cause many different kinds of movements by being the object of wishes present in many different kinds of beings? Why can't all the heavenly bodies be moved directly by God in just the way that an entire audience can be moved directly by the same tragedy?

An explanation that doesn't work is this: the heavenly bodies move in different orbits, so they must be moved by different unmoved movers. It doesn't work, because differences in those bodies themselves (such as differences in the purity of their understandings resulting from differences in the ether they contain) can explain the differences in their orbits, even if the other factor in the explanation, namely PM, is common to all of them. Different members of an audience can be moved in different ways by the same tragedy, because of differences either in their understandings or in their other psychological potentials.

The real explanation here lies in the Identity Thesis, and in the natures of the heavenly bodies as divine, living substances. To see this, we must first return to a text we looked at in 8.1: "Suppose someone were to say that what everyone desires is the apparent good, and does not control how it appears; but rather the end appears to him in accordance with the kind of person he is" (*EN* III 5 1114^{a}31–^{b}1). Take from it just this: it is how the good appears to an agent (it is the intentional object of his understanding and desire) that is crucial in explaining his actions or movements.

Second, a familiar fact about the understanding: Just as an eye affected by glaucoma, into whose jelly too much white matter is mixed, cannot accurately take on visible forms, so a passive understanding whose base contains too much earthy matter cannot accurately take on some intelligible forms.

Third, a familiar fact about the structure of the universe: The further we get from the center of the earth, the less earthy is the divine ether that is the base of passive understanding and of all forms. When we leave the sublunary realm behind, however, though we also leave earthy matter behind, we continue to find increasing clarity (or thinness) in the ether, increased value in the beings whose ether it is, until at the outermost sphere of the universe, at the primary heaven, we find the clearest ether, the most valuable being (*Cael.* I 2 269^{b}13–17).

Fourth, a new fact about God's location in the universe: "This movement [i.e., the movement of the primary heaven] alone is uniform—or [is so] to the highest degree—since the mover [i.e., God] does not undergo any change at all. But in order that the movement remain the same, what is moved must not undergo change in relation to it. Hence it must be either in the center or on the circumference, since these [center and circumference] are the first principles [of the sphere]. But the things closer to the mover are moved fastest, and the movement of the circumference is like that [i.e., fastest]. That, therefore, is where the mover is" (*Ph.* VIII 10 267^{b}3–9).[24] God, then, is located on the circumference of the sphere that is the primary heaven. And he must be located there to cause its continuous and uniform circular movement.

Starting with this last fact, we may work backwards. If God were an efficient cause of the movement of the primary heaven, we could understand why Aristotle might think that he had to be in contact with it in order to move it. But since he is a teleological cause, who moves the primary heaven by being the intentional object of its understanding and wish, God's location seems problematic. But is it? Consider our own case. How is it that the intentional object of Socrates' productive understanding and wish moves his body but not Callias'? Let us answer in just this boring way: Socrates' understanding stands *in the right sort of relation* to his body, but not to Callias'. Moreover, since ether naturally moves to the uppermost region possible, let us say, for a reason that will no doubt be immediately clear, that Socrates' productive understanding must be located as close to the circumference of his cranial sphere as possible, if it is to move his body.[25] So, if the primary heaven were related to God as our body is

---

[24] Also *Cael.* I 9 278^{b}11–15: "In one way, we call 'heaven' the substance of the outermost circumference of the whole . . . which we take to be the seat of all that is divine."

[25] *HA* I 15 494^{a}26–^{b}1: "In man more than in all the other animals the upper and lower parts are determined in accord with their natural places, for upper and lower in him are arranged in relation to upper and lower in the universe as a whole. . . . Of course, in all animals the head is up above in relation to its own body; but, as I have said, man alone, when completely developed, has this part up above in relation to the universe as a whole."

related to our productive understanding, we would have the kind of explanation of its location relative to the primary heaven that we are seeking.

Now God is apparently related to the primary heaven in just that way:

> Cael. II 3 286^{a}8–12 [^{a}8] Each thing, if it has a function, is for the sake
> of its function. [^{a}9] The activity of God is immortality, i.e., eternal
> life. It follows that [^{a}10] the movement of God must be eternal. But
> since [^{a}11a] the movement of [the primary] heaven is such (since it is a
> divine body), because of that [^{a}11b] he has *(echei)* a spherical body, the
> nature of which is always to move in a circle.[26]

We may set it alongside the following: "What is the first principle of
change in the soul? It is now clear: in exactly the way that *(hôsper)* in the
whole universe it is God, so too it is in the soul. For in a sense the divine
element in us [i.e., our productive understanding] moves everything" (*EE*
VIII 14 1248^{a}24–27). Take the *hôsper* seriously—lean on it, so to speak—
and it leads one to expect just what *Cael. II 3* seems to provide. But does it
really provide it? We must work through it to be sure.

^{a}8 is familiar doctrine. ^{a}9's bearing on it emerges when we recall that
God's essence is the eternal life activity of understanding, and that a thing's
function is its essence. Whatever movement God has, then, must be for the
sake of his eternal activity, and so must itself be eternal (^{a}10). But, as we
know, only one kind of movement can be eternal—movement in a circle.
Moreover, one thing that has such a movement is the primary heaven,
which, as something divine, is eternal (^{a}11a). ^{a}11b concludes that God
must have the primary heaven, whose nature is always to move in a circle,
as his body. Notice, that he, not the primary heaven,[27] must be the subject
of the verb *echei*. For the primary heaven *is* a divine body; it doesn't *have*
one. Besides, if the primary heaven were the subject, *Cael. II 3* as a whole
would go precisely nowhere.

It is a presupposition of *Cael. II 3,* on this reading, that God has a body.
But how can he have one when he is in essence an activity? The answer
must lie in the line of thought that leads Aristotle to conclude that human
beings are most of all their productive understandings—most of all super-

---

[26] Also *DA* I 5 409^{b}31–410^{a}1: "How will it [the soul] know or perceive *the
composite thing, e.g., what God is,* or man, flesh, bone, or any other composite thing?"
The reasons a spherical body is naturally best adapted for circular movement are
discussed in *Cael.* II 11.

[27] As in the *Revised Oxford Translation.*

natural entities. God has a body, the primary heaven, but he is in essence an activity all the same, just as we are.

That, then, is how God can have a body and still be in essence an activity. But why must he have one? After all, even we can shuffle off our bodies, can't we? Yes and no. We can shuffle of our natural or sublunary bodies, but we cannot treat the ether that is the base of our understandings (our ethereal bodies) in that way. The same, then, goes for God, since the primary heaven is an ethereal body. If we press our question, and ask why he must have an ethereal body, *Cael. II 3* itself provides the answer: God must have an ethereal body because he cannot have either a movement or a magnitude without one (*Ph.* VIII 10 267ª22–23). But that seems just to postpone the question. For why must God have a movement in the first place? Aristotle's response is that he is active, and "all actions are accompanied by movements" (*Met.* III 2 996ª27). For just as "a movement is held to be a sort of activity, but incomplete" (*Ph.* III 2 201ᵇ31–32), so "the name 'activity', which we connect with complete actuality *(entelecheia)*, has been extended most of all from movements to the other things, since an activity is held to be what is most of all a movement" (*Met.* IX 3 1047ª30–32). Activities, in turn, are most of all movements because every activity is the actualization of a second potential, and movement, as "the actuality of the potential as such" (*Ph.* III 1 201ª10–11), is just what a second potential is.[28] If we try to press even further, therefore, what we are asking is why the actual and the potential are so tied together that every actuality is the actualization of a potential. And there Aristotle's spade is turned.

Though we are not out of the woods yet, we are at least in a position to see why *1073ª36* follows from *ª29*. Every eternally moved thing needs an eternal unmoved mover of its own for just the reason that Socrates and Coriscus each needs a productive understanding of his own.

Ph. VIII 10 is our next target. Part of it—that the movement of the primary heaven is fastest—is argued for as follows: "The spheres move,

---

[28] Look at *EN* VII 14 1154ᵇ26–27: *ou gar monon kinêseôs estin energeia alla kai akinêsias.* It does not mean as the *Revised Oxford Translation* has it: "there is not only an activity of movement but an activity of immobility." For an activity must be the activity or actualization of a second potential, of a movement. The correct translation, therefore, is Irwin's: "activity belongs not only to change but also to unchangingness." The movement of which God is the actualization is the unchanging circular movement of the primary heaven.

while the stars are at rest [relative to them] and move with the spheres to which they are attached . . . and for the faster movement to be of the larger sphere is reasonable when all the spheres are attached to the same center. For just as in the case of other things, when they are moving with their own proper movement,[29] the larger body moves faster, so too in the case of the things [i.e., the spheres] that are moving in circles. For the arc intercepted by two radii will be larger in the larger circle, and hence it is reasonable that the revolution of the larger circle should take the same time as that of the smaller [and so be faster] " (*Cael.* II 8 289^{b}32–290^{a}5). The sphere of the primary heaven moves fastest, then, because it is connected to the center of all the other spheres, and so covers a greater distance in the time that they take to cover a shorter one, and "the faster of two things covers a greater distance in an equal time" (*Ph.* VI 2 232^{a}25–26). But why is it that God, as a teleological cause of the movement of that sphere, must be closest to it? Why, so to speak, does his influence on wish diminish with distance?

The primary heaven moves faster than any of the other spheres and is also bigger than any of them (since it encloses them). Hence it's capacity to move—the strength of its wish—must be strongest. For a greater capacity is one that "always produces an equal [result] in less time" (*Ph.* VIII 10 266^{a}26–27). But why is its wish so strong? Generally speaking, "we desire something because it seems [good] rather than its seeming [good] because we desire it" (*Met.* XII 7 1072^{a}29). Presumably, then, the better we think something is, the more we desire it, everything else being equal. Hence for a being like the primary heaven, which has no base appetites to cloud its understanding of the good (God), only the intrinsic clarity of its understanding can affect the strength of its wish. But that clarity is a function of its distance from the center of the universe (which is also the center of the earth). For the further the base of an understanding is from that center, the clearer (or brighter) is the ether in it; and the clearer the ether is, the clearer is the understanding whose base it is. It follows that the primary heaven's wish is strongest, and so its movement fastest, because it is closest to God. The very intentionality of wish, therefore, far from being a liability, has proved to be the key to explaining why God has a location in the universe, why it is where it is, and why there are as many eternal unmoved movers as there are eternally moving things *(1073^{a}36)*.

---

[29] I.e., not being caused to move in a non-natural way by something else, as fire, which naturally moves upward, might be forced to move down.

Just how many that is, however, is a question for astronomy, which is the mathematical science "most akin to philosophy," since it "provides theoretical knowledge of substance that is perceptible but eternal, whereas the others, viz., arithmetic and geometry, don't deal with substance at all" (*Met.* XII 8 1073^{b}5–8). Since astronomy is not our topic, we shall not explore Aristotle's self-admittedly speculative solution to it (1073^{b}10–1074^{a}17). But so that our thought may have "some definite number to grasp" (1073^{b}12–13), we should at least record that in his view forty-nine heavenly spheres,[30] each with its own unmoved mover, are needed to account for all the eternal circular movements present in the cosmos.

Aristotle's final argument returns us to philosophy proper, and to an apparently difficult problem:

> *Met.* XII 8 1074^{a}31–38 That there is one heaven is evident. For [^{a}31] if there are many heavens, as there are [many] men, the first principles of each will be one in form but many in number. But [^{a}33] all things that are many in number have matter (for the account of the many is the same, e.g., that of man, but Socrates is one [thing]). But [^{a}35] the primary essence has no matter, since it is a complete activity. Therefore, [^{a}36] the unmoved first mover is one both in account and in number; and, therefore, [^{a}37] that which is moved always and continuously [is one]. Therefore, [^{a}38] there is only one heaven.

The heaven referred to here is the entire connected system of forty-nine spheres (*Cael.* I 9 278^{b}9–21). The problematic move is ^{a}35–^{a}36. For if the fact that God, as PM, is matterless shows that he is unique, how can there be as many eternal unmoved movers as there are heavenly spheres? Aren't these movers also matterless?[31] To answer these questions, we need to determine what the various unmoved movers actually are.

As superlunary bodies, the heavenly spheres are without sublunary matter. But as visible substances, studied by astronomy, they are not without ethereal superlunary matter—ether. Hence their wishes can only be as strong, and their understandings as clear, as the ether in their bases permits. Since the spheres lack sublunary matter, however, their souls cannot perceive or remember. What, then, are the contents of their productive understandings? If our own case is to provide the model, as surely it should,

---

[30] Reading ἐννέα for ἑπτά at 1074^{a}13. See Ross, *Aristotle's Metaphysics,* ad loc.

[31] Ross, *Aristotle's Metaphysics,* ad loc., notes that the problem goes back to Plotinus, *Enneads* V. 1. 9.

the answer must be: their own productive self-understandings. But the contents of their understandings are also the contents of their wishes. Hence these contents must just be their unmoved movers.

Resorting again to the symbols we introduced in 7.5, the picture that emerges is this. Consider the secondary heaven (SH). Because its essence, $|SH|$, contains ether, $|m_2|$, the actualization of it in SH's active self-understanding, $|SH|^\star$, like the actualization of it in reality, contains a particular material element, $|m_2|^\star$. SH is the secondary heaven, however, rather than the primary one (PH), because $|m_2|^\star$ is less clear than $|m_1|^\star$, which is the material element of $|PH|^\star$. It follows that SH's wish is weaker than PH's. But if $|m_2|^\star$ is less clear than $|m_1|^\star$, $|PH|^\star$ and $|SH|^\star$ are distinct intelligible particulars. And the reason they are distinct is that, unlike God, they are not matterless.

Switching terminology, the same point might be made yet more perspicuously as follows. Matter is potential; form actuality. As we move outward from the center of the earth, therefore, we encounter substances that are getting closer and closer to being complete actualities, because what is potential in them (their matter) is increasingly actualized. When we reach God, who is a complete actuality, we reach a substance who, since he contains no unactualized potential, contains no matter.

The inference in 1074^a31-38 goes through, therefore, since the assumption that made $^a35-{}^a36$ seem problematic, namely, that all eternal unmoved movers are matterless, has turned out to be false. Moreover, it has turned out to be false because of a feature of essences, which we have been finding to be more and more crucial, namely, that many of them involve matter of some sort.

Aristotle's account of the number of eternal unmoved movers, then, far from being some sort of bizarre accretion to his theology, springs from the very core of his understanding of how God, as prime mover, moves the primary heaven. Hence it illuminates his theology in dramatic and unexpected ways. It shows, first, that God has a perceptible, though ethereal, body. For transparent ether, the stuff of the heavens, is perceptible—more precisely, visible—matter of a sort. Second, it provides us with a recipe for determining what is in God's direct sphere of influence. For the primary heaven, it is agreed, is within that sphere, since God is at once the intelligible object of its understanding and the object of its wish. Presumably, then, anything else he moves in that way will also be in that sphere.

But is there anything besides the primary heaven that God so moves? Yes. Consider SH again. $|SH|^\star$ is the content of its understanding and wish. It follows that |SH|* must be SH's apparent good. For, like us, SH is most of all its productive self-understanding. Hence its content is its own form or essence actualized. Unlike us, however, SH does not need the virtues of character, since it has no appetites or emotions to oppose its wish. But because it is a productive understanding, it does have theoretical wisdom—the virtue expressed in theoretical understanding. More exactly, it has a degree of theoretical wisdom, this being determined by the clarity of the ether in the base of its understanding. Happiness is activity express-ing the best or most complete virtue. Hence, by actualizing its essence in its productive understanding, SH achieves the highest level of happiness available to it. The content of SH's wish, therefore, is its apparent good, |SH|*.

This apparent good has an analysis, however: it is God—the real good—as he appears to a being the ether in the base of whose understand-ing is of a degree of clarity which places that being at such-and-such a distance from God. Thus while the intentional object of SH's wish is its own form or essence actualized, because of the opacity of its understanding of that object, another object lies concealed within in it: "Unqualifiedly and in truth what is wished for is the good, but to each what is wished for is the apparent good" (*EN* III 4 1113ᵃ23–24). Hence, unqualifiedly and in truth what SH wishes for is the real or best good—God. What it achieves, however, because it fails to understand that object clearly, and so fails to actualize it completely, is less than perfect or complete happiness: "While it is best of all for each being to attain the uttermost end, or if not, the closer it is to the best the better its state will always be. It is for this reason that the earth does not move at all, while the things close to it have few move-ments. For they do not attain the final [end], but are [only] able to come as close as their share in the divine first principle permits. But the primary heaven shares in it immediately through a single movement, whereas those intermediate between the first and last attain [a share of it] indeed, but they attain [it] through many movements" (*Cael.* II 12 292ᵇ17–25). The *scala naturae,* therefore, is also a scale of decreasing happiness, on which at least those beings that possess understanding—such as God, ourselves, and the forty-nine heavenly spheres—are ranked.

Because perceptual imagination is an analog of understanding, the story can also be extended, in an attenuated form, to all living things: "It is the most natural function in those living things that are complete [i.e., com-pletely developed] and not deformed or spontaneously generated, to pro-duce another like itself—an animal producing an animal, a plant a plant—

in order that they may partake in the eternal and divine to the extent possible. For all things desire that, and it is for the sake of it that they do whatever they do by nature. . . . Since, then, they cannot share in what is eternal and divine by continuous existence, because nothing that admits of passing-away can persist as numerically one and the same living thing, they share in them to the extent that each can; and what persists is not the thing itself but something like itself—not one in number, but one in form" (*DA* II 4 415^{a}26–^{b}7).[32] It can even be extended, indeed, albeit in a yet more attenuated way, to the elements themselves: "Beings that cannot pass-away are imitated by those that are involved in change, e.g., earth and fire. For these are also ever in activity, since they have their movement intrinsically and within themselves" (*Met.* IX 8 1050^{b}28–30).[33] The *scala naturae,* in other words, goes all the way down and all the way up.

It is important to be clear, however, that this does not mean that God obviates the need for the other unmoved movers (or their analogs in other beings). To think so would be to confuse the contents of their productive understandings with God himself. For good, as Aristotle is at pains to emphasize, "is spoken of in as many ways as being is spoken of" (*EN* I 6 1096^{a}23–24). There is a good in the category of substance (God or understanding), in quality (for example, the virtues), in quantity (the intermediate or mean amount), in relation (what is useful), in time (the opportune), and so on. The good, therefore, has as many different accounts as there are categories, and so is homonymous. But it is "not homonymous by mere chance," since all these different categories of goods are unified either "by all being derived from a single source, or by all being related to one joint end, or instead by analogy" (1096^{a}26–28). In the case of goods in the first of these groups, this end is the good in the category of substance—God (*Met.* IV 2 1003^{a}33–^{b}19). But even within that category, there are different substantial goods, as we have seen, which are like God, but are not identical to him. Hence he is not the teleological cause of their movements in the direct way that he is of the movement of the primary heaven. Instead, he is their teleological cause because their direct teleological causes (their own unmoved movers) are related to him in the relevant way: they are unclear understandings of him—something the definitions of their essences must make clear on pain of misrepresentation. God's direct sphere of influence,

---

[32] Also *GA* II 1 731^{b}20–732^{a}9.

[33] Also *Met.* IX 8 1050^{b}5–6, XII 4 1070^{b}34–35, 10 1075^{a}11–25.

then, is (to use a handy Aristotelianism) in one way, the primary heaven, and, in another, pretty well everything.[34]

8.3 God's Essence

God is the prime unmoved mover, at once the intelligible object of the primary heaven's active understanding and of its wish. But what is his essence? What, in other words, is the content of the primary heaven's active understanding?[35] That is the problem to which Aristotle now turns:

Met. XII 9 1074^{b}15–35 Matters concerning [^{b}15a] the understanding involve certain problems; for [^{b}15b] it is held to be the most divine of the visible things *(tôn phainomenôn theiotaton)*, but [^{b}16] what character it must have to be such, involves difficulties. For either [^{b}17] it understands nothing, in which case in what would its august character lie? It would be just like someone asleep. Or [^{b}18] it understands [something], in which case something else controls this. For, in this case, what it is, its substance, isn't active understanding, but potential [or passive understanding], and it would not be the best substance, for it is due to [active] understanding that its value [actually] belongs to it. And furthermore whether it is [passive] understanding or active understanding that is its substance [essence], what does it understand? For it [understands] either [^{b}22] itself or something else. And if something else, [^{b}23a] always the same thing or [^{b}23b] sometimes this and sometimes that. Does it, then, make a difference or not at all [whether it] understands [^{b}24a] the good or [^{b}24b] some chance object? Or would it not be absurd for [it] to be understanding certain kinds of things? It is clear, then, that [^{b}25] it understands what is most divine and most valuable, and [^{b}26] it does not change [its content], since change would be for the worse, and would at the same time be a sort of movement. [Going back to the] first [alternative], then, if it is not

---

[34] A similar conclusion about the extent of God's teleological causation is ably defended in Kahn, "The Place of the Prime Mover in Aristotle's Theology."

[35] Notice the switch from 'productive' to 'active'. Our understandings are productive because they turn second potentialities into second actualities by actualizing them (7.3). The first heaven's understanding, by contrast, is active not productive, since God, its content, is in essence an activity, a second actuality, and so is never a mere second potentiality.

active understanding [that is its substance] but potential [understanding], *[ᵇ28]* it is reasonable to suppose that the continuity of its active understanding is wearisome to it. Next, *[ᵇ29]* it is clear that something else would be more valuable than [passive] understanding, namely, what is understood [by it]. *[ᵇ31]* And indeed *(kai gar)* [passive] understanding and *(kai)* active understanding will be possessed by what understands even the worst thing, so that if this is to be avoided (since there are even things that it is simply better not to see than to see), the active understanding would not be the best thing. *[ᵇ33]* It is itself, therefore, that it understands, if indeed it is the best thing, and *[ᵇ34]* it is an active understanding that is an active understanding of active understanding *(hê noêsis noêseôs noêsis).*

To whom does the understanding mentioned in ᵇ15a belong? One might answer: God. But that would be a mistake. God *is* an understanding; he doesn't *have* one. What has the divine understanding is the primary heaven, which, in turn, is the body that God (who is that understanding) has. The importance of being clear about this emerges when we turn to the characterization of this understanding as "the most divine of visible things" *(ᵇ15b).*

God is an intelligible substance, the activity of understanding, a matterless form or essence. How, then, can he be a visible thing at all?[36] One might ask the same question about a human being, since he too is in essence an understanding. Not surprisingly, the answer is the same in both cases. We are visible because we have visible bodies. God is visible because "the [primary] heaven," which is his body, is "the most divine of

---

[36] Elders, *Aristotle's Theology,* 248–249, while rightly skeptical of other treatments of the expression, resorts in the end to a counsel of despair: "In Aristotelian terminology τὰ φαινόμενα are the visible things and observed facts. Since the first principle is mind [i.e., *nous*], which has itself as its object, it is strange that these lines seem to consider it as one of the visible things. Bonitz [*Aristoteles Metaphysik,* Bonn, 1848–9], 515, suspects a corruption in the text. In his paraphrase of the text, ps. Alexander, 710, 37–38, reformulates the wording so as to avoid the difficulty. Ross [*Aristotle's Metaphysics,* ad loc.] tries to solve the problem by suggesting that τῶν φαινομένων means here 'of all the things discovered by reason' (i.e., not by sense). Although the expression does not exclusively mean 'the visible things' or 'the observed facts', but also 'the common views of people', it is difficult to give it the meaning 'discovered by reason' . . . [I]t is also possible that an editor who brought together the various parts of Λ wrote the first line of chapter nine by himself so as to connect it with the preceding chapters. In that case τῶν φαινομέ-νων would just be a careless expression."

visible things *(ta theiotata tôn phanerôn)*" *(Ph.* II 4 196ᵃ33–34).[37] The divine understanding *is* being described in ᵇ*15b,* then, but the description is metonymic—it characterizes the whole in terms that literally apply only to a part.

The remainder of the argument is concerned with the question of how—in the face of the difficulties soon to be cataloged—God can be the most divine of visible beings. It is a good question. But, because God is an understanding, it boils down to what his relationship is to the intelligible object that is his content. Central to it—and to the entire argument—is the distinction between passive understanding and active understanding. For if God—the divine understanding—has no content, he is like someone asleep (ᵇ*17).* But if he is awake, he must have some content, since "understanding is moved by intelligible objects" *(Met.* XII 7 1072ᵃ30). Apparently, then, if God lacks content, he cannot have the august character of being the most divine of visible things, since his active or waking state would be yet more divine (1072ᵇ22–23). On the other hand, if God is understanding some intelligible object, *it* controls whether or not he is active (ᵇ*18).*[38] Apparently, then, he is not an understanding that is in substance or essence an activity, but a passive or potential one. If he is merely a potential understanding, however, he must be related to some other understanding that is in essence an activity in just the way that the primary heaven is in fact related to him. The value (mis-)ascribed to him in ᵇ*15b,* therefore, is value he actually possesses because of that other understanding, which is in fact the best and most divine of beings. Hence if God has a content, he is not the best or most divine substance.

The remainder of the argument is surprisingly intricate in structure, and has not been well understood.[39] I shall begin by sketching its overall structure, leaving the details for subsequent discussion. By the end of ᵇ*18,* Aristotle has argued that God cannot be either a passive understanding or an active one without falsifying ᵇ*15b.* That is one of the difficulties mentioned in ᵇ*16*—it concerns God's essence, not his content. The difficulties

---

[37] *Met.* VI 1 1026ᵃ18: "what is visible among things divine"; VII 8 1073ᵇ5–6: "astronomy theorizes about substance that is perceptible but eternal".

[38] Notice that ᵇ*17* and ᵇ*18* are exclusive possibilities. The latter must, then, be presupposing that God has some content, and that it is what controls him.

[39] By far the best discussion is Brunschwig, "Lambda 9: A Short-Lived Thought-Experiment."

concerning God's content are those that arise, first, on the assumption that God is in essence an active understanding. The discussion in $^b23a-26$, however, concerns an active understanding that, unlike the one mentioned in $^b22$, has something other than itself as its content. It excludes all possible contents except the good (^b24a)—in other words, what is most divine and most valuable $(^b25)$. No problems are raised for ^b24a. $^b28-29$ takes up the second possibility regarding God's essence, namely, that he is a passive or potential understanding. His content, in this case, must be something other than himself—for his actual content cannot be a mere second potential, but must be an actual intelligible particular. Hence there is a kind of continuity between $^b23a-26$ and $^b28-29$, since the latter shows that there are difficulties in reconciling ^b15b with any of the contents that God can be assigned. $^b31$ is a problem that arises for God's content, whether he is an active understanding whose object is not himself or a passive understanding whose object is other than himself. $^b33-34$ reaches the only conclusion that avoids all these difficulties.

So much for the outline sketch of Aristotle's argument, now for the details. If God is in essence an active understanding, what he understands must be the best and most divine good $(^b24a, ^b25)$. For if his content were anything else, any chance object, his august character, as most divine, would be threatened (^b24b).[40] Moreover, the good must be God's unchanging content, since any change of content would be a change for the worse, and would, in any case, constitute a sort of movement impossible in an unmoved mover $(^b26)$. For while thinking of the good, God would have to have the potential to think of his new content, F. Then, he would have to stop thinking of the good and start thinking of F. This sequence of stops and starts is a movement, since it is not complete at every instant.

If God is not an active understanding, however, but a second potential or passive one, he must be continuously activated by his content, since he is the actual mover of the continuously moving primary heaven $(^b28)$. But a second potential, as something that can by nature be inactive, has a natural limit to its period of activity: "For things that have a natural function, when they exceed the time for which they have the potential to do something must lose the potential. . . . If, then, perceiving is the function of a thing, it too, if it exceeds the time for which it has the potential to perceive continuously, will lose its potential and do this [i.e., perceive] no longer" (*Somn.* I 454^{a}26–32). Hence God's content, by keeping him con-

---

[40] $^b31$ adds further support for this conclusion.

tinuously active, would constrain him contrary to his nature as a second potential. Such constrained activity, however, "is necessarily wearisome— the more so, the more eternal it is—and is an arrangement without any share in what is best" (*Cael.* II 1 284ᵃ16–18).[41]

ᵇ29 is correlated with *ᵇ18*, making explicit an implication already implicit in the latter. If God were a passive understanding, he would, as we saw, be related to what he understands as the primary heaven is in fact related to him. What he would understand, then, would be the best and most divine good. Since it (as essentially an activity) is not identical to him, what he understands would be more valuable than the passive understanding he would be.

ᵇ31 presents difficulties mostly because its relationship to *ᵇ29* is initially hard to grasp. Its syntactic structure seems to be *kai gar . . . kai . . .*, which yields the meaning: "For both [passive] understanding and active understanding. . . ." Hence it seems to be giving an argument in support of *ᵇ29*. Just how it could be doing so, however, is obscure. For *ᵇ29* is assuming that God is a passive understanding whose content must, in consequence, be better than he is, while *ᵇ31* concerns (indifferently) a passive or active understanding whose content is the worst thing. It is more likely, therefore, that *ᵇ31* is a new difficulty altogether. The syntax of *ᵇ31* permits this, provided we treat the initial *kai* as a conjunction, *gar* as an adverb, and the second *kai* as an independent conjunction. This yields the meaning given in the translation: "And indeed *(kai gar)* [passive] understanding and *(kai)* active understanding will be possessed by what understands even the worst thing."

What *ᵇ31* does, in effect, is to consider the possibility that God owes his value to his essence—whether as a passive or as an active understanding— and not to his content at all. If so, he could be understanding the worst thing. But since actively understanding such a thing is to be avoided, it is clearly worse, not better, than only potentially understanding it. It follows that active understanding is not the best thing. That is a problematic consequence, however, since we have just seen an argument that the best thing *is* such an understanding.

The solution to all these difficulties is proposed in *ᵇ33*. If the understanding that is God is the best or most divine thing, as *ᵇ15b* claims, he must have himself as his content. *ᵇ33* follows immediately: God is *noêsis noêseôs*

---

[41] Also *DA* I 3 407ᵃ34–ᵇ12; *Met.* IX 8 1050ᵇ6–28.

noêsis—an active understanding that is an active understanding of active understanding.

Three problems with *^{b}33* complete Aristotle's discussion. The first two are as follows:

> *Met. XII 9 1074^{b}35–38* But *[^{b}35]* it seems that scientific knowledge, perception, belief, and understanding are always of something other [than themselves], and of themselves [only] as a by-product *(en parergô)*. Moreover, *[^{b}36]* if understanding and being understood are different, in respect of which does it [the divine understanding] possess the good? For the being [essence] of understanding [something] is not the same as that of what is understood.

Aristotle's solution to these problems is already familiar to us—though not as such. It is the Identity Thesis. *^{b}35* is generally speaking true, but "in the case of things that have no matter, they—understanding and the intelligible object—are the same" (*Met. XII 9 1075^{a}4–5*). What we need to do here, then, is not re-evaluate that doctrine, but see just how it is supposed to solve our two problems.

If *^{b}35* were true, *1074^{b}34* would be immediately threatened, since God could not have himself as his sole content. Instead, he would understand himself only as a by-product of understanding something else, which would lead to all the difficulties already raised in *^{b}23a–31*. *^{b}35* would not be threatening, however, if God had no matter—if, that is to say, he were a matterless form or essence. For *any* understanding that understands such an essence is identical to it. Since God is such an essence, the same holds, therefore, when he is understanding himself.

The question raised in *^{b}36* requires some scene-setting. Teaching and learning are different potentials: the teacher cannot teach what he does not already know; the learner cannot learn what he does already know. But, like seeing and being seen, they are the same in actuality, since teaching a thing cannot be actualized unless learning it is, and vice versa. Learning and teaching, then, are the same in actuality, but because they are different potentials, they have different accounts, and so are different in essence (*Ph. III 3*). God-the-understander should, therefore, be related to God-the-understood in just that way. But if so, the essences of the two must be different, even though they themselves are identical. There is a genuine question, therefore, as to whether God-the-understander is *in essence* the good or is the good only because he has the same actualization as God-the-understood. For if he were not in essence the good, if he owed his value to something with a different essence, then ^b15b would be false. Hence to solve this problem, Aristotle must show not just that God-the-understander and God-the-understood are one, but that they are one *in essence*. And that is just what he does show. For the Identity Thesis entails that God-the-understander is the very same matterless essence as God-the-understood.[42]

The third and final problem with 1074^b34 has to do with whether God's content is simple or composite. It is raised and answered in the following crabbed and opaque text. My more than usually literal translation is intended to convey its difficulty, while begging as few questions as possible:

> *Met. XII 9 1075^{a}5–10* A further problem remains—whether [$^a5$] the intelligible object is composite *(suntheton)*, since then [^a6a] it [the divine understanding] would undergo change in [understanding] the parts of the whole *(en tois meresi tou holou)*. Or [^a6b] is not everything that has no matter indivisible, [$^a7$] just as the human understanding [of such things] is, or [^a8a] the [understanding] even of composites in a certain time *(ê ho ge tôn synthetôn echei en tini chronô)*?[43] [^a8b] Indeed, it doesn't possess the good in this or that *(ou gar echei to eu en tôde ê en tôdi)*, but [^a9a] in a certain whole [it possesses] the best *(all' en holô tini to ariston)*, [^a9b] being something other *(on allo ti)*. [$^a10$] Isn't it the same for this understanding which, for all eternity, is an understanding of itself?

The problem raised in $^a5$ concerns the intelligible object of divine understanding. *Prima facie,* then, intelligible objects should be the focus of Aristotle's solution. The problem itself is this: if the intelligible object of divine understanding is composite, if it is a whole composed of distinct parts, God

---

[42] Elders, *Aristotle's Theology,* 262, somewhat unconfidently proposes the same solution, while failing to notice that it is Aristotle's own: "Aristotle does not give an answer to this objection. . . . It would seem that a solution of the difficulty has to be sought in this direction: in the first being even the formal essence of thinking [i.e., *noêsis*] and that of being thought are the same." Ross, *Aristotle's Metaphysics,* ad loc., also claims that this question is "left unanswered."

[43] Most scholars take *ê* as specificatory and *ge* as restrictive. The *Revised Oxford Translation* is typical: "We answer that everything which has not matter is indivisible. As human thought, or rather the thought of composite objects, is in a certain period of time." I think it is better to treat *ê* as a genuine disjunction and *ge* as intensive.

will change as first one and then another of these parts is the focus of his understanding (*6a).

*6b reminds us that if this intelligible object is matterless, as in God's case it is, it is not divisible into parts, just as the human understanding of such an object, which is—because of the Identity Thesis—identical to it, is not. That, by itself, would seem to solve the problem. *8a, however, introduces an additional consideration. Its gist is plain enough: even the human understanding of composite objects is complete in a certain time. But getting to that gist takes some work. The occurrence of *suntheton* in *5 and *sunthetôn* in *8a makes it natural to think that the latter is talking about an object of human understanding.[44] Moreover, since this object is composite, it cannot be matterless—*6b has ruled that out. It must, then, be an essence that involves matter of some sort.

What about the phrase *en tini chronô*, what is its role? Consider a composite intelligible object O, the parts of which are o_1, o_2, and o_3. Now imagine a human being, S, that at t_1 has o_1 as the content of its understanding, at t_2 o_2, and at t_3 o_3. If S's going though that temporal process is how we conceive of him understanding O as a whole, we will consider his understanding of O as divisible into a series of stages, and S himself as undergoing change in understanding it. But we shouldn't conceive of S's understanding O in that way: "The states of the understanding part [of the soul] are not qualitative changes, nor is there any coming-to-be of them . . . the potential knower becomes an [actual] knower not as a consequence of having undergone change itself, but rather through the presence of something else *(allo)* [viz., its object]. For when the part comes to be [known], [the knower] somehow knows the universal whole by knowing the part.[45] And again, there is no coming-to-be of their use, or activity,

---

[44] It is grammatically possible, however, that *suntheton* refers to composite understandings rather than to composite understoods. Ross, *Aristotle's Metaphysics,* ad loc., following Ps. Alexander, understands it in this way: "the human reason [i.e., *nous*], or rather the understandings of beings composed of matter and form."

[45] *Hotan gar genêtai to kata meros, epistatai pôs ta katholou tô en merei:* Usually *to kata meros* is understood to refer to particulars, so that the entire sentence is taken to be about how knowledge of a universal is reached from knowledge of particulars. It is more likely, I think, that it is about how knowledge of the parts of a composite intelligible object is involved in knowledge of the whole. For the "something else *(allo)*" in the previous sentence is clearly the intelligible object that activates the state of knowledge, and not a perceptible particular that activates a different percep-

unless one supposes that there is a coming-to-be of both catching sight and of touching, since the use, or activity, are similar to these. And the original acquisition of scientific knowledge is neither a coming-to-be nor a qualitative change, since we are said to know and to understand *(phronein)* as a result of our understanding's having come to rest and being still, and there is no coming-to-be of being at rest, or indeed of any change *(metabolê)* at all" (*Ph.* VII 3 247^{b}1–13). Thus understanding O is like winning a race (catching sight of something) rather than running it (looking for it)— "more like a sort of rest or a coming-to-a-halt than a movement" (*DA* I 3 407^{a}32–33). So we must think of S's understanding O as follows: As a result of successively grasping o_1 at t_1, o_2 at t_2, and o_3 at t_3, S's understanding grasps O as a whole at t_4: "in the case of understanding *(dianooumenois)* and making deductions about unmoving objects . . . the end is an intelligible object, for when one understands the two premises, one understands and puts together the conclusion" (*MA* 7 701^{a}9–11). The certain time in which S's understanding of O is indivisible is t_4, the moment at which he grasps it as a whole. That, I think, is why Aristotle describes it as he does in ^{a}8a.

Our next target is ^{a}8b–^{a}9b. Compare *en tois meresi tou holou* in ^{a}6 to *en tôde ê en tôdi, all' en holô tini* in ^{a}8b–^{a}9a. Surely, the closeness of their wording requires that they be understood in the same way.[46] Since the sense of ^{a}6 is not in any doubt, ^{a}8b–^{a}9a should, therefore, be interpreted as follows: "For it doesn't possess the good by understanding this or that part, but by understanding a certain whole it possesses the best."

Now focus on ^{a}8b–^{a}9a. If these two texts explain and elucidate ^{a}8a,[47] *to eu* in the former and *to ariston* in the latter must be composite intelligible objects, since ^{a}8a is exclusively concerned with such objects. Moreover, on

---

tual state. The focus of the entire passage is the understanding. The text supports my point in any case.

[46] Though, so far as I am aware, no one has understood them in this way. Instead, deceived by *en tini chronô*, which immediately precedes ^{a}8b, they have given *en tôde ê en tôdi* and *en holô tini* a temporal interpretation. Again, the *Revised Oxford Translation* is typical: "for it [human understanding] does not possess the good at this moment or at that, but its best, being something different from it, is attained only in a whole period of time."

[47] From the grammatical point of view, *gar* is treated as a causal or explanatory conjunction meaning 'for' or 'since'.

the face of it, they must be the same object, since ^a8b tells us that understanding does not possess in one way the very thing that ^a9a tells us that it
does possess in another way. Earlier in XII 9, however, *to ariston* refers to
God (1074^{b}20, ^{b}33), and within a mere two lines, the phrase *to agathon kai
to ariston* (10 1075^{a}11–12) has precisely this significance, with *to eu* used as a
stylistic variant two lines later (^{a}14). It seems, then, that both *to eu* and *to
ariston* refer to God.[48] The trouble is that God, being matterless, is *not*
composite (^a6b). It follows that ^a8b–^a9a cannot be taken as supporting ^a8a,
but must be taken as a separate point.[49] Its gist, therefore, is this: the human
understanding of an incomposite essence, such as the good or the best, is
by contrast with its understanding of a composite one, not a matter of
understanding one part and then another until the whole is grasped, but
simply a matter of grasping the whole.

The interpretation of ^a9b now becomes relatively routine. The point
made is that the good or best grasped by the human understanding in the
way described in ^a9a is not identical to the human understanding, but is
something else altogether, which marks a contrast with the divine understanding that is the main topic of 1075^a5–10 as a whole. This is confirmed
by the following text: "It is not in that way [i.e., by understanding something different from himself] that God possesses the good *(eu echei)*, rather
he is too good to understand anything besides himself, and the reason for
this is that while the good *(to eu)* for us has reference to something different, in his case he is his own good *(to eu)*" (*EE* VII 12 1245^{b}16–19). God
achieves the good by understanding himself, then, but we achieve it by
understanding something besides ourselves, namely, him.

The problem raised in $^a5$–6 has now been doubly answered. It is not a
problem for God, since his intelligible object is matterless. Hence $^a10$, and
so 1074^a34, are unthreatened by it. But the problem is not decisive in any
case. For even a composite object must be understood as a whole.

The God portrayed in *Metaphysics* XII 6–9 has been characterized as a
heavenly Narcissus, who finds nothing more worth understanding than
himself.[50] The characterization is meant as a criticism of any interpretation

---

[48] Notice that *to eu* is so used in *EE* VII 12 1245^{b}16–19, quoted below.

[49] From the grammatical point of view, *gar* is treated as an adverb, meaning
'indeed' or 'in fact'.

[50] Norman, "Aristotle's Philosopher-God," 63–64.

that would attribute such a view to Aristotle. In the following text, Aristotle raises—and answers—it himself:

MM II 15 1212*b*35–1213*a*7 [*b*35] If God is self-sufficient and needs no [friends], it does not follow from this that we need none. For [*b*36] the following sort of argument, too, is expressed about God. Since God, it is said, possesses all good things and is self-sufficient, what will he do, since he will not [simply] sleep? He will have theoretical knowledge of something, it is replied. For this is the best and most appropriate thing [for him to do]. Of what, then, will he have theoretical knowledge? If he has theoretical knowledge of something other than himself, it must be something better than he is. But it is absurd that there should be anything better than God. Therefore, he will have theoretical knowledge of himself. But that is absurd. For if a human being scrutinizes himself, we criticize him for lacking common sense. It will [also] be absurd, therefore, it is said, for God to have theoretical knowledge of himself.

If we focus on *b*36 in isolation, it might seem that Aristotle is rejecting 'narcissistic' theology in *propria persona*. But when we factor *b*35 into the equation, a wholly different picture emerges, whose point is that we cannot draw immediate inferences about ourselves from truths about God, or vice versa. God is indeed self-sufficient, and so does not need friends, but it does not follow that a self-sufficient human being has no need of them. To think so—and now we are in *b*36—would be like arguing that because a human being who spends all his time in self-scrutiny is senselessly narcissistic, so a God who has himself as the content of his active understanding would be similarly senseless. The argument is invalid precisely because Narcissus is not God, not the best thing, and so is not a proper object of eternal scrutiny. God, by contrast, is the best thing and is worthy of it. For him to have theoretical knowledge of himself alone, therefore, is, as it were, good sense, not foolishness.

To describe Aristotle's God as a heavenly Narcissus, then, is to misdescribe him, since it is to suggest that his self-absorption is a defect in the way that Narcissus' is. Nonetheless there is a core of truth in it: God does understand only himself. Even that core, however, is somewhat misleading. For God is the final or teleological cause of everything in the universe, which is, in turn, a teleological system that has him as it ultimate *telos* or end. But every such system is most of all its end (*EN* IX 8 1168*b*31–32). So the universe is most of all God. In understanding himself, therefore, God is understanding, if not the universe itself, then what the universe most of all is. There is, therefore, a sort of omniscience involved in his self-understanding.

Used as we are to genuinely omniscient gods, who are also omnipotent and omnibenevolently concerned about—at least our moral—well-being, Aristotle's God seems strange and discomfiting. How dare he not be focused on us is our concealed thought. It is our own narcissism, in other words, that is operative in our reaction, not his. Were the history of theology our topic, there would be much more to say on this head. I shall content myself with just one comment. In 1074^b31 Aristotle offers a criticism of divine omniscience: there are some things that it is unseemly for anyone, let alone God, to know. He thereby undercuts some of the ground on which we stand to criticize his God. Those who value highly the privacy that a literally omniscient God violates should find his criticism somewhat compelling.

8.4 God and "the Nature of the Whole"

God's nature has been defined, as has his relationship to the primary heaven, and the other beings in the universe: he is an active self-understanding; the primary heaven is his body; he moves it, as he moves everything, by being the object of wish and desire, the best good. What remains to discover is his relationship to the "nature of the whole":

> *Met. XII 10 1075ª11–25* We must consider too *[ª11]* in which way the nature of the whole possesses the good and the best—whether *[ª12]* as something separate and intrinsic, or *[ª13a]* as its organization *(taxis).* Or *[ª13b]* is it in both ways just like an army? For the good of an army is in its organization and is also the general. And *[ª14]* more so the latter, since he does not exist because of the organization, but it does exist because of him. *[ª16a]* All things (even swimming creatures, flying creatures, and plants) are jointly organized, though *[ª16b]* not in the same way, and are not of such a character that one thing has no relation to another. Instead, there is some [relation between them]. For *[ª18]* all things are jointly organized in relation to one thing. But *[ª19a]* it is just like in a household, where *[ª19b]* the free men least of all do things at random, but all or most of the things they do are organized, while *[ª21]* the slaves and beasts can do little for the sake of the common thing *(to koinon),* but mostly [do] things at

random. For [*22] that is the kind of first principle that nature is of each of them.[51] I mean, e.g., that [*23] all must at least come to be dissolved [into their elements] ; and similarly [*24] there are other things which they all share for the sake of the whole *(to holon)*.

The analogy with the household drawn in *19a*–*22 provides the best way into this complex text, though it is perhaps truer to say that it is the household's own connection to the city *(polis)* that is really illuminating.

A city "is prior in nature to the household, since the whole *(to holon)* is necessarily prior to its parts" *(Pol.* I 2 1253ª18–20), and "every household is part of a city" (I 13 1260ᵇ13). Since "the virtue of a part must be determined by looking to the virtue of the whole," it follows that the virtues of the household and its parts must be determined by looking to "the constitution *(politeia)*" of the city of which it is a part (1260ᵇ14–15). A constitution, however, is itself "a certain organization *(taxis)* of the inhabitants of a city" (III 1 1274ᵇ38). We may infer that the sort of organization referred to throughout *1075ª11–25* is relevantly similar to a constitution, and that the whole referred to in *11* is relevantly similar to a city.

In *21–*22, the behavior of the free men in the household is contrasted with that of the slaves and beasts that are also parts of it. The former is mostly "organized," the latter mostly "at random." The impression created—especially if we are unclear about the particular sort of organization at issue—is that the behavior of slaves is somehow freer than that of the free men. Nothing, obviously, could be further from the truth. What is meant, as we shall see, is that the behavior of the free men is more determined than that of slaves and animals by the constitution of the city of which the household is a part.[52]

The most important way in which the constitution determines the behavior of citizens is by providing public education that inculcates the kind of virtue that suits them to be citizens of the particular sort of constitution it is—whether aristocratic, oligarchic, democratic, or what have you.[53] This education is primarily, and often exclusively, provided to

---

[51] Reading τοιαύτε γὰρ ἑκάστου ἀρχὴ αὐτῶν ἡ φύσις ἐστίν with the mss.

[52] *Pol.* I 5 1254ᵇ24–26: "The difference in the use made of them [in the household] is small, since both slaves and domestic animals help provide the necessities with their bodies."

[53] *Pol.* VIII 1 1337ª11–24: "No one would dispute, therefore, that legislators should be particularly concerned with the education of the young. . . . For educa-

males, many of whom will eventually marry and become heads of households in their turn. When they do, one of their primary tasks will be to
educate the other members of the household in the kind of virtue that will
complete or perfect their different natures: "The deliberative part of the
soul is entirely missing from a slave; a woman has it but it lacks authority;[54]
a child has it but it is incompletely developed. We must suppose, therefore,
that the same necessarily holds of the virtues of character too: all must share
in them, but not in the same way; rather, each must have a sufficient share
to enable him to perform his own task. Hence a ruler must have virtue of
character complete, since his task is unqualifiedly that of a master craftsman, and reason is a master craftsman, but each of the others must have as
much as pertains to him. It is evident, then, that all those mentioned have
virtue of character, and that the temperance, courage, and justice of a man
are not the same as those of a woman, as Socrates supposed: men have the
courage and similarly the other virtues appropriate in a ruler, whereas
women have those appropriate in an assistant, and similarly in the case of
the other virtues too" (*Pol.* I 13 1260^{a}12–24). Thus the *scala naturae*
manifests itself within the household as a difference in the degree to which
education and habituation can develop the natural basis for the virtues into
the full-blown virtues themselves.[55] Moreover, the scale does not stop

---

tion should suit the particular constitution. In fact, the character peculiar to each
constitution usually safeguards it as well as establishing it initially (e.g., the
democratic character, a democracy, and the oligarchic one, an oligarchy), and a
better character results in a better constitution in all cases. . . . Since the whole city
has one single end, however, it is evident that education too must be one and the
same for all, and that its supervision must be communal."

[54] Part of what this implies may be that a woman, having arrived through
deliberation at what she judges is the best thing to do in particular circumstances,
may sometimes deliberately choose to do something else, because she tends to be
less able to control her own appetites and emotions than a man. This would explain
why those who are weak-willed are likened to women (*EN* VII 7 1150^{a}32–^{b}16).
On the other hand, it may be that what women lack authority over is not themselves so much as *other people,* since females generally have less spirit than males (*HA*
IX 1 608^{a}33–^{b}12; *PA* III 1 661^{b}33–34), and spirit is responsible for the ability to
command (*Pol.* VII 6 1328^{a}6–7).

[55] *EN* VI 3 1144^{b}4–9: "Virtue is similar to practical wisdom: as practical
wisdom is related to cleverness—not the same but similar—so natural virtue is
related to full. For each seems to possess his type of character somehow by nature,

with the human members of the household; it extends downwards to the domestic animals as well: "Domestic animals are by nature better than wild ones, and it is better for all of them to be ruled by human beings, since this will secure their safety" (5 1254ᵇ10–13).[56] Their virtues—which suit them to perform household tasks, such as plowing the fields or guarding the hen house at night—are not far removed, therefore, from the virtues of (at any rate, lower grade) slaves.

But to reiterate, as we move from one type of political constitution to another, the virtues of *all* the members of the household change: "Women and children must be educated with an eye to the constitution, if indeed it makes any difference to the virtue of a city that its children be virtuous, and its women too. And it must make a difference, since half the free population are women, and from children come those who participate in the constitution" (*Pol.* I 13 1260ᵃ15–20). What this means, in effect, is that when the nature of a household member has been completed or perfected through education and habituation in, for example, an aristocracy, he thereby acquires a specific sort of *second nature*—one that identifies him as a member of just such a household, since its constitution, in the shape of the relevant virtues, has been stamped into his soul. In addition to our individual *first natures,* therefore, which differ in all sorts of ways from one another as a result of the natural lottery, we also, as members of a household, have second natures. These are not the same in all members of the household, yet they are sufficiently similar to justify us in speaking of the members of the household as sharing a common second nature.[57]

It is because the members of a household share such a nature in this way that the behavior that expresses it is organized to different degrees by the constitution of which the household is a part. A free male head of household has virtue complete; his free wife, something very close to it. Hence

---

since we are just, temperate, and courageous immediately from birth. However, we still search for something else—full goodness—and expect to possess these characteristics in another way. For these natural states are possessed by children and beasts as well, but without understanding they are apparently harmful."

[56] *Pr.* X 45 895ᵇ23–896ᵃ6: "All domestic (or tame) animals are at first wild rather than domestic. . . . But the tame are better and the wild worse. . . . Under certain conditions of locality and time sooner or later all animals can become tame." Presumably, then, it is better even for wild animals to be ruled by man.

[57] I have developed this account more fully in *Aristotle: Politics,* especially xlvii–lxxii.

their behavior is to a very high degree organized by the constitution, in that almost everything they do expresses the complete virtue they possess. A slave, by contrast, since he possesses only a minimal amount of virtue, has his behavior only minimally organized in this way. His behavior is more random, therefore, than that of his master and mistress. The behavior of domestic animals, more so still.

Since the type of virtue each possesses has turned out to explain the difference between free and slave with respect to the organization of their behavior, it must also explain why slaves and beasts can do little for the sake of "the common thing *(to koinon)*" (*21). And if we understand *to koinon* by reference to its political analog, it does precisely this. For *to koinon* in a constitution is *to koinon sumpheron*—"the common benefit" (*Pol.* III 7 1279ª28–29). And one shares in, or contributes to, it to the degree that one shares in "living well" (1278ᵇ20–23)—in happiness. One shares in happiness, however, just to the degree that one shares in the virtues whose expression in one's behavior just is happiness. Slaves and animals can "do little for the sake of" this, then, because they have so small a share of the virtue that makes it possible to do more.

The differences in the first natures of slaves and free men is the basis of the differences in their second natures, and these, in turn, explain why each contributes to the common benefit in a different way and to a different extent. Nonetheless, they all do contribute to some extent. For though their first natures differ, the differences are complementary—attuned to one another, so to speak: "Those who cannot exist without one another necessarily form a couple, as female and male do for the sake of procreation (they do not do so because they deliberately choose to, but, like other animals and plants, because the urge to leave behind something of the same kind as themselves is natural), and as a natural ruler and what is naturally ruled do for the sake of survival. For if something is capable of rational foresight, it is a natural ruler and master, whereas whatever can use its body to labor is ruled and is a natural slave. That is why the same thing is advantageous for both master and slave" (*Pol.* I 2 1252ª26–34). Because their first natures have this feature, their second natures, too, must be so developed as to preserve and enhance it: "As for man and woman, father and children, the virtue relevant to each of them, what is good in their relationship with one another and what is not good, and how to achieve the good and avoid the bad—it will be necessary to go through all these in connection with the constitutions" (13 1260ᵇ8–13). It is not enough that the members of the household be organized, in other words, they must be so *jointly* organized as to fit together well. Moreover, as we are about to see, they must also be jointly organized in relation to a single thing—one that is intrinsic and separate from the smooth functioning of the household itself, from harmonious domestic life.

Household-management is the science that enables one to manage a household well, and mastership of slaves is a part of it. But a free man will not act as a slave master unless he has to: "there is nothing grand or august about this science. . . . Hence for those who have the resources not to bother with such things, a steward takes on this office, while they themselves engage in politics or philosophy" (*Pol.* I 7 1255ᵇ33–37). But even politics has its downside: "Among actions expressing the virtues, those in politics and war are preeminently fine and great, but are unleisurely and aim at some [further] end, and are not chosen [solely] because of themselves" (*EN* X 7 1177ᵇ16–18). The further end in question is the leisured activity of philosophy itself (or theoretical understanding), through which we participate in God, the best good and greatest happiness.⁵⁸ This end is pursued not just by the individual, however, but by the city as a whole and by the household which is a part of it: "Does this [practical wisdom] rule over all the things that are in the soul, as is held and also thought to cause problems? Surely not. For over the things that are better [than it is] —such as theoretical wisdom—it would seem not to do so. But it is said that this oversees everything, and has the authority to give orders. But presumably it is like the steward in the household. For such a person has control over everything and directs everything. But he does not rule over everything, instead he arranges leisure for his master, in order that the latter may not be tied down by the necessary [tasks] and turned aside from doing something that is noble and appropriate to him" (*MM* I 34 1198ᵇ8–17).⁵⁹ The rule of

---

⁵⁸ *Pol.* II 7 1267ᵃ10–12: "if anyone wants to enjoy things because of themselves, he should not look for a cure beyond philosophy"; VII 15 1334ᵃ22–25: "Courage and endurance are required for unleisure, philosophy for leisure, and temperance and justice for both."

⁵⁹ *EN* VI 13 1145ᵃ6–11: "It [practical wisdom] does not have authority over theoretical wisdom or the better part [i.e., the scientific part of the soul], just as medicine does not have authority over [someone who has] health; for it [medicine] does not use it [health], but provides for its coming-to-be; it gives orders for its sake, but not to it. Besides, it [saying that practical wisdom has authority over wisdom] would be like saying that political science has authority over the gods because it gives orders about everything in the city." Also *EE* VII 15 1249ᵃ21–ᵇ25, *Pol.* VII 15 1334ᵇ17–28.

the head of a household, therefore, is primarily the rule of a final or teleological cause, rather than that of an efficient one. It is because his end is theoretical understanding that all the things in the household are jointly organized by practical wisdom in the way that they are, namely, in relation to that one end. But he, though part of the household himself, is also an intrinsic being—a primary substance, separate not just from it, but from his own body.

So much for the household. Our next task is to see how it illuminates "the nature of the whole" (^{a}11), and the two ways in which the latter possesses God or the best good. It was antecedently clear to us, because of our earlier discussion, that God is a separate, intrinsic being who is the teleological cause of all movement in the universe (^{a}12), and that the universe is for his sake, not he for its (^{a}14). ^{a}13a, on the other hand, is new and somewhat surprising. But I think we can now see how to understand it. For just as all the members of a household share a second nature, which ensures that they are jointly organized in relation to a single thing, namely, the head of household, so all beings in the universe also share a first nature that ensures that they are jointly organized in relation to God (^{a}16a, ^{a}18). But because this nature is somewhat differently realized in each of them, they are not all jointly organized in the same way. Fish, birds, and plants, for example, do things more at random, and so less as a result of the constitutional organization of the universe, than either the heavenly spheres or rational human beings.

The reality, if I may put it that way, of this shared first nature emerges forcefully if we reflect again on the relationship between the household and the city. For just as the particular kind of constitution that a city has leaves its distinctive mark on the *second* natures of the members of its constitutive households, so the particular organization of this universe leaves its distinctive mark on the *first* natures of the beings that are its members, identifying them as such. For our universe does have a distinctive constitution—it is a monarchy: "Those [Platonists, Pythagoreans] who say that mathematical number is primary . . . give us many first principles. But the beings must not be governed badly. 'The rule of many is not good; let there be one ruler'" (*Met.* XII 10 1075^{b}37–1076^{a}4). Hence, like a sublunary monarchy, it marks its members as belonging, in particular, to a monarchical universe. Were there a democratic universe it would mark its members in a quite different way. This is what ^{a}22 is claiming. For the nature it refers to is "the nature of the whole"[60]—in other words, the

---

[60] The word order of the mss, adopted by Ross, *Aristotle's Metaphysics,* makes this

monarchical constitution of the universe, the presence of which in the first natures of its citizens explains their different levels of participation in it.

Given the analogy between the nature of the whole and the household, and between God and the household's head, we should expect that the household steward will also have a cosmic analog. This is the primary heaven. For just as its eternal circular movement, as prior to all other movements, is their efficient cause, so he is the efficient cause of the movements in the household.

8.5 God as Primary Substance$_m$?

In 7.6, we saw that human productive self-understanding could not be primary substance$_m$, since it could not be primary in account, knowledge, and time. God—divine active self-understanding—is a better candidate, therefore, since he is clearly prior to everything in at least one of these ways. For as in essence an actuality he is prior to all potentiality, and so is prior in time to all moving substances, whether eternal or subject to coming-to-be and passing-away. The problems arise when we turn to primacy in account and in scientific knowledge.

If God is primary in account (definition), prior in this way to all other beings, his definition "must be present in the account of each of them" (*Met.* VII 1 1028ᵃ35–36). Is this so? Look again at Socrates' essence:

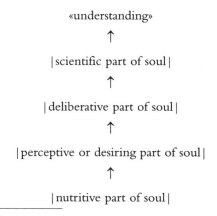

«understanding»

↑

|scientific part of soul|

↑

|deliberative part of soul|

↑

|perceptive or desiring part of soul|

↑

|nutritive part of soul|

clear: *toiaute gar hekastou archê autôn hê phusis estin.* If, with OCT and Zeller, we reverse the order of *archê* and *autôn*, ᵃ22 makes reference only to individual natures: "For that is the kind of first principle that the nature of each of them is." I was led to appreciate the significance of this by Sedley, "Metaphysics Lambda: Chapter 10."

Take it as a representative natural essence—in other words, ignore the fact that Socrates is really a (partly) supernatural being identical to his productive understanding. Where is God in it? As yet, nowhere. But that is because this essence is incompletely presented. For it doesn't reveal the ontological dependence of Socrates on God, or (equivalently) that Socrates is a citizen of this monarchic universe. Nonetheless, that is an essential a feature of his—as essential as the fact that he is not a mathematical object, but a living being. What we need to do, therefore, is add a new element to Socrates' essence that reflects the fact that God is his teleological cause. This element is a new topmost node connected to the rest of the essence in the appropriate way. The resulting essence—Socrates' *expanded essence*—will thus be represented as:

«God»

↑

«understanding»

↑

|scientific part of soul|

↑

|deliberative part of soul|

↑

|perceptive or desiring part of soul|

↑

|nutritive part of soul|

Suppose, then, that this expanded essence is Socrates' essence. Since God is a part of it, his definition is part of its definition. Hence God is prior in definition to Socrates, and, since Socrates is only an example, to all the other substances as well.

But are expanded essences really essences? If they are, if Socrates' expanded essence is a genuine essence, possessed of the requisite tight unity, it must be the ontological, and its definition the epistemological, first principle of some science, S. But since Socrates' essence is only an example, the expanded essences of all beings will, on the same grounds, also be first principles of S. Hence S will apparently be a universal science of all beings. But Aristotle's views on science seem to exclude the possibility of such a science. For a single science must deal with a single genus, and "being is not a genus" (*APo.* II 7 92^{b}13–14). So since "the genera of the beings are different," it seems that "none of the [principles] common [to all beings] is such that from them everything can be proved" (I 32 88^{a}36–^{b}2).[61]

Moreover, if there were such a science as S, its first principles would have to be primary in scientific knowledge, since as a universal science, nothing could be prior in knowledge to it. But then God could not be primary in scientific knowledge, since he would not be prior to everything else in that way. Put the other way around, if he were prior in scientific knowledge, it could only be because his science, theology, was somehow identical to S. But how could that be? How could the special science of one kind of being—God—be the universal science of being as such? How, in Scholastic idiom, could *metaphysica specialis* be *metaphysica generalis*?[62]

The Primacy Dilemma is not yet solved, therefore, even though some apparent headway has been made on it. For we can now see that primacy in scientific knowledge is the real stumbling block to resolving the dilemma, just as scientific knowledge itself is its real driving force. To science, then, we must return.

---

[61] Also *Top.* VI 12 149^{b}18–23.

[62] One other problem worth mentioning, though its solution will perhaps stand or fall with those already mentioned, is this. God is the real good, so if theology were some sort of universal science, it seems that there would have to be a single science of all goods. But Aristotle explicitly rejects such a science as a Platonic myth: "If a number of things are in accord with a single [Platonic] idea, there is also a single science of them; hence [if there were a Platonic idea of good], there would be a single science of all goods. But in fact there are many sciences even of the goods under one category; for the science of the opportune moment, e.g., in war is generalship, in disease medicine. And similarly the science of the moderate amount in food is medicine, in exertion gymnastics" (*EN* I 6 1096^{a}29–34).

NINE

THE SCIENCE OF BEING QUA BEING

9.1 Primary Science and Its Problems

Our investigations of the exact and inexact sciences (2.5), led us to investigate the different sorts of essences—penmattered, intelligibly mattered, and matterless—that are their ontological, and the definitions that are their epistemological, first principles (3.1–11). Our route was from science to being, from epistemology to metaphysics. Then we reversed direction, investigating being, substance, and essence, so as to arrive at a promising, though still somewhat problematic, candidate for the title of primary substance$_m$—God (4.1–8.5). Now we reverse direction a second time, turning from being to primary science, which is at once the science that "provides theoretical knowledge of being qua being, and of the [attributes] that belong to it intrinsically" (*Met.* IV 1 1003^{a}21–22) and the science of the primary substance—theology. By gaining insight into it, and by seeing how it can have both these feature, we shall finally discover how Aristotle's solution to the Primacy Dilemma is supposed to achieve its goal.

First, though, it will be useful to go through the entire set of problems, cataloged in *Metaphysics* III, that primary science faces. Aristotle's solutions to many of these will be easily recognizable. Nonetheless, by seeing them as a whole, we shall see how central to them, and so to the very conception of a primary science, the Primacy Dilemma is. At the same time, our grasp on what primacy science itself is will be tightened. For those, as we know, "who do not go through the problems before they begin their search are like people who do not know where they have to go" (*Met.* III 1 995^{a}33–36). I list the problems in the order in which they appear in the prospectus (III 1), not in the slightly different order in which they (or all but one of them) are subsequently discussed.

1. Whether it belongs *[a]* to one or *[b]* to more sciences to provide theoretical knowledge of the causes [of the beings qua beings]. (*Met.* III 1 995^{b}4–6)

240

Problems for 1a: "How can there be one science of first principles if these are not opposites [belonging to a single genus]" (2 996ᵃ20–21)? How can the good, which is a first principle of moving things be a first principle of everything when it is not a first principle of unmoving mathematical objects (996ᵃ21–ᵇ1)?

Problems for 1b: If there are many sciences dealing with first principles, which is the primary one that provides "the most scientific knowledge" of them (996ᵇ1–5)? Is it knowledge of efficient causes, or of final, formal, or material ones (996ᵇ5–8)? If it is "the most architectonic and authoritative," it will be the science of the good—a final cause (996ᵇ10–13). If it deals with the first and most scientifically knowable causes, it will be the science of substance—a formal cause (996ᵇ13–22). If it deals with coming-to-be, action, and change, it will be the science of efficient causes (996ᵇ22–24).

2. Whether it belongs to this science to know *[a]* the first principles of substance only, or *[b]* also the first principles from which everyone proves things. (*Met.* III 1 995ᵇ6–10)

Problems for 2a: If the science of substance and that of the axioms are different, "which of them is by nature more authoritative and prior" (2 997ᵃ11–12)? It would seem to be that of the axioms. For they are the most universal principles of all things, and it seems to belong to the philosopher (the one who deals with first principles) "to provide theoretical knowledge of what is true or untrue about them" (997ᵃ12–15). (But substance is ontologically primary, and so its science should be epistemologically primary.)

Problems for 2b: Since the axioms are common to all sciences, why should they be the special subject-matter of any one of them (2 996ᵇ33–34)? On the other hand, if they are the common subject-matter of all sciences, why should it be special to the science of substance to provide theoretical knowledge of them (996ᵇ35–997ᵃ2)? Moreover, "if there is a demonstrative science of them, there must be an underlying genus, and some of them must be attributes and others axioms (for it is impossible for there to be a demonstration of everything) . . . it follow that all the things proved must belong to a single genus, since all demonstrative sciences use the axioms" (997ᵃ5–11).

3. If [primary science] is concerned with substance, whether *[a]* there is

241

one concerned with all of them or *[b]* more than one, and if *[c]* there are more than one, whether they are all of the same type *(suggeneis)*, or *[d]* some of them types of theoretical wisdom, while others are to be called something else. (*Met.* III 1 995^{b}10–13)

Problems for 3a: If there is one science of substance, there will be "one demonstrative science dealing with all [intrinsic] coincidental attributes, since every demonstrative science provides theoretical knowledge of the intrinsic coincidental attributes of some subject" (2 997^{a}17–21). And that is unreasonable. (This is a version of the problem raised in 8.5.)

Problems for 3b: If there are many such sciences, to what sort of substance should the primary one be assigned (997^{a}16–17)?

Problems for 3c–d: These problems are not discussed in *Metaphysics* III although a solution is implied elsewhere.[1]

4. Whether *[a]* perceptible substances should alone be said to exist, or *[b]* also others in addition to them, and whether these others are of one type *(genê)* or many (as in the view of those who count as substances both forms and mathematical objects intermediate between forms and perceptible things). (*Met.* III 1 995^{b}14–18)

No problems are raised for *4a.* Those raised for *4b* are narrowly focused on Platonic forms, and the like, and are already familar from 1.3. Since Aristotle denies that such things are separate substances, his primary science is immune to them.

5. Whether [primary science] must provide theoretical knowledge of *[a]* substance only or *[b]* also about the intrinsic coincidental attributes of the substances [viz, the transcategorial ones]. (*Met.* III 1 995^{b}18–20)

Problems for 5a: If primary science provides theoretical knowledge of substance alone, what science provides such knowledge of its attributes (2 997^{a}32–33)?

Problems for 5b: Theoretical knowledge of attributes is demonstrative,[2] so if the science of substance and of its attributes are the same, there

---

[1] *Met.* IV 3 1005^{b}1–2, XI 4 1061^{b}27–33, 9.7–8.

[2] See *Problems for 3a.*

will be demonstrative knowledge of substance (essence), "but it is held that there is no demonstration of the essence *(ti estin)*" (997ª30–32).

6. Whether the first principles and elements of things are *[a]* the genera, or *[b]* the [parts] present in each particular thing, those into which it is divided. (*Met.* III 1 995ᵇ27–29)

Problems for 6a: Previous thinkers, such as Empedocles, who have investigated the matter, "say that the parts of which bodies consist and out of which they are compounded are the first principles" (3 998ª28–30). Moreover, "if we want to examine the nature of anything else, e.g., a bed, we examine the parts of which it consists and how they are put together, and then we know its nature" (998ª32–ᵇ3).

Problems for 6b: We have scientific knowledge of each thing when we know its definition. But genera are first principles of definition, and so "must also be first principles of definable things" (3 998ᵇ4–6).

Problems for 6a–b: "It is not possible to describe the first principles in both ways; for the account of the substance [essence] is one, but the definition by genera will be different from that which states the constituent parts" (3 998ᵇ11–14).

7. If they [the first principles] are the genera, whether *[a]* they are the ultimate ones, those applying to [perceptible[3]] individuals *(atomois)*, or *[b]* the first ones, e.g., whether animal [first] or man [ultimate] is a first principle, and more [a thing] that is over and above *(para)* what is particular *(to kath' hekaston)*. (*Met.* III 1 995ᵇ29–31)

Problems for 7a: "The first principle or cause must be over and above the things of which it is the first principle, and must be capable of existing separate from them," but a principle that applies to particulars will be ontologically dependent on them, and so not separate (3 999ª17–21).

Problems for 7b: If being and unity are genera, a genus will be predicable of its own differentiae, since all differentiae have both being and unity. But this is ruled out by the requirements on definition (3 998ᵇ19–27). If, on the other hand, being and unity are not genera, they won't be first principles, if the latter have to be genera (998ᵇ27–

---

[3] That only perceptible ones are being considered is made clear at III 4 999ᵇ1–6.

28). The intermediate types that include the differentiae, and so those that are individuals, will also be genera, since they are first principles. But "as it is, some are held to be genera, and others not" (998^{b}28–30). Indeed, "the differentiae are first principles even more that the genus" (since the ultimate differentia is the substance or essence). But if these are principles, and so genera, there will be "practically an infinite number of principles—especially if we suppose the primary genus to be a principle" (998^{b}30–999^{a}1).[4]

8. Whether there is an intrinsic cause over and above matter, or not, and, if there is, whether or not it is separate, and whether one or more in number, and whether it is over and above the compound. (*Met.* III 1 995^{b}31–35)

In the discussion this problem is combined with the following one:

9. Whether the first principles are limited *[a]* in number or *[b]* in kind *(eidei)*, both those in the account and those in the subject [viz., matter]. (*Met.* III 1 996^{a}1–2)

Problems for 9a: If there are only particulars, and an unlimited (or infinite) number of them, how is scientific knowledge of them possible? For it is "qua its being one thing and the same, and qua having some universal [attribute] that we know a thing" (4 999^{a}26–29). On the other hand, if attributes are first principles (and so substances, since substances are prior to other beings), genera (whether ultimate or primary) will be over and above particulars, which is impossible (since they are ontologically dependent on them) (999^{a}29–32). If there is a thing "over and above the compound (I mean by compound, whenever something is predicated of the matter), . . . is there one over and above each compound, or over and above some and not others, or over and above none?"[5] (999^{a}33–999^{b}1). Besides, if there is nothing over and above particulars, "so that there is no intelligible

---

[4] Ross, *Aristotle's Metaphysics,* ad loc.: "The higher up the scale of genera one begins in enumerating the ἀρχαί, the more ἀρχαί one will have to recognize."

[5] The final disjunct is puzzling, but may refer to universal first principles—such as perfect equality or beauty—that are not instantiated by hylomorphic compounds at all.

object, but only perceptible ones, there will be no scientific knowledge of anything" (999^{b}1–4). Furthermore, perceptible compounds, since they come-to-be, must come-to-be from something that does not itself come-to-be, namely, the matter (999^{b}4–8). But to make sense of coming-to-be, in addition to the compound and the matter, we need the form (999^{b}8–16). On the supposition that only particulars exist, however, these forms will themselves be particulars. But since "we could not suppose that there is a house over and above the particular houses," in which cases will there be such forms, and in which ones not (999^{b}17–20)? Besides, "will the substance [form] of all things be one [particular] e.g., [that] of all men?" (999^{b}20–22). If, on the other hand, these forms are many and different, "that too is unreasonable" (since it lands us back in the very first problem) (999^{b}22–23). Finally, there is a problem about how the matter becomes each of the particulars, and how the compound can be both matter and form (999^{b}23–25).

Problems for 9b: If the first principles "are one only in kind, none will be one in number, not even unity itself or being itself [i.e., the very things that seem to be ones over the greatest manys]" (4 999^{b}25–26). Besides, if there isn't *one* thing common to many, how will scientific knowledge be possible? (999^{b}26–27). On the other hand, if there is such a thing as numerical unity, and each of the first principles is one only in this sense, there will be nothing besides the principles—since there will be only one of each of them to go around (999^{b}31–1000^{a}4).

10. Whether the first principles of things that pass–away and things that don't are *[a]* the same or *[b]* different. (*Met.* III 4 1000^{a}5–7)[6]

Problems for 10a: If the first principle of both are the same, why is it that "some things pass-away and others don't, if indeed they are [constituted] out of the same [principles]" (1000^{b}20–21)?

---

[6] This problem merits special attention, because Aristotle claims that things that pass-away "belong to natural science (for they involve movement)," whereas those that don't, belong "to a different one, if *there is no first principle common to it and the other kinds of substance*" (*Met.* XII 1 1069^{a}30–^{b}2). Apparently, then, natural science and theology cannot have a common first principle, on pain of being a single science. The threat to the primacy of theology is manifest.

Problems for 10b: If the first principles of things that pass-away and things that don't are different, do they pass-away or not? If they do, they must consist of elements (since all things pass away into their elements), so that "prior to the first principles there are other principles, which is impossible" (1000^{b}24–27). If they do not pass-away, however, the problem raised for *10a* comes into play (1000^{b}29–1001^{a}3).

11. Whether *[a]* being and unity are first principles of the beings, as the Pythagoreans and Plato claimed, and not [attributes] of something else, or *[b]* whether this is not the case, but rather their subject is something else. (*Met.* III 1 996^{a}5–8)

As in the case of (4), the problems raised under *11a* presuppose views that Aristotle rejects, since he denies that being and unity are separate substances. No problems are raised for *11b.*

12. Whether *[a]* the first principles are universals or *[b]* like particulars among the beings. (*Met.* III 1 996^{a}9–10)

This is the Primacy Dilemma. We are already intimately acquainted with the problems that each alternative faces.

13. Whether the first principles of things . . . are *[a]* potentialities or *[b]* actualities, and, besides, *[c]* whether [potential or actual] in another way or *[d]* with regard to movement. (*Met.* III 1 996^{a}9–11)

Problems for 13a: If the elements are potentialities only, "it is possible that none of the beings exists" (6 1003^{a}2–3). This is a problem, as we know, because it leaves us unable to explain why anything actually exists (8.1).

Problems for 13b: "Potentiality is prior to actuality, and it is not necessary for everything potential to be actual" (1003^{a}1–2).

Problems for 13c–d: These are not discussed in *Metaphysics* III, though we know from 6.1 that *11c* is the alternative Aristotle defends.

14. Whether *[a]* numbers, lengths, figures, and points are substances of some sort, or *[b]* not, and if they are, whether *[c]* separated from perceptible things or *[d]* present in them. (*Met.* III 1 996^{a}12–15)

As in the case of (4) and (11), problems are raised against Platonists and Pythagoreans who hold *14a* and *c,* but no problems are raised for *14b* and *d,* which comprise Aristotle's own view.

With these problems to hand, we can see how central to all of them the Primacy Dilemma is. It is the theme, so to speak, on which they are the variations. For suppose, for example, that the first principles are perceptible particulars only. Then there will be no mathematical objects (14); no potentialities (and so no actualities) (13); no unity or being (11); no beings that pass-away (since no passing-away) and no beings that don't (since no intelligible beings) (10); no first principles, besides parts (9, 6), since other principles must be over and above the things whose principles they are, and so no definitions (7); no definitions means no sciences, and so no science of substance (1, 4), intrinsic coincidentals (5), or axioms (2)—in general, no primary science. Suppose, then, that they are universals only. Then there will be no substance, and so no attributes, and so no beings, and so nothing to be the ontological correlates of axioms or definitions, and so no science, and so no primary science.

We are now in a position to try to find the primary science—if there is one—that will show us how to solve these problems in a compelling way.

9.2 Special and Universal Sciences

In this section, we begin our search with an inductive survey of the special natural and mathematical sciences:

Met. VI 1 1025^{b}3–18 We are seeking [^{b}3] the first principles and causes of beings, and, clearly, qua beings. For [^{b}4a] there is a cause [e.g.,] of health and of good condition, and [^{b}4b] the objects of mathematics have first principles, elements, and causes, and in general [^{b}5] every science that is based in understanding or that shares in understanding to some extent deals with causes and first principles, whether more exactly or more simply. But [^{b}8] all these sciences mark off some being—i.e., a genus—and investigate it, but not as a being in the unqualified sense or qua being, and [^{b}10] for the essence they give no argument (logon) whatsoever, instead, starting from it—some making it clear to the senses, others assuming the essence as a hypothesis—they then demonstrate the intrinsic attributes of the genus, either in a more or in a less strictly necessary way. [^{b}14] It is evident from this induction, therefore, that there is no demonstration of the substance or essence [in these sciences], but some other way of making it clear [viz., those mentioned in ^{b}10b]. Similarly, [^{b}16] they say nothing as to the existence or nonexistence of the genus they

investigate, and this is because it belongs to the same [sort of] understanding to make clear the essence and whether or not it exists.[7]

b8 identifies the sciences referred to in *b5* as the familiar special sciences,
each of which deals with a single genus (2.1). Induction reveals that all of
them are to some degree demonstrative in structure, have essences as their
causes or first principles, and give no arguments for these (*b10*). That is why
they "say nothing" about the existence of the genus of beings with which
they deal (*b16*). For the existence of the genus presupposes the existence of
essences that are generically identical (3.8), and essences, as *first* principles,
are not demonstrable by any special science (PROBLEM 3a). Since a special
science considers beings only qua members of the genus it marks off as its
special subject matter, it does not consider them qua beings (*b8*), and so
cannot be the science that deals with the first principles and causes of them
qua beings (*b3*).

The subject matter of primary science is not, we may infer, some strange
thing—being qua being. Instead, it is just the beings themselves studied in
a certain way, namely, insofar as they are beings and nothing else.[8]

The inductive search among the sciences also reveals that they fall into
three distinct types, which are determined by the sorts of essences they
have as first principles: "But since natural science, too, deals with beings of
one type *(genos)* (for it deals with that sort of substance which has a first
principle of movement and rest present in itself), and since it is clear that it

---

[7] Notice that *logos* cannot mean account or definition at *b10a,* since the various
sciences do, of course, provide definitions of their first principles. What they do not
provide are *arguments* for them. Compare *Met.* XI 7 1063^{b}36–1064^{a}10: "Every
science seeks certain first principles and causes in relation to each of the things of
which it is the science, e.g., medicine and gymnastic training and each of the
others, whether productive or mathematical. For each of these marks off a certain
genus of things for itself and busies itself about it as something that exists, i.e., as a
being—not however qua being; the science that does this is another distinct from
these. Of the sciences mentioned each somehow gets hold of the essence *(to ti estin)*
and tries to prove the rest, either in a more or in a less strictly necessary way. Some
get the essence through perception, others by hypothesis; so that it is clear from an
induction of this sort that *there is no demonstration of the substance, i.e., the essence, [in
them].*" The parallels with *Republic* 510c–511e are manifest.

[8] As Barnes, "Metaphysics," 71 points out: "In phrases of the form 'to study Fs
qua G', the term replacing F fixes the domain of the study, and the term replacing G
fixes the aspect or the *focus* of the study."

is neither practical nor productive . . ., then, if all understanding is either practical or productive or theoretical, natural science must be theoretical science; but it provides theoretical knowledge only about being that admits of being moved, and only about substance that according to its account is for the most part, not being separate [from matter].[9] Now, we must not fail to notice the mode of being of the essence and of its account. For, without this, inquiry achieves nothing. . . . Mathematics too is theoretical, but whether its objects are unmoving and separate is not clear at present. What *is* clear, however, is that some parts of mathematics theorize about them qua unmoving and qua separate. And if there is some being that is eternal and unmoving and separate, the knowledge of it belongs to a theoretical science" (*Met.* VI 1 1025^{b}18–1026^{a}11). When we look at the different modes of being of the essences that are the first principles of the various special sciences, then, we see that there is a group of them that are penmattered. The type of beings that have such essences cannot constitute a genus of the sort relevant in $^{b}3$–$^{b}18$, however, since natural beings fall into multiple genera. Similarly, the essences that are the first principles of the mathematical sciences are distinctive in being intelligibly mattered, but, again, the beings that have them—numbers, lines, spheres, and so on—fall into multiple genera (1026^{a}23–27). Beings studied by the third unnamed theoretical science—which we know to be theology—also have a distinctive type of essence, namely, one that is matterless. But that science we may leave aside for now.

Finally, induction reveals the existence of two *universal* sciences, universal mathematics and universal natural science.[10] Since these study the beings of the correlative type as a sort of whole, they have some claim to be considering them qua being. Though their claim too will prove baseless, their existence will turn out to be of considerable importance.

Many theorems in mathematics are special to some branch of it, such as arithmetic or geometry, but there are also "certain mathematical theorems of a universal character" (*Met.* XIII 2 1077^{a}9–10). Here is an example, a problem about it, and a solution: "That proportionals alternate[11] might be

---

[9] The text and translation of the final clause is discussed, with the section omitted below, in 3.7.

[10] Aristotle calls the latter simply natural science *(phusikê)*. I have added 'universal' to distinguish it from the collective title of the special natural sciences.

[11] I.e., A:B = C:D ↔ A:C = B:D.

thought to apply [to numbers] qua numbers, [lines] qua lines, [solids] qua solids, and [times] qua times, as used to be demonstrated of these separately, although it is possible to prove it of all cases by a single demonstration. But because all these things—numbers, lengths, times, solids—do not constitute a single named [type] and differ in form from one another, they were treated separately. But now it is demonstrated universally: for what is supposed to hold of them universally doesn't hold of them qua lines or qua numbers but qua this [unnamed type]" (*APo.* I 5 74^{a}17–25). The theorem that proportionals alternate, then, belongs to universal mathematics. But its universality is open to challenge on the grounds that lines and numbers differ in genus. For, given the tight unity of the definitions that are scientific first principles, "it is necessary for the extreme and middle terms in [a demonstration] to come from the same genus" (I 7 75^{b}10–11). As a result, transgeneric demonstrations are ruled out: "it is impossible that what is proved should cross from one genus to another" (I 23 84^{b}17–18). Hence "the explanation [of why the theorem about proportionals holds] in the case of lines and of numbers is different" (II 17 99^{a}8–9), and so separate demonstrations seem to be needed in the case of each.

There is, however, an escape route from this predicament. For though the explanation of why the universal theorem holds is indeed different in the case of lines qua lines and numbers qua numbers, "qua such-and-such an increase in quantity, it is the same" (*APo.* II 17 99^{a}9–10). Hence the theorem "holds in common of all *quantities*" (*Met.* XI 4 1061^{b}19–21). For the attributes studied in mathematics hold of quantities, and of them alone: "while the genera of the beings are different, some [attributes] hold of quantities and others of qualities alone, with the help of which we can prove things by means of the common [principles]" (*APo.* II 32 88^{b}1–3).

But though the universal theorem does indeed hold of all quantities, it does so only *by analogy:* "Of the items used in the demonstrative sciences some are special to each science and others common—but common by analogy, since they are only useful in so far as they bear on the genus falling under the science. Proper: e.g., that a line is such-and-such, and straight so-and-so. Common: e.g., that if equals are taken from equals, the remainders are equal" (*APo.* I 10 76^{a}37–41). The type to which lines, numbers, and so on belong, then, which is the ontological correlate of a theorem of universal mathematics, isn't a genus, but a sort of analogical unity—a quantity.[12]

---

[12] *APo.* II 14 98^{a}20–23: "In order to grasp problems one should select both the

Moreover, because such theorems hold of all quantities, the mathematical sciences are ranked in order of priority and posteriority (*Met.* IV 2 1004^{a}7–9), and so of exactness and inexactness: "nor can one prove by any other science the theorems of a different one, except such as are so related to one another that the one is under the other—e.g., optics in relation to geometry and harmonics in relation to arithmetic" (*APo.* I 7 75^{b}14–17). We have already had intimations that the same is true of the natural sciences (3.8).

Universal natural science is a science of the same sort as universal mathematics: "It is the same with [universal] natural science as with [universal] mathematics. For [universal] natural science provides theoretical knowledge of the attributes and first principles of the beings qua moving [or changing] and not qua beings, whereas the primary science, as we have said, deals with the subjects [of the universal sciences] qua beings and not qua something else. For this reason, both [universal] natural science and [universal] mathematics should be regarded as parts of theoretical wisdom" (*Met.* XI 4 1061^{b}27–33). We may infer, then, that neither of these universal sciences is sufficiently broad in scope to be the primary one. That's the first point. The second is that there must be theorems of universal natural science, which, like those of universal mathematics, require distinctive ontological correlates. For otherwise universal natural science wouldn't be a science like universal mathematics with theorems of its own, but simply a taxonomic class, whose members are special natural sciences. Since universal natural science deals with substances qua moving and changing, these theorems must hold of all such substances, and so be transgeneric. (We shall consider one in 9.4.)

Since "things that are not all in one genus are one by analogy" (*Met.* V 6 1017^{a}2–3), it seems that the theorems of universal mathematics must also be in some way analogical. The discussion in *Metaphysics* XII 4–5 of the first principles and causes of natural beings—the definitions of which are

---

[correct] anatomies and the [correct] divisions; and in this way, laying down the genus common to all the subject-matter, one should select (if, e.g., animals are under consideration) whatever belongs to every animal. . . . Again, another way of selecting is by analogy; for you cannot get one identical thing that pounce [internal shell of the cuttlefish] and fishspine and bone should be called; but there will be things that follow from them too, as though there were some single nature of this sort."

the epistemological first principles of the special natural sciences—explains why and in what way this is so:

Met. XII 4 1070*31–*35 The causes and first principles of different things are in a way different, but if we speak somehow universally, i.e., analogically, in a way they are the same for all. For [*33] we might raise the problem of whether the first principles and elements are the same for substances and for relatives, and similarly in the case of each of the categories.[13] But it is absurd if they all have the same ones. For then relatives [non-substances] and substances will be [constituted] out of the same things. What then will this [common element] be? For there is nothing besides substance and the things in the other categories that are predicated that is common [to all of them]; but elements are prior to the things of which they are elements. But again substance is not an element of relatives [non-substances], nor is any of these an element of substance. Besides, how can all things have the same elements? For none of the elements can be the same as that which is composed of elements, e.g., BA [cannot be the same as] B or A. (None, therefore, of the intelligible beings, e.g., unity or being, is an element; for these are predicable of each of the compounds as well.) None of the elements, then, will be either a substance or a relative [non-substance]; but it must be [one or the other]. Therefore, it is not the case that all things have the same elements. [*10] Or, as we usually say, in a way they do, and in a way they don't, e.g., the elements of perceptible bodies, presumably, are as form, the hot, and, in another way, the cold, which is the privation; and, as matter, that which, primarily and intrinsically, is potentially these; and these things are substances, and also the compounds of them, of which they are the first principles (i.e., any unity that comes-to-be out of the hot and the cold, e.g., flesh or bone); for what comes-to-be must be different from its elements. Of these things, then, the same things are elements and first principles (but of different ones different things are), and if we speak in that way, not all things have [literally] the same principles, but by analogy [they do], i.e., in the way in which one might say that there are three principles—the form, the privation, and the matter. But each of these is different for each genus, e.g., in color, they are white, black, and surface. Again, there is light, dark, air; and out of these day and night. [*22] But since the elements

---

[13] Thus relatives are standing proxy for any non-substance.

present in a thing are not its only causes, but also something outside it, i.e., the moving [efficient] cause, it is clear that while first principle and element are different both are causes; and that which moves or halts is a first principle and a substance. *[^b25]* It follows that by analogy there are three elements and four causes and first principles; but the elements are different in different things, and the primary moving cause is different for different things. Health, disease, body; the moving cause is medicine. Form, disorder of a sort; the moving cause is house-building. And since the moving cause in the case of natural things is what is the same in form (e.g., for man, man, and in the products of thought the form or its opposite), in one way there will be three causes, in another four. For the craft of medicine is in a way health, and that of building the form of a house, and man begets man. *[^b34]* Moreover, besides these there is that which as first of all things moves all things.

This text divides the causes of natural beings into elements and first principles. These overlap, but are not identical, because the efficient cause is not an element, though the other causes—material, formal, final—are ($^b22$, PROBLEM 6). The elements of flesh and bone, then, are formative heat, the underlying matter, and the cold that is mastered to some degree by the formative heat in the process of concoction that produces homoeomerous stuffs ($^b10$, 3.2). Since the elements cannot be elements of themselves, it follows that not all natural beings can have the same elements, literally speaking ($^a33$). More particularly, beings in different genera have different ones. Nonetheless, these different elements constitute the analogical unities form, matter, and privation ($^b10$), which permit the formulation of an account of change that applies to all natural beings, and so enables natural science to formulate theorems about all of them (PROBLEM 8, 9, 5.1).

Since three of the four causes are also elements, the same story applies to them. Moreover, it also applies to efficient causes ($^b22$). For the primary efficient cause, the one that is the immediate cause of movement or change, is different for different things ($^b25$). Thus the efficient cause of health is the craft of medicine, that of a house, the craft of house-building, that of day and night, the sun. These causes are different, and yet they are analogically the same, since they all play the same sort of causal role. Again, this fact permits natural science to frame generalizations about all natural beings and their causes.

In addition to these, there is God, who is the final cause of the movements of all beings (*b*34). But God, of course, as an intelligible substance, is not part of the subject matter of universal natural science. He, therefore, is like the intelligible beings mentioned parenthetically in *a*33 only to be excluded. All things are beings and unities, all are caused by God, but these factors—which are the same for all beings—fall outside the purview of universal natural science.

The natural first principles and causes of perceptible, natural substances seem, then, to constitute analogical unities. But is this true of all of them? The following suggests (falsely as we shall see) that it is not: "Since some things are separate, whereas others are not separate, the former are substances. And because of this all things have the same causes, because without substances it is not possible for attributes or changes to exist. Furthermore, these will be soul, presumably, and body, or understanding and desire and body" (*Met.* XII 5 1070b36–1071a3).[14] The natural beings in non-substance categories, then, have natural substances among their first principles, and so they seem to have as causes the very things that cause such substances to come-to-be, pass-away, and undergo other sorts of changes.[15]

Nonetheless the apparent identity of such causes is an illusion—a product of an illegitimate focus on causally inert universals rather than their causally efficacious instances:

> *Met.* XII 5 1071a24–29 Next [a24] the causes and elements of substances (but different ones for different ones) are already, as has been said,[16] causes and elements of things that are not the same in type (*genei*)—[e.g.,] colors, sounds, substances, quantities—except by

---

[14] My understanding of this text and of XII 5 as a whole is indebted to Code, "Some Remarks on Metaphysics *Lambda* 5," though I part company with him in claiming that even the causes of natural substances, mentioned here, are causes of all natural beings only by analogy.

[15] Why these causes are soul, body, and understanding is explained as follows: "Since all non-living things are moved by something else, and since we have set forth in our work on primary philosophy our views about how the primary and eternally moved [heaven] is moved, and how the prime mover moves [it], it remains for us to consider how the soul moves the body, and what is the first principle of an animal's movement. For if we exclude the movement of the universe, living things are the causes of the movement of everything else, except such things as are moved by mutual impact" (*MA* 6 700b6–13).

[16] At *Met.* XII 4 1070a31–b35.

analogy. And *[ª27]* those of things that are the same in species *(eidei)* are different, not in species, but in that of different particulars [the cause] is different, [e.g.] your matter and form and mover and mine, but they are the same in universal account.

This text looks at two different cases. In *ª24* the causes and elements being considered are those of nonsubstantial changes (qualitative, quantitative, and so on) in a substance. In these cases, therefore, the causes and elements are the same only by analogy. In *ª27,* on the other hand, the causes and elements are those of changes (coming-to-be, passing-away) of sub-stances—moreover, of substances that are the same in species. Here the causes and elements are indeed the same in universal account. What is defined by such an account is a universal, however, and universals are causally inert: "one must observe that while some [causes] can be stated universally, others cannot. Indeed, the [particular] this that is first in actu-ality and a different thing [that is first in] potentiality are the first principles of all things. These, then, are not universals; for the particular is the first principle of particulars; for man is [the first principle] of the universal man, but no one [man] is, but rather Peleus of Achilles, and your father of you, and this very B of this very BA, whereas B in general is [the first principle] of BA unqualifiedly" *(Met.* XII 5 1071ª19–24). Thus the causes and ele-ments of different substances—even of those belonging to the same species (or having the same form)—are really different, and are the same only by analogy (1071ª33–35 below).[17] They are *like* one another in having the same universal account, but they are not identical.

When we turn from efficient causes to formal and material ones, the story is the same:

Met. XII 5 1071ª3–17 In another way, however, the first principles are the same by analogy, for example, actuality and potentiality. But these, too, are not only different for different things, they apply differently. For *[ª6]* in some cases the same thing exists at one time actually and at another potentially, e.g., wine or flesh or man does so (but these too fall under the previously mentioned causes; for the form is in actuality, if it is separate [from matter], and so does the compound and the privation, e.g., dark or diseased, but the matter is in potentiality, since it is what is capable of becoming both). *[ª11]* But actuality and potentiality differ in another way in the case of things of which the matter is not the same [and] of which the form is not the

---

[17] Contrast the case of God.

same but different, just as the cause of man is both its elements, fire and earth as matter and the special form, and some external thing, besides, e.g., its father, and [*15] beyond these the sun and its oblique course, which are not matter or form or privation, nor [are they] the same in form, but movers.

The matters of the beings discussed in *6 are different. As a result, the actuality of one is different from that of another: "the actuality of one matter is different from that of another, and [so is] the account; for of some things it's the composition, and of others it's the mixing" (*Met.* VIII 2 1043*12–14). Of a given harmony, for example, the matter is such-and-such notes, and the actuality is a certain mixture, whereas of a house the matter is bricks and wood and the actuality is a certain composition— "bricks and wood lying like *this*" (1043*7–11). Hence these first principles are simply the ones discussed in *1070*31–*35* under different names. The parenthetical material explains why: form separate from matter is actuality; matter when it actually has the privation (disease) has the opposite (health) potentially, and vice versa. Potentiality and actuality in these cases, we may infer, are the same only by analogy.

When *both* form and matter are different, however, potentiality and actuality differ "in another way" (*11). Socrates' father is his efficient cause. He differs in matter not form from Socrates. Hence he is in actuality what Socrates' matter is in potentiality. The sun is also Socrates' efficient cause, though in a different way than his father is. For it differs from Socrates both in matter and in form, and so is not in actuality what his matter is potentially. These efficient causes are different, therefore, though they are functionally analogous.

Notice that one efficient cause mentioned in this text is really the same for all natural beings, namely, the sun (*15). But like God and the intelligible beings mentioned in *1070*31–*35,* the sun is not a natural being studied by universal natural science, but a supernatural one studied by astronomy, which is a theoretical mathematical science (*Met.* XII 8 1073*5–8).

Having completed this discussion of the first principles of natural beings, Aristotle sums up: "If we inquire, then, what are the first principles and elements of substances and of relations and of qualities, [and] whether they are the same or different, it is clear at least that each is said in many ways, and that when these are distinguished, they [the principles and causes] are not the same but different—except in a way. That is, by analogy matter, form, privation, the mover belong to all things, and in this way the causes of substances are causes of all things, and when they are removed all things are removed. Further, that which is primary in actuality [is a first principle of all things]. In another way, however, there are different first principles, viz., the opposites which are neither [said of things] as belonging to same genus nor said in many ways; and, in addition, the [different] matters [of things]. We have stated, then, what are the principles of perceptible things, how many they are, and in what way they are the same and in what way different" (*Met.* XII 5 1071ª29–1071ᵇ2). The upshot for universal natural science is that the ontological correlates for its theorems are not species or genera, but beings which, as a type, are characterized in terms of such analogical unities as the three elements (matter, form, privation), and the four analogically characterized causes (material, formal, final, and efficient).

Because Aristotle doesn't trumpet it, it is easy to overlook the epistemological significance of the existence of universal mathematics and universal natural science. This emerges forcefully, however, if we focus again on the problem we raised for Aristotle's incipient solution to the Primacy Dilemma in 8.5. An inductive survey of the special sciences shows that each successful one deals with a particular genus. Consequently, the very idea of a transgeneric science seems like a cheat. A solution to the Primacy Dilemma that appealed to such a science, therefore, would be bound to seem arbitrary—like a solution to Russell's Paradox that precluded the formation of self-membered totalities without explaining what is wrong with the fundamental axioms of set theory that permit it. The existence of other successful universal sciences undercuts this criticism.

By the same token, the existence of these sciences serves to legitimate the analogical unities on which they rely. For without it, analogies by themselves can accomplish very little—a point Aristotle makes himself: "The celebrated natures found in numbers and their opposites, and in mathematical objects generally, as described by some people [Platonists, Pythagoreans], who make them causes of nature, seem . . . to vanish away. For none of them is a cause in any of the ways we distinguished in connection with the first principles [of natural beings]. The way they proceed does, however, make it evident that the good has application [to numbers, etc.], and that we do find odd, straight, equal-by-equal, and the capacities of certain numbers in the column of the beautiful. At the same time, indeed, the seasons and certain numbers go together, and this is the force of all the other examples they collect from mathematical theorems. Hence they are all like chance associations *(sumptômasin)*, since they are coincidental, but appropriate to one another, and one by analogy. For in each category of being there is the analogous thing, as the straight is in length, so is the plane in surface, the odd perhaps in number, and the white in color" *(Met.* XIV 6 1093^{b}7–21). Streplodites, then, were we to introduce them, would be idle. Why? Because there are no theorems that apply to all and only what is *st*raight or *pl*ane or *od*d or wh*ite*. Analogies, in other words, have a role in philosophy only so long as they honestly earn their scientific or explanatory keep. Mere flights of fancy founded on nothing more than chance associations are no good.

9.3 Theoretical Philosophies and First Principles

Aristotle sometimes applies the term *philosophia* to any of the sciences *(epistêmai)* that aim at theoretical truth rather than some practical end: "It is also right that philosophy should be called scientific knowledge of the truth. For the end of theoretical knowledge is truth, while that of practical knowledge is action" *(Met.* II 1 993^{b}19–20). In this sense of the term, all the (even loosely) theoretical sciences, whether special or universal, count as branches of philosophy, and so are sometimes referred to as the "philosophical sciences" *(Top.* I 2 101^{a}27–28). In this sense of the term, then, *philosophia* is more or less equivalent to *epistêmê,* and so is used in the strictest sense to apply to the most exact sciences, but is extended on occasions, as *epistêmê* itself is, to less exact ones.

Philosophia also has a narrower, more specialized sense, however, which is our concern here. In this sense, it applies exclusively to sciences that provide theoretical knowledge of first principles. Thus "theoretical wisdom *(sophia),*" of which *philo-sophia* is the love, "is a science concerned with first principles" *(Met.* XI 1 1059^{a}18). That is why there are as many types of philosophy as there are types of science, and so of types of essences (or substances): "There are precisely as many parts of philosophy as there are [types] of substances, and so there must be a primary philosophy, and [a secondary] one following it; for being is divided immediately into types *(genê),* which is why the sciences will also conform to these. For the philosopher is spoken of in the same way as the mathematician is, since it [mathematics] too has parts, and in mathematics there is a first and a second science and others succeeding them order" (IV 2 1004^{a}2–9). Hence, because there are three types of essences to serve as scientific first principles, there are "three theoretical philosophies, mathematical, natural, and theological" (VI 1 1026ᵃ18–19).[18] Which of these is primary, which secondary, and which tertiary will emerge in a moment.[19]

The following helps us to understand better what these philosophies do: "[The theorem] that when equals are taken from equals the remainders are equal is common to all quantities, but mathematics marks off a part of its proper [subject-] matter and provides theoretical knowledge of it, e.g., lines, or angles, or numbers, or some other sort of quantity—not, however, qua being, but qua being continuous in one, two, or three dimensions. But philosophy does not investigate the attributes that belong to a part qua part, but provides theoretical knowledge of each part qua being" (*Met.* XI 4 1061ᵇ19–27). The mathematician, then, provides us with theoretical knowledge about the various types of quantities, and even— when he does universal mathematics—about quantity in general. But he doesn't tell us anything about the attributes that belong to quantities qua being. That is what the philosopher does.

Since quantity is a category, it seems reasonable to infer that what the philosophers provides in its case is the sort of account given in *Categories* 6. If so, we can understand to some extent at least what it is to provide theoretical knowledge of quantity qua being. It is, first of all, to provide the sort of dossier on it that distinguishes it from all the other categories— something that universal mathematics, in being restricted to a single category, cannot do. Second, it is to uncover its ontological dependence on substance. For this constitutes at least part of the proof of its existence that universal mathematics cannot provide—a quantity exists, remember, when it is in a substance as subject.

In providing such theoretical knowledge of quantity, moreover, philosophy is also providing it of the lines, angles, and numbers that are the first principles of the special mathematical sciences. For each of these is a type of quantity. That, indeed, is why the theorems of universal mathemat-

---

[18] Also *Ph.* I 7 198ᵃ28–31.

[19] It should be said, too, that Aristotle occasionally recognizes various nontheoretical philosophies, such as "the philosophy of human affairs" (*EN* X 9 1180ᵇ15) or "political philosophy" (*Pol.* III 12 1282ᵇ23), and so classifies his own ethical writings as "those philosophical works of ours dealing with ethical issues" (1282ᵇ19–20). These philosophies seem to play the same role in relation to the first principles of the practical sciences that the theoretical philosophies play in relation to the theoretical ones.

ics apply equally well to all of them. We might see universal mathematics, therefore, as paving the way, in its very universality, for the science of being qua being.

The same sort of story, presumably, also applies in the case of natural science, which provides "theoretical knowledge of things not qua beings, but qua having a share in change" (*Met.* XI 3 1061^{b}6–7). Natural philosophy, therefore, should provide theoretical knowledge of natural substances qua beings, first, by providing accounts of the various elements and causes that are their first principles, and, second, by establishing their ontological dependence on substance.

Granted the ontological dependence of mathematical entities on *natural* substances in particular (*Met.* XIV 6 1093^{b}24–29), and of the latter on intelligible ones (XII 6–10), we can see that theological philosophy should be primary, natural philosophy secondary, and mathematical philosophy tertiary. And this is plainly Aristotle's own view. Thus "natural, i.e., secondary, philosophy has the task of providing theoretical knowledge of perceptible substances" (VII 11 1037^{a}14–16), whereas "the determination of the unmoving first principle of these [natural substances] is a task for a different and prior philosophy" (*GC* I 3 318^{a}5–6).[20] Tertiary philosophy is never mentioned by name, but elimination alone entails that it must be mathematical philosophy.

9.4 Primary Philosophy and Non-Contradiction

With this much as a partial account of philosophy's function with regard to the first principles of the special and universal sciences, it is time to focus more narrowly on *primary* philosophy. We have seen that—though not in detail why—it is theological philosophy, and we may infer, that it must therefore provide theoretical knowledge of the first principles of theology proper. It comes as a bit of a shock to discover, however, that it must also provide theoretical knowledge of the logical axioms—such as the principle of non-contradiction (PNC)—which, because they apply to all beings as such, are first principles of the science of being qua being: "We must state whether it belongs to one science or to different ones to provide theoretical knowledge about the axioms (as they are called in mathematics)

---

[20] Also *Ph.* I 9 192^{a}34–^{b}2, II 7 198^{a}21–31; *Cael.* I 8 277^{b}9–12; *PA* I 5 644^{b}23–645^{a}36; *MA* 5 700^{a}6–9.

and about substance.[21] It is evident, of course, that [it belongs to] one [science], and indeed the philosopher's as well, to investigate them. For these [axioms] hold of all beings and not of a certain genus, separate and distinct from the others. Everyone uses them, it is true, because they hold of being qua being, and each genus is a being. But each uses them to the extent he needs them, i.e., so far as the genus extends about which he presents his demonstrations. Hence, since it is clear that they hold of all things qua beings (for this [being a being] is what all things have in common), it follows that it also belongs to the one who knows being qua being to provide theoretical knowledge of the axioms. That is why none of those who investigate a special area undertakes to say anything about them, as to whether they are true or not. Neither geometers nor arithmeticians [do so], though some students of nature do. This is not surprising, since they were the only ones who thought they were investigating the whole of nature and of being. But since there is someone still higher than the student of nature, since nature [consists of] only one type of being, the investigation of these [axioms] must fall to the student of what is universal, the one who provides theoretical knowledge of primary substance. Natural science is also a type of wisdom, but it isn't primary" (*Met.* IV 3 $1005^a19-1005^b2$). Aristotle assumes, notice, that primary philosophy provides theoretical knowledge of PNC, and of primary substance, because both are universal first principles. What is puzzling about this assumption, of course, is that it entails that theology is the universal science of being qua being. And that was just the apparent absurdity that left the Primacy Dilemma unresolved in 8.5. Nonetheless, if we could see how theology could be this science, we could also see why PNC would fall within primary philosophy's purview: primary philosophy deals with the first principles of theology; theology is the science of being qua being; PNC is a first principle of the science of being qua being; so primary philosophy deals with PNC. But, of course, we cannot see this. For the moment, then, let us focus on PNC itself.

PNC is a universal principle that applies to beings as such. But that is a feature it shares with the law of excluded middle and all the other logical axioms that are "the first principles of deduction" (*Met.* IV 3 1005^b5-8). What is really distinctive about PNC, and what justifies the particular attention Aristotle pays to it, is revealed in the following text:

---

[21] A problem raised at *Met.* III 2 996^b25-33, to which Aristotle is now offering a solution.

Met. IV 3 1005ᵇ10–20 The one whose subject matter is the beings qua beings must be able to discuss the most secure first principles of things. This person is the philosopher. And *[ᵇ11]* the most secure first principle of all is one we cannot think falsely about. For this sort of first principle must be known best (since it is invariably what people don't know that they make mistakes about) and *[ᵇ14]* must be un-hypothetical. For a first principle that we must possess in order to understand anything at all about beings is not an hypothesis, and what we must know in order to know anything at all is a first principle we must already possess. Clearly, then, this sort of first principle is the most secure of all. *[ᵇ18]* And what it is we must next say, namely, that it is impossible for the same thing to belong and not to belong to the same thing at the same time and in the same respect.

Look first at *ᵇ11*. We cannot think falsely about PNC—indeed, we must "always do the opposite, I mean, think truly" (XI 3 1061ᵇ34–36). The basis of this claim lies in the distinction between saying something because, for example, one is confused, and actually thinking it when not confused: "It is impossible for anyone to suppose that the same thing is and is not, though some people take Heraclitus to say this; for what one says need not be what one supposes to be true" (IV 3 1005ᵇ23–34). Thus had Heraclitus been helped to see clearly just what he was saying, even he might have been led to recant: "Perhaps if we had questioned Heraclitus himself in this way, we might have forced him to confess that opposite statements can never be true of the same things. But, as it is, he adopted his opinion without understanding what his statement involved" (XI 5 1062ᵃ31–35). What would lead him to recant, however, would be just his inability—once unconfused—to have opposite beliefs at the same time: "The opposite of a belief is the belief in its contradictory. Hence it is evident that it is impossible for the same person at the same time to believe that the same thing is and is not, since someone who makes this mistake would have opposite beliefs at the same time. This is why all those who demonstrate refer back to this belief as ultimate; for this is by nature the first principle of all the other axioms as well" (IV 3 1005ᵇ28–34).

The unhypothetical status of PNC is next *(ᵇ14)*. "Demonstration," as Aristotle understands it, "is not related to external argument, but to the one in the soul, since deduction isn't either. For one can always object to external argument, but not always to internal argument" (*APo.* I 10 76ᵇ24–25). There is no obstacle, we may infer, to treating PNC as an hypothesis in an external argument. But there is an obstacle to so treating it in an internal one. For one cannot treat as a hypothesis in an internal argument what one cannot—clearheadedly—suppose to be false.

Someone who denies PNC must believe it, then, even though in words he disavows doing so. Hence a defense of PNC against him can at most get him to recognize his commitment. It cannot—except in cases of confusion—constitute his reason for believing it in the first place, since there is no reason more basic than it. Moreover, if he is recalcitrant, it may do no more than convince those who do accept PNC that he is committed to it, whether he admits as much or not.[22]

As a first principle of all sciences, PNC cannot be unqualifiedly demonstrated, since no science can demonstrate its own first principles: "There is no unqualified demonstration of such things [PNC] . . . For it is not possible to deduce this from a more reliable first principle, yet it must be [possible to do so] if indeed one is to demonstrate it unqualifiedly" (*Met.* XI 5 1062ª2–5). Nonetheless, PNC can, Aristotle claims, be demonstrated "by refutation *(elegktikôs)*" (IV 4 1006ª12) or "against someone" (XI 5 1062ª3). The following text explains what such a demonstration is and how it is possible:

> *Met. IV 4 1006ª15–28 [ª15]* I distinguish demonstration by refutation from [unqualified] demonstration. For in attempting to demonstrate [PNC], one might be taken to be assuming what is at issue, but [ª17] if someone else [the denier of PNC] is responsible [for the assumption], it will be a refutation [of him], and not a[n unqualified] demonstration. [ª18] The starting-point *(archê)* for all such [demonstrations by refutation] is not the demand that he [the opponent] speak of something either as being or as not being (for this one might take as assuming what is at issue), but the demand that he signify something both to himself and to another. For he must do this if he says something. For if he does not, no statement *(logos)*[23] is [possible] for him, either in response to himself or to anyone else. But [ª24] if he

---

[22] A point made by Code, "Metaphysics and Logic," 145, and by Lear, *Aristotle and Logical Theory,* 98–114. I have benefited generally from their resourceful discussions.

[23] 'Statement' is probably a better translation of *logos* here than 'argument', since the way the denier of PNC destroys argument is by destroying the determinate statements that serve as its premises.

does grant this [demand], there will be a demonstration [by refutation against him], since something will be definite as soon as he grants this.[24] But *[ª25]* the one responsible [for the starting point] is not the one who demonstrates [by refutation], but the one who allows [this to take place]; for eliminating statement he allows statement. Furthermore, *[ª26]* in allowing this, he has allowed that something is true independently of demonstration, so that not everything will be F and not-F.

[ª]18 characterizes *the say-or-signify-something requirement* (S) as "the starting point" common to all demonstrations by refutation of PNC. If the denier meets this requirement, Aristotle claims, he takes on the responsibility that allows the philosopher to escape the charge of "assuming what is at issue" *(ª15)*. What is at issue in the argument, however, is PNC itself. Hence the denier, in complying with S, must unwittingly reveal his commitment to it: "To demonstrate to an asserter of opposites why he speaks falsely one must obtain from him something that is equivalent to 'the same thing cannot both be and not be at one and the same time,' but which does not seem to be equivalent to it. For only in that way can one demonstrate [PNC] to someone who says that opposite statements can be truly made about the same thing" (XI 5 1062ª5–11). It follows that PNC can be no more metaphysically freighted, so to speak, than S is.

Prima facie, however, S seems to be just a principle of univocity. In *Metaphysics* IV 4, this is all but stated: "Suppose he [the denier of PNC] says that, e.g., 'man' signifies many things, not just one, and that twofooted animal is the account of one of the things signified [by it], but that there are also several other accounts, though a definite number. His saying this makes no difference, since a different name can be assigned to correspond to each account" (1006ᵇ2–5). In XI 5, it is yet more explicit: "Those who are to join in argument with one another must have some common understanding. For if they don't, how can they join in argument with one another? Hence each of the words must be familiar and must signify something—not many things, but one only. If it signifies many, it must be made evident to which one it applies" (1062ª11–16). Apparently, then, the

---

[24] *Met.* IV 4 1008ª15–18: "If this is so [viz., that the negation of is true of everything of which the affirmation of is true, but the affirmation is not true of everything of which the negation is true], then something will be fixed [determinate] as not being, and this will be a secure belief."

demand that 'man' "signify one thing" (IV 4 1006ª31) is designed simply to guard against equivocation and cross-purposes.

The dialectical benefits of understanding S in so unfreighted a way are no doubt mostly obvious, but two merit brief discussion. The first is that the requisite equivalence between S and PNC is guaranteed. For suppose the denier agrees that 'man' does signify just this one thing—twofooted animal. Then he cannot also believe that it does not signify this, or that it signifies something else as well. The second benefit is that PNC is indeed a principle that applies to *all beings* as such. To see why, and why it is significant, a contrast is useful. Suppose that in order to comply with S 'man' must signify the Aristotelian real essence of man.[25] How, then, would Aristotle deal with a denier of PNC of the following sort? He concedes that if 'F' signifies a secondary substance, such as man or horse, it satisfies PNC, so that nothing can be both F and also not-F. Nevertheless, he denies PNC, because he thinks it is sometimes false when 'F' signifies qualities, relations, or whatever.[26] Such a denier may admit that there are substances and essences, yet he may still consistently deny PNC. Does it follow that he is irrefutable? Is Aristotle's defense of PNC powerless against him? If so, the version of PNC actually defended will not be a first principle of the science of being qua being, since it will apply to substances only and not, as required, to all beings.

With the univocity of 'man' agreed to, in any case, the denier says that it is possible that something is a man and also that it is not a man. Is he making a *de re* claim or a *de dicto* claim? Is he saying of some man that it is possible for him to be not a man? Or is he saying of the propositions "*x* is a man" and "*x* is not a man" that they can both be true? The following passage sends somewhat mixed signals:

> *Met. IV 4 1006ᵇ28–34 [ᵇ28]* Necessarily, . . . if it is true to say of something that it is a man, it is a twofooted animal, since this we saw is what 'man' signifies. And *[ᵇ30]* if this *(touto)* is necessary, it is not possible at that time for the same thing *(tote to auto)* not to be a twofooted animal; for 'necessary for it to be' signifies precisely that it

---

[25] As Code, "Metaphysics and Logic," 146–148, and Lear, *Aristotle and Logical Theory,* 98–114, both claim. Code notices that this affects the generality of Aristotle's defense: "Aristotle never gives us an extension of the proof to the non-substance cases" (148).

[26] *Republic* 523a–524d describes someone of this sort.

is impossible for it not to be. *[^{b}33]* It cannot, therefore, be at the same time true to say that the same thing is a man and is not a man.

The necessity in ^{b}28 and ^{b}33 seems to be the necessity of the consequence (a *de dicto* necessity). But that in ^{b}30 seems to be the necessity of the consequent (a *de re* necessity). Hence the mixed messages. Since *de dicto* necessities do not entail *de re* ones, the argument seems to trade on a modal confusion.[27]

The only way to rescue it, therefore, has seemed to be to treat both ^{b}28 and ^{b}30 as making *de re* (r) modal claims. Since the *touto* ('this') in ^{b}30 will then refer to the consequent of the conditional in ^{b}28, we will get the following inference:

(^{b}28r) □-man *(x)* → □-twofooted-animal *(x)*
(^{b}30r) □-twofooted-animal *(x)* → not-◇-not-twofooted-animal *(x)*
(^{b}33r) Therefore, not-◇ (man *(x)* and not-man *(x)*)

—where, as usual, □ symbolizes necessity and ◇ possibility. Since (^{b}28r) entails (^{b}30r) and—by substitution of 'man' for what it signifies—(^{b}33r), this argument is clearly valid. (Substitution in a modal context—often problematic—is legitimate here because of the necessary equivalence of 'man' and what it signifies.)

The problem with this proposal, however, is that S does not entail (^{b}28r). For S, we argued, is just a principle of univocity, and so cannot entail the sort of essentialism (^{b}28r) embodies. If, on the other hand, we revise S, so as to guarantee that it does entail (^{b}28r), we lose its equivalence with PNC. For PNC cannot reasonably be supposed to entail essentialism.

There seems to be little for it, then, but to go back to the text and start over. Taken at face value, as we said, ^{b}28 is a *de dicto* necessity (d), which we may represent as follows:

(^{b}28d) □(man *(x)* → twofooted-animal *(x)*).

Since the *touto* in ^{b}30 can now only refer to this entire conditional, ^{b}30 will have to be understood as:

---

[27] 'If x is a bachelor, he is an unmarried men' is a *de dicto* necessary truth, but it does not follow from it that 'if x is a bachelor, he is necessarily an unmarried man'. To think that it does is to confuse '□(p → q)' with 'p → □q'. Such confusion is allegedly a feature of Aristotle's modal syllogistic—e.g., Hintikka, "On Aristotle's Modal Syllogistic."

(^{b}30d) □(man *(x)* → twofooted-animal *(x)*) → not-◇-not-
twofooted-animal *(x)*.

The question, then, is whether (^{b}30d) is true. And the answer seems to be
that it is not. If we resort for a moment to the normal possible world
semantics for modality, we can see why. There are worlds in which □ (man
(x) → twofooted-animal *(x)*) is true because its antecedent is false (either
because *x* does not exist or because it exists but is not a man). Since in some
of these worlds *x* is not a twofooted animal, (^{b}30d) as a whole is false.

What we have left out of the picture, however, is the anaphoric adverbial
phrase *tote to auto* ('at that time for the same thing') in ^{b}*30*. What it does is
restrict the claim made in ^{b}*30* to those worlds in which what is being
considered is the very same thing referred to in ^{b}*28* at the time at which it is
a man and so a twofooted animal.[28] Think of those worlds, therefore, as all
the (relevantly) possible worlds, so that something is necessary in the
pertinent sense if it holds in all of *them*. When we evaluate (^{b}30d) in those
worlds, however, we see that it is true. For in no such world can *x* fail to
exist or be a man or a twofooted animal. From (^{b}30d) by substituting 'man'
for what it signifies, we reach ^{b}*33*. Like the *de re* version, then, this mixed
modality version is valid. But it also has a feature that the *de re* version lacks:
its first premise is entailed by S.

Look back now to *1006^{a}18*. It gives the philosopher's demonstration of
PNC a 'transcendental' flavor.[29] It suggests that S *must* be met if
statement—or, indeed, private thought (*Met.* IV 4 1006^{b}5–11)—is to be
so much as *possible*. And this is the type of conclusion characteristic of the
transcendental arguments we associate most particularly with Kant. Just
what such arguments amount to, however, or whether any of them are
sound, is itself a controversial issue. So rather than pursue what may well be
a will o' the wisp, let's adopt a safer tactic. Let's suppose that Aristotle's
demonstration by refutation of PNC is a transcendental argument, and ask
what it establishes. The answer depends, as we saw, on S. Since S does not

---

[28] That *tote* plays just such a role in other of Aristotle's modal principles was first
discovered by Tad Brennan, "Two Modal Theses in the Second Half of *Metaphysics*
Theta.4," 167–173. I am indebted to his important paper.

[29] Capitalized upon with great resourcefulness in Irwin, *Aristotle's First Principles*.
I note, without wanting to make anything of it, that this flavor is missing from *Met.*
XI 5 1062^{a}5–11 (quoted in the text above), which merely claims that *any* premise
equivalent to PNC, but not thought to be so by the denier, is sufficient for the
philosopher's purpose.

commit the denier of PNC to essentialism, therefore, PNC can't either. And that is surely how it should be, given the goal of the demonstration. For no denier of PNC should have to give too many hostages to the philosopher in order to ensure his own refutability.

Two other pieces of evidence support this way of looking at S, and so PNC. The first has to with the further effects of denying PNC:

> *Met. IV 4 1007ª20–33* In general those who speak in this way [viz., denying PNC] do away with substance, i.e., essence. For they must say that everything is coincidental and that there is no such thing as just what the being *(einai)* for a man is [e.g., twofooted animal] or just what the being for an animal is. For [ª*23]* if there is something that is just what being *(einai)* a man is, it will not be what being not a man is or what not being a man is (for these are the negations of being a man). For, as we saw, one thing is signified [e.g., by 'man'], and this is the thing's substance [essence]. But [ª*26]* to signify a thing's substance [essence] is to signify that what the being for that thing is is nothing other [than its essence]. But if just what the being for a man is is the same as just what the being for not a man is or as just what the not being for a man is, then the being for that thing will be something other [than its essence]. Hence they [viz., the ones who deny PNC] must say that nothing has this sort of account [viz., the sort that defines a thing's substance or essence], but that everything is coincidental. For pale is a coincidental attribute of man in that he is pale but not just what pale is.

Notice that this text claims only that a denier of PNC does away with substance in the sense of essence. It does not claim that someone committed to PNC is thereby committed to essence. The commitment, in fact, runs in the other direction. Moreover, the argument would apparently be no different if an attribute, such as spale, were employed instead of man, since spale too has both an essence (albeit not in the unqualified sense) and coincidental attributes (4.4). The denier of PNC, in other words, does away with the distinction between the essential and the coincidental quite generally, and not just with the distinction between the essential and coincidental attributes of Aristotle's own substances.

'Man' is in compliance with S, ª*23* tells us, if it signifies one thing, such as twofooted animal. This one thing, in Aristotle's own view, is a real essence: "A definition is a phrase which signifies the essence. It is given either as a phrase in place of a word or a phrase in place of a phrase" (*Top.* I

5 101^{b}38–102^{a}1).[30] But it need not be that the denier of PNC shares this view. For if he does away with the general distinction between the essential and the coincidental, he will also do away with the narrower one in which, because of its interest to science as he conceives of it, Aristotle is most interested. *a26* then establishes the desired conclusion in a straightforward way.

The second piece of evidence, which also allows us to make a larger point, looks away from PNC to a principle that has a comparable status, namely, the *principle of natural kinesis* (PNK). This principle states that "the things that exist by nature are, either all or some of them, subject to change" (*Ph.* I 2 185^{a}12–13). It is a transgeneric first principle of universal natural science on a par with the principles of universal mathematics. Since it is a first principle, however, a discussion of whether or not it is true "is not a contribution to natural science" (184^{b}25–185^{a}1), but belongs instead not to primary (since PNK does not apply to all beings as such), but to natural philosophy. Hence natural philosophy should provide a demonstration of it like the one primary philosophy provides for PNC. The following seems designed to fill just this bill: "Even if it is really the case that being is infinite and unchanging, it certainly does not appear to be so according to perception, rather [according to it] many beings undergo change. Now if indeed there is such a thing as false belief or belief at all, there is also change; similarly if there is imagination, or if anything is thought to be one way at one time and another at another. For imagination and belief are thought to be changes of a sort" (VIII 3 254^{a}24–30). Notice that this argument too can be given a transcendental cast: if opinion or imagination is to be possible, change must exist. But PNK is weak. It is the sort of principle that even a subjectivist skeptic about substance, essence, and the rest could accept. There must be change of some sort, he may be forced to agree, but the only sort that occurs is psychological change. PNC should be no more metaphysically freighted, therefore, than PNK.

Transcendental arguments are thought to be very important, epistemologically speaking. It is supposed to be a scandal not to have one to support one's first principles, since this leaves them open to skeptical attack. Yet this is not at all Aristotle's attitude to his demonstration of PNK. Instead, he suggests that to demand a demonstration of it—or indeed an argument of any kind at all—shows not intellectual probity, but poor judgment: "But to investigate this [PNK] at all—to seek an argument *(logos)* in a case where

---

[30] Also *Met.* IV 7 1012^{a}21–24, VIII 6 1045^{a}26–27.

we are too well off to require argument—implies bad judgment of what is better and what is worse, what commends itself to belief and what does not, what is a first principle and what is not. It is likewise impossible that all things should be changing or that some things should always be changing and the remainder always at rest. For against all these this one thing provides sufficient assurance: we *see* some things sometimes changing and sometimes at rest" (*Ph.* VIII 3 254ª30–ᵇ1). He says essentially the same thing about PNC: "Some people actually demand that we demonstrate even this [PNC], but their demand is the result of lack of general education. For we lack general education if we do not know what we should and should not seek to have demonstrated. For it is in general impossible to demonstrate everything. . . . But if there are some things of which we must not seek a demonstration, these people could not say what principle is more appropriately left without demonstration than this one" (*Met.* IV 4 1006ª5–11).³¹ Education, then, and not a transcendental argument is what the denier of such principles really needs. From the perspective of the well-educated philosopher's bureau of internal affairs, therefore, demonstrations by refutation of first principles like PNC and PNK will have a small (though perhaps not entirely negligible) role to play, though his foreign relations department may well need to make extensive use of them. The contrast with Kant could hardly be sharper. And we can see why. The principles that demonstrations by refutation can establish are much weaker than those needed for significant metaphysical purposes—mere schemata on whose bare bones an inductive investigation of the special and universal sciences themselves must put the requisite flesh. Such demonstrations are not nothing. But it would be a mistake to see them as doing more work in primary philosophy than they can properly manage. They may block the skeptic, or help clear away the sort of intellectual confusion that can make PNC seem false or questionable. They may, to use a favorite Aristotelian distinction, make PNC clearer *to us,* but they don't make it *intrinsically*

---

³¹ Since Aristotle mentions only demonstration in this text, he might be referring only to those people who seek an *unqualified* demonstration of PNC, and not to those who seek a demonstration by refutation. But given his comments about PNK, which is less secure than PNC, this is surely unlikely. For if those who ask *for any sort of argument* for PNK are uneducated, those who would settle for less than an unqualified demonstration of PNC could hardly escape being included in the same class.

clearer, or more epistemologically secure. It is already, in advance of such argument, as clear and secure as can be.[32]

Suppose I am wrong, however, and that S is a more freighted principle than I have represented it as being. All that follows is that Aristotle's refutation of the denier of PNC becomes more controversial and more limited in scope. It will work, if it works at all, only against certain rather compliant deniers, not against others. The form of the argument and the reconstruction of it I propose in the next section will remain unaffected.

9.5 Non-Contradiction Demonstrated

The actual demonstration of PNC is our next topic. I shall set it out in stages as a dialectical or aporematic exchange more-or-less of the sort described in the *Topics*. The questioner is the philosopher; the one who answers—by plain assent or dissent as the rules of dialectic demand—is the denier of PNC.

> *Stage 1:* Is PNC true of all beings, or not? Not. Is it false of all the beings, or not? Not. Is it false of all the beings except the G_1s, G_2s, . . ., G_ns, or not? Yes. Excluding the Gs, is the following principle (PNCC)—the contrary of PNC—true: it is possible for F to belong and not to belong to the same thing at the same time and in the same respect? Yes. In particular, is it possible for 'man' to belong and not belong in this way? Yes. Does 'man' signify something, or not? Not.

Then "it is absurd for us to seek to engage in argument with someone who does not engage in argument about anything, qua not engaging in it; for qua not engaging in argument, he is like a vegetable" (*Met.* IV 4 1006ᵃ13–15). Since neither the philosopher nor PNC has anything to fear from vegetables, the philosopher is justified in abandoning the argument. If, on the other hand, the denier answers in the affirmative, the demonstration can proceed.

---

[32] Irwin, *Aristotle's First Principles*, 181–188, argues that Aristotle's demonstration of PNC must meet the standards characteristic of a demonstration within a science. In part this is because he ignores the distinction between science and philosophy. The former must, indeed, be demonstrative, but the latter is aporematic not demonstrative.

Stage 2: Does 'man' signify something, or not? Yes. Does it signify one thing, or not? Not. Does it signify a definite number of things, or not? Not.

Then again, but for a different reason, argument is undermined: "If he says the name signifies an indefinite number of things, it is evident there will be no argument. For not to signify one thing is to signify nothing, and if names do not signify [anything], discussion with one another, and indeed even with oneself, is destroyed (for we cannot understand *(noein)* without understanding one thing, and if we can [understand], one name can be assigned to this one thing)" (*Met.* IV 4 1006^{b}5–11). As in Stage 1, therefore, the philosopher is justified in abandoning the argument. If, however, the denier does not answer in this way, the demonstration can continue.

Stage 3: Does 'man' signify a definite number of things, or not? Yes. Of the definite number of things that 'man' signifies, does 'man$_1$' signify twofooted animal, or not? Yes. Is it possible for 'man$_1$' to belong and not belong to the same thing in such a way as to make PNCC true, or not? Yes. Does 'man$_1$' signify the same thing as 'twofooted animal', or not? Yes.

The remainder of the argument is stated in a rather roundabout way by Aristotle. So it will be well to look at what he actually says before attempting any further reconstruction:

Met. IV 4 1006^{b}11–34 Suppose, then, that as we said at the beginning, [^{b}12] the name ['man'] signifies something, and some one thing; it follows that the being for a man cannot signify just what not being for a man is. . . . And [^{b}18] it will not be possible for the same thing to be [a man] and not to be [a man], except [^{b}19] by homonymy of the sort that would arise if, for instance, others called not-man what we call man. [^{b}20] The problem, however, is not about whether the same thing at the same time can both be and not be a man *in name,* but whether this is possible *in fact.* Now if 'man' and 'not man' do not signify something different, it is clear that the not being for a man signifies what the being for a man signifies [viz., twofooted animal], so the being for a man will be not being for a man, since they will be one thing (for being one signifies being [one] as cloak and cape are [one], if they have one account), and if these are one, then the being for a man and the not being for a man will signify one thing. But it has been shown that they signify different things. [^{b}28] Necessarily, therefore, if it is true to say of something that it is a man, it is a twofooted animal, since this we saw is what 'man' signifies. *[b30]* And if this is necessary, it is not possible for the same thing in that case not to be a twofooted animal; for 'necessary for it to be' signifies precisely that it is impossible for it not to be. Hence *[b33]* it cannot be at the same time true to say that the same thing is a man and is not a man.

b18 reaches the desired conclusion from *b12,* which is the one reached at the end of Stage 3. But *b19* allows an exception, namely, that 'man$_1$', though it does signify one thing, signifies the same one thing as 'not man$_1$'. This is ruled out in *b20*. If 'man$_1$' and 'not man$_1$' did signify the same one thing (twofooted animal), man$_1$ and not man$_1$ would have the same account, as cloak and cape do. Hence to say that something is man$_1$ and also not man$_1$, or to apply both 'man$_1$' and 'not man$_1$' to it, would simply be to say twice over that it is (not) a twofooted animal. It follows either that PNCC is not the contrary of PNC or that 'man$_1$' is not an instance of PNC. *b28–b33* explains, in the way we looked at in 9.4, why *b12* entails *b18*.

Omitting the material on homonymy, we can express this final stage of the argument in proper aporematic style as follows:

Stage 4: If 'man$_1$' signifies twofooted animal, does it follow that necessarily, if *x* is a man$_1$, *x* is a twofooted animal, or not? Yes. If this is necessary, does follow that it is not possible that, at that time, *x* is not a twofooted animal? Yes. Then does it follow that it cannot be that *x* is a man$_1$ and at the same time not a man$_1$, or not? Yes.

The denier is thereby refuted. He has been forced to concede that PNCC is false in the case of man$_1$. But man$_1$ is only a representative member of the class of beings to which the denier alleges PNCC applies. Hence in being forced to concede that PNCC is false of man$_1$ the denier is being forced to concede that it is false of the entire class. In other words, he is being forced to accept that PNCC is false—period. Hence, he is being forced to accept that PNC is true. Deniers of PNC show their commitment to it, therefore, in the very process of significantly denying it.

9.6 Primary Philosophy as Primary Science?

Now that we have seen how primary philosophy demonstrates PNC, we must consider how this mode of demonstration is to be extended to all other first principles. For if it is this sort of demonstration that provides theoretical knowledge of first principles, then a similar sort of demonstration must also be provided for them. Since the logical axioms are clearly in this class and are already familiar, we may begin with them.

According to Aristotle, PNC "is a first principle even of all the other axioms" (*Met.* IV 3 1005^{b}33–34). Hence, in particular, it is a first principle of the law of excluded middle. But why so? One explanation might be that PNC entails excluded middle, since we can demonstrate it from PNC, using DeMorgan's Laws. Aristotle himself assumes these laws when he argues as follows: "It also follows [from the denial of PNC] that it is not necessary either to affirm or deny. For if it is true that he is a man and not a man, clearly, he will also be neither a man nor not a man. For each of the affirmations has a negation; and if one of the affirmations has two components, it will be opposed by one negation [that also has two components]" (4 1008^{a}3–7).[33] The trouble is that we can also use DeMorgan's Laws to run the demonstration the other way around. That's the problem with Aristotle's claim. All logical axioms are logically equivalent and interderivable, just as PNC and excluded middle are. Hence there seems to be no basis—at least not in logic proper—for assigning primacy to any one of them.

When we turn from logic to aporematic primary philosophy, however, things change. For while it may well be true that PNC and excluded middle are interderivable, it is far from obvious that excluded middle can be directly demonstrated by refutation in the way that PNC can. Reflection on this fact could allow PNC to be accorded an *epistemological* status even in logic that no other principle could have. In any case, the general point remains that primary philosophy can assign priority to principles for its own reasons.

In addition to providing theoretical knowledge of the logical axioms, however, primary philosophy must also provide such knowledge of the following attributes: being, unity, similarity, sameness, equality; their op-

---

[33] Irwin and Fine, *Aristotle: Selections,* explain: "The affirmation with two components is 'He is a man and not a man', which opponents of PNC must accept. Since they reject PNC, they must also accept the negation of this compound affirmation. The negation is the compound 'He is neither a man nor not a man'; and this negation conflicts with the Principle of Excluded Middle." Aristotle assumes, therefore, that 'Not(he is a man and he is not a man)' is equivalent to 'Not(he is a man) or not(he is not a man)', which is (a special case of) one of DeMorgan's Laws.

posites, plurality, negation, privation, difference, unlikeness, inequality; opposition itself (*Met.* IV 2 1003^{b}22–1004^{a}25); "priority and posteriority, genus and species, whole and part, and the others things of that sort" (1005^{a}16–18). These are readily recognized, no doubt, as the trans-categorial attributes or "common things *(koina)*" mentioned in 2.2. It is because all the beings share some of these—specifically, being—that the axioms hold of them (3 1005^{a}27–28).

The reason such attributes come within primary philosophy's purview is this: "If not to the philosopher, indeed, to whom does it belong to investigate whether Socrates and Socrates-seated are the same thing, or whether one thing has [just] one opposite, or what opposition is, and in how many ways it is said, and similarly with other such questions? Therefore since these things are intrinsic [attributes] of that which is one qua one, and of being qua being, but not qua numbers or lines or fire, clearly it belongs to this science to know both what it [being] is and its [intrinsic] coincidental attributes. . . . For just as there are attributes special to number qua number—e.g., oddness, evenness, commensurability, equality, excess, deficiency—and these belong to numbers both intrinsically and with reference to one another (and similarly there are others special to the solid, being moved or unmoved, being weightless or possessing weight), so too there are attributes special to being qua being, and it belongs to the philosopher to discover the truth about these" (*Met.* IV 2 1004^{b}1–17). We see, then, that both being (and so substance) and its intrinsic coincidental attributes are dealt with by primary philosophy (PROBLEM 5). At the same time, however, we see that primary philosophy is not restricted to dealing with attributes that all beings share. For just as no number is both odd and even, so no being is both one and many (in the same way). Instead, primary philosophy deals with those attributes, which, because they are transcategorial, can be possessed by any beings, regardless of what genus or type they belong to, and so which cannot be the exclusive subject matter of any of the special or universal sciences we have discussed so far.

Again, the aporematic nature of primary philosophy offers us a compelling explanation of why this should be so. For the dialectical problems it considers are those that, not being proper to a science, can arise with regard to any science. But problems of this sort are just the ones that can arise for every being, regardless of genus or type, since "for every single genus there is a single [sort of] perception and a single science" (*Met.* IV 2 1003^{b}19–20).

Furthermore, sophistic and dialectic also deal with the transcategorial attributes: "dialectic and sophistic deal with the attributes of the beings, but not qua beings or with being itself just insofar as it is being" (*Met.* XI 4 1061^{b}7–10).[34] Hence they share both their methods and their subject matter with primary philosophy, and so can readily assume its guise: "It is a sign of this [viz., that it belongs to the philosopher to provide theoretical knowledge of the transcategorial attributes] that dialecticians and sophists assume the same guise as the philosopher. For sophistic has the appearance—only—of wisdom, and dialecticians discuss everything, and being is common to everything, and they discuss these because it is clear that to do so is proper to philosophy. Sophistic and dialectic do indeed deal with the same type *(genos)* [of things] as philosophy, then, but differ from it in the latter case in the sort of capacity it has and in the former in the life deliberately chosen. For dialectic is peirastic concerned with the things about which philosophy is knowledge, while sophistic has the appearance [of knowledge] but not the reality" (IV 2 1004^{b}17–26).[35] We have good reason to think, then, that primary philosophy is aporematic in nature. For if it is not, it will be hard to explain the primacy it attributes to PNC, its concern with the transcategorial attributes, or its similarity to sophistic and dialectic.

If primary philosophy is aporematic, however, it must, it seems, be quite different from the special or universal sciences. Indeed, it seems that it cannot really be a science in the strict sense at all. For a science is a structure of unqualified demonstrations from first principles, whereas primary philosophy provides demonstrations by refutation of first principles themselves. In both its mode of demonstration, therefore, and in its direction of proof, primary philosophy is apparently nonscientific.

---

[34] Also *APo.* I 11 77^{a}26–32: "All the sciences associate with one another on the basis of the common [principles] (by common, I mean those they use as the things from which [as principles of proof] they prove, but not about which they prove [things] or what they prove [as conclusions]); and dialectic [associates with] all of them, and so would any science that attempted to prove the common [principles] universally [of all beings]—e.g., that everything is either affirmed or denied [viz., excluded middle], or that equals from equals leave equals, or any things of that sort. But dialectic is not in this way concerned with [viz., as trying to prove] any determinate [class] of these, nor with any one genus. For then it would not ask questions; for one cannot ask questions when demonstrating because when the opposites are assumed the same thing is not proved."

[35] Also *SE* 11 171^{b}5–7, *Met.* III 1 995^{b}18–25.

Moreover, even a universal science must deal with something analogous to a genus. But it is hard to see even that much unity in primary philosophy's area of interest—consisting, as it does, of primary substance, the logical axioms, and the transcategorial attributes. For that reason too, then, it seems that primary philosophy cannot be a science. Aristotle calls it a science, to be sure (*Met.* IV 2 1004^{b}7, quoted above). But he is wont, as we know, to call other things sciences, which are not sciences in the unqualified sense that the exact sciences are (2.3–5).

There is a problem, however, with all these conclusions. Primary philosophy provides demonstrations by refutation of first principles, such as PNC, which are first principles of being qua being, as well as of the intrinsic attributes of being qua being. If such demonstration constitutes theoretical knowledge, it seems that primary philosophy must just be the science of being qua being—the primary science (*Met.* IV 1 1003^{a}21–22). The primary science, however, simply in virtue of being primary, must be the most exact science, for primacy and exactness must go hand-in-hand (2.5). How, then, can primary philosophy, which is not a science at all, be the primary science? That is one problem. Another is that if the Primacy Dilemma is to be solved, theology must be the primary and most exact science. But primary philosophy, which provides theoretical knowledge of theology's first principles by demonstrating them by refutation, seems not to be identical to theology proper, any more than natural philosophy seems to be identical to universal natural science, or mathematical philosophy to universal mathematics.

These problems are clearly little more than notational variants, however, of the problem of how theology can be the science of being qua being. It is presumably to theology, then, that we must turn for a solution to them.

9.7 Theology as Primary Science?

Theology, as we think of it, is the subject that deals primarily with the existence and nature of God or gods and his or their role in the cosmos and our lives. Aristotle more-or-less agrees. Unlike us, however, he also thinks that theology is in some sense or other God's own science: "The most divine science is also the most valuable, and it alone is most divine in two ways: for the divine science [may be thought of] as the one that God most of all would possess, or as the science of divine things. But only this [science of first causes] is so in both ways. For God is held to be among the causes of all things and a first principle, and such a science God alone—or

277

he most of all—would possess" (*Met.* I 2 983ª5–10). Are we to suppose, then, that God practices theology? If so, we may argue as follows. All God does is actively understand. Hence, if he practices theology, it can only be in understanding it. Moreover, all God understands is his own essence. It follows that theology, when actively understood, must just be God's essence. But that essence is simple and incomposite (XII 7 1072ª30–32, XII 9 1075ª5–10). Hence theology cannot have the inferential complexity characteristic of a demonstrative structure. For, if it did, God would undergo change, as he first understood the first principle of theology, and then came to have demonstrative scientific knowledge of another of its theorems (8.3). If we leave aside PNC and the other principles common to all sciences, therefore, it follows that theology's one distinctive first principle must be its sole content. Since God is identical to his essence, it also follows that God must just be theology fully actualized in an active understanding. The *perfect* mesh of theology with its subject-matter is thereby assured.

In fact, however, there is no need to suppose that theology is quite so circumscribed. For all Aristotle says is that theology is the science that God "most of all" would possess. But that, as we know, means that the science God does possess isn't identical to theology at all (7.5). Rather, in the way that any "system seems to be most of all its most supreme part" (*EN* IX 8 1168ᵇ31–32), so the universe is most of all God (*Met.* XII 10 1075ª11–15), and theology—which, like other realistically conceived Aristotelian sciences, mimics the structure of the universe (*Cael.* II 13 293ª15–ᵇ15)—is most of all its first principle.

Aristotle also has a second thought about theology, however, which seems yet more problematic, namely, that it is identical to primary philosophy. Here is the apparent proof text:

> *Met.* VI 1 1026ª21–30 [ª21] the most valuable science must deal with the most valuable type *(genos)*, so that the theoretical sciences are more choiceworthy than the others, and it [theology] than them. . . . Now [ª27] if there were no substances besides those constituted by nature, natural science would be the primary science, [ª29] but if there is an unmoving substance, the science of it would be prior and would be primary philosophy.

Focus, first, on ª29. It seems to confuse theology, which is the science that deals with an unmoving substance, with the philosophy that deals with the first principles of that science. This apparent confusion is further dramatized by *27. For it claims that if there were no other substances besides those constituted by nature, natural science would be the primary science. Apparently, then, the cognate claim about theology should be that it is the primary science, not that it is primary philosophy. Moreover, this is what *21 also seems to require. For it is theology itself—not theological philosophy—that is "most valuable" (I 2 983ª5).

The possibility arises, therefore, that *29 is simply a slip—something its near doublet in *Metaphysics* XI 7 in fact suggests: "If natural substances were primary among beings, natural science would be primary *among sciences,* but if there is another nature, a separate and unmoving substance, the science of it [viz., theology] must be different from and prior to natural science, and universal because prior" (1064ᵇ9–14). Apparently, then, it is theology, not theological philosophy, that is the primary science.

But can theology have that status. Can it really be prior to all other sciences? To answer, we must look again at the conditions it must satisfy if it is to fill the bill:

> *APo.* I 27 87ª31–35 One science is more exact than, and prior to, another [ª31] if it is at the same time knowledge of the that and the why, but not of the that separate from the why; and [ª33] if it is not said of a subject and the other is said of a subject, e.g., arithmetic and harmonics; and [ª34] if it depends on fewer [posits], the other on an additional posit, e.g., arithmetic and geometry.

If we focus on ª33 and ª34 alone, theology does seem to have what it takes to be primary, since it is clearly prior to natural science, which would supposedly be primary if it were not *(1026ª27).* For, first, the formal element of God's essence is not said of anything else, whereas the formal element of a natural essence is said of the material element (5.3). And, second, theology does not have to posit perceptible matter, whereas natural science does (5.1).

When we factor ª31 into the picture, however, theology's primacy seems to be threatened. For no science seems to provide theoretical knowledge of its own first principles. But that is just what the primary science must do if it is to satisfy ª31. If we take this condition seriously, therefore, it seems that primary (or theological) philosophy, not theology, is the primary science. But for the reasons we gave at the end of 9.6 that conclusion raises problems.

The peculiar nature of God, however, and so of his science, seems to offer a way through them. The first principle of theology is God's essence.

Since it is an activity, a matterless, unmoving, intelligible form identical to the good, no other principle or cause can be prior to it. For God, as unmoving, has no efficient cause, and, as matterless, has no material one. That leaves just his formal and final causes to consider. And it is clearly God's essence that plays these roles. For, as a matterless form, it is his formal cause, and, as the good, it is his final one. But God is identical to his essence. Hence in actively understanding it, he is understanding both himself and—insofar as he can be said to have any—his first principle and cause: "of some things the cause of their necessity is something else, of others nothing [else], but rather it is because of them that others things are necessary. It follows that what is necessary in the primary and strict sense is what is simple [viz., God], since it does not admit of more than one state, so that it does not admit even of one after the other, since it would thereby admit of more than one. If, then, there are certain eternal and unmoving things, nothing in them is forced and nothing against nature" (*Met.* V 5 1015^{b}9–15). In God's case, then, the fact that he exists and the reason why he does are the same and inseparable. Apparently, then, theology meets all three of the conditions for being the primary science.

But where does that leave primary philosophy? God has perfectly clear, problem-free understanding of theology always and eternally. Hence he does not need primary philosophy to clarify his understanding. For him, therefore, theology itself fulfills primary philosophy's function. With us, of course, it is different. *Our* understanding of theology can be darkened by problems, so that we do need primary philosophy. In the limit, however, that need evaporates even for us. For the most exact scientific knowledge of theology comes only at the end of the aporematic process that renders our understanding clear and problem free: "Theoretical wisdom is the most exact form of scientific knowledge. The one who has it must not only know what is derived from the first principles of a science, therefore, but must also grasp the truth about the first principles themselves. It follows that theoretical wisdom is understanding plus scientific knowledge—scientific knowledge of the most valuable things having a crown, as it were" (*EN* VI 7 1141^{a}16–20).[36] In the end, then, primary philosophy is replaced by theology in our case too. (Notice that this conclusion fits with our findings about the relative unimportance for the well-educated of primary philosophy's defense of PNC.)

---

[36] Also *MM* I 34 1197^{a}20–30.

It seems, then, that *1026ª29* may not be a slip at all, but rather an acknowledgment that, in the case of theology, at least, the distinction between science and philosophy is, as it were, overcome. But, in fact, the same is also true of the distinction between the other universal sciences and their respective philosophies. "Both natural science and [universal] mathematics," Aristotle claims, "should be regarded as parts of theoretical wisdom" (*Met.* XI 4 1061ᵇ32–33). Since "theoretical wisdom is the most exact form of scientific knowledge," it follows that natural science must be the most exact of the natural sciences and universal mathematics of the mathematical ones. Because of what such exactness amounts to, however, it also follows that universal natural science must provide theoretical knowledge of the first principles of the special natural sciences and universal mathematics of those of the special mathematical sciences (9.6). Once we have truly mastered these higher-level sciences, therefore, and our understanding is no longer darkened by problems, we should not need mathematical and natural philosophies, except when we have to deal with those who, because they lack proper education, stand in need of refutation. It is important, all the same, not to conflate the aporematic tasks of these philosophies with the very different demonstrative ones of their associated sciences. To be overcome, so to speak, the distinction must first of all be fully appreciated.

It is one thing to claim that the distinction between theological philosophy and theology proper is overcome, of course, and another to justify that claim. To accomplish that Aristotle must convince us that *a single science* provides theoretical knowledge about substance, the axioms, and the transcategorial attributes, and that the science in question is theology (PROBLEMS 1, 2, 5). For otherwise the sciences of these things might be prior to theology, and their first principles prior to its first principle. The Primacy Dilemma would then come into play yet again, putting theology's claim to primacy in jeopardy.

If theology *is* the science of being qua being, however, another problem arises, namely, of how natural science and universal mathematics could then qualify as branches of theoretical wisdom (PROBLEM 3c–d). For if theology's first principle is a first principle of them, don't they stand to theology as the various special sciences stand to them? Since the latter aren't branches of theoretical wisdom, why, then, should universal mathematics and universal natural science be any different?

Even after so long a journey, then, the Primacy Dilemma must still be declared unsolved.

9.8 The Primacy Dilemma Solved

Though the transcategorial attributes seem to be a somewhat diverse and unrelated lot, they are in fact unified in an important way:

> *Met.* IV 2 1004^{a}25–1 Since [^{a}25] all things are referred to the primary thing (e.g., all things that are called one are referred to the primary unity), this is also what we should say about sameness, difference, and the opposites. And so [^{a}28] we should distinguish how many ways each is said, and then show how each of the things we have distinguished is said with relation to the primary thing in each predication; for some things will be so called because the have the primary thing, others because they produce it, others in other such ways. [^{a}31] It is evident, then, that it belongs to one [science] to have an account of these things and substance (and this is [the solution to] one of the problems we listed [viz., PROBLEM 5]), and it belongs to the philosopher to be able to provide theoretical knowledge of all of them.

Suppose, then, that spale is F—where F is a transcategorial attribute. In order to explain why this is so, we will, first, have to distinguish all the different ways in which something can be said to be F (^{a}28). This is the task attempted in *Metaphysics* V.[37] Once we have settled on which kind of F-ness spale is being said to have, we are ready to carry out the second task, which is described in ^{a}25.

So suppose, for concreteness, that F is unity, and that we have determined that the relevant sort of unity possessed by spale is the sort of intrinsic unity something has when it is one in form, and so in account (*Met.* V 6 1016^{b}33). Since spale is an attribute, this account will reveal its ontological dependence, first, on surface, and then on substance (4.4). Spale will thus owe its being to substance. But "being and unity are the same and a single nature . . . since one-man, man-that-is, and man are the same thing" (IV 2 1003^{b}22–27). Hence spale also owes its *unity* to sub-

---

[37] The table of contents makes this plain: 1 first principle; 2 cause; 3 element; 4 nature; 5 necessity; 6 unity; 7 being; 8 substance (essence); 9 sameness; 10 opposites; 11 prior and posterior; 12 capacity; 13 quantity; 14 quality; 15 relatives; 16 completeness; 17 limit; 18 the 'in virtue of which' *(to kath' ho);* 19 disposedness *(diathesis)* (= position *(keisthai)* in *Categories?*); 20 state *(hexis);* 21 affection (attribute); 22 privation; 23 having; 24 'the from which' *(to ek tinos);* 25 part; 26 whole; 27 mutilated; 28 genus (type); 29 false; 30 coincidental.

stance. But if substance is to explain the unity of spale, it too must have some sort of unity, which we know to be the sort it possesses in virtue of its form or essence. Hence it is more particularly substance's unity that explains the unity of spale. If all the other sorts of unity possessed by spale (and so by other qualities) can also be traced back to the unity of substance, therefore, it will be "the primary unity" (*a25*). For it will figure in the explanation "in each predication" of unity of a quality (*a28*).

On the supposition that a similar story can be told about all the other categories and all the other transcategorial attributes, substance—or their predication of it—will play the same role in explaining why they hold of each thing. It will follow immediately that if there is only one science of substance, it will also deal with the transcategorial attributes (*a31*). We have now brought the transcategorial attributes into the science—if there is only one—that deals with substance (PROBLEM 5).

With substance and the transcategorial attributes brought almost within the confines of a single science, we must next consider the logical axioms. What mathematical philosophy, as we know, is to provide us with theoretical knowledge of quantity, which is the analogical unity that is the first principle—because truth-maker or ontological correlate—of the theorems of universal mathematics. Now axioms have a status in primary science analogous to that of theorems in universal mathematics. By parity of reasoning, therefore, what primary philosophy must do for them is provide us with theoretical knowledge of their ontological correlates. The axioms, however, are true not just of quantities, but of all beings as such, so that their truth-maker—their ontological correlate—is simply being. Hence it is of it that primary philosophy must provide theoretical knowledge. If it does that, however, it will provide us with theoretical knowledge of a first principle of the axioms: "Since even the mathematician uses the common [theorems] in a special application, it must belong to primary philosophy to provide theoretical knowledge of the first principles of these" (*Met.* XI 4 1061^{b}17–19).

On the assumption that primary philosophy is indeed a science, and that substance is indeed a first principle of all beings, we have now brought both the logical axioms and the transcategorial attributes within the ambit of the science of substance—if, indeed, there is just one such science (PROBLEM 2).

In order to explain the existence of actualized potentialities in the universe, we have make reference to an intelligible substance that is in essence an activity—a sort of actuality that is not the activation of a potential in the way that a process or movement is (PROBLEM 13c–d)—and that is the teleological cause of all actual beings (PROBLEM 4). It follows that natural beings, which pass-away, and supernatural ones, which don't, share a first principle. If this principle were the only one, and if it were an element of all beings, that would be a serious problem (PROBLEM 10a). Moreover, the distinction between natural science and theology, legitimated by a difference in their essences, and explaining why some pass-away and some don't, would collapse (*Met.* XII 1 1069ᵃ30–ᵇ2). By dint of drawing the distinctions cataloged in *Metaphysics* V 1, however, between the various ways in which something can be said to be a first principle, these consequences are avoided. God is a cause and (as we shall see) an element of the natural beings. But he is not their only first principle—penmattered essences, perceptible matter, and the sun are also such. They can undergo change, therefore, including substantial change, even though he cannot.

God is a cause and first principle of all the substances, but he is himself a substance. And in the way that substances unify the transcategorial attributes, he unifies the substances: "Being is said in many ways, but always with reference to one thing—i.e., to some one nature—and not homonymously . . . [and] in all cases with reference to one first principle. For some things are called beings because they are substances, others because they are attributes of substances, others because each is a way to a substance: either passings-away or privations or qualities or productive or a cause of the coming-to-be of a substance, or things said with reference to it, or negations of one of these or of substance. That is why we even say that not-being *is*—not-being. . . . It belongs to one science, indeed, not only to provide theoretical knowledge of things said in one way [viz., things in a single genus], but also things said with reference to a single nature, since these things too are *in a sense* said in one way. It is clear, then, that it also belongs to a single science to provide theoretical knowledge of the beings qua beings" (*Met.* IV 2 1003ᵃ33–ᵇ16).[38] The explanatory role of God in the universe, therefore, guarantees that the substances have a single

---

[38] It is often claimed that Aristotle is arguing here that because the word *on* or *einai* ('being') has a certain semantics, a primary science exists. This seems to me to be a mistake. What Aristotle is actually arguing is that because science has revealed that being has a certain structure (which is reflected to some extent in the semantics of the word 'being') it follows that there is a single science of being qua being.

substantial first principle, and that theology is the science that provides theoretical knowledge of it (PROBLEMS 1, 3).

As a result of uniting all the beings into a single universe, in other words, God also unites all the sciences into a single structure that as a whole characterizes that universe. For God, as a teleological cause of all substances, has a place at the topmost node of their (extended) essences, and so in the (extended) essences of all the other beings that are ontologically dependent on them. In 8.5 we considered one of these, namely, the essence of a (partly) natural being—Socrates:

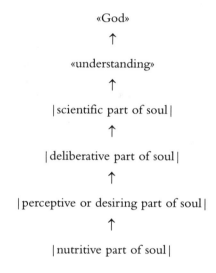

«God»

↑

«understanding»

↑

|scientific part of soul|

↑

|deliberative part of soul|

↑

|perceptive or desiring part of soul|

↑

|nutritive part of soul|

Now we should add the essences that are first principles of a productive and a practical science:

«God»

↑

«happiness»

↑

|house|

and

«God»

↑

«happiness»

↑

|X|

—where |X| is an essence like that of Socrates, which is a first principle of a practical science (3.5). Clearly, theology plays a role in these sciences similar to the one it plays in universal natural science: by providing us with theoretical knowledge of God, it removes the guillemets that the other sciences cannot remove. When it does so, moreover, it reveals that God (the primary object of theoretical understanding) is identical to happiness (the primary object of practical understanding), thereby uniting the theoretical, practical, and so productive sciences (PROBLEM 1a, 8.1). In the case of the latter sciences, however, natural science also has a role to play. This is obvious in the former case, since |X|, a (partly) natural essence, is manifestly a part of the essences that are their first principles. But, of course, the essences of these sciences are also first principles of the productive ones: to build a house in which *human beings* are happy, a builder must draw on the natural science of humans (3.5).

Since mathematical objects do not have teleological causes, the mathematical sciences cannot be brought into this emerging structure in quite so direct a way (PROBLEM 1b). What brings them in is that, unlike artifacts and agents, they are not substances. Hence they are ontologically dependent on the substances that are already in the structure—specifically, on the natural substances from which they are inseparable (*Met.* XIV 6 1093^{b}27–29).

Theology, then, is prior to and more exact than universal natural science, since it provides theoretical knowledge of God, and God is a component of natural essences. (For the same reason it is prior to astronomy and whatever other strictly theoretical sciences of substance there may be—for instance, the one that provides theoretical knowledge of separate human productive understanding.) But it also has this status because, in providing knowledge of God, it provides theoretical knowledge of a first principle of the logical axioms and transcategorial attributes that all sciences use. Universal natural science, in turn, is prior to and more exact than the special natural sciences, since it provides theoretical knowledge of their first principles—for example, formal, final, material and efficient causes, form, perceptible matter, and privation, and PNK. Similarly, it is prior to universal mathematics, since it provides theoretical knowledge of the natural substances on which mathematical objects are ontologically dependent. It is prior to the practical sciences in providing such knowledge of (the natural parts of) human beings, and these, in turn, are prior to the productive sciences. Finally, universal mathematics is prior to and more exact than the special mathematical sciences, since it provides theoretical knowledge of their first principles, namely, quantities, and the various universal theorems that apply to them.

We can now understand why Aristotle claims that "if there is an unmoving substance, the science of it would be prior and would be primary philosophy, and it would be universal in this way—because it would be primary" (*Met.* VI 1 1026^{a}29–31).[39] For God is a first principle of *all* beings, and so theology is—in that way—universal. Theology does not, however, deal with "a single genus, i.e., a single nature" (1026^{a}24–25). It is not a universal science of the being genus in the way that ornithology is a universal science of the bird genus. For God's differentia is immortal, "immortal is a differentia of [the genus] living being" (*Top.* IV 2 122^{b}12–14), and no special science deals with that genus. Instead, theology is more like universal mathematics and natural science, only broader in scope, since it provides theoretical knowledge of the first principles of all the beings—not just of the quantities or of those with penmattered essences. What the existence of universal mathematics and natural science as genuine transgeneric sciences with theorems of their own has legitimated, in other words, is theology's claim to be itself just such a science. And this, in turn, has made its existence compatible with the claim that "being is not a genus" (*APo.* II 7 92^{b}13–14).

God, then, is both ontologically primary and primary in scientific knowledge. He, therefore, is the primary substance—the hard-won solution to the Primacy Dilemma (PROBLEM 12).

9.9 Post Dilemma Metaphysics

With Aristotle's solution to the Primacy Dilemma to hand, it remains for us to determine what effect, if any, it has on the overall shape of his metaphysics—which we can now think of as consisting of universal mathematics, universal natural science, theology, and (insofar as they are dis-

---

[39] Also *PA* I 1 641^{a}32–^{b}10.

tinct) their associated philosophies. In the following text, Aristotle himself provides, if not the answer, at least a significant suggestion as to what it is:

> *Met. XII 7 1072ª30–32* Intrinsically intelligible objects are *[ª30]* in one of the two columns [of opposites], and *[ª31]* in this [column] substance is primary, and *[ª32]* in this [sub-column] the simple one and an activity [is primary].

Of the columns mentioned in ª30, one consists of the categories of intrinsic beings, the other of the coincidental beings that are their opposites. In the former, substance$_m$ is primary (ª31), since it is prior to quality, quantity, and the rest in account, knowledge, and time. In the category of substance$_m$, the substance that is simple and an activity, God, is prior either to some other substances in the same category as himself or to some substances in some other category of substance (ª32). Without prejudice, let us call God's category *primary substance$_m$* and the other category *secondary substance$_m$*. This results in the following table:

INTRINSIC BEINGS					PRIVATIONS
SUBSTANCE$_m$			QUALITY	QUANTITY . . .	
PRIMARY$_m$		SECONDARY$_m$			
MOST PRIMARY	LESS PRIMARY				
GOD	?	?			

The question is what members (if any) do primary substance$_m$ and secondary substance$_m$ now have?

We may begin with species. If a species or species essence is a *suniversal*—a way matter might be—it is certainly not a primary substance$_m$, since it is not a particular. But it is not a universal either—not a way particular substances might be. Hence it cannot belong in any of the non-substance categories, since their members are all universals. The only remaining possibility, therefore, is that it is in the category of secondary substance$_m$. Species are secondary substances in the *Metaphysics,* then, just as they were in the *Categories.*

In the *Categories,* genera too are secondary substances. But in the *Metaphysics,* Aristotle may seem to have undergone a change of heart where they are concerned: "In general, if a man and things spoken of in that way are substance, it follows that nothing in their account is the substance of any of them or exists separate from them or in anything else. I mean, e.g., that there is no animal, nor anything else mentioned in the accounts, in addition to the particular ones" (*Met.* VII 13 1038^{b}30–34).[40] All he is really claiming, however, is that there is no generic animal, separate from and in addition to particular animals belonging to different species. If there were, the unity of definition, and so of substance, would be threatened, since each particular substance would be identical to the many particular substances included as parts of its essence (IV 6 1003^{a}9–11). All he is precluding, therefore, is that genera should belong in the category of primary substance$_m$, not that they should belong in that of secondary substance$_m$. For separation is a mark only of primary substance$_m$, not of all substance. And, in fact, secondary substance$_m$ is where genera must belong. For a genus, as no more than its constituent species taken generically, is not a universal belonging to a nonsubstance category, but some sort of determinable suniversal, some sort of secondary substance. Hence the category of secondary substance$_m$, since it contains both genera and species, contains the very same members as secondary substance$_c$. Arguably, then, they are the same category.

Turn now to primary substance$_m$. God—who is simple and an activity—is a primary substance$_m$. But so, too, are the various unmoved movers of the other heavens, since they, though epistemologically and ontologically posterior to God, and so less primary than he is, are neither universals nor suniversals, but substantial particulars of the same sort as him—forms actualized in understandings. Unlike God, however, these unmoved movers involve unactualized potential—matter. In other words, they are hylomorphic compounds—though their matter is ether, not ordinary sublunary matter (8.2). Socrates himself, as most of all a supernatural being, is just like these unmoved movers, so he too should be included in primary substance$_m$ (7.5). Presumably, then, other species essences actu-

---

[40] Also *Met.* VIII 1 1042^{a}12–22: "Some arguments imply that the essence *(to ti ên einai)* is substance, others that the subject is, still others that the genus is substance more than the species are, and the universal more than the particulars. . . . But since the essence *is* substance, and the definition is an account of it [the essence], because of that we discussed definition and what it is intrinsically. And since the definition is an account, and the account has parts, we also had to see about its parts, about what sorts of parts are parts of the substance, and what sorts aren't, and whether the same parts are also part of the definition. Further, then, neither the universal nor the genus is substance."

alized in matter, which are also substantial particulars—but of a lower grade of actuality, because constituted of more earthy, less ethereal, matter—are also included in that same category. Where else, to put it bluntly, could they possibly belong? It follows, then, that the category of primary substance$_m$ contains the very same beings as that of primary substance$_c$.

Was God, then, always Aristotle's candidate for the exalted position of the most primary of primary substances? I think so. What happens of ontological consequence as we move from the *Categories* to the *Metaphysics* is that, through metaphysical analysis, the category of primary substance gains in structure and complexity. It doesn't change its inhabitants. God was a member in the *Categories;* Socrates and Bellerophon remain members in the *Metaphysics.*

Aristotle developed his metaphysics over time, no doubt, since something so immensely rich and complex, so much the fruit of aporematic engagement with other philosophers and philosophies, hardly sprang full blown even from a head as amazing as his. But as we have it in the writings he bequeathed us, it does not much develop. Instead, as I have tried to show, it is a consistent whole, constructed very largely in response to a single deep and difficult problem, the Primacy Dilemma, and offering a solution to it so daring and ingenious that it is one of the greatest creations of the philosophical imagination.

TEN

ARISTOTELIANISM

10.1 The Primacy Dilemma Revisited

I have taken for granted, with Aristotle, that the Primacy Dilemma is a serious philosophical problem. I have accepted that ontological first principles and epistemological ones must be the same. Yet modern philosophy, beginning more-or-less with Descartes, seems simply to ignore the dilemma altogether, by separating—to speak evocatively rather than precisely—the epistemological (ideas or sense data) from the ontological (material objects, minds, God). Why not follow the moderns, then, and consign the Primacy Dilemma, and Aristotle's resolution of it, to the junk heap of history? The answer, in a nutshell, is what happens subsequently. For without simply parodying what is, after all, a very complex story, one might with some justification say that the Primacy Dilemma has not gone away, but has instead haunted Descartes' heirs, shaping their philosophical theories from behind the scenes. Skepticism, for example, has thrived largely by exploiting the gap between ideas and things, threatening to confine a thinker to the former, and deprive him of warranted access to the latter. Reductionism of some kind then tries to close the gap again by constructing ontological first principles out of epistemological ones, material objects out of ideas or sense data. Realism, as a result, has invariably been under attack. It is the Eden from which skepticism has driven us, and to which we long to return. For no reductionist project has ever satisfied robust common sense for long, and none has succeeding even in its own terms.

The same arguments that have made the world outside our minds seem forever beyond our legitimate epistemological reach have made universals—including Aristotelian immanent universals—seem especially objectionable and inaccessible. For judgments that import them seem to involve the kind of ampliative inferences skepticism targets. Even in reporting the contents of our own minds, indeed, universals seems to raise these problems. For if I judge that I am being appeared to redly, I imply that I am being appeared to in a way that is (objectively) similar to other ways I was (will be) appeared to about which I made (will make) the same judgment. I thereby commit myself to something beyond the immediately given contents of my thoughts, something subject to skeptical attack. Some form of nominalism or a reduction of universals to sets or the like then beckons. Perhaps, something is red just in case it is a member of a particular set, or part of a particular aggregate, and so on. These reductionist strategies, too, have proved unsatisfactory. All seem plagued by the occurrence somewhere within them of a universal, such as similarity, that has not been—and cannot be—appropriately reduced.

Problems with universals multiply, if anything, when we consider what seem on the face of it to be relations between them, especially, such 'external' relations as causal ones. 'Calcium deficiency causes osteoporosis', for example, seems to report the existence of a universal relation holding between two other universals or properties: *being deficient in calcium* and *having osteoporosis*. Again skepticism challenges us to produce the inferential route that leads from our epistemological first principle to such relations and universals. Failing to meet the challenge we resort to reductionism once again—for example, to counterfactual conditionals about sets or aggregates of particulars, and to possible worlds as an account of their truth conditions.

The effects of allowing ontological first principles to come apart from epistemological ones are also palpable in the philosophy of language. For example, the sentence 'There are two prime numbers between 2 and 7' seems to have the same sort of truth conditions, the same logical form, as 'There are two houses between ours and the mail box'. The first commits us to the existence of prime numbers, therefore, just as surely as the second commits us to the existence of houses. When we turn to epistemology, however, the former causes problems that the latter does not. For while our epistemic access to houses (or to houses appropriately reduced) seems relatively unproblematic, our access to such apparently 'Platonic' entities as prime numbers seems, by comparison, entirely suspect. The temptation to find a saving semantic difference between the two sentences thus becomes very strong. Perhaps, all the former really commits us to is the existence of a proof or a construction or the like. If so, that must be reflected in its truth conditions or logical form, with the result that philosophical grammar forces us to change the apparent subject in a disconcerting way—one, moreover, that the relevant experts (semanticists of natural languages) reject.

Just as numbers, universals, and causal relations all become creatures of semi-darkness once the need to reduce them to our favored skeptic-proof, epistemological primitives becomes intellectually urgent, so also do minds and values. It is perhaps unnecessary to elaborate on this, except to say that here, too, no clear way out of the darkness has been found.

The conclusion I want to draw from this potted bit of history is modest enough, I hope, not to overstrain its justificatory resources. It is just this: setting aside the Primacy Dilemma is not a cost-free but a high-cost stratagem. Hence we have ample reason, beyond whatever intrinsic pleasures they may offer, to take seriously philosophical theories like Aristotle's, which attempt to defend realism by actually solving the dilemma.

But how seriously can we really take Aristotle's own solution, ridden as it seems to be, with so much that we are bound to find arcane? That is a hard question. I shall approach it, as Aristotle does, by starting with Platonism, and seeing if and how it improves on that.

10.2 Aristotelianism or Platonism?

Platonic substantial forms, as Aristotle sees then, have two liabilities: (1) they are particular-universal hybrids; (2) they are not identical to their essences. The first renders them unfit for ontological primacy; the second for primacy in scientific knowledge. Could Plato reduce these to acceptable levels? Presumably he could at least try. He could abandon both (1) and keep (2). He could identify the human being-itself (or the form of a human being) not with a paradigm particular, but with the human form or essence, treating it as separate from particular perceptible human beings. In other words, he could allow forms to exist altogether uninstantiated. He could become not an Aristotelian Platonist—a substantial paradigmatist—but a Platonist as we understand the term, someone who advocates an *ante rem* theory of universals. Forms would then be eligible, at least, for both ontological and epistemological primacy.

Uninstantiated universals are themselves somewhat problematic entities, of course. For example, any attempt to explain how they are related to the particulars that instantiate them seems to lead to paradox. For suppose the relationship in question is participation$_1$, so that Socrates is a human being by participating$_1$ in the form of human being. Participation$_1$ is itself clearly a universal, the particular instances of which are ordered pairs, such as

⟨Socrates, form of human being⟩ and the like. But these pairs participate$_2$ in the Platonic form of participation$_1$, and so on. If participation$_1$ is not identical to participation$_2$, we have an infinite, vicious regress. If the two are identical, we have a circular explanation, in which participation$_1$ is explained in terms of itself.

Such criticisms are certainly troubling, but they can often be met (or at least tamed somewhat) by being co-opted. For it is open to the Platonist to agree that participation cannot be explained in a non-circular way, but to claim that this is not a problem. Participation cannot be explained by any theory because it is presupposed in any explanation of anything. It is *sui generis* and must simply be grasped from examples—analogically, as he might somewhat provocatively say.

Every philosophical theory has its primitive notions. No theory can explain absolutely everything. These notions will be good primitives, as we saw, if, like potentiality and actuality, we can use analogies to enhance our intuitive grasp of them, and if they fit well with what we already know, with science in the broad Aristotelian sense, which includes bodies of productive and practical knowledge as sciences. But no theory can afford to have too many primitives, or to have particularly opaque or mysterious ones.

Aristotelian epistemology has a potentially non-mysterious account of our scientific knowledge of universals and suniversals: experience-based scientific investigation of the natural world, abstraction from it, induction—including higher level induction—and aporematic are sufficient to provide it. Platonic epistemology, by contrast, seems much more mysterious, since somehow our minds must be able to grasp uninstantiated universals—objects with which it apparently cannot be in causal contact. The ontological advantages that makes Platonism a perennially attractive option, for example, in the philosophy of mathematics, are therefore threatened by apparently intractable epistemological liabilities.

These liabilities carry over, too, into the philosophy of mind. For in order to explain how a mind could have knowledge of uninstantiated universals it is tempting—if not actually mandatory—to assign a status to it that no mere product of nature could intelligibly have. Mind-body dualism of some sort typically results. Aristotle, on the other hand, is free to embrace what we can recognize as at least a forerunner of functionalist theories of the mind. (Once ether is removed from the picture, as it will be in a moment, a full-blooded functionalism will be even more within Aristotelian reach. For ether—as intrinsically formative—is the major obstacle to treating psychological states as potentially realizable in a variety of different material bases in the way that functionalist theories require.[1])

No one is naive enough to consider any of this a killing blow to Platonism, but it does seem to put Aristotelianism somewhat ahead on points in all these areas.

Aristotelian immanent (or *in re*) universals, as ontologically dependent on particulars, explain their own instantiation, since if they exist at all, they *must* be instantiated. But this is not true where Platonic universals are concerned, since they can exist uninstantiated. To fill the explanatory gap in his theory, therefore, Plato appeals (and perhaps must appeal) to the existence of God—a divine craftsman who puts forms (or something resembling them) into appropriate, already existing matter. It follows that Plato's God is an ontological first principle. Universal forms, however, are supposed to be the primary objects of scientific knowledge. Since Plato's God is not a universal form, he cannot be such an object. Platonic metaphysics thus leaves its correlative epistemology threatened with self-refutation, and the Primacy Dilemma unsolved. No doubt here too there are ways to maneuver, but each of them represents a cost that Aristotelianism does not have to pay.

Though there is no general problem about why Aristotelian universals are instantiated, there is a problem about why, for example, species essences are among the ones that are. Aristotle handles this problem by accepting in effect that it is unsolvable. No forms or essences come-into-being and none pass-away. They are either eternally in the world or they aren't ever there. Animals come from other actual animals with the same species essence as themselves, so that there must always have been just the species essences, just the species of animals, that there are now.

Plato's solution to this problem appeals again to God and to the forms. But it also needs something else: an explanation of why God causes some forms to be instantiated rather than others. As in the case of Leibniz, God's rationality and goodness are supposed to provide it. God puts just these forms into the world, because he is a wise being, striving to realize the good as far as he can. Aristotle, on the other hand, needs no such further explanation, since, on his view, there are no forms that aren't instantiated.

Still, Aristotle does have a substantial cost to pay in this area, since he

---

[1] Code and Moravcsik, "Explaining Various Forms of Living," 138–141, have seen that Aristotle's conception of matter is inhospitable to functionalism, but not that ether is ultimately what makes it so.

must explain why any universals exist at all. Platonism avoids this cost, since its universals are necessary existents. Thus the problem Plato has with the instantiation of necessarily existent universals, Aristotle has with the existence of contingently instantiated ones. It is here that Aristotle must invoke ether as a formative element present in the world that guarantees the existence there of forms and universals. Ether is thus an immanent analog of Plato's divine craftsman. For it must not just be intrinsically formative, but it must carry out its formative operations in a way that promotes the good. Moreover, ether is problematic not only in its operations and teleology, but also in its intrinsic nature. For example, the fact that, when separate from sublunary body, it can be so fully actualized that no residual potential remains strongly suggests that it is an illegitimate reification of the concept of (second) potentiality itself. For when a second potential is actualized it is, indeed, actualized without remainder. But, then, such a potential is not an actual being that can play any sort of causal role. At the end of the day, therefore, we might not see Aristotle as further ahead here. But that would be to underestimate the resources of his theory.

The assumption that there is a good-promoting, formative element that is an eternal presence in our eternal world is not one that we would grant. From our perspective, or at any rate from that of our professionalized sciences, such an assumption is not much of an improvement on Plato's. Indeed, our religious views may lead us to favor Plato here. It is important to see, therefore, that Aristotle has the resources in his metaphysics to do much better than he himself is able to recognize.

Here again is (one representation of) Socrates' form or essence:

|animal| + |human being| + |male| + |Socrates|

M, a male baboon, has a similar form:

|animal| + |baboon| + |male| + |M|

Focus on |baboon|. When it tries to transmit its formative motions to the menses of F, a female baboon, it slackens or degrades so much that the resulting offspring is a monster (*teras*)—MM. Fortunately for MM, he meets a female monster FF, and they have a male monstrous offspring, MMM. He meets FFF, and so on. Now all these monstrous births are just dramatic cases of the normal variations present in normal offspring: "anyone who does not take after his parents is in a way already a monster" (*GA* IV 3 767^{b}5–6). But when there have been enough of them over a long enough time what one gets—fudging Darwin a fair bit—is a new species, such as that to which Socrates belongs, whose adaptedness to some available natural environment promotes its long-term stability. Relative to the species *homo sapiens* that has thereby emerged, we can define a notion of goodness: what is good for human beings is what promotes their survival and flourishing in their natural environment. It is a small, though different, step from there to the notion of persons, as essentially rational beings, relative to which a notion of moral or ethical goodness may be defined.

Worries about the status of understanding aside, then, and whether or not it could be the product of Darwinized teratology (worries our own evolutionary biology has not entirely banished), Aristotle's theory, only slightly modified, has the resources needed to explain the emergence and evolution of new species essences that did not exist anywhere before, and to explain what is good or valuable for the beings that have them. Moreover, Darwinized teratology extended all the way down shows us how elements on the order of earth, air, fire, and water could—without the aid of ether—give rise to more complexly formed substances. Platonism, by contrast, lacks these resources. It needs a God to explain why form and value exist in the world in a way that Aristotelianism, appropriately Darwinized, does not need any equivalent assumption. That is a significant comparative advantage.

In theology too Aristotle seems to come out ahead of Plato. Creator Gods usually tend to do double duty as enforcers of morality. Plato himself is cagey on this topic, but in the Myth of Er he imagines an afterlife where the evil are punished and the good rewarded. In Christianity, this idea gets fully elaborated into a complex theory of the afterlife, in which eternal punishment in Hell is provided for hardened sinners, and eternal rewards in Heaven for those who seek forgiveness. There is something repugnant, however, about the idea of a perfect God running an eternal torture chamber or creating someone to run it for him. Certainly, the idea has inspired a literature that curdles the blood, and reaches its nadir in the idea—entertained even by St. Thomas[2]—that one of the joys of heaven consists in awareness of the suffering of the damned.

The idea has also had a problematic effect in ethics. For it is very

---

[2] *Summa Theologica*, III, *Supplementum*, Q. 94, Art. 1.

tempting for Christian ethics to lapse into thinking of moral principles as simply a set of maker's instructions backed with threats. Or perhaps, as I should say, it is very easy for that idea to be appealed to when explanations of the intrinsic badness of immorality seem to wear a bit thin: the thinness doesn't matter so much, we are inclined to think, because there is always heavenly reward and hellish punishment to provide the necessary incentive to the unconvinced.

It is a great merit of Aristotle's theology that his God is neither a creator nor a judge. Yet in a way that is not always sufficiently appreciated, his God is a moral God, a God with a role to play in morality. For he is identical to happiness, which is the moral end. Failure to know and love him, therefore, failure to achieve the moral end, is its own punishment. The badness of immorality is, therefore, intrinsic to it. It is noticeable, too, that while Aristotle believes that we are—or are most of all—immortal, supernatural beings, he says nothing about our postmortal fate. But one thing we can straightforwardly infer from what he does say is that it is the same for the virtuous and the vicious. For once human productive self-understandings are separate from their bodies they are all—absent any cosmic rewarders or punishers—in the same boat, all as happy as can be. Their punishment on earth, the result of their own bad characters, is implicitly treated as punishment enough.

10.3 Aristotle Without God?

While it isn't quite true to say that the only philosophy we need is philosophy of science, it is surely true that a metaphysics out of touch with science in the broadest sense—out of touch with well-established bodies of systematic knowledge, whether empirical or *a priori*—is simply out of touch. The reliance of Aristotle's metaphysics on science, then, is a measure of its epistemological respectability. But the price it pays for such respectability is that of making itself somewhat hostage to science. To the extent that our science does not need Aristotle's God, therefore, or any of the other unmoved movers of the heavenly spheres, or those spheres themselves, it somewhat undercuts his metaphysics. Since the cut seems deep, we must wonder how much is left once it has been made. Is there any more than a marvelous but intellectually uninhabitable ruin? This question is really twofold. First, it asks whether, or how much of, Aristotle's metaphysics can survive if his theology is deprived of its subject matter. Second, it asks whether what does survive is underwritten or undercut by our science.

Aristotle tells us himself that "if there were no other substances besides those constituted by nature, natural science would be the primary science" (*Met.* VI 1 1026ᵃ27–29). He has thereby provided us with a recipe for constructing a naturalistic and Godless primary science on his behalf: it will simply be universal natural science, as he conceives of it.[3] Form, therefore, just to take one pertinent example, will still be identified as an analogical unity present in all natural essences. The five-stage analogical account of actuality and potentiality, which is conceptually independent of theology, will still be used to explain it. Happiness, now understood as human happiness, will also be explained in such terms, so that just as it is the teleological cause of the household and city, it will become the potential teleological cause of as much in the cosmos as we can shape to further it.[4] That may not result in the same degree of unification of the sciences as God did, but it may serve to unify many of the natural sciences, and all of the productive and practical ones.

It is hard to see, to be sure, how this new naturalistic primary science will solve the Primacy Dilemma. For, in Aristotle's view at least, "if there are no beings besides the perceptible ones, there will be no first principle, no order, no coming-to-be, and no heavens, but each first principle will have a principle before it" (*Met.* XII 10 1075ᵇ24–26). But perhaps the difficulty we face here is just that of not being able to see how a realist solution to the Primacy Dilemma is in fact possible.

It is this inability, too, that makes the second question we distinguished earlier hard to answer. For we cannot say whether an adequate realist philosophy of our science would be even roughly Aristotelian or not, until we have one to hand. We can, however, put the question in a useful light by recalling that the distinction between matter and form, which must surely be central to any Aristotelian primary science, is a particular case of a much broader distinction: that between potentiality (possibility) and actu-

---

[3] I am assuming for simplicity that if God goes, superlunary physics (astronomy) will become part of natural science.

[4] Indeed, as *Pol.* I 8 1256ᵇ15–22 makes explicit, this is already true of all the natural or sublunary beings: "Clearly, then, we must suppose in the case of fully developed things too that plants are for the sake of animals, and that the other animals are for the sake of human beings, domestic ones both for using and eating, and most but not all wild ones for food and other kinds of support, so that clothes and the other tools may be got from them. If then nature makes nothing incomplete or pointless, it must have made all of them for the sake of human beings."

ality. And the latter looks like a distinction that no thought about the world—scientific or otherwise—can do without.

10.4 Aristotle's Conception of Philosophy

Central to Aristotle's conception of philosophy is the idea of it as being a science of first principles, and central to his methodology—to his style of doing philosophy—are the constraints thus imposed on philosophy.

Philosophy's task, on this conception, is in part to defend the first principles of the various sciences, crafts, and other bodies of knowledge by solving the problems that skeptics and others raise against them. If it cannot solve them, however, it does not simply succumb to skepticism itself, rather it sees the situation as a stand-off: the problem threatens the foundations, but the existence and successful functioning of the building stands on the other side, giving philosophy good reason to think that the problem cannot in the end be fatal.

To carry out this task, however, philosophy must meet the same episte-mological standards that it sees as the key to the success of other bodies of knowledge. Hence it cannot do what Anaxagoras is described as doing in the following moving passage: "A saying of Anaxagoras to some of his friends is also recorded—'that the beings would be for them as they sup-posed them to be' . . . Hence it is clear that if both [i.e., that x seems F and that x seems not-F] are types of wisdom, then beings too are at the same time F and also not-F. And this result is the hardest to accept. For if those who more than any others have seen such truth as it is possible to see (i.e., those who seek and love it most)—if *they* believe and affirm such views about the truth, how can we expect beginners in philosophy not to lose heart? For the search for truth would be a wild goose chase" (*Met.* IV 5 $1009^b26-1010^a1$). Philosophy must, in other words, be epistemologically self-substantiating, allowing for the pursuit of the truth it prizes in the ways it sees to be successful elsewhere. Its own first principles, therefore, must be ones that it can defend aporematically. Since any such defense will involve argument of some sort, the first principles of argument—for this reason as well as because of their centrality to science—are bound to be among philosophy's first principles. A threat of circularity seems immediately to arise: a deductive argument in favor of deduction is circular, an inductive one is too weak; an inductive defense of induction is circular, a deductive one is too strong. An escape from this sort of circularity, if one is possible, must surely be along the lines of Aristotle's defense of the principle of non-contradiction.

Given the diversity of kinds of sciences and types of knowledge, moreover, it is unlikely that a unified or reductionistic science of everything is possible. Philosophy's own first principles, therefore, are almost certain to involve something like analogy. In this respect, it will be like some sciences, perhaps, but not like others: they will directly investigate different bits or regions of being producing non-analogical explanations of it; it will investigate all of the sciences, producing an analogical account of being as whole—of being qua being.

Though philosophy must meet the standards it sees as required for success in science, it cannot be like science in every respect. For, first, it must remain open, as science need not, to almost all comers. This is because its aspiration to be a science of first principles imposes on it an obligation to defend those first principles against even those objections which may seem to come from far left field. The Darwinian biologist, by contrast, can be a creationist in religion by dint of separating his professional scientific self from his everyday religious one. The philosopher is allowed no such luxury. He cannot, Hume-like, worship one god in his study, and another when he is playing backgammon with his friends.

A second way in which Aristotelian philosophy differs from science has to do with its relationship to history. By solving its problems, science kills their scientific interest, so that they become of historical interest only. Philosophical problems, by contrast, seldom suffer this fate. For philosophy is always young, always returning to first principles, and so always reencountering problems that seemed solved when different first principles seemed more defensible or attractive. Philosophy must always be actively involved with its history for this reason, and so is committed to keeping the great philosophers of the past readily available to it by translating them into the idiom it finds most intelligible. It is no accident, in other words, that Aristotle is the first historian of philosophy, that he invariably begins with the thought of his eminent predecessors, and that he invariably recasts their thought in his own terms.

These brief comments on Aristotle's conception of philosophy do scant justice to it. To grasp it with any real appreciation of its resourcefulness, and sure self-conscious methodology and architectonic, we need to see it in operation on a problem with which we struggle ourselves. Philosophy, notoriously, is not a spectator sport. By focusing on the Primacy Dilemma that is one of the needs I have tried to satisfy. To a large extent, therefore, what I have written might be regarded as a treatise for participants on Aristotle's conception of philosophy. For even if we reject outright the conclusions about substance Aristotle defends, we might still see merit in how he goes about constructing that defense. If so, he will surely have provided us with substantial knowledge, even if not of the kind that he himself thought most valuable.

REFERENCES

Ackrill, J. L. *Aristotle Categories and De Interpretatione.* Oxford: Clarendon Aristotle Series, 1963.

———. "Aristotle's Distinction between *Energeia* and *Kinêsis.*" Reprinted in his *Essays.*

———. "Aristotle's Definitions of *Psuchê.*" Reprinted in his *Essays.*

———. *Essays on Plato and Aristotle.* Oxford: Clarendon Press, 1997.

Allan, D. J. *Aristotelis De Caelo.* Oxford: OCT, 1955.

Annas, Julia. *Aristotle Metaphysics Books M and N.* Oxford: Clarendon Aristotle Series, 1976.

Armstrong, D. M. *Universals and Scientific Realism.* 2 vols. Cambridge: Cambridge University Press, 1978.

———. *What is a Law of Nature?* Cambridge: Cambridge University Press, 1983.

Balme, D. M. *Aristotle De Partibus Animalium I and De Generatione Animalium I.* Oxford: Clarendon Aristotle Series, 1992.

———. "The Snub." Reprinted in Gotthelf and Lennox, *Philosophical Issues in Aristotle's Biology,* 306–312.

———. "Aristotle's Use of Division and Differentiae." In Gotthelf and Lennox, *Philosophical Issues in Aristotle's Biology,* 69–89.

———. *Aristotle: History of Animals Books VII–X.* Cambridge: Loeb, 1991.

Barnes, Jonathan, ed. *The Complete Works of Aristotle: The Revised Oxford Translation.* Princeton: Princeton University Press, 1984.

———. "Aristotle's Philosophy of the Sciences." *Oxford Studies in Ancient Philosophy* XI (1993): 225–241.

———. *Aristotle Posterior Analytics.* 2 ed. Oxford: Clarendon Aristotle Series, 1994.

———. "Metaphysics." In Barnes (ed.) *The Cambridge Companion to Aristotle.*

———. ed. *The Cambridge Companion to Aristotle.* Cambridge: Cambridge University Press, 1995.

Bolton, Robert. "Aristotle's Method in Natural Science: *Physics* I." In Judson, *Aristotle's Physics,* 1–30.

———. "Aristotle's Account of the Socratic Elenchus." *Oxford Studies in Ancient Philosophy* XI (1993): 121–152.

Bonitz, Hermann. *Index Aristotelicus.* Berlin: De Gruyter, 1975.

Bostock, David. *Aristotle Metaphysics Books Z and H*. Oxford: Clarendon Aristotle Series, 1994.

Brennan, Tad. "Two Modal Theses in the Second Half of *Metaphysics* Theta. 4." *Phronesis* XXXIX (1993): 160–173.

Brentano, Franz. "*Nous Poiêtikos:* Survey of Earlier Interpretations." Reprinted in Nussbaum and Rorty, *Essays on Aristotle's De Anima,*" 313–341.

Brunschwig, Jacques. "Lambda 9: A Short-Lived Thought-Experiment." In Charles and Frede, *Proceedings of the Thirteenth Symposium Aristotelicum.*

Burnyeat, M. F., et al. *Notes on Book Zeta of Aristotle's Metaphysics.* Oxford, 1979.

———. "Is an Aristotelian Philosophy of Mind Still Credible? A Draft." In Nussbaum and Rorty, *Essays on Aristotle's De Anima,*" 15–26.

Charles, David. "Aristotle: Ontology and Moral Reasoning." *Oxford Studies in Ancient Philosophy* IV (1986): 119–144.

———. "Aristotle on Hypothetical Necessity and Irreducibility." *Pacific Philosophical Quarterly* 69 (1988): 1–53.

———. "Teleological Causation in the *Physics.*" In Judson, *Aristotle's Physics,* 101–128.

———. "Aristotle on Meaning, Natural Kinds and Natural History." In Devereux and Pellegrin, *Biologie, Logique et Metaphysique chez Aristote,* 145–167.

———. "Aristotle on Substance, Essence, and Biological Kinds." *Proceedings of the Boston Area Colloquium in Ancient Philosophy* 7 (1993): 227–261.

———. "Aristotle and the Unity and Essence of Biological Kinds." In Kullmann and Föllinger, *Aristotelische Biologie,* 27–42.

———, and Michael Frede, eds. *Proceedings of the Thirteenth Symposium Aristotelicum.* Oxford: Clarendon Press, forthcoming.

Charlton, William. *Aristotle Physics Books I and II.* Oxford: Clarendon Aristotle Series, 1970.

———. "Did Aristotle Believe in Prime Matter?" Appendix to *Aristotle Physics Books I and II.*

Code, Alan. D. "The Aporematic Approach to Primary Being in *Metaphysics* Z." *Canadian Journal of Philosophy* Supplementary Volume 10 (1984): 1–20.

———. "Aristotle: Essence and Accident." In Richard Grandy and Richard Warner, *Philosophical Grounds of Rationality: Intentions, Categories, Ends.* Oxford: Clarendon Press, 1986.

———. "Metaphysics and Logic." In Mohan Matthen, *Aristotle Today: Essays on Aristotle's Ideal of Science* (Edmonton: Academic Printing and Publishing, 1987).

———. "Aristotle's Metaphysics as a Science of Principles." *Revue Internationale de Philosophie* (1997): 345–366.

———. "Some Remarks on Metaphysics *Lambda* 5." In Charles and Frede, *Proceedings of the Thirteenth Symposium Aristotelicum.*

————, and Julius Moravcsik. "Explaining Various Forms of Living." In Nussbaum and Rorty, *Essays on Aristotle's De Anima,* 129–145.

Cohen, S. M. *Aristotle on Natural and Incomplete Substance.* Cambridge: Cambridge University Press, 1996.

Cohen, S. Marc. "Aristotle and Individuation." *Canadian Journal of Philosophy* Supplementary Volume 10 (1984): 41–65.

————. "Hylomorphism and Functionalism." In Nussbaum and Rorty, *Essays on Aristotle's De Anima,* 57–73.

Coles, Andrew. "Animal and Childhood Cognition in Aristotle's Biology." In Kullmann and Föllinger, *Aristotelische Biologie,* 287–323.

Cooper, John M. *Reason and Human Good in Aristotle.* Cambridge, MA: Harvard University Press, 1975.

————. "Hypothetical Necessity and Natural Teleology." In Gotthelf and Lennox, *Philosophical Issues in Aristotle's Biology,* 243–274.

————. "Metaphysics in Aristotle's Embryology." *Proceedings of the Cambridge Philological Society* 214 (1988): 14–41.

Devereux, Daniel. "Separation and Immanence in Plato's Theory of Forms." *Oxford Studies in Ancient Philosophy* XII (1994): 63–90.

————, and Pierre Pellegrin, eds. *Biologie, Logique et Metaphysique chez Aristote.* Paris: CNRS, 1990.

Driscoll, John. A. "ΕΙΔΗ in Aristotle's Earlier and Later Theory of Substance." In Dominic J. O'Meara, *Studies in Aristotle.* Washington, DC: Catholic University of America Press, 1981.

Düring, Ingemar. *Aristotle's Protrepticus: An Attempt at Reconstruction.* Göteborg: Studia Graeca et Latina Gothoburgensia XII, 1961.

Elders, Leo. *Aristotle's Theology: A Commentary on Book Λ of the Metaphysics.* Assen: Van Gorcum, 1972.

Everson, Stephen. *Aristotle on Perception.* Oxford: Clarendon Press, 1997.

Ferejohn, Michael. *The Origins of Aristotelian Science.* New Haven: Yale University Press, 1991.

Fine, Gail. *On Ideas: Aristotle's Criticism of Plato's Theory of Forms.* Oxford: Clarendon Press, 1993.

Frede, Dorothea. "The Cognitive Role of *Phantasia.*" In Nussbaum and Rorty, *Essays on Aristotle's De Anima,* 279–295.

Frede, Michael. "The Title, Unity, and Authenticity of the Aristotelian *Categories.*" Reprinted in *Essays.*

————. "Categories in Aristotle." Reprinted in *Essays.*

————. "Individuals in Aristotle." Reprinted in *Essays.*

————. *Essays in Ancient Philosophy.* Minneapolis: University of Minnesota Press, 1971.

————. "The Definition of Sensible Substances in *Met. Z.*" In Devereux and Pellegrin, *Biologie, Logique et Metaphysique Chez Aristote,* 113–139.

————, and Gunther Patzig. *Aristoteles Metaphysik Z*. Munich: C. H. Beck, 1988.

Freeland, Cynthia. "Accidental Causes and Real Explanations." In Judson, *Aristotle's Physics*, 49–72.

Freudenthal, Gad. *Aristotle's Theory of Material Substance: Heat and Pneuma, Form and Soul*. Oxford: Clarendon Press, 1995.

Furth, Montgomery. *Aristotle: Metaphysics Books VII–X*. Indianapolis: Hackett, 1985.

————. *Substance, Form and Psyche: An Aristotelian Metaphysics*. Cambridge: Cambridge University Press, 1988.

Geach, Peter. *Mental Acts*. London: Routledge and Kegan Paul, 1957.

Gill, Mary Louise. *Aristotle on Substance: The Paradox of Unity*. Princeton: Princeton University Press, 1989.

————. "Comments On Charles." *Proceedings of the Boston Area Colloquium in Ancient Philosophy* 7 (1993): 262–269.

Gotthelf, Allan, ed. *Aristotle On Nature and Living Things*. Pittsburgh: Mathesis Publications, 1985.

————. and James G. Lennox, eds. *Philosophical Issues in Aristotle's Biology*. Cambridge: Cambridge University Press, 1987.

Graham, Daniel. *Aristotle Physics Book VIII*. Oxford: Clarendon Aristotle Series, 1999.

Grice, Paul. "Method in Philosophical Psychology." Reprinted in *The Conception of Value*.

————. "Reply to Richards." Reprinted in *The Conception of Value*.

————. *The Conception of Value*. Oxford: Clarendon Press, 1991.

Hamlyn, D. W. *Aristotle De Anima*. Rev. ed. Oxford: Clarendon Aristotle Series, 1993.

Hankinson, R. J. "Philosophy of Science." In Barnes, *Cambridge Companion to Aristotle*, 109–139.

Heath, Thomas. *A History of Greek Mathematics*. Vol. 1. Oxford: Clarendon Press, 1921.

Heinaman, Robert. "Activity and Change in Aristotle." *Oxford Studies in Ancient Philosophy* XIII (1995): 187–216.

Hicks, R. D. *Aristotle De Anima*. Cambridge: Cambridge University Press, 1907.

Hintikka, Jaakko. "On Aristotle's Modal Syllogistic." Reprinted in his *Time and Necessity: Studies in Aristotle's Theory of Modality*. Oxford: Clarendon Press, 1973.

Hussey, Edward. *Aristotle Physics Books III and IV*. Oxford: Clarendon Aristotle Series, 1983.

————. "Aristotle's Mathematical Physics." In Judson, *Aristotle's Physics*, 213–242.

Irwin, T. H. *Aristotle's First Principles*. Oxford: Clarendon Press, 1988.

————, and Gail Fine. *Aristotle: Selections*. Indianapolis: Hackett, 1995.

Jaeger, Werner. *Aristotelis Metaphysica*. Oxford: OCT, 1957.

Judson, Lindsay. "Chance and 'Always or For the Most Part'." In Judson, *Aristotle's Physics,* 73–100.

———, ed. *Aristotle's Physics: A Collection of Essays.* Oxford: Clarendon Press, 1991.

Kahn, Charles. "The Place of the Prime Mover in Aristotle's Theology." In Gotthelf, *Aristotle On Nature and Living Things,* 183–205.

Kirwin, Christopher. *Aristotle Metaphysics Books* Γ, Δ, *and* E. Oxford: Clarendon Aristotle Series, 1971.

Kosman, Aryeh. "Perceiving that we Perceive: *On the Soul* III, 2." *Philosophical Review* 84 (1975):499–519.

———. "What does the Maker Mind Make?" In Nussbaum and Rorty, *Essays on Aristotle's De Anima,* 343–358.

Kullmann, Wolfgang, and Sabine Föllinger, *Aristotelische Biologie: Intentionen, Methoden, Ergebnisse.* Stuttgart: Franz Steiner Verlag, 1997.

Lear, Jonathan. *Aristotle and Logical Theory.* Cambridge: Cambridge University Press, 1980.

———. "Aristotle's Philosophy of Mathematics." *Philosophical Review* 91 (1982):161–192.

———. *Aristotle: The Desire to Understand.* Cambridge: Cambridge University Press, 1988.

Lennox, James G. "Kinds, Forms of Kinds, and the More and the Less in Aristotle's Biology." In Gotthelf and Lennox, *Philosophical Issues in Aristotle's Biology,* 339–359.

Lewis, David. "New Work for a Theory of Universals." Reprinted in Mellor and Oliver, *Properties,* 188–227.

McKirahan, Jr., Richard D. *Principles and Proofs: Aristotle's Theory of Demonstrative Science.* Princeton: Princeton University Press, 1992.

Mellor, D. H. "Properties and Predicates." Reprinted in Mellor and Oliver, *Properties,* 255–267.

———. *The Facts of Causation.* London: Routledge, 199.

———, and Alex Oliver, eds. *Properties.* Oxford: Oxford University Press, 1997.

Menn, Stephen. "Metaphysics, Dialectic and the *Categories.*" *Revue de Metaphysique et de Morale* (1995): 311–37.

Minio-Paluello, L. *Aristotelis Categoriae et Liber De Interpretatione.* Oxford: OCT, 1949.

Mueller, Ian. "Aristotle on Geometrical Objects." *Archiv für Geschichte der Philosophie* 52 (1970): 156–171.

Norman, Richard. "Aristotle's Philosopher-God." *Phronesis* 14 (1969): 63–74.

Nussbaum, Martha Craven. *Aristotle's De Motu Animalium.* Princeton: Princeton University Press, 1978.

———, and Amélie Rorty, eds. *Essays on Aristotle's De Anima.* Oxford: Clarendon Press, 1992.

Owen, G. E. L. "Inherence." Reprinted in his *Logic, Science and Dialectic.*

———. *Logic, Science and Dialectic: Collected Papers in Greek Philosophy.* Ithaca: Cornell University Press, 1985.

Parfit, Derek. *Reasons and Persons.* Oxford: Clarendon Press, 1984.

Peck, A. L. *Aristotle: Generation of Animals.* Cambridge: Loeb, 1953.

———. *Aristotle: Parts of Animals.* Cambridge: Loeb, 1961.

———. *Aristotle: Historia Animalium.* Vol. 1. Cambridge: Loeb, 1965.

———. *Aristotle: Historia Animalium.* Vol. 2. Cambridge: Loeb, 1970.

Pellegrin, Pierre. "Aristotle: A Zoology without Species." In Gotthelf, *Aristotle On Nature and Living Things,* 95–115.

———. *Aristotle's Classification of Animals: Biology and the Conceptual Unity of the Aristotelian Corpus.* Berkeley: University of California Press, 1986.

Quine, W. V. O. *Word and Object.* Cambridge, MA: MIT Press, 1960.

Reeve, C. D. C. *Practices of Reason: Aristotle's Nicomachean Ethics.* Oxford: Clarendon Press, 1992.

———. *Aristotle: Politics.* Indianapolis: Hackett, 1998.

———. "Philosophy and Dialectic in Aristotle." In Jyl Gentzler, ed. *Method in Ancient Greek Philosophy.* Oxford: Clarendon Press, 1998.

———. "Aristotelian Education." In Amélie Rorty, ed. *Philosophers on Education.* London: Routledge, 1998.

Ross, G. R. T. *Aristotle De Sensu and De Memoria.* Cambridge: Cambridge University Press, 1906.

Ross, W. D. *Aristotle Metaphysics.* 2 vols. Oxford: Clarendon Press, 1924.

———. *Aristotelis Physica.* Oxford: OCT, 1956.

———. *Aristotelis De Anima.* Oxford: OCT, 1956.

———. *Aristotelis Politica.* Oxford: OCT, 1957.

———. *Aristotelis Analytica Priora et Posteriora.* Oxford: OCT, 1968.

———. *Aristotelis Topica et Sophistici Elenchi.* Oxford: OCT, 1970.

Schofield, Malcolm. "Aristotle on the Imagination." Reprinted in Nussbaum and Rorty, *Essays on Aristotle's De Anima,* 249–278.

Sedley, David. "Is Aristotle's Teleology Anthropocentric?" *Phronesis* 36 (1991): 179–196.

———. "Metaphysics Lambda: Chapter 10." In Charles and Frede, *Proceedings of the Thirteenth Symposium Aristotelicum.*

Shoemaker, Sydney. "Identity, Properties, and Causality." In his *Identity, Cause, and Mind.* Cambridge: Cambridge University Press, 1984.

Silverman, Allan. "Color and Color-Perception in Aristotle's *De Anima.*" *Ancient Philosophy* 9 (1989): 271–292.

Smith, Robin. *Aristotle Topics Books I and VIII.* Oxford: Clarendon Aristotle Series, 1997.

Sorabji, Richard. *Aristotle On Memory.* London: Duckworth, 1972.

———. "Body and Soul in Aristotle." *Philosophy* 49 (1974): 63–89.

Strawson, P. F. *Individuals.* London: Methuen, 1959.

van der Eijk, Philip J. "The Matter of Mind: Aristotle on the Biology of 'Psychic' Processes and the Bodily Aspects of Thinking." In Kullmann and Föllinger, *Aristotelische Biologie,* 231–258.

Walzer, R. R., and J. M. Mingay. *Aristotelis Ethica Eudemia.* Oxford: OCT, 1991.

Wedin, Michael. *Mind and Imagination in Aristotle.* Yale: Yale University Press, 1988.

Whiting, Jennifer. "Metasubstance: Critical Notice of Frede-Patzig and Furth." *Philosophical Review* 100 (1991): 607–639.

Williams, Bernard. "Hylomorphism." *Oxford Studies in Ancient Philosophy* IV (1986).

Williams, C. J. F. *Aristotle De Generatione and Corruptione.* Oxford: Clarendon Aristotle Series, 1982.

INDEX LOCORUM

GENERAL INDEX

abstraction, 39; in mathematics, 64
Ackrill, J. L., 97 n. 10, 119 n. 2, 140 n. 3
action, 145
activity, 138; end of, 145; unimpeded, 201
actuality, first and second, 136
analogy, 250; and actuality and potentiality, 134, and elemental change, 121
Anaxagoras, 7 n. 14, 300
anthrôpos, meanings of, 184
aporematic, 21
Armstrong, D. M., 59
artifact problem, 118
artifacts, 60
astronomy, 36, 215
attributes, *ante rem* v. *in re* theory of, 3; ontological dependence of, 1; transcategorical, 275
axioms, 260, 274

babble, 127
Balme, D. M., 46 n. 7, 56 n. 20, 127 n. 14
Barnes, Jonathan, 70 n. 34, 90 n. 1, 170 n. 33, 248 n. 8
Beckett, Samuel, 142 n. 5
being, actual v. potential, 134; coincidental, 92; and matter, 137; intrinsic, 89; intrinsic nonsubstantial, 96; -qua-being, 248
biology, order of *HA, PA,* and *GA,* 77
body, sublunary v. superlunary, 59
BODY-body problem, 119
Bolton, Robert, 18 n. 3, 27 n. 12

Bostock, David, 127 n. 14
Brennan, Tad, 265 n. 28
Brentano, Franz, 116 n. 19
Brunschwig, Jacques, 221 n. 39, 178 n. 37, 221 n. 39
Bryson, 23
Burnyeat, Myles, 3 n. 7, 153 n. 8

capacities, active v. passive, 46
Categories, unity and title of, 111
category, 259; definition of, 106
cause, 252; final 76; 'as if', 28; intrinsic v. coincidental, 27
chance, 28
change, 110, 115; attribute, 116; canonical recipe for, 116; elemental, 120; existence, 116; pseudo-attribute, 156; substantial, 117; types of, 116
Charles, David, 37 n. 29, 44 n. 4, 77 n. 40, 146 n. 9
Charlton, William, 122 n. 7
Code, Alan, 8 n. 16, 15 n. 29, 130 n. 17, 254 n. 14, 263 n. 22, 265 n. 25, 295 n. 1
Cohen, S. M., 62 n. 25
Cohen, S. Marc, 55 n. 19, 122 n. 6, 153 n. 8
Coles, Andrew, 46 n. 7, 47 n. 11, 164 n. 26
color, 150; proto-, 151
coming-to-be, 117
common things, 24, 275
concoction, 46
consistency, 27
content, 174

319

C.D.C. REEVE is Professor of Philosophy and the Humanities at Reed College. He is the author of *Philosopher-Kings* (Princeton, 1988), *Socrates in the Apology* (Hackett, 1990), and *Practices of Reason* (Oxford, 1992). Also available from Hackett are his revision of G.M.A. Grube's translation of Plato's *Republic* (1992), and his translations of Plato's *Cratylus* (1998) and Aristotle's *Politics* (1998).